Regarding the Significance of Lexicography /
Zur Bedeutsamkeit der Lexikographie

LEXICOGRAPHICA

Series Maior

Supplementary Volumes to the International Annual for Lexicography
Suppléments à la Revue Internationale de Lexicographie
Supplementbände zum Internationalen Jahrbuch für Lexikographie

Volume 169

Regarding the Significance of Lexicography / Zur Bedeutsamkeit der Lexikographie

Europe and Australia / Europa und Australien

Edited by / Herausgegeben von
Idalete Dias, Rufus H. Gouws, Anja Lobenstein-Reichmann,
Stefan J. Schierholz

DE GRUYTER

ISBN 978-3-11-914594-7
e-ISBN (PDF) 978-3-11-221664-4
e-ISBN (EPUB) 978-3-11-221671-2
ISSN 0175-9264

Library of Congress Control Number: 2025943478

Bibliographic information published by the Deutsche Nationalbibliothek
The Deutsche Nationalbibliothek lists this publication in the Deutsche Nationalbibliografie; detailed bibliographic data are available on the internet at http://dnb.dnb.de.

Typesetting: Integra Software Services Pvt. Ltd.
Printing and binding: CPI books GmbH, Leck

www.degruyterbrill.com
Questions about General Product Safety Regulation:
productsafety@degruyterbrill.com

Contents/Inhalt

Idalete Dias, Rufus H. Gouws, Anja Lobenstein-Reichmann, Stefan J. Schierholz

Regarding the Significance of Lexicography: Europe and Australia

Lexicography is a cultural practice whose goal is the creation of dictionaries. Lexicography is both a practical and a scientific activity that requires a considerable degree of philological, subject-specific, didactic, and technical skills and expertise. Dictionaries used to be printed reference works, but today they are almost always online dictionaries (or both), which usually provide extensive and complex data, so that they are referred to as lexical information systems. Lexicographical practice is embedded in the theory of dictionary research, which has the task, among other things, of critically accompanying lexicographical activities, optimizing lexicographical processes, systematizing lexicography, and researching user needs. Thus, lexicography fundamentally strikes a balance between theory and practice. The products of lexicography are monolingual and multilingual, general and specialized, historical, diachronic, and contemporary reference works, standard and regional dictionaries, pronunciation, valency, learner, spelling, neologism, frequency, synonym, dialect, etymology, and sign language dictionaries, to name just a few types of dictionaries.

Reference works are produced in almost every country in the world, for almost every language, for many varieties, for national languages, for minority languages, and also for endangered languages.

The contributions in this volume selectively highlight the diversity and breadth of lexicography in relation to the areas mentioned, including theoretical approaches and outlooks on the future of the discipline. The gap between Europe and Australia may seem surprising at first glance, but it is justified by the global activities of the European Master in Lexicography (EMLex).[1] The EMLex consortium[2] regularly organizes international colloquiums and workshops on current topics in the field and regularly

1 Cf. https://emlex.eu.usc.gal/web/emlex-home (last access: 29 July 2025).

2 Since 2015, with the coordination and organizational headquarters at the Friedrich-Alexander Universität Erlangen-Nürnberg, and since 2024 at the Universidade de Santiago de Compostela.

Idalete Dias, University of Minho, School of Arts and Humanities, Campus de Gualtar, 4710-057 Braga, Portugal, e-mail: idalete@elach.uminho.pt

Rufus H. Gouws, Stellenbosch University, Department of Afrikaans and Dutch, Private Bag X1 Matieland 7602, South Africa, e-mail: rhg@sun.ac.za

Anja Lobenstein-Reichmann, Niedersächsische Akademie der Wissenschaften zu Göttingen. Frühneuhochdeutsches Wörterbuch, Geiststraße 10, 37073 Göttingen, Germany, e-mail: anja.lobenstein-reichmann@adwgoe.de

Stefan J. Schierholz, Universität Erlangen, Department für Germanistik und Komparatistik, Bismarckstr. 1B, 91054 Erlangen, Germany, e-mail: stefan.schierholz@fau.de

https://doi.org/10.1515/9783112216644-001

seeks to establish new professional contacts around the world. The contributions in this volume originate from a symposium held in the fall of 2023 at the Universidade do Minho (Braga) and from an EMLex tour of Australia, during which the program was promoted and numerous lectures were given at Macquarie University Sydney, the University of Melbourne, Monash University Melbourne, the Australian National Dictionary Centre at the Australian National University in Canberra, and the University of Adelaide (in cooperation with the University of South Australia). The compilation and selection of contributions clearly shows how diverse and varied lexicography and dictionary research are in the two antipodes. In Europe, lexicography is a well-established field with a long tradition of high-quality dictionaries, thoroughly underpinned by multiple and diverse theoretical approaches. Speakers of various European languages and speech communities are accustomed to having easy access to extensive typological categories of dictionaries in print and online formats. In contrast to the languages of the Old World, lexicography, both practical lexicography and dictionary research, is much younger in the New World and has not yet reached the same scope and diversity as in Europe.

The countries of the New World (in Africa, America, and Australia) generally have diverse multilingual and multicultural populations. Due to daily language contact and constant linguistic influence, such a multilingual environment can be considered a linguistic and lexicographical laboratory. From a metalexicographical perspective, some existing and successfully tested dictionary models can be implemented and used effectively. However, the exciting challenges lie in the diversity of languages and cultures and the potential for developing innovative lexicographical projects. These projects enrich lexicographical practice on the one hand, and on the other hand offer metalexicography the opportunity to adapt, modify, and expand its theories through a transformative lexicographical approach, thus transcending the boundaries of what is already known.

The importance of lexicography in Australia can be seen in the context of innovative efforts to create dictionaries that reflect the languages and cultures of all Australian ethnic groups. Since English is the only national language, local dictionaries complement British and international English dictionaries to achieve a good lexicographical representation of Australian languages and varieties. The Australian National Dictionary, which plays a pioneering role in this regard, together with other products from commercial and educational lexicography, has played an important role in establishing Australian English as a significant variety of English and continues to contribute to maintaining and improving its status. At the same time, due to growing linguistic nationalism, Australia has a deep-rooted interest in the country's indigenous languages and varieties and, therefore, in dictionaries on these topics. Lexicography in Australia therefore plays an important role in documenting individual languages and varieties, some of which have only a few speakers left, so that in some cases even a revival is within reach. However, Australia is particularly important for lexicography because its linguistic and cultural diversity offers numerous opportunities to plan and compile dictionaries that not only enhance the quality of lexicographical practice on this continent, but also serve as a model for dictionary compilation in the rest of the world.

The core significance of lexicography in Australia is the establishment of a bidirectional dictionary culture. Lexicography adapts to society by producing user-friendly dictionaries that are aimed at target groups with real lexicographical needs. However, the expansion of dictionary production also means that society adapts to lexicography by becoming aware of the achievements of professionally produced reference works, acquiring skills in using dictionaries, and recognizing and using them as useful tools in their daily lives. These dictionaries are not only reference works, but also represent the language of a people, thus securing the status of that language and filling the members of the language community with pride. Good dictionaries honor and confirm the importance of the language they cover.

While members of speech communities with a long lexicographical tradition (Europe) sometimes view dictionaries uncritically and take their availability for granted, lexicography in Australia reveals innovation, excitement, emotion, and the gratitude of speech communities gaining access to a dictionary of their native language for the first time. This illustrates not only the academic, social, and educational value of dictionaries, but also the life-changing impact they can have on a language and, above all, on a speech community.

Of great importance in current Australian lexicographical work is the expansion of the typological network of dictionaries for indigenous languages. In addition to general monolingual and bilingual dictionaries, lexicographical work has been expanded to include, for example, encyclopedic dictionaries and terminological resources. This is only the beginning of a process to create dictionaries that meet the challenges and opportunities of a multilingual environment.

The important social and cultural-historical role of lexicography in Australia can be enhanced through a stronger interactive relationship between dictionary research and lexicographic practice. The planning and publication of theory-based lexicographic products driven by a committed user perspective could ensure a long and prosperous future for Australian lexicography and make this continent a pioneer in lexicography for multilingual and multicultural environments. The scholarly exchange that took place between Europe and Australia in the spring of 2024 may therefore have been an important step towards a lasting connection. This anthology sees itself as a building block in this process.

The contributions are arranged thematically, with contributions from Braga and Australia appearing in irregular succession. A general overview of the development of lexicography in Australia is followed by historical lexicography, sign language lexicography, terminology and terminography, the treatment of indigenous languages and colloquial language in Australia, as well as an outlook on artificial intelligence in dictionaries, the individual cognitive skills and achievements of human lexicographers, and the future of dialect lexicography.

In the first article, "Australian Lexicography and the Australian Story: Historical Perspectives and the Current Scene", Amanda Laugesen (Canberra) divides Australian lexicography into three areas: (a) general/educational dictionaries, which are often published by specialist and educational publishers; (b) popular dictionaries and word collections, which are often available in stores; (c) research/scientific dictionaries, which are often produced in academic contexts. In addition to a historical overview, the influence of Australian national and cultural identity on Australian lexicography is highlighted, and current challenges are identified.

Anja Lobenstein-Reichmann (Göttingen) provides a discussion and an attempt at an answer to the question posed in the title, "Warum brauchen wir historische Lexikographie?" ('Why do we need historical lexicography?'). Against the backdrop of the possibilities offered by modern language and information technologies (in short: AI), the question of the tasks of historical lexicography and its fundamental justification is of educational and professional importance. Every discipline in the humanities faces the task of questioning its own activities, making its theoretical and methodological premises transparent, and thus legitimizing them for a supposedly general and specialist audience.

In his article "Zur Berechtigung historischer Lexikographie: Fakten und Überlegungen" ('The justification of historical lexicography: facts and considerations'), Oskar Reichmann (Göttingen) distinguishes between lexicography focused on individual words, and lexicography focused on the entire vocabulary of a language. The former is based on a theory of dictionaries founded on representation theory and aims to process as many isolated lemmas as possible. The second approach has a more pragmatic and communicative basis and aims to link all lemmas according to semantic, syntactic, and word-formation aspects. In the lexicography of German and its neighboring languages, this approach is found primarily in the Early New High German Dictionary (FWB).

In "Signed language lexicography and the Auslan dictionaries in print and online", Trevor Johnston (Sydney) describes the Auslan (Australian Sign Language) dictionaries and the lexical database on which they are based. Since the 1980s, this database has spread across multiple software platforms as the types of data that can be included in newer databases (text, graphics, video) have been improved and expanded, allowing the dictionaries to appear in three formats: print, multimedia (CD-ROM), and online. Lexicographical and lexicological principles, the types and contents of the data fields used in the database, and the way in which the data is displayed in each edition are presented. The linking of the examples to the Auslan corpus is described, as well as how the architecture of the Auslan Signbank can accommodate data from any sign language and how this can then be used for cross-linguistic studies of the lexicology and phonology of sign languages.

In "Terminology from a Lexicographic Perspective", Pius ten Hacken (Innsbruck) draws on Eugen Wüster's general terminology theory, which is considered the prevailing guideline for the work of standardization institutes. He examines the extent to which this dominance can be explained from a lexicographical perspective. The challenges discussed are based on corpus-based terminology work, terminology work for the purpose of language preservation, and the relationship between precisely defined terms and prototype semantics. The extent to which definitions consisting of necessary and sufficient conditions can be replaced or supplemented by a more flexible selection of information is discussed. A user-oriented lexicographical evaluation of terminological resources should recognize that Wüster's theory is primarily useful for experts.

In her contribution "Online Terminography for Indigenous Australians", Pam Peters (Sydney) uses an online term database for Australian family law terms to show how user-based lexicography can be designed in terminography to make content accessible to indigenous users with low literacy skills. Instead of semasiological order, an onomasiological structure is used in the design of dictionaries and term banks, which focuses on the conceptual structure for users. A variety of media (graphics, audio, language) and links are used to make it easier for users to access unfamiliar terms and concepts in family law.

In the article "The AIATSIS Dictionary Program: Supporting the Strengthening of Australian Indigenous Languages", Lauren W. Reed, Alison L. Mount, Alexandra Marley, Kira Davey, Mahesh White-Radhakrishnan, Grace Smith, Jason Chong, Kaitlyn Lodewikus, and Tamarind Meara (Canberra) present the dictionary program of the Australian Institute of Aboriginal and Torres Strait Islander Studies (AIATSIS), which is part of the Australian government's efforts to support these endangered languages. A historical overview is followed by a description of the program's history and a discussion of the particular challenges of dictionary compilation given the linguistic characteristics of the two indigenous languages.

In "Encyclopaedic Lexicography: the Warlpiri Encyclopaedic Dictionary", Mary Laughren (Queensland) discusses the Warlpiri encyclopedic dictionary, which is the result of a collaboration between Warlpiri speakers and linguists that began in 1978. The form and content of the dictionary were largely determined by the linguistic, historical, and social context. The role of bilingual education programs, which were introduced in Warlpiri community schools in 1973, proves to be an essential factor alongside the existing documentation of the Warlpiri language. The expansion of purely linguistic aspects to encyclopedic content proves to be necessary and valuable, especially where languages and cultures diverge.

In "Behind the lingo – slang and the dictionary", Kate Burridge and Howard Manns (Melbourne) demonstrate the complexity of colloquial language, focusing on its fleeting nature, its unpredictable development, and the challenges of lexicographical documentation. Using Australian slang as an example, they discuss historical examples such as the 19th-century convict glossary, modern slang innovations, and the results of a survey on so-called Australian expressions. By analyzing linguistic remnants and fleeting trends, they highlight the cultural, socio-historical, and linguistic forces that shape the life cycle of slang. Technology, globalization, and Australia's penchant for informality complicate the task of understanding and defining slang. As an expression of linguistic creativity, slang exemplifies the interplay between formal and informal language and reflects a dynamic, ever-changing lexicon that lexicographers must master with increasing complexity.

In their article "People, machines, and dictionaries: Is artificial intelligence killing dictionaries?", Iván Arias-Arias, María José Domínguez Vázquez, and Carlos Valcárcel Riveiro (Santiago de Compostela) examine the relationships between people, dictionaries, and computer systems in the lexicographical process, as well as the actions of dictionary creators and users. They present the influence of artificial intelligence on lexicographical activities and the results of new experiments that demonstrate the reliability of AI-generated results depending on the type of user. Finally, they discuss the current social and cultural value of dictionaries and their influence on society.

Konan Kouassi (Erlangen) reports in his article "Wörterbücher von heute und morgen. Von den Ausgangsdaten zum Wörterbuchartikel" ('Dictionaries of today and tomorrow. From the source data to the dictionary article') on a research project in Erlangen that examines the achievements and competencies of lexicographers in modern lexicographical practice. The performance complexes are divided into concrete and abstract elements and determine the role and significance of lexicographers, as well as their knowledge and skills for successful lexicographical practice. The cognitive performance of lexicographers is linked to the quality of dictionary articles, whereby high quality is to be regarded as the goal and cognitive performance as the prerequisite.

In the last article, "Dialektwörterbücher als Wörterbücher der Zukunft" ('Dialect dictionaries as dictionaries of the future'), Christine Ganslmayer (Erlangen) highlights the importance of dialect dictionaries from the perspective of the early 21st century. After a brief overview of the current state of academic German-language dialect lexicography, the fifteen Villa Vigoni Theses on Lexicography (2018) are applied to dialect dictionaries of the Bavarian region. The analysis considers dialect dictionaries as "dictionaries of the future" and highlights their potential for future-oriented lexicography.

The editors would like to thank the contributors for their patience in the production of this anthology.

Idalete Dias, Rufus H. Gouws, Anja Lobenstein-Reichmann,
Stefan J. Schierholz

Zur Bedeutsamkeit der Lexikographie: Europa und Australien

Die Lexikographie ist eine kulturelle Praxis, deren Ziel die Erstellung von Wörterbüchern ist. Die Lexikographie ist zum einen eine praktische, zum anderen eine wissenschaftliche Tätigkeit, die ein beträchtliches Maß an philologischen, einzelfachlichen, didaktischen sowie technischen Fähigkeiten und Kompetenzen erfordert. Die Wörterbücher waren früher gedruckte Nachschlagewerke, sind heute fast immer Online-Wörterbücher (oder beides), die meistens ein umfangreiches und komplexes Datenangebot bereitstellen, so dass sie als lexikalische Informationssysteme bezeichnet werden. Die lexikographische Praxis ist eingebettet in die Theorie der Wörterbuchforschung, die u. a. zur Aufgabe hat, lexikographische Aktivitäten kritisch zu begleiten, lexikographische Prozesse zu optimieren, die Lexikographie zu systematisieren und Benutzungsbedürfnisse zu erforschen. Somit bewegt sich die Lexikographie grundsätzlich in einer Balance zwischen Theorie und Praxis. Die Produkte der Lexikographie sind ein- und mehrsprachige, allgemeine und fachliche, historische, diachrone und zeitgenössische Nachschlagewerke, Standard- und Regionalwörterbücher, Aussprache-, Valenz-, Lerner-, Rechtschreib-, Neologismen-, Häufigkeits-, Synonym-, Dialekt-, Etymologie-, Gehörlosenwörterbücher, um nur eine Auswahl an Wörterbuchtypen zu nennen. Nachschlagewerke werden in nahezu jedem Land der Welt, für fast jede Sprache, für viele Varietäten, für Nationalsprachen, zu Minderheitensprachen und auch zu bedrohten Sprachen erstellt.

Die Beiträge dieses Bandes zeigen mit Bezug zu den genannten Bereichen selektiv die Vielfalt und Breite der Lexikographie, einschließlich theoretischer Ansätze und unter Einbeziehung von Ausblicken auf die zukünftige Situation des Fachs. Der Spagat zwischen Europa und Australien mag in der ersten Betrachtung verwundern, ist aber mit den weltweiten Aktivitäten des Europäischen Masters für Lexikographie (EMLex)[1]

1 Vgl. https://emlex.eu.usc.gal/web/emlex-home (letzter Zugriff: 29.7.2025).

Idalete Dias, University of Minho, School of Arts and Humanities, Campus de Gualtar, 4710-057 Braga, Portugal, e-mail: idalete@elach.uminho.pt
Rufus H. Gouws, Stellenbosch University, Department of Afrikaans and Dutch, Private Bag X1, Matieland 7602, Südafrika, e-mail: rhg@sun.ac.za
Anja Lobenstein-Reichmann, Niedersächsische Akademie der Wissenschaften zu Göttingen. Frühneuhochdeutsches Wörterbuch, Geiststraße 10, 37073 Göttingen, Deutschland, e-mail: anja.lobenstein-reichmann@adwgoe.de
Stefan J. Schierholz, Universität Erlangen, Department für Germanistik und Komparatistik, Bismarckstr. 1/1B, 91054 Erlangen, Deutschland, e-mail: stefan.schierholz@rzmail.uni.erlangen.de

https://doi.org/10.1515/9783112216644-002

begründet. Regelmäßig veranstaltet das EMLex-Konsortium[2] internationale Kolloquien und Workshops zu aktuellen Themen im Fach und bemüht sich regelmäßig um neue fachliche Kontakte in der ganzen Welt. Die Beiträge dieses Bandes stammen zum einen aus einer Fachtagung im Herbst 2023 an der Universidade do Minho (Braga), zum anderen aus einer EMLex-Rundreise in Australien, in der in der Macquarie University Sydney, der University of Melbourne, der Monash University Melbourne, dem Australian National Dictionary Centre an der Australian National University in Canberra und an der University of Adelaide (in Kooperation mit der University of South Australia) Werbung für den Studiengang gemacht worden ist und zahlreiche Vorträgen gehalten worden sind. In der Zusammenstellung und Auswahl der Beiträge ist deutlich geworden, wie unterschiedlich und vielfältig die Lexikographie und Wörterbuchforschung in den beiden Antipoden vorliegt. In Europa ist die Lexikographie ein gut etabliertes Fachgebiet mit einer langen Tradition hochwertiger Wörterbücher, die durch mehrere und unterschiedliche theoretische Ansätze gründlich untermauert sind. Angehörige verschiedener europäischer Sprachen und Sprachgemeinschaften sind daran gewöhnt, dass sie einen leichten Zugang zu umfangreichen typologischen Kategorien von Wörterbüchern in gedruckter Form und im Online-Format haben. Im Gegensatz zu den Sprachen der Alten Welt ist die Lexikographie, sowohl die praktische Lexikographie als auch die Wörterbuchforschung, in der Neuen Welt wesentlich jünger und hat derzeit nicht den gleichen Umfang und die gleiche Vielfalt wie in Europa erreicht.

Die Länder der Neuen Welt (in Afrika, Amerika und Australien) haben in der Regel eine vielfältig mehrsprachige und multikulturelle Bevölkerung. Aufgrund des täglichen Sprachkontakts und des ständigen Spracheinflusses kann ein solches mehrsprachiges Umfeld als ein linguistisches und lexikographisches Laboratorium betrachtet werden. Aus metalexikographischer Sicht können einige bestehende und erfolgreich getestete Wörterbuchmodelle implementiert und sinnvoll eingesetzt werden. Die spannenden Herausforderungen liegen jedoch in der Vielfalt der Sprachen und Kulturen und dem Potenzial für die Entwicklung innovativer lexikographischer Projekte. Diese Projekte bereichern zum einen die lexikographische Praxis, bieten zum anderen der Metalexikographie die Möglichkeit, ihre Theorien durch einen transformativen lexikographischen Ansatz anzupassen, zu modifizieren und zu erweitern, und somit die Grenzen des bereits Bekannten zu überschreiten.

Die Bedeutung der Lexikographie in Australien ist im Rahmen innovativer Bemühungen bei der Erstellung von Wörterbüchern zu sehen, die die Sprachen und Kulturen aller australischen Ethnien widerspiegeln. Da Englisch die einzige Landessprache ist, ergänzen lokale Wörterbücher die britischen und internationalen englischen Wörterbücher, um eine gute lexikographische Darstellung der australischen

2 Seit 2015 mit der Koordination und Organisationszentrale an der Friedrich-Alexander-Universität Erlangen-Nürnberg, seit 2024 an der Universidade de Santiago de Compostela.

Sprachen und Varietäten zu erreichen. Das Australian National Dictionary, das in dieser Hinsicht eine Vorreiterrolle einnimmt, hat zusammen mit anderen Produkten aus der kommerziellen und pädagogischen Lexikographie eine wichtige Rolle bei der Etablierung des australischen Englisch als bedeutende Varietät des Englischen gespielt und trägt auch weiterhin dazu bei, deren Status zu erhalten und zu verbessern. Gleichzeitig hat Australien aufgrund eines wachsenden Sprachnationalismus ein tief verwurzeltes Interesse an den indigenen Sprachen und Varietäten des Landes und daher auch an Wörterbüchern zu diesen. Somit hat die Lexikographie in Australien eine hohe Dokumentationsfunktion, wenn einzelne Sprachen bzw. Varietäten, zu denen es manchmal nur noch wenige Sprecher gibt, lexikographisch bearbeitet werden, so dass in einigen Fällen sogar eine Wiederbelebung in Reichweite steht. Australien ist aber für die Lexikographie gerade deshalb von hoher Bedeutung, weil die sprachliche und kulturelle Vielfalt zahlreiche Möglichkeiten bietet, Wörterbücher zu planen und zu erstellen, die nicht nur die Qualität der lexikographischen Praxis auf diesem Kontinent erhöhen, sondern auch für den Rest der Welt bei der Wörterbucherstellung wegweisend sind.

Der Kern der Bedeutung der Lexikographie in Australien ist die Etablierung einer bidirektionalen Wörterbuchkultur. Die Lexikographie passt sich der Gesellschaft an, indem sie benutzerfreundliche Wörterbücher herstellt, die sich an Zielgruppen mit realen lexikographischen Bedürfnissen richten. Die Ausweitung der Wörterbuchproduktion bedeutet aber auch, dass sich die Gesellschaft an die Lexikographie anpasst, indem sie sich der Leistungen von professionell erstellten Nachschlagewerken bewusst wird, sich Fertigkeiten im Umgang mit Wörterbüchern aneignet und diese als nützliche Hilfsmittel in ihrem täglichen Leben anerkennt und einsetzt. Diese Wörterbücher sind nicht nur Nachschlagewerke, sondern sie stellen die Sprache eines Volkes dar und sichern so den Status dieser Sprache, und sie erfüllen die Mitglieder der Sprachgemeinschaft mit Stolz. Gute Wörterbücher würdigen und bestätigen die Bedeutung der Sprache, die in ihnen behandelt wird.

Während Mitglieder von Sprachgemeinschaften mit einer langen lexikographischen Tradition (Europa) Wörterbücher manchmal unkritisch und als selbstverständlich verfügbar ansehen, offenbart die Lexikographie in Australien Innovationen, Aufregung, Emotionen und die Dankbarkeit von Sprachgemeinschaften, die zum ersten Mal Zugang zu einem Wörterbuch ihrer Muttersprache erhalten. Dies verdeutlicht nicht nur den akademischen, sozialen und pädagogischen Wert von Wörterbüchern, sondern auch die lebensverändernden Auswirkungen, die auf eine Sprache und vor allem auf eine Sprachgemeinschaft wirken können.

Von großer Bedeutung in der aktuellen australischen lexikographischen Arbeit ist die Erweiterung des typologischen Netzes von Wörterbüchern für die indigenen Sprachen. Neben allgemeinen ein- und zweisprachigen Wörterbüchern ist die lexikographische Arbeit z. B. um enzyklopädische Wörterbücher und terminologische Ressourcen erweitert worden. Dies ist nur der Anfang eines Prozesses zur Erstellung von

Nachschlagewerken, die den Herausforderungen und Möglichkeiten des mehrsprachigen Umfelds gerecht werden.

Die wichtige gesellschaftliche und kulturhistorische Rolle der Lexikographie in Australien kann durch eine stärkere interaktive Beziehung zwischen Wörterbuchforschung und lexikographischer Praxis intensiviert werden. Die Planung und Veröffentlichung theoriebasierter lexikographischer Produkte, die von einer engagierten Benutzerperspektive angetrieben werden, könnte der australischen Lexikographie eine lange und erfolgreiche Zukunft sichern und diesen Kontinent zu einem Vorreiter in der Lexikographie für mehrsprachige und multikulturelle Umgebungen machen. Der wissenschaftliche Austausch, der im Frühjahr 2024 zwischen Europa und Australien stattgefunden hat, mag daher ein wichtiger Schritt für eine dauerhafte Verbindung gewesen sein. Dieser Sammelband versteht sich als ein Baustein in diesem Prozess.

Die Zusammenstellung der Beiträge folgt einer thematischen Ordnung, so dass Beiträge aus Braga und aus Australien in unregelmäßigem Wechsel hintereinanderstehen. Nach einem allgemeinen Überblick zur Entwicklung der Lexikographie in Australien folgen die Historische Lexikographie, Gebärdensprachenlexikographie, Terminologie und Terminographie, die Behandlung indigener Sprachen und der Umgangssprache in Australien sowie ein Ausblick auf die Künstliche Intelligenz in Wörterbüchern, die individuellen kognitiven Kompetenzen und Leistungen des Human-Lexikographen sowie auf die Zukunft der Dialektlexikographie.

Im ersten Beitrag „Australian Lexicography and the Australian Story. Historical Perspectives and the Current Scene“ unterteilt Amanda Laugesen (Canberra) die australische Lexikographie in drei Bereiche: (a) allgemeine/bildende Wörterbücher, die häufig von Fach- und Bildungsverlagen herausgegeben werden; (b) populäre Wörterbücher und Wortsammlungen, die häufig im Handel erscheinen; (c) Forschungs-/Wissenschaftswörterbücher, die oft in akademischen Kontexten entstehen. Neben einem historischen Überblick wird der Einfluss der australischen nationalen und kulturellen Identität auf die australische Lexikographie aufgezeigt, und es werden aktuelle Herausforderungen herausgestellt.

Anja Lobenstein-Reichmann (Göttingen) liefert zu der Frage im Titel „Warum brauchen wir historische Lexikographie?“ eine Diskussion und den Versuch einer Antwort. Gerade vor dem Hintergrund der Möglichkeiten moderner Sprach- und Informationstechnologien (zusammengefasst: KI) ist die Frage nach den Aufgaben der Historischen Lexikographie und ihrer grundsätzlichen Begründung von pädagogischer und fachlicher Bedeutung. Jede geisteswissenschaftliche Disziplin steht vor der Aufgabe, ihre eigenen Aktivitäten zu hinterfragen, ihre theoretischen und methodischen Prämissen transparent zu machen und damit vor einem vermeintlich allgemeinen wie fachlichen Publikum zu legitimieren.

Oskar Reichmann (Göttingen) unterscheidet in seinem Beitrag „Zur Berechtigung historischer Lexikographie: Fakten und Überlegungen“ zwischen einer auf einzelne Wörter und einer auf den gesamten Wortschatz einer Sprache gerichteten Lexikographie. Erstere stützt sich auf eine repräsentationstheoretisch fundierte Theorie des Wörterbuchs und möchte eine möglichst große Anzahl von isoliert behandelten Lemmata bearbeiten. Der zweite Ansatz hat eher eine pragmatisch-kommunikative Basis und die Vernetzung aller Lemmata unter semantischen, syntaktischen und wortbildnerischen Aspekten zum Ziel. In der Lexikographie des Deutschen und seiner Nachbarsprachen findet sich dieser Ansatz vor allem im Frühneuhochdeutschen Wörterbuch (FWB).

Trevor Johnston (Sydney) beschreibt in „Signed language lexicography and the Auslan dictionaries in print and online" die *Auslan*-Wörterbücher (Australian Sign Language) und die lexikalische Datenbank, auf der sie basieren. Seit den 1980er Jahren hat sich diese Datenbank über mehrere Softwareplattformen verbreitet, da die Arten von Daten, die in neueren Datenbanken enthalten sein können (Text, Grafiken, Video), verbessert und erweitert wurden, so dass die Wörterbücher in drei Formaten erscheinen können: Gedruckt, multimedial (CD-ROM) und online. Es werden lexikographische und lexikologische Grundlagen, die Arten und Inhalte der Datenfelder, die in der Datenbank verwendet werden, sowie die Art und Weise, wie die Daten in jeder Ausgabe angezeigt werden, präsentiert. Es wird die Verlinkung der Beispiele mit dem Auslan-Korpus geschildert und auf welche Weise die Architektur der Auslan Signbank Daten aus jeder beliebigen Gebärdensprache aufnehmen kann, und wie diese dann für sprachübergreifende Untersuchungen der Lexikologie und Phonologie von Gebärdensprachen genutzt werden können.

Pius ten Hacken (Innsbruck) stützt sich in „Terminology from a Lexicographic Perspective" auf die Allgemeine Terminologielehre von Eugen Wüster, die als vorherrschende Richtschnur für die Arbeit der Normungsinstitute gilt. Es wird untersucht, inwieweit sich diese Dominanz aus lexikographischer Sicht erklären lässt. Die diskutierten Herausforderungen basieren auf korpusbasierter Terminologiearbeit, terminologischer Arbeit zum Zwecke der Sprachbewahrung und dem Verhältnis zwischen genau abgegrenzten Termini und prototypischer Semantik. Dabei wird diskutiert, inwieweit Definitionen, die aus notwendigen und hinreichenden Bedingungen bestehen, durch eine flexiblere Auswahl von Informationen ersetzt oder ergänzt werden können. Eine benutzerorientierte lexikographische Bewertung von terminologischen Ressourcen sollte anerkennen, dass Wüsters Theorie in erster Linie für Experten nützlich ist.

Pam Peters (Sydney) zeigt in ihrem Beitrag „Online Terminography for indigenous Australians" anhand einer Online-Termdatenbank für Termini des australischen Familienrechts, wie benutzerbasierte Lexikographie in der Terminographie gestaltet werden kann, um den Inhalt für indigene Nutzer mit geringer Lese- und Schreibkompetenz zugänglich zu machen. Anstelle der semasiologischen Ordnung wird bei der Gestaltung von Wörterbüchern und Termbanken ein onomasiologischer Aufbau verwendet, der die konzeptionelle Struktur für die Benutzer in den Vordergrund stellt. Dabei werden vielfältig Medien (Grafik, Audio, Sprache) und Verlinkungen eingesetzt, um den Benutzern den Zugang zu unbekannten Termini und Konzepten im Familienrecht zu erleichtern.

In dem Beitrag „The AIATSIS Dictionaries Program: Supporting the strengthening of Australian Indigenous Languages“ von Lauren W. Reed, Alison L. Mount, Alexandra Marley, Kira Davey, Mahesh White-Radhakrishnan, Grace Smith, Jason Chong, Kaitlyn Lodewikus und Tamarind Meara (Canberra) wird das Wörterbuchprogramm des Australian Institute of Aboriginal and Torres Strait Islander Studies (AIATSIS) vorgestellt, das Teil der Bemühungen der australischen Regierung ist, diese bedrohten Sprachen zu stützen. Nach einem historischen Überblick folgen eine Beschreibung der Geschichte des Programms und eine Diskussion der besonderen Herausforderungen bei der Wörterbucherstellung angesichts der sprachlichen Besonderheiten der beiden indigenen Sprachen.

Mary Laughren (Queensland) behandelt in „Encyclopaedic Lexicography: the Warlpiri Encyclopaedic Dictionary“ das enzyklopädische Wörterbuch der Warlpiri, das das Ergebnis einer 1978 begonnenen Kooperation zwischen Warlpiri-Sprechern und Linguisten, die Form und den Inhalt des Wörterbuchs zu einem großen Teil durch den sprachlichen, historischen und sozialen Kontext bestimmt haben. Die Rolle der zweisprachigen Bildungsprogramme, die ab 1973 in den Warlpiri-Gemeinschaftsschulen eingeführt worden sind, erweist sich dabei neben den vorliegenden Dokumentationen der Warlpiri-Sprache als wesentlicher Faktor. Die Erweiterung der rein sprachlichen Aspekte auf enzyklopädische Inhalte erweist sich insbesondere dort, wo die Sprachen und Kulturen divergieren, als notwendig und wertvoll.

Kate Burridge und Howard Manns (Melbourne) zeigen in „Behind the lingo – slang and the dictionary“ die Komplexität der Umgangssprache und konzentrieren sich dabei auf deren flüchtige Natur, ihre unvorhersehbare Entwicklung und die Herausforderungen bei der lexikographischen Dokumentation. Am Beispiel des australischen Slangs werden historische Beispiele wie das Sträflingsglossar aus dem 19. Jahrhundert, moderne Slang-Innovationen sowie die Ergebnisse einer Umfrage zu sog. australischen Ausdrücken diskutiert. Durch die Analyse von sprachlichen Überbleibseln und flüchtigen Trends werden kulturelle, soziohistorische und sprachliche Kräfte hervorgehoben, die den Lebenszyklus des Slangs prägen. Technologie, Globalisierung und Australiens Vorliebe für die Informalität erschweren die Aufgabe, Slang nachzuvollziehen und zu definieren. Als Ausdruck sprachlicher Kreativität ist Slang ein Beispiel für das Zusammenspiel zwischen formeller und informeller Sprache und spiegelt ein dynamisches, sich ständig veränderndes Lexikon wider, das Lexikographen mit zunehmender Komplexität beherrschen müssen.

Iván Arias Arias, María José Domínguez Vázquez und Carlos Valcárcel Riveiro (Santiago de Compostela) befassen sich in ihrem Beitrag „People, machines and dictionaries: Is artificial intelligence killing dictionaries?“ mit den Beziehungen zwischen Menschen, Wörterbüchern und Computersystemen im lexikographischen Prozess und mit den Handlungen von Wörterbucherstellern sowie Benutzern. Es wird der Einfluss Künstlicher Intelligenz auf lexikographische Aktivitäten vorgestellt sowie Ergebnisse neuer Experimente, in denen die Zuverlässigkeit von KI-generierten Ergebnissen in Abhängigkeit vom Benutzertyp dargestellt wird. Schließlich wird der aktuelle soziale und kulturelle Wert von Wörterbüchern und ihren Einfluss auf die Gesellschaft diskutiert.

Im Beitrag von Konan Kouassi (Erlangen) „Wörterbücher von heute und morgen. Von den Ausgangsdaten zum Wörterbuchartikel" wird aus einem Erlanger Forschungsprojekt berichtet, in dem die Leistungen und Kompetenzen des Lexikographen in der modernen lexikographischen Praxis untersucht werden. Die Leistungskomplexe teilen sich in konkrete und abstrakte Elemente und bestimmen die Rolle und Bedeutung des Lexikographen sowie dessen Erkenntnisse und Kompetenzen für eine gelungene lexikographische Praxis. Die kognitiven Leistungen des Lexikographen werden mit der Wörterbuchartikelqualität verknüpft, wobei die hohe Qualität als das Ziel und die kognitiven Leistungen als die Voraussetzung zu betrachten sind.

Im letzten Beitrag „Dialektwörterbücher als Wörterbücher der Zukunft" beleuchtet Christine Ganslmayer (Erlangen) die Bedeutung von Dialektwörterbüchern aus der Perspektive des frühen 21. Jahrhunderts. Nach einem kurzen Überblick über den aktuellen Stand der akademischen deutschsprachigen Dialektlexikographie werden die fünfzehn Villa Vigoni Thesen zur Lexikographie (2018) auf Dialektwörterbücher des bayerischen Raums bezogen. Die Analyse betrachtet Dialektwörterbücher als „Wörterbücher der Zukunft" und zeigt ihr Potenzial für eine zukunftsorientierte Lexikographie auf.

Die Herausgeberinnen und Herausgeber danken den Beiträgerinnen und Beiträgern für ihre Geduld bei der Produktion dieses Sammelbandes.

Amanda Laugesen

Australian lexicography and the Australian story: Historical perspectives and the current scene

Abstract: Australian lexicography can be understood to consist of three traditions: general/educational dictionaries, often produced by trade and educational publishers; popular dictionaries and word collections, often trade publications; and research/scholarly dictionaries, often produced within academic contexts. In this article, I provide an historical overview of these three Australian lexicographical traditions and examine how Australian lexicography has been shaped and informed by ideas of Australian national and cultural identity. I conclude by exploring some of the contemporary challenges that are faced in Australian lexicography.

Keywords: Lexicography, Australian English, Australian dictionaries, Australian identity, Australian culture

Schlagwörter: Lexikographie, Australisches Englisch, Australische Wörterbücher, Australische Identität, Australische Kultur

1 Introduction

The Australian continent was colonised by the British at the end of the eighteenth century, but it would not be until well into the twentieth century that an established lexicographical tradition would be put into place and the Australian variety of English considered as the standard. In this article, I provide an overview of the development of Australian lexicography and consider how it has been shaped by (and informed) the close relationship between language and identity in Australia. I will also consider how lexicography contributed to the legitimation of the Australian variety of English, as well as examine how contemporary Australian lexicography is evolving in a period where the idea of an 'Australian identity' has become more complicated and problematic.

Australian lexicography currently has three main lexicographical areas or traditions: the first being educational and reference dictionaries, usually produced by commercial publishers, for the school and general market; the second consists of popular dictionaries and word studies, often produced as commercially-published (trade) texts

Amanda Laugesen, Australian National Dictionary Centre, AD Hope Building, Australian National University, ACTON, 0200, e-mail: Amanda.laugesen@anu.edu.au

https://doi.org/10.1515/9783112216644-003

that may or may not be based on rigorous research or accurate information; and the third tradition is of research-based dictionaries often produced within scholarly contexts and informed by rigorous research and understanding of how dictionaries function. These three traditions of lexicography have developed over time, with each of them having their own specific history in Australia. Each type of dictionary has its own purposes and uses for its audience; all three have shaped how Australian English is understood by the general Australian public. At times, these traditions overlap and draw on each other – for example, educational and general reference dictionaries have been closely informed by work done on research dictionaries.

It should be noted that this article only examines English-language lexicography, but there is also a long tradition of First Nations language lexicography in Australia. Many hundreds of First Nations languages and dialects existed when Europeans first arrived on the Australian continent. As colonisation proceeded, First Nations peoples were dispossessed and communities dramatically reduced through violence and illness. There were attempts to strip First Nations peoples of their culture, including language. The result has been that while some work was done in the nineteenth and into the early twentieth century to document some Aboriginal languages – for example, by missionaries – the number of speakers of those languages was decimated. Many languages became extinct or 'went to sleep'. Attempts are now being made to preserve languages that are still spoken and increase the number of speakers, and to revive 'sleeping' languages (see Commonwealth of Australia 2020). In this context, dictionaries are a vital resource for documentation, educational, and revitalisation purposes.

While dictionaries produced for these languages in the twentieth century tended to be scholarly productions compiled within Linguistics departments and often having limited circulation beyond this, in recent decades, much more work has been done to both address the needs of communities in terms of producing lexical resources that are of value and utility to First Nations communities, and that are also produced with collaboration, consultation, and input by community. Consultation with community and producing resources that are useful to community is now considered a first priority. However, the need for trained First Nations lexicographers remains (Woods 2023).

The establishment of Australian English lexicography must be understood as a complement and a tool to the entrenchment and exercising of settler-colonial power in Australia. It has served to underpin a 'naturalising' of the variety as the de facto 'national language'. I mention this because it is important to consider the contribution of dictionaries in the functioning of broader language ideologies which, as Debra Spitulink (1988: 164) has observed, are 'among many things, about the construction and legitimation of power, the production of social relations of sameness and difference, and the creation of cultural stereotypes about types of speakers and social groups'. Language ideologies are 'universalising' and 'naturalising', she argues, 'disguising conditions of production and their intimate and often strategic ties to power'. English-language dictionaries in Australia are thus part of the entrenchment of English as the colonising language.

2 Early dictionaries in Australia

The first European settlements in Australia were convict colonies, with the first of these established in what was named New South Wales. Early settler populations were made up of many convicts who were transported from the United Kingdom to the Australian colonies. Once there, convicts might be sent out to work 'on assignment', working for the free settlers who began to arrive in the colonies. They could earn their freedom and from there establish themselves as farmers or in business. It is in this milieu of convictism that the first English-language dictionary appears. This was a lengthy glossary entitled 'A new and comprehensive vocabulary of the flash language' appended to the *Memoirs of James Hardy Vaux*, published in England in 1819. James Hardy Vaux was what was called a 'gentleman convict', that is, he had some education and had worked as a clerk and served in the navy (Fink 1967; see also McLachlan 1964: xxxiv).

Vaux's glossary consisted largely of 'flash' language: that is, language, primarily slang, that was purportedly spoken by members of the criminal underworld. Vaux dedicated the vocabulary to Thomas Skottowe, the commandant of the Newcastle penal settlement. He noted that 'in the course of a chequered and eventful life, I have intermixed with the most dissolute and unprincipled characters' and so he was now 'familiar with their language and system of operations'. From these experiences, he had collected his lexicon. He sought to ingratiate himself with Skottowe, suggesting in his foreword that the glossary would both amuse him and 'from the correctness of its definitions, you may occasionally find it useful in your magisterial capacity' (Vaux 1964: 223).

As a dictionary of 'flash' language, the vocabulary is a valuable record of the kind of language that may have been used among convicts and that was exported to the colonies. The dictionary belongs to a genre of dictionaries that recorded the language of the 'criminal classes', popular in Britain in the eighteenth and nineteenth centuries with middle-class readers who took a prurient interest in the ways of life of the so-called criminal 'underworld'. While only a small number of words from Vaux's glossary actually entered the general Australian English vocabulary, such as *swag*, Vaux's dictionary was arguably the earliest in the tradition of popular and slang dictionaries that would be an important facet of the broader Australian lexicographical scene.

Dictionaries were of value to colonial society through the nineteenth century, as the population and cities grew. But these were all imported into the colonies, mostly, but not exclusively, from Britain. Dictionaries were advertised as being for sale in colonial newspapers. Advertisements from the time indicate the availability of 'Johnson's dictionary' as well as 'Walker's pronouncing dictionary' (*Geelong advertiser*, 28 June 1849: 1).[1] 'Webster's dictionary' was also available (*Sydney gazette*, 24 June 1830: 2). Dictionaries were useful

1 Exact editions of these dictionaries are not mentioned in newspaper advertisements.

for the business and education of the colonies. There are also some early mentions of 'Johnson's dictionary' being used as an authority in colonial court cases (see for example, *Colonial times*, 10 December 1833: 2; *Cornwall chronicle*, 9 May 1846: 358; and *Sydney herald*, 6 July 1835: 4).

Australian-produced dictionaries first appear nearer the end of the nineteenth century. This reflected several developments in the Australian colonies during the nineteenth century: a growth in print culture that included newspapers, periodicals, and books that accompanied a growing Australian literary culture with an interest in Australian subjects; a related and growing readership for such texts with the growth of the Australian population, especially in urban areas; a developing sense of Australian identity as something distinctive and separate from a British identity; and related to that, an awareness of a distinctive 'language' being spoken in the colonies. As evidence of this last, we can see that the term *Australian English* is first recorded in 1870, *Australian language* (meaning Australian English rather than an Aboriginal language) in 1880, and *Australianese* in 1898. The term *Australian accent* first appeared in 1856, suggesting that an awareness of the accent preceded a more general idea of an Australian variety of English (Moore 2016: vol. 1).

The dictionaries that were produced in Australia towards the end of the century helped to establish both the popular and research lexicographical traditions. In the popular tradition, three dictionaries/dictionary projects are worth mentioning: *The Sydney slang dictionary*, published in 1882; *The Australian slang dictionary*, published in 1895; and an unpublished manuscript for a slang dictionary compiled by A.G. Stephens and Stephen O'Brien which is dated as ca. 1910, but the material for which had been collected over several years. The two that found publication were published in Australia, not in Britain. Most Australian texts were still published in Britain in this period, but small printers had started to set up in Australia and there was a growing market for locally produced texts.

The Sydney slang dictionary and *The Australian slang dictionary* were both primarily focused on collecting the language of criminals and the underworld. *The Sydney slang dictionary* was advertised as documenting the 'elegant colloquial peculiar to denizens of the dark retreats of Sydney' (Robertson 2005: 23). Cornelius Crowe's *The Australian slang dictionary* was published in Melbourne, and included slang words used by the 'criminal classes' with a professed aim of translating them for the police, courts, and public (see Crowe 1895: Preface). While much of the slang contained therein was not exclusively or uniquely Australian (Robertson 2005: 12),[2] these dictionaries nevertheless captured something of the slang in use in urban colonial Aus-

2 Robertson argues that nearly all the terms were copied from English or American sources, probably Hotten's slang dictionary. More recently, James Lambert (2022) has argued that despite these terms not being exclusively Australian, there is evidence of Australian use for many of them.

tralia, especially among the working-classes and those engaged in activities such as sex work. They also helped to connect the idea of Australian English to slang.

The lexical material collected by Stephens and O'Brien was never published. Stephens and O'Brien both worked for the popular Australian periodical *The bulletin*: A.G. Stephens wrote for the periodical and was the manager of *Bulletin publications* from 1896; S.E. O'Brien was a freelance writer who wrote for *The bulletin* from 1898 to 1907 (Lee 1990; Robertson 2005: 166). *The bulletin* was an aggressively Australian publication that championed an independent Australian culture. Both Stephens and O'Brien were keen to capture the Australian vernacular, embracing what they perceived to be the unique Australian flavour of the language. This kind of language was actively promoted, if not coined, in *The bulletin*'s pages. While a study suggests only around half of the lexical items included in the manuscript are uniquely Australian (Robertson 2005: 181), it reflected – as with the dictionaries just discussed – the development of a popular lexicographical tradition (and broader cultural discourse) that intimately linked 'slang' with 'Australian English'. And while this manuscript never found publication, the promotion of slang and informal language within the pages of popular periodicals such as *The bulletin* also contributed to the idea that an 'Australian language' was one that consisted of slang and colloquial language.

The popular tradition of Australian lexicography established by the end of the nineteenth century, therefore, was one that focused very much on the idea of slang and colloquialisms, and which connected that to an idea of what the Australian English lexicon was. Beyond that, there was only a limited recognition of what, other than the accent, might mark an Australian variety of English.

The appearance of a scholarly dictionary based on research into just this question, Edward Ellis Morris' *Austral English: A dictionary of Australasian words, phrases and usages*, opened up a new tradition of lexicography in Australia, that of research or scholarly dictionaries. *Austral English* was published in 1898 and was an attempt to capture a distinctive vocabulary that was understood to be developing in the Australian colonies and in New Zealand (the colonies were collectively referred to as Australasia). Morris was a scholar of languages who taught at the University of Melbourne, and his dictionary was a product of work that he did in contributing to the 'New English dictionary' project, later the *Oxford English dictionary*. He also contributed to the work of American dictionary publisher Funk and Wagnalls as a member of their 'Advisory Committee on disputed spelling and pronunciation' (Morris 1898: x).

Morris' lexicographical approach was based on an OED-style methodology, that is, he collected written quotations to illustrate usage of a given vocabulary item. His dictionary identified and recorded major areas of the Australian English vocabulary, including flora, fauna, and words borrowed from Aboriginal languages. In his introduction, Morris was keen to assert that '[t]he phrase "Australasian English" includes something much wider than slang' (Morris 1898: xii). He described Australasian English as made up of 'altered English' or 'words new to the language' (Morris 1898: xiii–xiv). Interestingly, A.G. Stephens took Morris to task for his decision not to include slang in his dictionary in the pages of *The bulletin* (Robertson 2005: 167). For Stephens, a radical Australian nationalist, what was distinctive about the Australian language was that it was indigenous to Australia and that it was made up of colourful words and idioms.

Morris' work established a connection between Australian lexicography and broader developments in English-language lexicography through the turn of the twentieth century. The principles upon which the *Oxford English dictionary* were based were scientific and scholarly. The dictionary was based on evidence, and it applied historical principles to the development of language, considering the origins of words and their evolution across time. While this reflected a Western, arguably colonialist, perspective to language – the English language was an instrument of the British Empire and its expanding lexicon reflected the processes of colonisation, conquest, and imperialism – it nevertheless forged an important methodology that would continue to be used by historical lexicographers in the twentieth century and beyond.

Morris' dictionary reflected both the close intellectual relationship that a nascent Australian lexicography (and more broadly scholarship) had with that being done in the 'motherland' as well as reflecting a sense that a distinctive culture was producing its own variety of English. In this period of Australian history, as Melissa Bellanta (2013: 236) writes, an interest in Australian national identity co-existed with a strong commitment to British culture and the empire. This was evident in the production of *Austral English*, the most significant contribution to Australian lexicography for quite some time to come.

3 Making an 'Australian language'

While Morris' *Austral English* was an important contribution to Australian lexicography, it surprisingly remained the only dictionary to attempt to record the Australian English lexicon for several decades. The next major contribution to Australian lexicography came through the work of Sidney Baker. Baker was a journalist from New Zealand who moved to Australia in 1935. He took a strong interest in the distinctive vocabulary of Australia (and New Zealand), especially slang and colloquialisms. His biographer suggests that his interest was piqued when he travelled to the UK and found that there were many words used in Australia and New Zealand that the British didn't understand (Ramson 1993). Receiving a Commonwealth Literary Fund grant, he dedicated much time to collecting and documenting what he perceived to be the unique vocabulary items used in Australian. This included collecting material from the general public, with the solicitation of contributions through calls in newspapers.

From this 'field research', as well as using the earlier collections of Crowe, Stephens and O'Brien, and Morris, Baker produced several important publications that are valuable documentations of slang and colloquial language. He published three editions of *A popular dictionary of Australian slang* through the early 1940s, and in 1945, his major work *The Australian language*[3] appeared. *The Australian language* was not a dictionary, but it recorded and discussed many terms that Baker believed to be Australian English, organised in thematic chapters, such as 'The Bush', 'The City', 'The Underworld', 'Peoples and Places' and 'Children' (Baker 1945).

Importantly, Baker sought to establish the idea of an independent 'Australian language' (the title of his book is modelled on H.L. Mencken's *The American language*) and to see this as something that Australians should have an awareness of, if not pride in. Baker argued in his book that Australian English was 'a living language, virile and colourful, and as richly Australian as the environment in which we live' (Baker 1945: 21). Baker also made the argument that knowledge of the idiom of Australia was essential to producing literature that was authentically Australian (Baker 1945: 23).

The first half of the twentieth century was a period in which Australian English, including the accent, struggled for legitimacy, but was slowly moving towards it. British English was generally considered the standard, and an accent that was closer to British Received Pronunciation (the 'BBC accent') was preferred in broadcasting and public speaking. However, through the 1930s and 1940s, the Australian accent and the Australian lexicon gained in legitimacy and slowly moved towards acceptability. Academic work into the accent began to be undertaken by scholar A.G. Mitchell who developed a framework for understanding the Australian accent, categorising it into 'Broad' and 'Educated' (later joined by 'General'). Mitchell also undertook much public work, such as public lectures and radio talks, where he argued that an Educated Australian accent was perfectly acceptable (Laugesen 2023; see also Leitner 2004). Meanwhile, Australian literary writers of the period between the two world wars made use of the Australian lexicon to help confer authenticity to a growing canon of literature that told Australian stories, which were often linked to the land and the bush.[4]

Posing a different sort of challenge to the primacy of the British standard in Australia was American English. During this period, American English was increasingly heard and read through movies, radio, and novels. American popular culture was generally viewed with suspicion in Australia. While popular with many people, cultural gatekeepers saw American culture as potentially corrupting due to its alleged immorality. American slang and use of language was also seen as substandard and unattractive. A fear that American slang would be taken up by (especially young) Australians became a topic of some commentary and debate in the Australian media throughout this period (Damousi 2007: 397). The presence of large numbers of American service personnel during the Second World War exacerbated concerns on the one

3 It should be noted that the term 'Australian language' is one that is now more properly used for an Aboriginal language. Using it to describe Australian English is generally inappropriate.

4 Examples include Katherine Susannah Prichard and Henrietta Drake-Brockman.

hand, but also saw attempts to share slang and promote friendships between Australians and Americans. The influence of the US on Australian speech (and popular culture more broadly) would continue to be a topic of perennial interest – and often concern – for the rest of the century and into the twenty-first century.

One consequence of this concern about the influence of American English and speech on Australia was, however, to further legitimise Australian English. This is not to say that Australian English was recognised as the norm yet, especially in formal contexts – British English remained the standard – but it is to say that Australian English was increasingly viewed either neutrally or positively. Importantly, it is through this period from the late nineteenth century to the years of the Second World War that Australian English increasingly came to be associated with Australian values and considered as integral to an idea of an Australian national identity. In addition, as an Australian identity evolved that spoke to things such as fairness, equality, a lack of pretension, and supporting others, Australian English terms such as *fair go*, *dinkum* ('genuine'), and *mateship* found increased traction in the national discourse and became core terms in Australian discourse.

Despite these cultural changes, by the middle of the century, Australian lexicography had made little progress in a formal sense, with no rigorous, research-based work being undertaken except for Baker's work in collecting and recording colloquialisms and slang. Progress was made on understanding the Australian accent, as we've seen with Mitchell's work. But these decades laid important groundwork in progressing the evolution of the general idea of 'Australian English', adding to public understanding of Australian English and further linking Australian speech and lexicon to ideas of Australian identity.

4 An independent Australia and a new lexicography

The period of the Second World War and the decades that followed saw some significant changes to the country. This included a much stronger sense of a culturally and politically independent Australia as a result of the war and a reorientation from Britain to the USA in foreign policy; a growth in non-Anglo-British migration (mostly from southern and eastern Europe) that required 'old' Australians to define themselves against these so-called 'new' Australians; and a growth in suburban and consumer life. Importantly also, higher education and academia grew, providing a basis for growth in academic research. All of this would provide the basis for the expansion of Australian lexicography in the second half of the twentieth century.

The second half of the twentieth century also saw a great deal of growth in the Australian publishing and literary scene; it also witnessed the development of a much stronger sense of an Australian national identity in the cultural sphere. Australian accents – including 'broad' Australian accents – were increasingly heard and celebrated on radio, television, on stage, and in film, and Australian cultural productions now commonly featured Australian slang and colloquial language. The 1970s and 1980s in particular saw a great surge in Australian nationalism, as Australia sought to define an identity that was separate from its British past.

It was in this context of change and the explosion in Australian cultural nationalism that Australian lexicography took off in unprecedented ways. Australians continued to use imported dictionaries into the 1970s, but it was becoming very clear that there was a real need and demand for dictionaries that reflected the language that most Australians spoke and wrote: Australian English. If English in Australia still often set British English as an aspiration (for example in the pronunciation of certain words), there was still a recognition that there was a need for a reliable source that represented Australian English. The last thirty years of the twentieth century were thus arguably the golden years of Australian lexicography, and this can be said of all three lexicographical traditions: academic, popular, and commercial/educational.

Academic work on the lexicon launched in the 1960s. In 1964, the Australian Language Research Centre (ALRC) was established at the University of Sydney, with one of its aims being to collect material for a future 'historical dictionary of Australianisms'. A series of short studies of the lexicon were subsequently produced that examined aspects of the Australian vocabulary such as sheep shearing, and historical periods such as the convict era. Some 30,000 quotations were collected by the ALRC team, but further work did not eventuate (Peter Davies. 'Towards a Dictionary of Australian English', AND Files 1966–75, ANDC, ANU).

The 1970s saw major developments in commercial and educational lexicography. The first school and reference dictionary projects were set into motion. These projects were largely driven by the educational publishing industry, which was prepared to invest money into such projects, as well as those in academia who were developing expertise in studying the lexicon. The *Australian pocket Oxford dictionary* was published in 1976, edited by Grahame Johnston, as was the *Heinemann dictionary of Australian English* (1976).

One of the biggest lexicographical projects underway in the 1970s was the dictionary that would become the *Macquarie dictionary*. This was a project led by Arthur Delbridge, a linguist at Macquarie University who had been involved with the ALRC, and with the goal of producing a general reference dictionary that would describe English as it was used in Australia. It started life as the 'Jacaranda dictionary', a project supported by a notable Australian educational publisher, Jacaranda Press. Jacaranda had initially approached Delbridge and another scholar, John Bernard, to initiate work on the dictionary (Manser 2021: 4).

But ultimately the project, which came to be based at Macquarie University, struggled to find a publisher due to changes to the ownership of Jacaranda and the cost of publication. A solution was found in Kevin Weldon, a rich businessman, who took on the task. He set up the Macquarie Publishing Company Ltd, to publish it; the dictionary would ultimately be sold through a type of mail order scheme and was hugely successful thanks to extensive marketing, as well as its ability to meet a significant gap in the market. The first edition of the *Macquarie dictionary* sold 50,000 copies within the first three months of publication (*Sunday Age*, 30 October 2005: 18).

The publication of the *Macquarie dictionary* in 1981 was a major cultural event. The new dictionary was widely publicised and discussed, and regarded as a cultural landmark. The first edition's production reflected a strong sense of Australian nationalism: for example, the dictionary cover's colour motifs were the Australian sporting colours green and gold. As Pat Manser writes (2021: 84), the dictionary 'combined the authority of a serious reference book with a strong Australian identity'. Sue Butler, a later chief editor of the *Macquarie* and then part of the editing team, has written that the publication of the first edition 'radically altered the filter through which Australians might view their variety of English' (2006: 337). This was the core of its importance: it legitimised once and for all the Australian variety of English. The *Macquarie* became the style standard used by the media, some publishers, and in the legal system.

The Macquarie team would also go on to produce a range of other dictionaries, including for the school market. These include the *Macquarie school dictionary* and the *Macquarie primary dictionary*. These are currently published by Jacaranda Press.[5] The *Macquarie dictionary* is now in its 9th edition, as well as being available through an online edition, and is published by Pan Macmillan. It remains a central dictionary of reference in the Australian market.

General reference and educational dictionaries would also be produced by Oxford University Press through the last decades of the twentieth century. From the 1970s, Oxford University Press Australia established a significant presence in the academic market, publishing many books in areas such as Australian history and Australian cultural and literary studies. Oxford also continued to develop its significant role in the educational market, increasingly producing textbooks and reference books that catered to and reflected an Australian readership.

Oxford dictionaries already had a presence and an authority in Australia before this period ('brand recognition'), but these were wholly imported texts from the UK. As mentioned above, the first of the Oxford Australian dictionaries to be produced was the *Australian pocket Oxford dictionary*, published in 1976 and edited by an academic in an English department, Grahame Johnston. The full suite of Australian Oxford Dictionaries was developed through the 1980s and 1990s, and was a product of the relationship that Oxford University Press Australia developed with the Australian National University and the establishment of the Australian National Dictionary Centre (ANDC).

5 For the current range of Macquarie dictionaries, see https://www.jacaranda.com.au/subjects/references-dictionaries/#1639986386742-7e163069-de19 (last access: 25 April 2025).

When the Centre was established in 1988 (see below), the ANDC began to take on the editing of the full range of Australian Oxford dictionaries from primary school level through to full general reference dictionaries. These included such dictionaries as *The Australian primary Oxford dictionary, The Australian middle primary Dictionary, The Australian pocket Oxford dictionary,* and *The Australian concise Oxford dictionary.* The majority of these editions were developed under Bruce Moore, director of the ANDC from 1994 to 2011, and have been continued under current ANDC director Amanda Laugesen and senior editor Mark Gwynn. One particular dictionary of note produced under Moore is the *Australian Oxford dictionary,* the first edition of which appeared in 1999. This was an encyclopaedic dictionary, with some 110,000 headwords, and a rival to the *Macquarie.*

Alongside the flourishing world of the general reference and school dictionaries was the development of an important academic research dictionary: the *Australian national dictionary: Australian words and their origins* (AND). This dictionary began as the project of W.S. 'Bill' Ramson, whose PhD thesis was a study of the Australian English lexicon of the nineteenth century, published as *Australian English: An historical study of the vocabulary 1788– 1898* in 1966. In his work on Australian English, Ramson was keen to demonstrate that the lexicon was made up of more than slang and colloquialisms, and to show the relationship of Australian English to British English. He worked with the team that produced the *Macquarie dictionary,* in particular contributing and working on historical material. But he soon dedicated his lexicographical career to realising the production of a stand-alone dictionary of Australianisms based on historical principles.

From the 1970s, Ramson received funding for moving his project forward, and a group of researchers – including a team that read vast tranches of Australian books, magazines, and newspapers – began to gather the quotations that would form the basis for a dictionary on historical principles.[6] Ultimately modelled on, and following the methodology of, the *Oxford English dictionary* and published by Oxford University Press Australia in 1988, AND provided a scholarly, research-based record of Australian English and its development from the time of the European invasion.

Lexical items gained inclusion to AND on the basis of evidence (a certain number of quotations over a period of time). A word or expression had to be proven to be of Australian origin, used more in Australia than elsewhere, or to have special significance to Australia. Several areas of the lexicon received special focus, including words borrowed from Aboriginal languages, flora and fauna, words to do with specific professions (such as shearing, farming, and so on), words to do with the colonisation process, and colloquial and proverbial phrases.

It is also worth noting that once it was established that Oxford University Press would publish the dictionary, a close relationship was established with the Oxford En-

6 For an account of the development of the first edition, see Ramson (2002). See also Laugesen (2014).

glish Dictionary team with Robert Burchfield and John Simpson providing advice and evidence. The project was located at Ramson's university, the Australian National University, and received financial support from the Press, the ANU, and the Australian Commonwealth government. The connection with Oxford conferred a certain level of academic prestige and authority. But it also attracted criticism. Kevin Weldon, who published the *Macquarie*, had put in a bid to publish AND, but was unsuccessful. He and others subsequently attacked the decision as 'non-nationalistic' (*Sydney morning herald*, 29 September 1983) and an example of 'cultural cringe' (Peter Donoghue and John Collins, Jacaranda Wiley, 30 September 1983, AND Files 1983, ANDC, ANU). This also reflected the fact that this was a particular moment in Australian publishing history when Australian publishers flourished – this would not be maintained into the twenty-first century where independent publishers struggled to survive against multinational conglomerates, and as evidenced by the fact that the *Macquarie* is now published by overseas-owned Pan Macmillan.

The first edition of the *Australian national dictionary* contained some 10,000 headwords, collocations, and compounds, with a strong focus on the nineteenth century and words that spoke to Australia's development as a settler-colonial nation. The marketing of the first edition reflected something of the ambiguity around Australian nationalism that was evident by the end of the 1980s. If the *Macquarie* and its success captured an historical moment of unalloyed Australian patriotism at the beginning of the 1980s, by the end of the decade, this idea of Australia had its challengers. AND was released in the bicentenary year, the two hundredth anniversary of the arrival of British settlers to a continent already occupied by First Nations people. The anniversary was thus a fraught moment for the country. Many Australians – including but not exclusively Indigenous people – campaigned against an uncritical celebration of the bicentenary. When AND was publicised, the marketing blurb quoted Ramson as saying that 'Australian English provides evidence of Australian racism, sexism and inhumanity, of the Australian's self-consciousness and insecurity of identity, but also reveals intention, pragmatism, heroism and idealism and the emergence of a distinctive national character.' This quote perfectly captured the ambivalent story of the nation that the dictionary represented.

Work began almost immediately on collecting material for a second edition under the leadership of Bruce Moore at the ANDC. This ongoing research into Australian English informed the Australian Oxford range of dictionaries produced over the same period. Numerous studies of the Australian English vocabulary appeared through the early 2000s including monographs on historical aspects of the vocabulary such as Moore's *Gold, gold, gold: the language of the nineteenth-century Australian gold rushes* (2000) and Amanda Laugesen's *Convict words: Language in early colonial Australia* (2002), and on Australian regional vocabularies, including Maureen Brooks's *Words from the west: A glossary of Western Australian terms* (1994) and Brooks and Joan Ritchie's *Tassie terms: Glossary of Tasmanian words* (1995). All of the work undertaken for these publications informed AND's second edition.

The second edition of AND was published in 2016, edited by Bruce Moore. It was almost double the page extent of the first edition, and contained some 16,000 headwords, compounds, and collocations. The edition rewrote the story of Australia's variety of English with more focus on slang and colloquialisms, more detailed etymologies, and a focus on twentieth and twenty-first century vocabulary items. Indigenous-related material was prominent, and work undertaken on etymologies related to Indigenous languages helped to tell a story that acknowledged First Nations people to a much greater extent.

Popular works that showcased aspects of the Australian vocabulary – sometimes in dictionary form – were a feature of the Australian publishing scene through the 1980s and 1990s. Publications included books such as *Aussie talk: the Macquarie dictionary of Australian colloquialisms* (1984), *The dinkum Aussie dictionary* (1986), Bill Hornadge's *The Australian slanguage* (1986) and *Fair dinkum Aussie lingo* (1995). Most of these highlighted slang and colloquialisms, which was what most Australians associated 'Australian English' with. Some were based on research being done by scholars and/or dictionary units, but there were also a number of publications that were less rigorous in their approach and paid less attention to accurate information on, for example, etymologies. Nevertheless, this genre boosted the idea of 'Australian English' generally and, if not quite adding to the process of making it legitimate from a formal language perspective, helped to further bed in the connection made between Australian English, colloquialism language, and national identity.

Australian lexicographical work flourished from the 1970s into the first decade or so of the twenty-first century. All three traditions became firmly entrenched in the Australian landscape, reflecting the recognition of the Australian variety of English as the standard for formal writing, speech, and education, as well as the celebration of Australian English – especially slang and colloquialisms – as the language of everyday Australians. Yet Australian lexicography retained ties to international scholarship, perhaps most obviously through the AND's close relationship with the OED, and there was at least some evidence of ambivalence over the 'nationalist' approach – at least within the scholarly tradition.

5 The contemporary scene

The twenty-first century has seen significant shifts that have complicated and challenged the work of Australian lexicographers. Some of this comes from the practical side of resourcing and publishing dictionaries in an increasingly challenging environment. Publishers have struggled to find financially sustainable models for lexicography as commercially-published dictionaries have moved from print to digital formats. Users have come to expect dictionaries to be open access or prefer to use Google as the means to find the answer to the typical questions asked of a dictionary user, such as the meaning of a word or its pronunciation. This has left dictionaries, especially those produced within the commercial/general reference/educational tradition, struggling to assert their ongoing relevance.

While lexical data has been licensed by large publishers such as Oxford University Press, many users increasingly no longer see the dictionary as an independent reference work, nor do they turn to a dictionary as a reliable source of information about language, except in specific educational contexts. In Australia at least there is a definite decline in the use, if not the authority, of dictionaries, especially outside of the classroom. While no-one would doubt the need for authoritative, trustworthy, information about language, finding the money to ensure the production of such knowledge is harder than ever. The rise of artificial intelligence has offered possibilities for some of the work of lexicographers to be taken over by machines (see De Schryver 2023), but what the outcome of this (especially for large publishers looking to save money) will be remains to be seen.

The two major dictionary publishers in Australia are Pan Macmillan, who produce the *Macquarie dictionary*, and Oxford University Press Australia and New Zealand, who continue to produce in partnership with the ANDC the range of Australian Oxford Dictionaries. However, the latter range is slowly declining. For example, whereas Oxford used to produce standalone dictionaries and thesauruses, along with combined editions, for some dictionaries, only the combined edition is still being produced. Larger dictionaries such as the *Australian Oxford dictionary* are no longer published in new editions, and even dictionaries such as the *Australian concise Oxford dictionary* are no longer financially viable and may similarly not find a new edition.

The AND continues as the major scholarly research dictionary in Australia, but it is no longer supported by Oxford University Press. Its financial situation remains precarious, and its future somewhat uncertain. Aside from financial sustainability pressures, there are broader epistemological questions surrounding its work. For example, a consultation session held by the ANDC with Indigenous experts in 2022 suggested that cultural sensitivities around certain words and expressions – such as offensive terms, but also including words relating to First Nations culture and ceremony – might require these terms to be removed from the dictionary or face scrutiny and criticism from Indigenous communities. The sexist, racist and misogynist nature of a significant proportion of Australian English that Ramson identified (and to which can be added homophobic), makes elements of the dictionary offensive and in an age of increased 'cancellation', this places pressure on any public-facing dictionary resource.

Australians undoubtedly continue to take a strong interest in Australian English and in language. This has allowed the popular lexicographical tradition to continue in Australia, with a variety of popular books and dictionaries, usually focused on Australian slang and colloquial language. These kinds of books range from those which are not strongly based on research or collection of evidence of use, to those that seek to promote their own unique Australianisms, to those based on research, including scholarly research. Despite periodic concerns about local slang being superseded by 'overseas' slang, there is no sign that Australians will lose interest in language generally, nor in Australianisms specifically. However, an uncritical celebration of the informal, slangy speech of Australians – which continues to be the way the press (for example) reports on Australian English and the way many people engage with discussions of the lexicon – could be regarded as problematic when that maintains a story of the nation that already tends to be overly masculine and white.

Whatever story of Australian English dictionaries tell into the future (if Australian dictionaries continue to exist) will need to be one that is responsive to changing ideas of Australian identity, while also being true to the need to accurately document and understand the evolution of the language.

Bibliography

Baker, Sidney (1945): The Australian language. Sydney: Angus and Robertson.

Bellanta, Melissa (2013): Rethinking the 1890s. In: Bashford, Alison/Macintyre, Stuart (eds.): The Cambridge history of Australia. Vol. 1: Indigenous and colonial Australia. Melbourne: Cambridge University Press.

Butler, Susan (2006): Case-study: Dictionaries and style guides. In: Munro, Craig/Sheahan-Bright, Robyn (eds.): Paper empires: A history of the book in Australia 1946–2005. St Lucia: University of Queensland Press.

Commonwealth of Australia (2020): National Indigenous languages report. Canberra: Commonwealth of Australia.

Crowe, Cornelius (1895): The Australian slang dictionary. Fitzroy: Robert Barr.

Damousi, Joy (2007): 'The filthy American twang': Elocution, the advent of American 'talkies' and Australian cultural identity. In: American historical review 112, no. 2 (April 2007): 394–416.

De Schryver, Gilles-Maurice (2023): Generative AI and lexicography: The current state of the art using ChatGPT. In: International journal of lexicography 36, (4 December): 355–387.

Fink, Averil F. (1967): James Hardy Vaux (1782–1841). In: Australian dictionary of biography, online 2006.

Lambert, James (2022): Everyone's a critic: Redeeming Cornelius Crowe. In: Green's dictionary of slang. https://blog.greensdictofslang.com/articles/2022/everyones-a-critic-redeeming-cornelius-crowe (last access: 25 April 2025).

Laugesen, Amanda (2014): Dictionaries for a nation: the making of The Macquarie dictionary and the Australian national dictionary. In: Journal of Australian studies 38, 1: 52–67.

Laugesen, Amanda (2023): Towards an 'Australian voice': A.G. Mitchell and debates over Australian speech, 1940–1960. In: History Australia 20, 2: 236–253.

Lee, Stuart (1990): Alfred George Stephens 1865–1933. In: Australian dictionary of biography, 1990, online: https://adb.anu.edu.au/biography/stephens-alfred-george-8642 (last access: 25 April 2025).

Leitner, Gerhard (2004): Australia's many voices: Australian English – the national language. Berlin/Boston: Mouton de Gruyter.

Manser, Pat (2021): More than words: The making of the Macquarie Dictionary. Sydney: Pan Macmillan.

McLachlan, Noel (1964): Introduction. In: Vaux, James Hardy (1964): The memoirs of James Hardy Vaux. London: Heinemann.

Moore, Bruce (2016) (ed.): The Australian National Dictionary: Australian words and their origins. Melbourne: Oxford University Press.

Morris, E.E. (1898): Austral English: A dictionary of Australasian words, phrases and usages reprinted as A Dictionary of Austral English. Sydney: Sydney University Press, 1972.

Ramson, W.S. (1993): Sidney John (Sid) Baker (1912–1976). In: Australian dictionary of biography, online 2006.

Ramson, W.S. (2002): Lexical images: The story of the Australian National Dictionary. Melbourne: Oxford University Press.

Robertson, Judith (2005): Australian lexicography 1880–1910: An evaluation. Canberra: ANU PhD thesis.

Spitulink, Debra (1988): Mediating unity and diversity: the production of language ideologies in Zambian broadcasting. In: Schieffelin, Bambi B./Woolard, Kathryn A./Kroskrity, Paul V. (eds.): Language ideologies: Practice and theory. New York: Oxford University Press.

Vaux, James Hardy (1964): The memoirs of James Hardy Vaux. Edtied by N. McLachlan. London: Heinemann.

Woods, Lesley (2023): Something's gotta change: Redefining collaborative linguistic research. Canberra: ANU Press.

Anja Lobenstein-Reichmann

Warum brauchen wir historische Lexikographie?

Abstract: Every discipline in the humanities has to face the task of questioning its own activities, explaining its theoretical and methodological premises transparently and thus legitimizing them before an assumed general as well as specialist audience. Especially against the background of the capabilities of modern language and information technologies, usually generalized as "artificial intelligence" (AI), the question of the tasks of historical lexicography and its fundamental why is of educational and professional im-portance. This article is both: A discussion and an attempt to answer this question.

Keywords: historical lexicography, Early New High German Dictionary, dictionary as a storage medium, lexicography and identity, historical comprehension, collective memory

Schlagwörter: historische Lexikographie, Frühneuhochdeutsches Wörterbuch, das Wörterbuch als Speichermedium, Lexikographie und Identität, historisches Verstehen, kollektives Gedächtnis

1 Einführung

Mit der Titelfrage[1] „Warum wir historische Lexikographie brauchen",[2] wird bereits die Präsupposition vorausgesetzt, dass historische Lexikographie wichtig ist und dies auch explizit begründet werden kann. Diese Vorwegnahme ist ehrenwert, offenbart aber gleichzeitig den Legitimationszwang unter dem die Lexikographie, vor allem die historische Lexikographie steht. Warum-Fragen sind offene Fragen, keine Entscheidungsfragen. Der Fragende eröffnet somit ein Gespräch, lässt dem Angesprochenen Raum zum Erzählen, gibt ihm die Möglichkeit, seine Position zu beleuchten, seine Mo-

1 Captatio benevolentiae: Der Vortragsduktus des vorliegenden Beitrags ist weitgehend beibehalten worden.

2 Man vgl. zu Wirkung, Funktion und Benutzung lexikographischer Werke Reichmann 2012; auch folgende Artikel im Handbuch Wörterbücher: Hausmann (1989A); Püschel (1989); außerdem Wiegand (1998); Kühn/Püschel (1990).

Anja Lobenstein-Reichmann, Niedersächsische Akademie der Wissenschaften zu Göttingen. Frühneuhochdeutsches Wörterbuch, Geiststraße 10, 37073 Göttingen, e-mail: anja.lobenstein-reichmann @adwgoe.de

https://doi.org/10.1515/9783112216644-004

tivationen offenzulegen und seine ganz persönlichen Begründungen für sein Denken oder Handeln zu reflektieren. In diesem Sinne sollen die nachfolgenden Ausführungen verstanden werden. Sie sind Reflexionen und Begründungen, die der lexikographischen Praxis entstammen und entsprechend an Beispielen des *Frühneuhochdeutschen Wörterbuches* (FWB) dargelegt werden.

Die Aufgabe vergangenheitsbezogener Lexikographie, unabhängig davon, ob diese diachron oder synchron ausgerichtet ist, besteht aufs Einfachste formuliert in der lexikographischen Aufbereitung des Wortschatzes eines historischen Autors, z. B. Johann Wolfgang von Goethes oder Martin Luthers, eines historischen Sprachstadiums, z. B. des Alt-, Mittel- oder Frühneuhochdeutschen, einer Sprachvarietät, die mit historischer Tiefe aufbereitet wird (s. *Schweizerisches Idiotikon*), einer historischen Sprachgruppe oder einer bestimmten historischen Fachsprache. Letzteres kann man am Beispiel des *Deutschen Rechtswörterbuchs* (im Folgenden: DRW) sehen, das die westgermanische Rechtssprache behandelt. Während das gesamtsprachbezogene *Deutsche Wörterbuch* (DWB) der Brüder Grimm bereits abgeschlossen ist, befinden sich andere wie z. B. das DRW, das Althochdeutsche Wörterbuch, das Schweizerische Idiotikon und nicht zuletzt auch das FWB noch in Bearbeitung.

Das FWB ist eines der großen Sprachstufenwörterbücher des Deutschen. Es behandelt den gesamten Wortschatz des Frühneuhochdeutschen, das heißt: des hochdeutschen Teils des deutschen Sprachgebietes des späten Mittelalters und der Frühen Neuzeit (ca. 1350 bis ca. 1650). Es beschreibt dem Anspruch nach alle Teilzeiten, alle Sprachräume und alle Textsorten dieser Epoche. Es ist also kein Spezialwörterbuch, sondern umfasst den gesamten überlieferten Wortschatz des Frühneuhochdeutschen. Die Benutzungsinteressen umfassen alle historischen Disziplinen, angefangen von der Literaturgeschichte, der Begriffsgeschichte, der Theologie-, Medizin- oder Rechtsgeschichte, bis hin zur spontan entstandenen Frage nach der Bedeutung oder der Genese bestimmter Wörter beim Stammtischgespräch. Der moderne Onlinezugriff auf das Wörterbuch macht die kompetente Beantwortung überall auf der Welt sogar für Handybenutzer möglich.

Bei der Herstellung der beispielhaft genannten, oft vielbändigen, von Wissenschaftlern verfassten Wörterbücher, die oft Jahrzehnte bis zur Fertigstellung brauchen, entstehen nicht unerhebliche Kosten. Wie sind diese zu rechtfertigen? Vor allem vor dem Hintergrund der scheinbar omnipotenten Fähigkeiten moderner, in der Regel verallgemeinert als „Künstliche Intelligenz“ (KI) bezeichneter Sprach- und Informationstechnologien ist die Frage nach den Aufgaben historischer Lexikographen und dem prinzipiellen Warum historischer Lexikographie wichtig. Etwas konkreter formuliert stellt sich die Frage wie folgt: In welchen Erkenntnis-, Motivations-, Handlungs- und sozialidentifikativen Zusammenhängen ist historische Lexikographie auch und gerade für eine moderne Gesellschaft von Bedeutung?

2 Eine sprachphilosophisch-anthropologische Antwort

Die erste, einfachste, vielleicht aber wichtigste Antwort, die man geben kann, lautet: Weil Gesellschaften aus sprechenden Menschen bestehen und weil das, was den Menschen fundamental und anthropologisch auszeichnet, seine Sprache ist. „Sprache", so schreibt der Basler Philosoph Emil Angehrn (2012: 53): „ist Grund und Horizont des Selbstseins. Dass der Mensch das sprechende Lebewesen ist, heißt zuletzt nicht nur, dass er die Sprache hat, sondern dass er in der Sprache ist und dank der Sprache Mensch ist" (ebd.). Wer also die Frage nach dem Menschen stellt, kommt an seinem Sprechen nicht vorbei. Denn, so Emil Angehrn zusammen mit Joachim Küchenhoff (2012: 7): „Sprechend beziehen wir uns auf die Dinge, auf andere Menschen und auf uns selbst; über Sprache dringen wir forschend in die Welt ein, sprechend vollziehen wir Handlungen, konstruieren wir Geschichten und begründen Institutionen, im Gespräch verständigen wir uns mit Fremden. Fast alles, was der Mensch tut, vermag er durch die Sprache. Sie scheint alles zu umfassen, nichts scheint ihr entzogen."

Das heißt: Ohne Sprache gibt es keinen Bezug auf vorsprachlich gedachte Gegebenheiten, in der Formulierung Angehrns (und Küchenhoffs) also auf *Dinge*, darunter auch auf *Menschen*, auf *uns selbst*. Wir setzen uns damit – ohne es zu merken – als ‚vorsprachlich' (übrigens auch ‚vorkognitiv gegeben') voraus; es geht hier um die Darstellungsfunktion von Sprache. Wenn es dann sinngemäß weiter heißt: Alles Tun *vermag* der Mensch *durch Sprache*, dann ist das als versteckte Aussage in dem Sinne zu lesen: Was *durch* etwas Anderes verläuft, erfährt bei diesem Durchlauf eine Prägung von Seiten des Durchlaufenen. Damit sind wir bei der Erkenntnisfunktion von *Sprache*, hier verstanden als ‚Einzelsprache'. Und wenn es weiterhin u. A. auch noch heißt, dass wir *sprechend Handlungen vollziehen*, dann ist offensichtlich, dass es keine Kommunikation mit anderen, keine Erkenntnis, keine Darstellung, keine Hervorbringung und Gestaltung der Welt, kein Verstehen und schon gar keine Sinnstiftung ohne Einzelsprache gibt. Zusammengefasst: Die gesamte soziokulturelle Welt in ihrer Prägung, in ihrer sozialen Sinngestaltung und ihrer Handlungsaufladung ist sprachlicher, aber eben auch einzelsprachlicher Provenienz. Es gibt schlechterdings nichts, das nicht (einzel)sprachlich geprägt wäre. Das ist gleichsam die ideologische Basis, der soziale Taufspruch, das religiöse Bekenntnis für Sprachwissenschaft generell und für Lexikographie als eine ihrer Einzeldisziplinen.

Mit lexikographischer Hilfe wird es dem Menschen ermöglicht, seine Sprache und sich selbst in einem individuellen wie in einem kollektiven Gewordensein zu verstehen. Lexikographie beschäftigt sich speziell mit dem Wort als dem wichtigsten sprachlichen Handlungsinstrument, das der Mensch hat. „Es gibt nichts Relevantes auf der Welt und im Kopf des Menschen, auf das man nicht mittels lexikalischer Zeichen Bezug genommen hätte", so pointiert Reichmann (2012: 21) dieses Bekenntnis. Der Mensch erkennt, beschreibt, gestaltet und konstruiert mit Worten seinen menschlichen Geist, seine soziale Welt, seine Beziehungen, seine Handlungen, seine kollektive wie seine individuelle Identität. Zwischen dem Streben nach Autonomie und nach Bindung gestaltet er in und mit Worten seine Abgrenzungen wie seine Gemeinschafts- und Sinnstiftungen. Zu den zentralen Sinnstiftungen gehören nicht nur politische oder religiöse Ordnungen, auch moralische und allseitige soziale Werte.[3] Wirklichkeitssetzendes *Verworten* der Welt ist „ein auf geteilter Interaktion basierendes, beständig vollzogenes qualifizierendes soziales Verorten der gesamten Gesellschaft durch die gesamte Gesellschaft" (Lobenstein-Reichmann 2019: 14). Das *Verworten* geschieht daher gerade nicht mit universeller Gültigkeit, sondern mit jedem Sprechen, zu jeder Zeit und in jeder Gruppe anders. Und genau das macht die Notwendigkeit wie die Faszination von Wörterbüchern aus. „Woher aber rührt die Faszination?" fragt Franz Josef Hausmann (1989: 20):

> Der Mensch (als soziales Wesen) hat den Eindruck, daß das Wörterbuch einen großen Teil seiner selbst schwarz auf weiß einschließt, fixiert, nachschlagbar und überprüfbar macht. Das ist deshalb so wichtig, weil kein Mensch ein präsentes Bewußtsein seines sprachlichen Wissens hat. Ich weiß, daß ich viel weiß. Aber ich kann mein Wissen nicht vor mir aufschlagen. Aufschlagen aber kann ich das Wörterbuch. Das Wörterbuch ist die präsente Synopsis des versteckten sozialen Wissens. Man findet darin sich selbst in einer Weise, wie man sich ohne das Wörterbuch nicht finden kann. Das macht die Faszination des Wörterbuchs aus.

Speziell die historische Lexikographie bietet den Blick zurück in vergangene Wortwelten, das heißt in die Gesamtheit geschichtlicher Sinngliederungen, Beziehungs-, Handlungs- und Weltgestaltungen. Sie hat die Aufgabe, die historische Sprachwelt so zu rekonstruieren, d. h. über das Lexikon zu resemantisieren und zu repragmatisieren, in allen ihren Sprachständen zu dokumentieren und einer späteren Generation verständlich zu vermitteln, dass die Nachwelt aus der historischen Differenz Erkenntnisse gewinnen kann, die weit über Sprachliches hinausgehen. Im Spiegel unserer sprachlichen Vergangenheit sehen wir die eigene Welt, die eigene Identität und das eigene Gewordensein.[4]

---

3 Worte konstituieren nicht zuletzt auch die Perspektive auf Raum und Zeit, z. B. auf die Erklärung der Vergangenheit oder die Visionierung von Zukunft.

4 Reichmann (2012: 2): „Die lexikographische Befassung mit dem so aufgefassten Wortschatz ist eine Tätigkeit im Dienste verschiedener Zwecke. Diese Zwecke sind mindestens: die wissenschaftliche Erkenntnis des Gegenstandes ‚Wortschatz', die kulturpädagogische Vermittlung der Resultate dieser Erkenntnis, die praktische Hilfeleistung an diejenigen, die mit dem Wortschatz einer Sprache fragend oder gestaltend umgehen. (3) Speziell die historische Lexikographie öffnet den Zugang zum Verständnis geschichtlicher Sprachstände, damit der sprachlichen Überlieferung generell und historischer Einzeltexte im Besonderen, über all dies zum Verständnis der historischen Gewordenheit heutiger Sprache und schließlich zum historischen Bewusstsein einer Gesellschaft, die sich (so jedenfalls innerhalb Europas) lange Zeit entscheidend über ihre Sprache und ihre Texte definiert hat, teilweise noch heute definiert und vermutlich weiterhin definieren wird."

> Am Anfang steht die Lexikographie als eine von sprachlich und literarisch interessierten Gesellschaften gewünschte Aufbereitung der eigenen Vergangenheit zu Zwecken der Sinngebung für die Gegenwart (Reichmann 2012: VII)

Das Wort **Sinn** im Kompositum **Sinngebung** ist in doppelter Bedeutung zu verstehen, zum einen linguistisch als darstellungsbezogene Bedeutung eines Wortes in einem komplexen Sinnzusammenhang von Texten und Diskursen und zum anderen als dasjenige, was den Menschen motiviert und antreibt, seinen Daseinssinn. Auch dieser Sinn wird sprachlich gestiftet und steht im Spannungsfeld von individueller Biographie und gesellschaftlichen Sinnstiftungen durch z. B. Ideologie oder Religion. Beide Sinngebungen fallen nicht vom Himmel, sondern sind, wie die Grundwörter -**gebung** bzw. -**stiftung** bereits ausdrücken, dynamisch und handlungsorientiert. Sinngebungen sind das Ergebnis kommunikativer Diskurse, die das ehemals Gesprochene in sich tragen und weitertragen, und doch im Sprechen immer wieder neu modifizieren und verändern. Das gilt auch für das vergangenheitszugewandte Bedeutungsverstehen, das von der gegenwartsbezogenen Werterfahrung und der zukunftsbezogenen Zwecksetzung kaum zu trennen ist. In einer semiotischen Weise veranschaulichen dies Stadtbilder, wie z. B. das der Stadt Prag. Wer in der Gegenwart durch die Straßen geht, macht auch einen Spaziergang durch vergangene Jahrhunderte. Das eine Gebäude ist karolinisch (aus der Zeit Karls IV), das andere barock, das dritte modern. Manche Gebäude repräsentieren architektonisch mehrere Jahrhunderte gleichzeitig. Man kann diese Gleichzeitigkeit des Ungleichzeitigen auch auf die Sprache übertragen. In jedem Sprecher wirkt das historisch Gesprochene nach. Es prägt die Art, wie wir heute sprechen, unsere Semantiken, unsere Sinngebungen. „[E]in Gespräch wir sind“ (2000: 638), schreibt Hölderlin. Dieses zu erkennen ist fundamentaler Teil menschlicher Selbstreflexion, ohne die Selbsterkenntnis unmöglich ist.

Lexikographisches Verstehen ist daher fundamental hermeneutisch. „Hermeneutik[5] ist die Kunst des *hermeneuein*, d. h. des Verkündens, Dolmetschens, Erklärens und Auslegens“, so Hans-Georg Gadamer (1974: 1061). „Die Leistung der H[ermeneutik] besteht grundsätzlich immer darin, einen Sinnzusammenhang aus einer anderen ‚Welt‘ in die eigene zu übertragen“ (ebd.). Das gilt auch umgekehrt, da man die eigene Weltsicht immer auch in die Erkenntnis der historischen Welt einbringt. Genau dies ist die vornehmste Aufgabe der historischen Lexikographie.[6] Der historische Lexikograph vermittelt einen geschichtlichen Sinnzusammenhang differenzsemantisch und differenzpragmatisch in seine eigene Sprach- und Diskurswelt. Gelingen wird ihm das entsprechend dem fundamental hermeneutischen Charakter der Lexikographie nie ganz

5 Vgl. auch Dilthey (1900: 189): „Solches kunstmässiges Verstehen von dauernd fixierten Lebensäußerungen nennen wir Auslegung oder Interpretation“.
6 Transformatiert man die Definition der Hermeneutik Wilhelm Diltheys „Kunstlehre der Auslegung von Schriftdenkmalen“ auf die Lexikographie (Dilthey 1990: 320), dann ist diese die Kunstlehre der Auslegung von Wörtern in Schriftdenkmälern; vgl. auch Angehrn (2004: 11).

vollständig, nicht ein für allemal *richtig*, nicht *objektiv*, sondern diskursiv gesprächsförmig, sozialbezogen und immer vermittelnd.

3 Eine (meta-)lexikographische Antwort

Aus dem Vorgetragenen zur ersten anthropologischen Antwort ergibt sich eine Reihe weiterer Begründungen, die speziell mit der lexikographischen Textsorte, ihrer Mikro- und Makrostruktur, vor allem aber mit den Verstehens- und Vermittlungsaufgaben des Lexikographen zusammenhängen. Wenn der genuine Zweck der historischen Lexikographie darin besteht, geschichtliche Sinnzusammenhänge im oben genannten doppelten Sinne zu vermitteln, muss sie die Datengrundlage sowohl aufbereiten wie zur Verfügung stellen, auf deren Basis semantische Fragestellungen wie gesellschaftliche Sinnstiftungen rekonstruiert werden können. Tatsächlich ist die historische Lexikographie der vornehmste Speicher- und Dokumentationsort für historische Wortwelten. Das DWB von Jacob und Wilhelm Grimm liefert mit seinen 32 Bänden das beste Beispiel für einen Speicher großer Nationalsprachen. Im Falle kleinerer historischer Sprachen, wie z. B. denjenigen indigener Völker umspannt der lexikographische Dokumentationsauftrag auf der Minimalseite das einfache Listen von Wörtern, die den Sprachverlust gerade noch überlebt haben und geht bis hin zur enzyklopädischen Aufarbeitung und Dokumentation ganzer Kulturen wie es zum Beispiel das *Warlpiri encyclopaedic dictionary* von Mary Laughren für die first Australians der Tanami-Wüste vorgelegt hat.[7] Im Unterschied zu Korpora bzw. Textsammlungen, die Wortmaterial nur akkumulieren, werden in der Lexikographie Wortdaten hermeneutisch aufbereitet dokumentiert, d. h., sie werden nicht nur in komprimierter Auswahl und dadurch leicht überschaubarer Form zugänglich gemacht, sondern wie oben schon erläutert auch hermeneutisch resemantisiert und repragmatisiert. Die Geschichtlichkeit des Menschen und seines Sprechens wird zudem in ihrer Systemhaftigkeit wie in ihrer Variabilität gezeigt, also diatopisch im Raum, diastratisch in der soziologischen Gebundenheit und diaphasisch durch Zeiten und Sprachwandel hindurch,[8] im Idealfall sogar im jeweiligen gesellschaftlichen Diskurs. Dabei gehen Sach- und Sprachbeschreibung nicht selten ineinander über. Am Beispiel des FWB sollen die genannten Funktionen Dokumentieren, Verstehbarmachen, Vermitteln und Erkennen im Folgenden genauer ausgeführt werden.

7 Vgl. Laughren (2022); siehe auch Troy (1994) sowie McConvell/Thieberger (2001).
8 Vgl. Coseriu (2007: 24 ff.).

3.1 Wörterbücher als Dokumentations- und Speichermedium von Kultur und Geschichte

Im FWB wie in den anderen genannten Wörterbüchern wird eine geschichtliche Sprachwelt am Beispiel ihres Wortschatzes für einen nachkommenden Benutzerkreis nachhaltig in einer einzelnen Publikation zusammengeführt und so für spätere Sprechergenerationen dokumentiert. Nur so kann zugänglich gemacht werden, was Sprache laut Berger/Luckmann (2004) ist, nämlich „der Speicher angehäufter Erfahrungen und Bedeutungen, die sie zur rechten Zeit aufbewahrt", um sie „kommenden Generationen zu übermitteln." (ebd.: 39). Nimmt man das soeben Formulierte ernst, so kann man im Sinne McLuhans Idee von Medien als ‚Extension of Man'[9] über das Wörterbuch sagen, dass es ein ausgegliedertes Sprachgedächtnis des Menschen sei, eine Art Kulturprothese, in der nachgeschlagen werden kann, was das eigene bzw. das kollektive Sprachgedächtnis nicht umfassend abrufen oder vergessen hat. Die historische Lexikographie ist entsprechend nicht einfach nur eine Textsorte mit ganz eigenem Format, das mit einer anspruchsvollen Methode erarbeitet und gefüllt wird. Das historische Wörterbuch ist ein Medium, mit dessen Hilfe das Sprachgedächtnis einer geschichtlichen Sprechergemeinschaft aus den überlieferten Texten gesammelt, in seinem historischen Sprechen mit seinen Kontexten gelesen, interpretiert, nach sorgfältiger Bearbeitung konserviert und für nachfolgende Generationen verstehbar dokumentiert wird. Auf diese Weise wird das sprachkulturelle Erbe einer Gesellschaft einer späteren Nachwelt nachhaltig und vor allem zugriffsfreundlich verfügbar gemacht. *Nachhaltig* auch deshalb, weil nur wenige sprachwissenschaftliche Werke in derselben Weise generationenübergreifend und unabhängig von allen möglichen programmatischen Strömungen mit derselben Intensität benutzt werden wie Wörterbücher. Stammen sie aus einer anderen Sprachepoche, wechseln sie im Lauf der Zeiten den Status von der Beschreibungsebene zur Objektebene und werden selbst zum Teil eines historischen Sprachkorpus. Dann überliefern sie explizit den Wortschatz mit allen Sinnstiftungen im zeithistorischen Wandel.

Man mag nun einwenden, dass auch Textkorpora als dokumentierende Speicher ausreichen könnten. Doch mit den Stichworten *zugriffsfreundlich/verstehbar* und *interpretiert* wird der zentrale Mehrwert von Wörterbüchern gegenüber modernen Korpora deutlich. Ist doch das Hauptanliegen lexikographischer Arbeiten, historische Quellentexte, also das Sprechen geschichtlicher Menschen komplexitätsreduziert lesbar und verstehbar zu machen, ohne die Rezipienten dabei mit unüberschaubaren Materialmassen eher zu belasten und zu verunsichern als kurz und prägnant zu informieren. *Zugriffsfreundlich* kennzeichnet geradezu prototypisch das Darstellungsformat, in dem Wörterbücher metalexikographisch gedacht werden. Makro- und Mikrostruktur von

---

9 McLuhan (2001: 26): „All media are extensions of some human faculty – psychic or physical". Vgl. dazu auch ebd. (7 f.; 23); vgl. im Hinblick auf das Medium Wörterbuch: Lobenstein-Reichmann (2007).

Wörterbüchern sollen den Lesern einen direkten, schnellen und effektiven Zugriff auf den Wortschatz bieten, während Korpora allein ihnen nur undurchdringliche Datenmassen konservieren. Sie stellen Texte als Lautfolgen und Ausdrucksseiten zur Verfügung, die man zwar durchsuchen kann, die vielleicht sogar halbautomatisch erzeugte systembezogene Oberflächensemantiken generieren können, doch bezogen auf kognitive Tiefen- und Handlungssemantiken gänzlich blind sind.

Das Medium Wörterbuch in seiner Dokumentations- und Speicherfunktion ist nicht nur sinnfälliger Träger von Informationen, sondern ist, auch dies im Sinne McLuhans, die Botschaft selbst.[10] Wörterbücher bedienen Erwartungshaltungen ihrer Benutzer, die mit einem kaum zu unterschätzenden Vertrauensvorschuss einhergehen. Weil sich das Wörterbuch über das Rauschen der Stimmen, über die semiotische Vielstimmigkeit des Alltags erhebt und die darin enthaltenen Informationen in der Regel von kompetenten, dazu ausgebildeten Lexikographen erstellt wurden, die die Deutungshoheit über die Interpretamente für sich beanspruchen, bekommen ihre Bedeutungszuschreibungen, ihre semantischen Setzungen normatives Gewicht. Wörterbücher haben somit einen Glaubwürdigkeits- und Geltungsvorschuss, der weit über objektsprachliche Vorbildlichkeit und Modellcharakter hinausgeht. Um diesen zu erhalten, bieten vor allem bedeutungsgeschichtliche Wörterbücher eine ausgefeilte Belegdokumentation zur Plausibilitätskontrolle durch den Benutzer. Sind diese Belege digital mit ihren Ausgangstexten verlinkt, bieten sie auch eine Tür zu weiteren Textwelten.

3.2 Wörterbücher als Verstehenshilfe im Umgang mit historischen Quellen

Die zweite Antwort auf die Eingangsfrage betrifft ganz grundsätzlich das Verstehen von Wörtern, von Texten und Textzusammenhängen. Wir brauchen historische Lexikographie, weil sie den Zugang zum Verstehen geschichtlichen Sprechens in seinen geschichtlichen Bedingungen von Raum, Zeit und sozialer Gruppe öffnet und so zum Verständnis geschichtlicher Sprachstände und Textsorten beiträgt. Die historische Lexikographie bietet also praktische Hilfeleistungen für all diejenigen, die mit dem

10 McLuhan (2001: 26): „All media work us over completely. They are so pervasive in their personal, political, economic, aesthetic, psychological, moral, ethical, and social consequences, that they leave no part of us untouched, unaffected, unaltered. The medium is the message. Any understanding of social and cultural change is impossible without a knowledge of the way media work as environments." Vgl. dazu auch ebd. (1964/2001: 7 f.; 23).

Wortschatz einer Sprache unter irgendeinem Gesichtspunkt fragend oder gestaltend umgehen.[11] Die Hilfe beginnt bei der Worterkennung.

3.2.1 Verstehen als ausdrucksseitige Worterkennung

Die doppelte (inhaltsseitige) Sinnstiftung, das Verstehen eines im geschichtlichen Text dokumentierten Ausdruckes setzt seine Wortidentifikation voraus. Oft genug scheitert der Leser geschichtlicher Texte aber bereits an der Worterkennung. Sebastian Brants Narrenschiff aus dem Jahre 1494/5 bietet eine Reihe von Beispielen, die zum Hindernis für einen modernen Leser werden können:

> Mancher den schlenttrianum tribt | Die blat er vff dem disch vmb schibt | Do mit das best für jn kum dar | Jch hab des vil genomen war | Das mancher treib sŏlch ofentür. (Lemmer 1968: 110a, 167)

Eine solche Hürde bietet der Satz: „Das mancher treib sŏlch ofentür". Was tut man, wenn man *ofentür* treibt? In solchen Fällen gewährt das historische Wörterbuch seinen Benutzern erst einmal Hilfe zur Selbsthilfe. Tatsächlich hilft FWB-online[12] mit seiner ausdrucksseitigen Spracherkennung beim Lemmatisieren des Wortes weiter. Gibt man das Wort buchstabengetreu in die Suchmaske ein, wird man auf den hochpolysemen Artikel **abenteuer** geleitet und erfährt, dass *ofentüre* nur eine Schreibung der elsässischen Lautung des als **abenteuer** Wortes lemmatisierten Wortes ist. In diesem Idealfall ist der Beleg zitiert und liegt dem Leser semantisch aufbereitet vor. Statt alle 17 Bedeutungsansätze durchlesen zu müssen, landet er zudem direkt auf Ansatz 8, in dem das Wort **abenteuer** im Sinne von 'Unrechtmäßigkeit jeder Art, Ungebührlichkeit, Unsittlichkeit, Betrug, Gaunerei, übles Treiben, Machenschaften' gebraucht wird (vgl. Abb. 1).

Abenteuer verweist hier also nicht auf die mittelhochdeutsche *Aventiure*, einer 'zum Beweis ritterlicher Tüchtigkeit, oft zugleich zur Heilung von Rechtsbrüchen unternommene ritterliche Bewährungsprobe', was Bedeutungsansatz 1 wäre. Wer bei Tisch *abenteuer* treibt, beginnt auch kein romantisches Liebesgeplänkel mit seiner Nachbarin, was wiederum eine moderne Bedeutung des Wortes wäre, sondern er schiebt die Platte mit dem Essen so herum, dass er immer von allem das Beste erhält. Er verhält sich also ausgesprochen ungebührlich und ungesittet. Der Blick auf die onomasiologische Vernetzung bestätigt dies nicht nur, sie zeigt auch die Öffnung hin zum Kriminellen. Bedeutungsverwandt zu **abenteuer** 8 sind **anschlag** 5, **büberei** 1, **laster** 1; 2, **lotterei**, **manszucht**, **schimpf** 7, **tuk** uvm. Jedes dieser Wörter assoziiert

11 Vgl. Reichmann (2012: 2).
12 Hierbei handelt es sich um das Online-Angebot des FWB, abrufbar unter www.fwb-online.de (letzter Zugriff: 27.01.2025).

abenteuer,

8. ›Unrechtmäßigkeit jeder Art, Ungebührlichkeit, Unsittlichkeit, Betrug, Gaunerei, übles Treiben, Machenschaften‹.

Gesamtgebiet; mittleres und späteres Frnhd.

Bedeutungsverwandte: *anschlag* 5, *büberei* 1, *laster* 1; 2.

Syntagmen: *a. vertragen / treiben / sehen / brauchen: a.* (Subj.) *geschehen: sich der a. berümen:* Idiom: *sein a. stehen* ›für die Folgen seines Verhaltens gerade stehen‹.

Belegblock:

Mon. Boica, NF. 2, 1, 299, 6 (nobd., 1464): *wie der herrschaft die awgen verclawbt sint worden und abenthewer geschehen.*

Enders, Eberlin 3, 37, 25 (Erfurt 1523): *darumb hab ich müssen [...] furtragen yr [munch] abentewr.*

Schade, Sat. u. Pasqu. 2, 210, 494 (nobd. 1524): *Der ban, der ablaß unds fegfeur, / Darneben sonst vil obenteur.*

Lemmer, Brant. Narrensch. 110a, 167 (Basel 1494): *Die blat er vff dem disch vmb schibt / [...] / Das mancher treib sölch ofentür.*

Barack, Zim. Chron. 3, 67, 38 (schwäb., M. 16. Jh.): *Die zwo frawen haben sich übel geschempt [...] und nit vil sich dieser abentür [...] berüempt.*

Dinklage, Frk. Bauernweist. 53, 19 (nobd., A. 16. Jh.): *sucht aber einer awßflucht, so sten einer seyn abethewer.*

Luther, WA 41, 398, 13;
Chron. Augsb. 9, 364, 25;
Müller, Nördl. Stadtr. 124, 36;
Mon. Boica, NF. 2, 1, 300, 1.

Abb.1: Bedeutung 8 zu **abenteuer** im FWB sowie ein Holzschnitt aus Brants *Narrenschiff.*

Betrug, Ränke, eben Büberei. Die Deontik des Wortes in dieser Bedeutung lautet: Pass auf! Demjenigen, der ein solches Verhalten zeigt, ist nicht zu trauen!

Man erkennt, wie im Laufe der Zeit ein elitäres Kulturkonzept zum Erwerb von Ehre und gesellschaftlichen Ansehen zu einem Attribut der Unkultur, gar der Kriminalisierung abgewertet wurde. Was im Ansatz 8 besonders offensichtlich wird, zieht sich auch in den anderen Bedeutungsansätzen wie ein roter Faden durch (z. B. 7: 'Lügengeschichte, Ammenmärchen'; 9: 'Posse, Gaukelspiel, Narretei, Zaubertrick, Kunststück, Mätzchen'). Das als moralische Matrix dahinter entfaltete Tugend- und Ordnungssystem des Frühneuhochdeutschen ließ wenig Raum für das unkontrolliert Abenteuerliche.

3.2.2 Verstehen als semasiologisches, differenzsemantisches Bedeutungserkennen

Die Identifikation der Schreibung *ofentüre* als **abenteuer** ist also nur der Einstieg in das eigentliche Verstehen der frnhd. Text- und Sprachwelt. Um diese differenzsemantisch zugriffsfreundlich und für einen modernen Leser verständlich aufzubereiten, bietet das FWB ein komplexes, aber übersichtliches Beschreibungsprogramm, in dessen Zentrum jedoch nicht die Ausdrucksseite steht, sondern die Semantik, das von kompetenten Lexikographen in fachkundiger Interpretation erarbeitete semasiologische Feld (vgl. Abb. 2). Dieses Bedeutungsfeld ist nicht isolationistisch auf das Einzel-

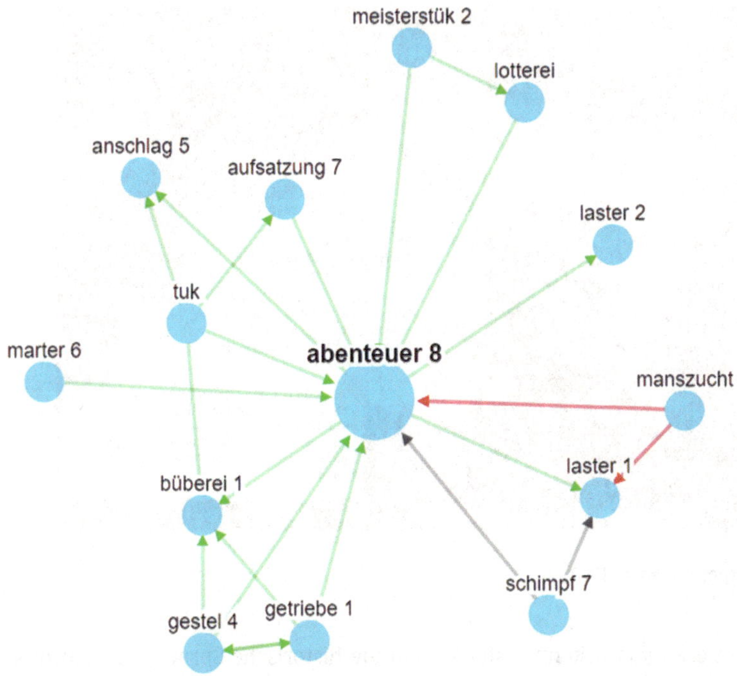

Abb. 2: Onomasiologisches Netz zu **abenteuer** 8.

wort bezogen, sondern eingebettet in die Gesamtsprache und ihre Gebrauchsfunktionen. Mit den beiden Informationspositionen der onomasiologischen Vernetzung *Bedeutungsverwandtschaft* und *Gegensatzbereich* wird dem Leser nicht nur vorgeführt, mit welchen anderen Wörtern der geschichtliche Autor auch hätte handeln können und welche genau das Gegenteil davon besagen, sie öffnen ihm die Tür in den zeitgenössischen Diskurs. Ähnliches gilt für die Syntagmen, die Wortbildungsfelder und nicht zuletzt die Symptomwertangaben.

Mit den genannten Informationspositionen (vgl. Abb. 3) ist der Blick auf eine hermeneutisches Bedeutungs- und Sinnverstehen gerichtet, das nur von Menschen in einem „wesentlich kommunikativen Vorgang" möglich ist, so Angehrn (2004: 11):

> Verstehen ist mehr als ein Aufnehmen, Entziffern und Bearbeiten von Informationen; weder Zeichen noch das System ihrer Differenzen sind der eigentliche Ort des Sinns. Verstehen enthält in der Tiefe ein Sich Ansprechenlassen durch ein anderes Subjekt, ein Antworten auf Fragen, die ein anderer aufwirft, ein Wiedererkennen eigener Fragen in dem, worauf der andere antwortet. Dies gilt nicht nur für die Situation des direkten Gesprächs, sondern ebenso für den Umgang mit Texten, wo der Autor abwesend ist, ja nicht einmal bekannt sein muß. Vom Fernsten sich ansprechen lassen und mit ihm in ein Gespräch zu treten, gehört zum Pathos hermeneutischen Verstehens. (Ebd.)

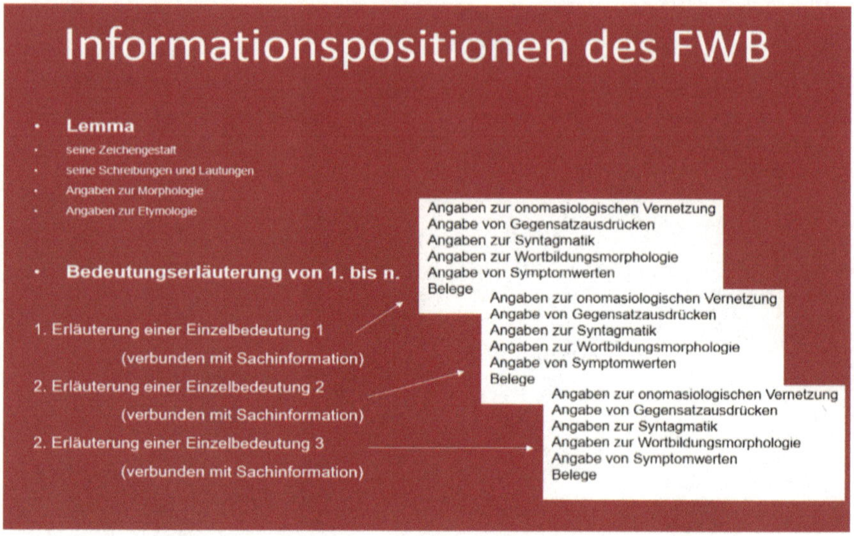

Abb. 3: Informationspositionen im FWB.

Die Lexikographin erkundet erkenntnisfunktional die historische Sprachwelt und fragt beim Verstehen der Quellentexte zunächst einmal nach der Referenzfunktion, danach, wie historische Sprecher welche Gegenstände und Sachverhalte bezeichnet haben (z. B. nach **kopf**, **hals**, **hand**, **fuß**, **katze**). Dabei erhält sie einen Einblick in die Sach- und Lebenswelt der Zeit. Sie erfährt, dass das Wort **Katze** eben nicht nur den beliebten 'Schmusetiger' bezeichnet, sondern zeitgenössisch auch eine 'Belagerungsmaschine', ein 'Ballspiel' oder ein 'Gefängnis'(vgl. Abb. 4). Der Blick in *Duden online* bietet differenzsemantisch nur das Tier und bei den Redewendungen die 'neunschwänzige Peitsche'.[13]

Auch wenn die Welt der Dinge ein zentrales Cluster im Wortschatz bildet, ist der Wortschatz der sozialfaktischen Welt umfassender. Die historische Lexikographin fragt nach der Gestaltungs- und Konstruktionsfunktion von Sprache, also danach, wie geschichtliche Sprecher mit ihren Bezeichnungen ihre soziale Welt konstituiert bzw. welche Sinnstiftungen sie mit den Worten vollzogen, bzw. wie sie mit Wörtern wie **Abenteuer**, aber auch mit **Gott**, **Recht**, **Treue**, **Knecht** oder **Tugend** ihre Welt *ertextet* haben.

Es geht in der Lexikographie aber nicht nur um Einzelbeispiele wie *ofentüre*. Viel wichtiger ist, welche sprachinhaltlichen Zusammenhänge sich hinter dem Gesamtwortschatz von rund 100000 Lemmaeinheiten und einem mehrere hunderttausend

13 Zum entsprechenden Artikel siehe unter https://www.duden.de/rechtschreibung/Katze (letzter Zugriff: 27.01.2025).

kattuniert

Bedeutungsindex »katze«

1. ›Hauskatze beider Geschlechter‹; gelegentlich
2. ›Belagerungsmaschine, Kriegsgerät‹; auch
3. ein Ballspiel.
4. ›Gefängnis‹.
5. ›Geldgürtel‹.

[1]katze,

die; -n/-n.

1. ›Hauskatze beider Geschlechter‹; gelegentlich auch Bezeichnung für andere Raubtiere der Katzenfamilie; im Volksglauben Begleitung der Hexe, auch ›Teufel‹; verschiedene dem Tier zugeschriebene Eigenschaften (Falschheit, Reinlichkeit, Gewandtheit) bilden die Grundlage für eine große Zahl von Phrasemen sowie für viele Komposita.

Phraseme (und Raa.; Auswahl): *die katze schreit alle tage reue; der katze den käse vertrauen; hüt dich vor der katze; katzen lecken vorne, kratzen hinten; sich abdrehen / abziehen mit eren wie eine katze aus dem taubenhaus; die katze bringt eine bache* ›etwas Unwahrscheinliches geschieht‹; *die katze lacht die maus an; die katze läst das mausen nicht; der katze schellen anhängen* ›vor einer unmöglichen Aufgabe stehen‹; *der katze gehen die haare aus* ›es wird ernst‹; *wie katze und hund gegeneinander sein; wie die katze der maus glauben halten; wie die katze aus dem haus, so reihen sich die mäuse; die katze wird das beste vieh* ›man kommt auf den Hund‹; *sich mit den katzen beissen* ›streiten; fremdgehen‹; *die katze puzt / schmückt sich* für Schönrednerei; *jm. läuft die katze den rücken hinauf; jm. tut die katze am rücken ach* u. ä. ›Angst haben‹; *jm. eine katze vor der tür hängen lassen* ein Zeichen, daß der Weg (zu einer Frau) frei ist; alte Rechtsbräuche wiederspiegeln sich in: *eine katze halten / heben* ›eine harte Strafe erleiden‹; *die katze durch den bach ziehen lassen* ›verlieren und die Kosten zahlen müssen‹.

Syntagmen: *eine k. braten / entweiden / fangen / jagen / schinden / streichen; einer k. die haut abziehen; betriegliche / böse / feiste / geschnittene / junge / kristallene / listige / reine / schwarze / tote / wilde k.*

Abb. 4: Artikel **katze** im FWB.

Seiten umfassenden Bedeutungsinventar verbergen. Damit kommen die in der linguistischen Fachdiskussion unter dem Terminus *Frame* laufenden Wortschatzstrukturen ins Spiel. Gerade aus Wörterbüchern lassen sich *Frames* als historisch-kultureller Horizont oder in der Anerkennungsterminologie Axel Honneths als „intersubjektiv geteilter Werthorizont einer Sprachgesellschaft“ (1992/2003: 196) rekonstruieren. In der Brechung des überlieferten Wortgebrauchs können Frames diachron für den gegenwärtigen Wörterbuchbenutzer differenzsemantisch und differenzpragmatisch zugänglich gemacht werden.[14] Vergliche man den Frame zu frnhd. **abenteuer** mit demjenigen in mhd. Zeit würde die Pejorisierung ebenso deutlich wie im Vergleich zum Gegenwartsdeutschen die Meliorisierung. Noch deutlicher wird die Differenz bei semasiologischen Feldern von Alltagswörtern wie z. B. **leben, das**. Ein Vergleich des Artikels im FWB mit seinem gegenwartssprachlichen Heteronym im *Digitalen Wörterbuch der deutschen Sprache* (DWDS) zeigt auf einen Blick, dass die Vorstellungen von Leben heute und Leben damals weiter auseinandergehen. Die Präsenz des Todes ist zentraler Kern des Lebens im späten Mittelalter und der frühen Neuzeit. Krankheit, Hunger und Todesstrafe machen das Leben in ganz anderer Weise fragil als heute. Selbstwirksamkeit und Genuss, heute maßgebliche Werte, kannten nur wenige und diese gehörten dann der sozialen Oberschicht an. Die frnhd. Phraseme und Syntagmen spiegeln in Nuce die existentielle Geworfenheit des Menschen, denn *Media vita*

14 Vgl. Lobenstein-Reichmann (2023: 224).

in morte sumus. Das gesamte Bedeutungsfeld zeigt, dass die Existenz und das Glück des Menschen ein durch das Göttliche bestimmte Wechselspiel zwischen fragiler Körperlichkeit und fragiler Psyche ist. Das Leben galt als dem Tod geweihte Geworfenheit mit offenem Ende, das im besten Fall im Paradies, im schlechtesten in der Hölle mündete. Der Blick der Menschen war vertikal auf Gott gerichtet und auf das ewige Leben danach, das diesseitige galt nur als Übergang. Der Blick der heutigen Menschen scheint dagegen eher profan horizontal ausgerichtet zu sein, geradezu hedonistisch auf sich selbst.

Doch der diachrone Vergleich der Frames bleibt unvollständig, wenn man ihn isolationistisch betrachtet. Wirklich aussagekräftig wird er, wenn man die Miniaturebene verlässt und die sprachliche Vernetzung eines Wortes mit seinen bedeutungsverwandten Ausdrücken im Hinblick auf den gesamten Substantivwortschatz sieht.[15] Dann wird der Lexikograph zum Kulturanthropologen und kann aus der Beschreibung des Gesamtwortschatzes heraus visualisieren, was Clifford Geertz (1983: 9) mit Kultur als „selbstgesponnenem Bedeutungsgewebe" meint:

> Der Kulturbegriff, den ich vertrete, ist wesentlich ein semiotischer. Ich meine mit Max Weber, daß der Mensch ein Wesen ist, das in ‚selbstgesponnene Bedeutungsgewebe' verstrickt ist, wobei ich Kultur als dieses Gewebe ansehe. Ihre Untersuchung ist daher keine experimentelle Wissenschaft, die nach Gesetzen sucht, sondern eine interpretierende, die nach Bedeutungen sucht.

Welchen Stellenwert hat z. B. der Ordnungs-, Rechts- oder Tugendframe im Bedeutungsgewebe des Gesamtwortschatzes, das heißt in der Kultur des späten Mittelalters und der frühen Neuzeit? Ist er marginal oder zentral? Wie sehr durchzieht seine Semantik den Sprachgebrauch? Die Vogelperspektive auf ein bestimmtes onomasiologisches Feld zeigt, wie sehr ein Frame das Bedeutungsgewebe einer Sprache durchfasert und entsprechend der oben genannten Kulturdefinition somit auch die Sprachgesellschaft des späten Mittelalters und der frühen Neuzeit konstituiert. Besonders anschaulich wird das am Lemma **recht**, das im FWB mit 20 Bedeutungen angesetzt ist. Ansatz 7 wird lexikographisch beschrieben als „moralische Berechtigung, gesellschaftlichen Normen entsprechende Befugnis, Erlaubnis zu etw."; „das jm. / e.S. Zustehende, e. P. gebührendes Anrecht auf Wertschätzung, Ehrerbietung"; mit Tendenz zu: „moralische Richtigkeit, Wahrheit"; eng anschließbar an 5, im Unterschied dazu eher auf ungeschriebene, aber gesellschaftlich und moralisch akzeptierte Normen bezogen". Extrem verdichtet zeigt sich in Abb. 5, wie diese Semantik den im Cluster rechts unten dargestellten Abstraktwortschatz durchfasert. Die zur onomasiologischen Vernetzung gehörigen Knoten sind mit den Farben gelb und rot sichtbar gemacht.

Es zeigt sich, dass das Rechtssystem des Frühneuhochdeutschen mit seinen Einzelaspekten, Wirkungen und Bewertungsakteuren abrufbar im Artikel selbst nicht nur hochfrequent und hochpolysem ist, es prägt auch den Gesamtwortschatz des Frühneuhochdeutschen insgesamt. Sein Vernetzungsgrad sticht mit seiner außerge-

15 Vgl. zur kulturgeschichtlichen Erkenntnis auch Lobenstein-Reichmann/Reichmann (2020).

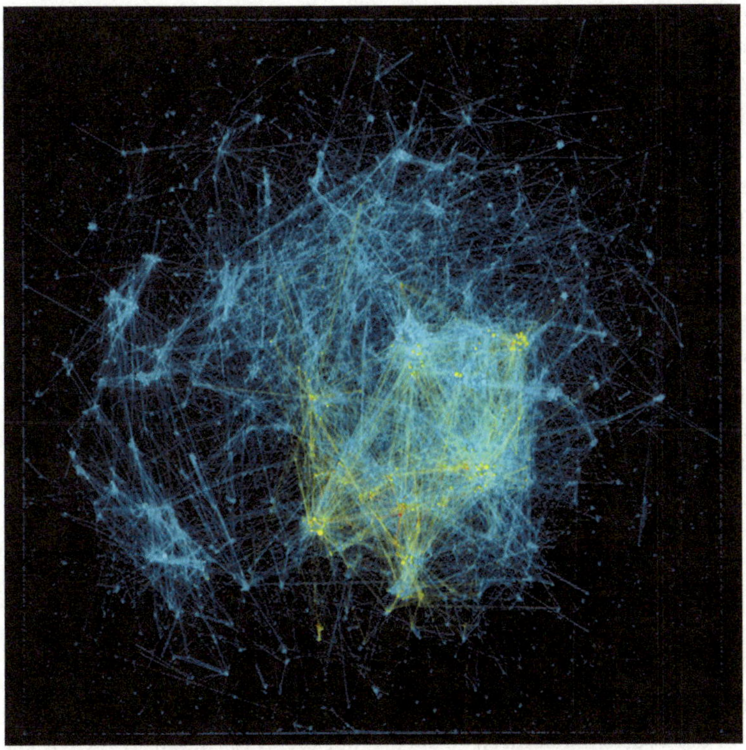

Abb. 5: Vernetzung des aktuell im FWB vorliegenden Substantivwortschatzes im Hinblick auf die Durchfaserung des Bedeutungsansatzes 7 von **recht.**

wöhnlichen Knotendichte deutlich heraus. Spannend ist entsprechend die Liste derjenigen Wörter, deren Ausgangssemantik mit hoher onomasiologischer Dichte vernetzt sind. Dazu gehören bestimmte Verben, aber eben auch **recht** und **ere**.

3.2.3 Verstehen als differenzpragmatisches Bedeutungs- und Handlungserkennen

Es wurde am Wort **abenteuer** schon deutlich, dass der Wortschatz neben einem konnotativen Bewertungshorizont auch denotative Dimensionen mit impliziten Handlungsperspektiven hat. Wer eine andere Person als **abenteurer** bezeichnete und dies im Sinne von Bedeutungsansatz 2 des FWB tat, denunzierte sie als 'herumziehenden Unterhaltungskünstler, Gaukler, Possenreißer, Trickkünstler'. Dies war, so kommentiert der Lexikograph „meist negativ bewertet" und meinte dann so viel wie: 'Schwindler, Gauner'; falls die angewendeten Tricks sprachlicher Art sind: 'Lügenbold, Sprücheklopfer'. Die Pejorisierung impliziert eine Deontik, eine Art Gebrauchsanweisung für so angesprochene Personen, die im Idealfall neben dem Werthorizont lexikographisch dargestellt werden sollte, damit diese mit dem Wort diskursüblichen Handlungsdimensionen kenntlich werden. Wer in frnhd. Zeit jemanden als **erlos** bezeichnet hat, wie es Bedeutung 3 beschreibt, dann hat er das Wort gebraucht „als *deonti*sches Kriminalisierungs- und Ausgrenzungsattribut: ‘die Ordnung der Gesellschaft missachtend, damit nicht vertrauenswürdig und gesellschaftlich ausgegrenzt’. Lexikographen dokumentieren in solchen Fällen, wie geschichtliche Sprecher interaktiv und deontisch mit Wörtern wie **abenteuer**, **hexe**, **mor**, **ketzer**, **dieb**, **sünde**, **notzucht**, **unzucht** oder dem Hochwertwort **ere** gehandelt haben. Wer eine andere Person in frnhd. Zeit als **hexe** bezeichnet hat, hat sie denunziert und damit einem möglichen Tod durch Verbrennen ausgeliefert (interaktive Handlungsfunktion).

Mit Wortverwendungen werden nicht nur Bewertungen der anderen kommuniziert. Symptomfunktional verrät der Wortsprecher viel über sich selbst. Bei der lexikographischen Beschreibung der Symptomfunktion wird aufgearbeitet, wie sich Menschen mit ihren Wortgebräuchen in ihrer Welt positioniert haben. Dies betrifft ihre räumliche, diatopische Position, indem sie sich sprachgeographisch mit ihrem Sprechen zu einer Varietät zuordnen lassen: *ofentüre* ist elsässisch, *aubenteuer* besonders im Schwäbischen überliefert. Symptomfunktional verraten sich Sprecher auch ideologisch, indem sie mit ihrem Wortgerbrauch offenlegen, wo sie sich z. B. im konfessionellen Kampf der Zeit positionieren: **gnadheinz** und **lutherisch** sind Fremdprädikationen der Katholiken, um die Protestanten zu verunglimpfen, mit **pfäffisch** entwerteten die Protestanten ihre katholischen Gegner. Das Adjektiv **evangelisch** wiederum ist eine Selbstbeschreibung, mit der Protestanten ihren Anspruch auf die evangelische Wahrheit zur Selbstermächtigung nutzten.

Die Aufbereitung im Wörterbuch zeigt jedem Benutzer außerdem sehr deutlich den Zusammenhang zwischen Textsorte und Wortsemantik bzw. zwischen Textsorte und Polysemie. Wird eine Frau mit dem Namen Maria in den religiösen Texten des Frnhd. als **bettlerin** bezeichnet, wird sie als ‘Gottesmutter’ verehrt, findet man das Wort *bettlerin* dagegen in Rechtstexten, selbst dann, wenn die so bezeichnete Frau Maria hieße, wird sie aus der Stadt verwiesen und rechtlos gemacht. Ähnliches gilt für programmatische Hochwertwörter der Reformation wie z. B. **gewalt**, **gnade**, **glaube**, **gerechtigkeit** usw., deren Verwendungen je nach Textsorten deutlich variieren. Die *Gewalt* Gottes (*gewalt* 1) konstituiert sich in der Regel in religiösen Textsorten, während die ‘juristische Vollmacht, Ermächtigung’ (**gewalt** 7), die in frnhd. Zeit ebenfalls als **gewalt** bezeichnet wurde, vorzugsweise in Rechtstexten vorkommt.

Gelingt dem Lexikographen die hermeneutische Rekonstruktion, d. h. das Resemantisieren und Repragmatisieren des historischen Kategorisierens, Sortierens, Fokussierens und Perspektivierens, kann er seinem Wörterbuchbenutzer kompakt vermitteln, wie historische Sprecher ihre Welt gesehen, konstituiert und nach welchen Deontiken, d. h. nach welchen Gebrauchsanweisungen sie in ihr gehandelt haben.[16]

---

16 Vgl. Lobenstein-Reichmann (2023: 227); Hermanns (1995: 84).

4 Wörterbücher als Ort selbstreflexiven Erkennens

Eine grundsätzliche Frage ist bislang noch gar nicht gestellt worden. Warum unternehmen Gesellschaften diesen Aufwand? Warum will man das alles überhaupt wissen? Was gehen den modernen Menschen z. B. die Menschen des 16. Jahrhunderts an? Tatsächlich liegt hierin wohl der entscheidende Antwortversuch. Historische Lexikographie ist deshalb wichtig, weil in der differenzsemantischen Brechung der Schlüssel zum Verstehen und Erkennen der Gegenwart liegt. Der lexikographische Blick zurück ermöglicht das Erkennen der Sprachlichkeit der Kultur und der Geschichte, aber auch andersherum, der Geschichtlichkeit des menschlichen Sprechens wie des Menschen selbst. Er eröffnet den Zeithorizont, das Bewusstsein von Kontinuität, Vergänglichkeit, Erfahrung des Erinnerns und Vergessens, des Beständigen wie des Wandels, sogar eine zu antizipierende Zukunft. Historische Wörterbücher bezeugen mit jedem Artikel genau diese Spannung zwischen Kontinuität und permanentem Wandel sowohl einer Sprache wie der soziofaktischen Welt, die durch kommunikatives Handeln der Sprecher genau in und mit dieser Sprache geschaffen wurde. Sie bezeugen zudem Pluralität, Variabilität und Vielfalt des Sprechens und Schreibens. Der Blick zurück entzaubert und entlarvt dabei pseudoholistische Normenpositionen. Indem Wörterbücher den modernen Benutzer von den scheinbar stabilen Pfaden der normativ gezügelten modernen Sprache auf Abwege führen hin zum Fremden, Nicht- bzw. Nichtmehreigenen der geschichtlichen Sprachwelt, zeigen sie ihm immer auch spiegelbildlich die eigene Gegenwart. Im Vergleich zum Hier und Jetzt erkennt er sein persönliches wie sprachkulturelles Gewordensein, die genutzten wie die verpassten Möglichkeiten sprachlichen Handelns, und lernt wie das dokumentierte sprachkulturelle Gedächtnis auch seine Identität, sein sprachliches Handeln biographisch geprägt hat bzw. noch prägt.

Wir brauchen die Historische Lexikographie, weil das geschichtliche Sprechen heute noch nachwirkt und wir in genau dieser Sprache und mit dieser Sprache weitersprechen. Coseriu (1974: 22) bringt dies auf den Punkt:

> Weil jeder Sprachzustand zum großen Teil Wiederherstellung eines früheren ist. Zum anderen, weil ein so genannter „Sprachwandel" nur in Bezug auf eine frühere Sprache Wandel ist, während er hinsichtlich der gegenwärtigen Sprache Kristallisation einer neuen Tradition bedeutet, das heißt gerade Nicht-Wandel: Diskontinuitätsfaktor in Bezug auf die Vergangenheit ist der Wandel zugleich Kontinuitätsfaktor in Bezug auf die Zukunft [...].

Sprache vermittelt das Gefühl der überzeitlichen Stabilisierung in einer an sich wandelhaften Welt. Als Teil dieser Sprechergemeinschaft wird der moderne Sprecher Teil einer Sprachgeschichte und verlängert seine eigene Geschichte damit um Jahrhunderte zurück, er bindet sich ein die in ihr geschaffene Kulturwelt, im Guten wie im Schlechten. Sprache „ermöglicht die continuity over time des Subjekts (resp. Personale Identität und Handlungskontinuität), selbst wenn es [wie Gregor Samsa in der *Verwandlung*, ALR] als Käfer erwacht." (Stoellger 2012: 98).

Denn Menschen werden in und durch Sprache sozialisiert und damit in den vorgegebenen Traditionen des Sprechens. Wörter wie **Recht**, **Gnade** oder **Ehre** umspannen Jahrhunderte des Gesprochenwordenseins. Die semantischen Kondensate dieser kulturellen Traditionen kann man im Wörterbuch nachlesen und in den Gesamtdiskurs einordnen. Dass **Ehre** eines der zentralen gesellschaftlichen Anerkennungswörter des Mittelalters und der Frühen Neuzeit ist, sieht man wieder am Netzwerk der üblichen Substantive(vgl. Abb. 6).

Ehre bedeutete in frühneuhochdeutscher Zeit zum Beispiel s.v. **ere** 3: ‘zur sozialen Identität e.P. gehörendes gesellschaftlich aushandelbares und ausgehandeltes Ansehen’ (allgemein); speziell: ‘e. P. zugeschriebene Anerkennung in und vor der Welt als soziales Kapital, als ethische, moralische Qualitätszuschreibung, als positives Image’; ‘jm. von der Gesellschaft aufgrund einer besonderen Leistung (z. B. aufgrund von Heldentum, künstlerischer bzw. schriftstellerischer Tätigkeit) zugesprochene Anerkennung, Ruhm, hohes Prestige’.[17]

Wörterbücher bezeugen im Zeigen der Differenzsemantik, dass man kulturellen Konzepten widersprechen kann. Denn genau in diesem Widersprechen liegt der Same des Wandels begründet. So widerspricht Falstaff in Shakespeares *König Heinrich IV.*

Abb. 6: Vernetzung des Wortes **ere** im FWB.

17 Siehe den Artikel zu *ere* in Bedeutung 3 unter https://fwb-online.de/lemma/ere.s.1f?q=ere%203&page=1#sense3 (letzter Zugriff: 27.01.2025).

seinem Prinz Heinrich, als dieser ihn um seiner Ehre wegen in den Krieg schicken will:

> Kann Ehre ein Bein ansetzen? Nein. Oder einen Arm? Nein. Oder den Schmerz einer Wunde stillen? Nein. Ehre versteht sich also nicht auf die Chirurgie? Nein. Was ist Ehre? Ein Wort. Was steckt in dem Wort Ehre? Luft. Eine feine Rechnung! – Wer hat sie? Er, der vergangenen Mittwoch starb. Fühlt er sie? Nein. Hört er sie? Nein. Ist sie also nicht fühlbar? Für die Toten nicht. Aber lebt sie nicht etwa in den Lebenden? Nein. Warum nicht? Die Verleumdung gibt es nicht zu. Ich mag sie also nicht. – Ehre ist nichts als ein gemalter Schild beim Leichenzug […]. (Shakespeare 1955, Erster Teil: V, 1).[18]

Das Hochwertwort *Ehre*, vor allen im Sinne von heldenhafter Soldatenehre, hat seit den letzten Kriegen deutlich an Hochwert und Sozialprestige verloren. In den 80er Jahren des 20. Jahrhunderts hatte es den Charakter eines Unwortes. „Doch was einmal gedacht worden ist, kann man nicht mehr zurücknehmen“ (1962: 72) sagt Dürrenmatt in den *Physikern*. Und so spukt es immer weiter in unserem kulturellen Gedächtnis, das eben immer auch unser sinnstiftendes Handlungsgedächtnis ist. Wir wissen nicht, ob das Wort **Ehre** nicht schon bald wieder zum gemalten Schild beim Leichenzug wird. Es sind eben die sprachlichen Gespenster in uns, die uns Lebende antreiben. Oder ganz profan linguistisch ausgedrückt:

> Gegenwartssprachlicher Wortschatz ist immer Resultat der Art und Weise, wie frühere Sprecher auf Realität Bezug genommen haben; er ist damit zugleich sprachliches Inhaltssystem, das allen gegenwärtigen Weisen der Bezugnahme zugrunde liegt. Dies zu erkennen und pädagogisch zu vermitteln, ist eine Aufgabe, die mit dem Selbstverständnis von Wissenschaft, darin bestehend, das eigene Tun reflexiv zu begleiten, harmoniert. (Reichmann 2012: 23)

Wörterbücher sind, wie ausgeführt wurde, anerkannte Verstehenshilfen, ja geradezu Sprach- und Welterklärungstexte. Genau das erwartet man von ihnen. Schon allein dadurch wirken sie auch normativ in ihre Zeit hinein und haben insofern einen doppelten Sinnstiftungscharakter. Sie erklären den Sinn von (geschichtlich) gesprochenen Wörtern und schaffen ihn dabei immer wieder neu.[19] Wörterbücher sind somit mehr als nur passiv gedachte Speicher bzw. Ablagen oder Schubladen, mehr als nur Medien der Weltwissenssammlung. Da sie mit ihrem Gegenstand Sprache die genannten Größen Kultur und Geschichte immer in einer spezifischen Fassung erschließen, und da

---

18 In der Übersetzung von Schlegel/Tieck. Englischer Originaltext: „'Tis not due yet. I would be loath to pay Him before His day. What need I be so forward with Him that calls not on me? Well, 'tis no matter. Honor pricks me on. Yea, but how if honor prick me off when I come on? How then? Can honor set to a leg? No. Or an arm? No. Or take away the grief of a wound? No. Honor hath no skill in surgery, then? No. What is honor? A word. What is in that word 'honor'? What is that 'honor'? Air. A trim reckoning. Who hath it? He that died o' Wednesday. Doth he feel it? No. Doth he hear it? No. 'Tis insensible, then? Yea, to the dead. But will it not live with the living? No. Why? Detraction will not suffer it. Therefore, I'll none of it. Honor is a mere scutcheon.“; unter https://www.folger.edu/explore/shakespeares-works/henry-iv-part-1/read/5/1/> (letzter Zugriff: 27.01.2025).

19 Vgl. dazu Lobenstein-Reichmann (2022).

der jeweilige Modus der Speicherung, der Erfassung, Be- und Verarbeitung, das Gespeicherte transformiert, haben sie aktiven Anteil an der Weltwissens- und Weltbildkonstruktion.

Literatur

Angehrn, Emil (2004): Interpretation und Dekonstruktion. Untersuchungen zur Hermeneutik. 2. Aufl. Weilerswist: Velbrück Wissenschaft.

Angehrn, Emil (2012): Die Sprachlichkeit der Existenz. Zwischen Kommunikation und Welterschließung. In: Angehrn, Emil/Küchenhoff, Joachim (Hrsg.): Macht und Ohnmacht der Sprache. Philosophische und psychoanalytische Perspektiven. Weilerswist: Velbrück Wissenschaft, 36–54.

Angehrn, Emil/Küchenhoff, Joachim (2012) (Hrsg.): Macht und Ohnmacht der Sprache. Philosophische und psychoanalytische Perspektiven. Weilerswist: Velbrück Wissenschaft.

Berger, Peter/Luckmann, Thomas (2004): Die gesellschaftliche Konstruktion der Wirklichkeit. Frankfurt a.M.: S. Fischer Verlag.

Coseriu, Eugenio (1974): Synchronie, Diachronie und Geschichte. Das Problem des Sprachwandels. München: Wilhelm Fink.

Coseriu, Eugenio (2007): Sprachkompetenz. Grundzüge der Theorie des Sprechens. Tübingen: Gunter Narr.

Dilthey, Wilhelm (1900): Die Entstehung der Hermeneutik. Tübingen: J.C.B. Mohr (Paul Siebeck).

Dilthey, Wilhelm (1990): Gesammelte Schriften V. Die geistige Welt. Einleitung in die Philosophie des Lebens. Erste Hälfte. Abhandlungen zur Grundlegung der Geisteswissenschaften. Göttingen: Vandenhoeck und Ruprecht.

DRW = Deutsches Rechtswörterbuch. Hrsg. v. Forschungsstelle der Heidelberger Akademie der Wissenschaften, https://drw.hadw-bw.de/drw-cgi/zeige (letzter Zugriff: 27.01.2025).

Duden online (o. J.): Artikel Katze, https://www.duden.de/rechtschreibung/Katze (letzter Zugriff: 27.01.2025).

Dürrenmatt, Friedrich (1962): Die Physiker. Eine Komödie in zwei Akten. Zürich: Die Arche.

DWb = Deutsches Wörterbuch von Jacob Grimm und Wilhelm Grimm (digitalisierte Fassung im Wörterbuchnetz). Hrsg. v. Trier Center for Digital Humanities, https://www.woerterbuchnetz.de/DWB (letzter Zugriff: 27.01.2025).

DWDS = Digitales Wörterbuch der deutschen Sprache. Das Wortauskunftssystem zur deutschen Sprache in Geschichte und Gegenwart. Hrsg.v. Berlin-Brandenburgische Akademie der Wissenschaften, https://www.dwds.de/ (letzter Zugriff: 27.01.2025).

FWB = Frühneuhochdeutsches Wörterbuch. Hrsg. v. Goebel, Ulrich/Reichmann, Oskar. Berlin/New York (später: Boston): De Gruyter, 1989 ff.

WB-online = Frühneuhochdeutsches Wörterbuch online. Hrsg. v. Niedersächsische Akademie der Wissenschaften zu Göttingen, https://fwb-online.de/ (letzter Zugriff 27.01.2025).

Gadamer, Hans-Georg (1974): Art. Hermeneutik, In: Ritter, Joachim (Hrsg.): Historisches Wörterbuch der Philosophie. Bd. 3. Basel: Schwabe Verlag, Sp. 1061–1073.

Geertz, Clifford (1983): Dichte Beschreibung. Beiträge zum Verstehen kultureller Systeme. Frankfurt a.M.: Suhrkamp.

Hausmann, Franz Josef (1989): Die gesellschaftlichen Aufgaben der Lexikographie in Geschichte und Gegenwart. In: Hausmann, Franz Josef, et al. (Hrsg.): Wörterbücher. Ein internationales Handbuch zur Lexikographie. Erster Teilband. Berlin/New York: De Gruyter, 1–19.

Hausmann, Franz Josef (1989a): Wörterbücher und Öffentlichkeit. Das Wörterbuch im Urteil der gebildeten Öffentlichkeit in Deutschland und in den romanischen Ländern. In: Hausmann, Franz Josef, et al.

(Hrsg.): Wörterbücher. Ein internationales Handbuch zur Lexikographie. Erster Teilband. Berlin/ New York: De Gruyter, 19–28.

Hausmann, Franz Josef, . (1989b/1990/1991) (Hrsg.): Wörterbücher. Ein internationales Handbuch zur Lexikographie. 3 Teilbände. Berlin/New York: De Gruyter.

Hermanns, Fritz (1995): Sprachgeschichte als Mentalitätsgeschichte. In: Gardt, Andreas/ Mattheier, Klaus J./Reichmann, Oskar (Hrsg.): Sprachgeschichte des Neuhochdeutschen. Gegenstände, Methoden, Theorien. Tübingen: Niemeyer, 69–102.

Hölderlin, Friedrich (2000): Sämtliche Werke. Frankfurter Ausgabe. Bd. 7: Gesänge. Hrsg. v. Sattler, D.E. Frankfurt a.M/Basel: Stroemfeld.

Honneth, Axel (1992/2003): Kampf um Anerkennung. Zur moralischen Grammatik sozialer Konflikte. Frankfurt a. M.: Suhrkamp.

Laughren, Mary (2022): Warlpiri encyclopaedic dictionary. Warlpiri yimi-kirli manu Jaru-kurlu. Canberra: Aboriginal Studies Press.

Lemmer, Manfred (1968): Sebastian Brant. Das Narrenschiff. Nach der Erstausgabe (Basel 1494) mit den Zusätzen der Ausgaben von 1495 und 1499 sowie den Holzschnitten der deutschen Originalausgaben. 2. Aufl. Tübingen: Niemeyer.

Lobenstein-Reichmann, Anja (2007): Medium Wörterbuch. In: Müller, Friedrich (Hrsg.): Politik, [Neue] Medien und die Sprache des Rechts. Berlin: Duncker & Humblot, 279–313.

Lobenstein-Reichmann, Anja (2019): Sprache und Geschichte. In: Bär, Jochen A./Lobenstein-Reichmann, Anja/Riecke, Jörg (Hrsg.): Sprache in der Geschichte. Berlin/Boston: De Gruyter, 7–43.

Lobenstein-Reichmann, Anja (2022): Sprachliche Ausgrenzung in der Lexikographie des Deutschen. In: Lexicographica 38, 7–38.

Lobenstein-Reichmann, Anja (2023): Beziehungslexikografie – Lexikografische Aufbereitung von gesellschaftsgeschichtlichen Anerkennungsrelationen am Beispiel des Frühneuhochdeutschen. In: Auteri, Laura, et al. (Hrsg.): Jahrbuch für Internationale Germanistik/Wege der Germanistik in transkultureller Perspektive. Akten des XIV. Kongresses der Internationalen Vereinigung für Germanistik (IVG). Bd. 10. Bern: Peter Lang. 223–244.

Lobenstein-Reichmann, Anja/Reichmann, Oskar (2020): Lexikographische Konzeption und kulturgeschichtliche Erkenntnis im digitalen Zeitalter. In: Lexicographica 36, 287–309.

McConvell, Patrick/Thieberger, Nicholas (2001): State of Indigenous languages in Australia – 2001. Canberra: Department of the Environment and Heritage.

McLuhan, Marshall (1964/2001): Understanding Media. The Extensions of Man. Berkeley, CA: Ginko Press.

Püschel, Ulrich (1989): Wörterbücher und Laienbenutzung. In: Hausmann, Franz Josef, et al. (Hrsg.): Wörterbücher. Ein internationales Handbuch zur Lexikographie. Erster Teilband. Berlin/New York: De Gruyter, 128–135.

Reichmann, Oskar (2012): Historische Lexikographie. Ideen, Verwirklichungen, Reflexionen an Beispielen des Deutschen, Niederländischen und Englischen. Berlin/Boston: De Gruyter.

Schweizerisches Idiotikon. Wörterbuch der schweizerdeutschen Sprache. Hrsg. v. Verein für das Schweizerdeutsche Wörterbuch. Bände I–XVI, Frauenfeld: Huber, Band XVII, Basel: Schwabe, https://www.idiotikon.ch/ (letzter Zugriff: 27.01.2025).

Shakespeare, William (1955): Werke in zwei Bänden. München/Zürich: Knaur.

Shakespeare, William (o. J.): Henry IV, Part 1. Folger Shakespeare Library, https://www.folger.edu/explore/shakespeares-works/henry-iv-part-1/read/ (letzter Zugriff: 27.01.2025).

Stoellger, Philipp (2012): Vom Sagen des Zeigens und Zeigen des Sagens. Die Macht der Sprache zwischen Sagen und Zeigen. In: Angehrn, Emil/Küchenhoff, Joachim (2012) (Hrsg.): Macht und Ohnmacht der

Sprache. Philosophische und psychoanalytische Perspektiven. Weilerswist: Velbrück Wissenschaft, 82–113.

Troy, Jakelin (1994): The Sydney Language. Canberra: Australian Dictionaries Project and the Australian Institute of Aboriginal and Torres Strait Islander Studies.

Wiegand, Herbert Ernst (1998): Wörterbuchforschung. Untersuchungen zur Wörterbuchbenutzung, zur Theorie, Geschichte, Kritik und Automatisierung der Lexikographie. 1. Teilband. Berlin/New York: De Gruyter.

Oskar Reichmann

Zur Berechtigung historischer Lexikographie: Fakten und Überlegungen

Abstract: The current paper distinguishes between lexicography directed at individual words and lexicography directed at the complete vocabulary of a language. The first approach relies on a representation-theoretical based theory of the lexicon and sees its assignment in the description of the highest possible number of headwords that are treated isolationistic. However, their presentation still displays a definite width. The second approach rather has a pragmatic-communicative base. It has the interconnectedness of all headwords regarding semantic, syntactic and word formation aspects as goal. In the lexicography of German and its neighbouring languages, this approach is predominantly found in the FWB. A justification question is directed at both these approaches in lexicography.

Keywords: Early New High German, Lexicography related to individual words and vocabulary as a whole, expressive and semantic orientation

Schlüsselwörter: Frühneuhochdeutsches Wörterbuch, isolationistische und gesamtwortschatzbezogene Lexikographie, Ausdrucksorientierte und semantikorientierte Lexikographie

1 Einführung zur Reichweite des Problems

Der hier vorgelegte Artikel ist zweifellos stark von meiner Arbeit und den dieser Arbeit entsprechenden Interessen am *Frühneuhochdeutschen Wörterbuch* (im Folgenden: FWB) geprägt. Demnach enthält er eine Reihe von persönlichen Urteilen, über die man geteilter Meinung sein kann, und verzichtet weitgehend auf die üblichen literaturgestützten Anmerkungen. Desto mehr bemühe ich mich um ein höchstmögliches Maß von Unvoreingenommenheit, Nachvollziehbarkeit, Begründbarkeit, letztlich auch um eine maximale eigenkritische Ehrlichkeit angesichts eines Problems, in dem auch *mea res agitur*, also meine eigene Angelegenheit verhandelt wird. Mit dem Blick auf die Gegenstände soll das hier heißen: Es geht um die bereits vorhandene sowie um die zukünftige historische Lexikographie, und zwar sowohl um synchron geschichtliche Sprach- und Varietätenlexikographie (etwa zum Alt- oder Mittelhochdeutschen, zum Altniederländischen, Frühneuenglischen, Altnordischen usw., denkbar auch z. B. zur deutschen Klassik) wie um geschichtliche Autorenlexikographie (denkbar z. B. zu Hartmann von Aue, zu Shakespeare, Goethe oder Karl Marx). Hintergrün-

Oskar Reichmann, Göttingen

https://doi.org/10.1515/9783112216644-005

dig (und deshalb nicht weiter ausgeführt) steht mit der Titelformulierung aber auch das gesamte akademische Gegenstandsfeld der historischen *Geisteswissenschaften*, darunter speziell der Sprach- und Literaturwissenschaft, zur Diskussion. Nochmals genereller und – hier ebenfalls nur angedeutet – geht es schließlich um die Gegenstände jeder Geschichtswissenschaft, seien sie theologischer, rechtlicher, philosophischer, sozialgeschichtlicher, ereignis- oder zustandsbezogener Art.

Mit dem Ausdruck *Berechtigung* in der Titelformulierung werden Existenzprobleme unterstellt. Diese oszillieren zwischen einerseits „typisch akademisch ausgerichtet" im Sinne ‚von auf eine Interessengruppe sozialspezifisch besonderer Prägung bezogen' und andererseits von 'allgemeingesellschaftlicher Relevanz', damit – so meiner Überzeugung nach – keineswegs gruppenbezogen und randständig, sondern von umfassender Bedeutung für die gesamte Bildungssoziologie und letztlich für die Konstitution einer Gesellschaft. Die Probleme sollen erkannt, benannt, erläutert, möglichst vorbehaltlos diskutiert, in Frage gestellt, relativiert, schließlich diskursiv abwägend als nur unter bestimmten und zu erfüllenden Voraussetzungen (möglicherweise) behebbar dargestellt werden. Angesichts der hier unterstellten Existenzproblematik, in der die historische Lexikographie (letztlich wie mitgesetzt: der historische Teil der Ausrichtung unseres Bildungssystems) steht, wundert es, dass dieser – zumindest nach meiner Einschätzung – immer noch eine quantitativ umfängliche Teildisziplin der Lexikographie des Deutschen bildet und – möglicherweise auch aufgrund der Konservativität der entscheidungsbefugten Geldgeber – bilden wird. Zur Erinnerung: Wir haben zum Beispiel das Leipziger *Althochdeutsche* (im Folgenden: AWB), trotz Lexer und Benecke/Müller/Zarncke (im Folgenden: BMZ) das neue *Mittelhochdeutsche* (im Folgenden: MWB) und das *Frühneuhochdeutsche Wörterbuch* (FWB), die zusammen genommen die volle geschichtliche Tiefe des Hochdeutschen erfassen, ferner das *Deutsche Rechtswörterbuch* (im Folgenden: RWB) mit speziell rechtswortgeschichtlichem Auftrag, außerdem *das Mittelniederdeutsche Wörterbuch* und immerhin die historisch orientierte Göttinger Arbeitsstelle für sog. *digitale Lexikographie* sowie das Berliner sog. *Große Wörterbuch der deutschen Sprache* (im Folgenden: GWdS); und wir hatten bis vor kurzem die partielle Neubearbeitung des *Wörterbuches von Jacob Grimm und Wilhelm Grimm* (im Folgenden: DWB*)* und des *Deutschen Fremdwörterbuches* (letzteres am IdS. Institut für deutsche Sprache; Mannheim), außerdem lange Zeit eine Dialektlexikographie, die für den Einbezug der Wortgeschichte durchaus offen war. Beispiele dafür bilden bzw. bildeten das *Rheinische Wörterbuch*, das *Hessen-Nassauische Volkswörterbuch*, das *Schlesische* und das *Preußische Wörterbuch*, das erst kürzlich eingestellte *Wörterbuch der bairischen Mundarten in Österreich* (der Österreichischen Akademie der Wissenschaften) sowie eine Reihe weiterer Dialektwörterbücher (etwa zum Niedersächsischen, Pfälzischen, Südhessischen, Fränkischen, Bairischen mit ihrer freilich je eigenen Geschichte). Das *Schweizerische Idiotikon* (im Folgenden: Schweiz. Id.) stellt mit seiner grundsätzlichen historischen Orientierung einen Sonderfall dar, der das Gesagte für den deutschsprachigen Teil der Schweizer Eidgenossenschaft aber bestätigt. Alle diese Arbeitsstellen, sowohl die noch laufenden wie die eingestellten, sind bzw. waren – wie speziell wiederum das um 1880 gegründete Schweiz. Id., aber auch einige andere – relativ langfristig (teils Generationen, teils auch ein Jahrhundert übergreifend) angelegt; sie verfügen (bzw. verfügten) über eine im Einzelnen zwar stark unterschiedliche, wenn auch teils nicht voll aufrechterhaltene, aber teils doch durchschnittliche Personalausstattung in mittlerer, teilweise auch geringerer einstelliger Höhe; sie leisten (bzw. leisteten[1]) sich im Vertrauen auf diese Absicherungen zumindest teilweise eine Publikationseffizienz, die Anlass zu kritischen Fragen hinsichtlich der Arbeitseffektivität gibt. Das heißt nicht zuletzt: Sie sind und waren im Einzelnen und allesamt relativ teuer[2] und werden dies auch weiterhin bleiben. Ich verstehe dies alles als allgemeine Kennzeichnung der Situation, nicht also als kritische Aussage zu den einzelnen Unternehmen.

2 Zur theoretischen Grundlage der historischen Lexikographie

Den Anlass für den vorliegenden Artikel bildet neben dem gerade Gesagten auch die folgende sprachtheoretische Zustandsbeschreibung der historischen Lexikographie des Deutschen: Sie steht immer noch – jedenfalls großenteils, also mit Ausnahmen – auf dem sprachtheoretischen Stand des 19. Jahrhunderts; und sie steht immer noch – natürlich ebenfalls nur großenteils –auf dessen benutzerbezüglichem Interessestand. Diesen sprachtheoretischen Stand sehe ich dann gegeben, wenn ein Wörterbuch den Wortschatz als eine Summe von schätzungsweise 100 000 Einzeleinheiten (Simplicia und Wortbildungen zusammengenommen) auffasst und aufgrund dieser Zahlenfixierung dazu tendiert, Qualitätsurteile in dem Sinne zu vertreten: „je mehr Stichwörter/Lemmaeinheiten, desto höher der Wert des Wörterbuches". Auch wenn dieses Urteil in der lexikographischen Fachliteratur nicht mit der hier vertretenen Deutlichkeit ausgesprochen wird, scheint es insbesondere dann, wenn die Anzahl der Lemmata in den jeweiligen Vorwörtern und sonstigen Rahmentexten besonders betont und mit derjenigen vorhandener oder befürchteter Konkurrenzunternehmen verglichen wird, doch immer wieder durch oder wenn neue bzw. laufende Unternehmen nur dann bzw. nur insoweit finanziert bzw. verlängert werden, wenn sie neue Lemmata, wie irrelevant sie auch sein mögen, versprechen. Ich belege diese Aussagen hier nicht mit Beispielzitaten, dies deshalb nicht, weil sie zutiefst mit dem Selbstverständnis und der

1 Diese Doppelformulierungen sowie Kennzeichnungen wie *teilweise* sollen zeigen, dass es mir hier nicht um eine regresspflichtige flächendeckende Zustandsbeschreibung historisch orientierter dialektaler Prägung, auch nicht um eine erschöpfende Aufzählung aller Unternehmen und schon gar nicht um Einzelurteile geht, sondern um allgemeine Tendenzen.

2 Mir ist natürlich bewusst, dass *teuer* je nach Vergleichsgröße unterschiedlich, aber doch auch selbstkritisch zu verstehen ist. Vergleichswerte mit den Kosten technischer Projekte anzugeben, zeugen jedenfalls von einer gewissen Verkennung der gesellschaftlichen Wertungen.

damit verbundenen sprachideologischen Grundlegung der historischen Lexikographie korrelieren und insofern mit einer unterschwelligen Zustimmung aufgenommen werden.

Damit ist die angesprochene sprachideologische, -theoretische Grundlage zu charakterisieren. Meine Aussage lautet: Lexikalische Einheiten werden relativ generell als *Darstellungen* vorsprachlich und vorkognitiv vorhandener Gegebenheiten verstanden. Man rufe sich nur die jahrzehntelange Diskussion um die vermeintlichen Probleme „Wörter und Sachen", „Sprach- und Sach- (= enzyklopädisches) Wissen" usw. in Erinnerung. Die Brücke zwischen „Vorgegebenheiten" der gerade mittels der Attribute *vorsprachlich* und *vorkognitiv* gekennzeichneten Art und der Lexik wird im vulgären *naiven* Realismus streng abbildtheoretischer Art als 1:1-Verhältnis gesehen: „so viele Vorgegebenheiten/Sachen, so viele Wörter". Da diese Gleichung schon bei oberflächlichem Blick auf *Sache*, außerdem auf innersprachliche (z. B. geschichtliche, dialektale, pragmatisch perspektivische usw.) Verhältnisse, erst recht beim Blick auf andere Sprachen als nicht haltbar erkannt wird, setzt man im sog. *kritischen* Realismus verschiedene Brechungsmöglichkeiten zwischen einerseits (vermeintlich) objektiv-sinnlicher und andererseits einzeldialektaler, pragmatisch einzelperspektivierter sowie languehaft differierender Semantik voraus. Wie immer man die jeweils angesprochene Perspektivität auch betonen mag: Der Objektivitätsgedanke bleibt gegenüber dem perspektivischen hintergründig, gleichsam als Urteilslatte, vorhanden und fließt – wie versteckt auch immer – in die semantischen Beschreibungen der Stichwörter ein, auch wenn diese offensichtlich gesellschaftliche Einrichtungen, Erkenntnisse, Ideologieeinheiten, soziale Beziehungen und ähnliche zweifellos *soziofaktische* Gestaltungen hintergründig gegebener (hier mal als *realfaktisch*[3] attribuierter) Unbestreitbarkeiten betreffen. Man könnte diese Haltung in dem Maße als *vulgäraufklärerisch* bezeichnen, in dem man vorkognitiv und vorsprachlich angenommene Gegenstände (aber auch Beziehungen wie z. B. Kausalität oder Finalität) annimmt, die auf einer letztlich doch objektiven, allen Menschen eigenen gleichen Wahrnehmung, einer ihnen ebenso eigenen schlechthinnigen Vernunft und daraus folgenden, vielleicht nicht ganz gleichen, aber doch vergleichbaren soziofaktischen Gegebenheiten sieht und sie als sprachlich so verfasst betrachtet, wie man sie als vorgegeben ansieht. Wie auch immer man zu dieser Problematik steht: Es geht nicht nur um die lexikographische Bedeutungserläuterung, sondern auch um einfachste Tagesbetriebe, um die Vermittlung von Textübersetzung und um jede sprachenübergreifende Verständigung. So wie jeder Pädagoge[4] bei der Vorbereitung jeder Unterrichtsstunde vor den Fragen steht: „*Was* genau (damit im strengen Sinne aber nur geprägt Vorausgesetztes) will ich als (nur *sogenannt)* gegenstandsbezogen behandeln? *Wie, mit welchen Gewich-*

3 Würde man versuchen, eine Grenze zwischen *sozio-* und *real*faktisch zu ziehen, so würde diese wohl sehr weit im Bereich von *sozio-* anzubringen sein.

4 Er sei hier als Beispiel für jeden Sprecher in jeder Sprechsituation gemeint.

tungen will ich es behandeln? *Wem* will ich es *wie* nahebringen? *Wie* will ich es in der Schulpolitik etwa gegenüber den Geldgebern verantworten? So steht auch der Lexikograph gegenüber angenommenen Nachschlagenden (den *usern*) vor vergleichbaren Fragen, darunter z. B.: *Was* will ich überhaupt oder vorwiegend und wie behandeln?" In Frage kommen gesamtwortbezogene (dies weiter unten mit den Siglen von a. bis e.) und semembezogene (dies unten von f. bis l.) Eigenschaften. Diese Unterscheidung bedarf eines einführenden Zusatzes: *Gesamtwortbezogen* kann *ausdrucks-* oder *signifikatbezogen* heißen; *semembezogen* betrifft nur die unterschiedenen sog. *Einzelbedeutungen* eines Wortes. Am Beispiel erläutert: Die Zeichengestalt (eines Stichwortes wie z. B. frnhd. *abenteuer* oder *minne*) gilt in der Regel für alle Bedeutungen/Sememe/Syntagmen/Wortbildungen eines Stichwortes bzw. mit einem solchen; *semembezogene* Unterscheidungen dagegen gelten nur pro Einzelbedeutungsansatz. Diese Unterscheidung ist in der Lexikographie allerdings systematisch unbeachtet geblieben: Störend ist dies vor allem dann, wenn z. B. in der Diskussion über die Bedeutung M. Luthers für die Entwicklung oder auch die sog. *Entstehung* der nhd. Schriftsprache durchgehend (gesamt)signifikatbezogen argumentiert und damit unterstellt wird, dass sich mit einem sogenannten *Lutherwort* in seiner ebenso nur sogenannten *eigentlichen* Bedeutung auch das gesamte semasiologische Feld mit allen seinen semantischen Differenzen, den tropischen Gebräuchen, seinen Syntagmen usw. gleichgerichtet verändert habe.

3 Behandlungsgegenstände: Sinn- und Identifikationsfrage

Es gibt gesamtwortbezogene und semembezogene Aussagen. Gesamtwortbezogen sind:

a. ein Lemma (üblicherweise verstanden als Konstrukt einer Zeichengestalt, also der Ausdrucksform),
b. geschichtliche Schreibungen (in je regionaler, zeitlicher, sozial üblicher Form, die aber durch das Lemmakonstrukt abgefangen sein können),
c. die Flexionsformen (der Absicht nach dokumentativ pro Raum, Zeit, Textsorte, teils variantenübergreifend normalisiert),
d. die Etymologie (wie auch immer gewichtet),
e. eine wie auch immer geartete Erläuterung der Gesamtbedeutung (des Signifikates).

Semembezogene Aussagen sind:

f. die Erläuterung jeder angenommenen Einzelbedeutung (jedes Semems), de facto der Bedeutungsansätze des Lexikographen,

g. die Angabe von Symptomwerten (zu Zeit, Raum, Textsorte),
h. die Angabe von Phrasemen,
i. die Angabe bedeutungsverwandter Wörter,
j. die Angabe von Syntagmen,
k. die Angabe von Wortbildungen mit dem Stichwort,
l. die Belegzitate.

Offensichtlich ist, dass diese Liste lexikographisch nicht pro Position je gleichberechtigt, sondern je unterschiedlich mindestens nach den Zielen gerade herrschender rezeptionszeitlicher Interessen, nach je wissenschaftlichen sowie kultur- und bildungsbezogenen Anliegen abgearbeitet werden wird: Auf nahezu alles kann verzichtet und nahezu alles kann als beschreibungsrelevant betrachtet werden. Nach meinem Urteil wird man dabei nicht um einige vorgängige Urteile und damit um einige Offenheiten herumkommen.

Im Hintergrund dieser Überlegungen steht die Sinn- und Ausgangsfrage des vorliegenden Textes, also der vorausgesetzte Zweifel an der Berechtigung historischer Lexikographie. Unterstellt sei dabei, dass jeder Wissenschaftler, so auch der historisch orientierte Lexikograph, „etwas gesellschaftlich Sinnvolles" tun will und tun sollte (so Reichmann 2012: 1), also etwas, das über die Schaffung bloß punktueller Nachschlagetexte hinausgeht und auf keinen Fall einem rein persönlichen Hobby der Angehörigen einer kleinen, sogenannten sozialen Elite ähnlich wäre. Das damit angesprochene Problem stellt sich desto offensichtlicher, je weniger sich eine Sprachgesellschaft aus ihrer Geschichte heraus definiert, umgekehrt gesagt: je mehr sie sich aus ihrem gegenwärtigen Funktionieren im Raum heraus identifiziert, wie dies entscheidend, aber nicht ausschließlich z. B. für das heutige Deutsche und für viele andere Sprachen gilt. Ich erinnere in diesem Zusammenhang an die grassierende Reduktion der historischen Komponente im Fächer- und Inhaltskanon selbst des Gymnasialunterrichts in allen Ländern der Bundesrepublik Deutschland, die natürlich darauf hinausläuft, dass geschichtliches Interesse gar nicht erst aufkommt und erst recht so etwas wie historische Lexikographie ihre gesellschaftliche Interessebasis verliert. Es geht folglich nicht mehr unter zeitlichen Aspekten um die historische Tiefe des Deutschen von seinen Uranfängen bis hin zu seiner Rolle als Ausbau-, Kultur- und Nationalsprache, anders gesagt: um seine Rolle als die Nation (im sprachnationalen Sinne) definierendes Verständigungssystem hohen, verehrungswürdigen, tendenziell sogar religiös unterlegten Eigenwertes, den man denn auch – wie oft gesagt wird – *verraten* und an dem man sich bei schlechtem Gebrauch – auch als *Sprachverhunzung* gesehen und so bezeichnet – *versündigen* kann (vgl. hierzu von Polenz 1999: 298); sondern es geht um seine Funktion als wertfrei pragmatisch gesehenes und großräumig bis weltweit einsetzbares Verständigungsmittel. Dass bei dieser Perspektive bestimmte Varietäten, speziell die Fachsprachen, aktuell in Konkurrenz mit dem Englischen, eine zumindest partielle Provinzialisierung, auf jeden Fall eine Peripherisierung erfahren, wird besonders dann als Selbstverständlichkeit verstanden, wenn Deutsche nicht nur über naturwissenschaftliche Gegenstände, sondern auch über ihre eigene Sprache selbst wissenschaftlich nicht mehr auf Deutsch schreiben oder gar sprechen, sondern englisch (dies oft schon als symbolfunktionales Erkennungszeichen ihrer Bildung) und damit jede Geschichtlichkeit unterlaufen. So viel zum Motivationshintergrund des Artikelthemas.

Zu den angesprochenen Offenheiten gehören Fragen wie: Was heißt überhaupt *brauchen*? *Wozu* braucht *we*r auch immer *was* auch immer? Ins Stammtischdeutsche übersetzt ist das die Frage: „Wozu ist das gut"? Etwas ernsthafter fragt sich: Wer sind *wir*, und was ist *was*? Ferner: Welcher Interesse- und Bildungsschicht gehören die überhaupt Interessierten an? Welche Argumente haben sie, ihre Interessen als allgemeinverbindlich voraussetzen und Steuergelder für ihre Tätigkeit in Anspruch nehmen zu dürfen? Man erkennt, dass es im Folgenden nicht um eine allgemeine Antwort im Sinne von „ja" oder „nein" der simplen Art geht: „Man braucht historische Lexikographie" bzw. „man braucht sie nicht", sondern um Differenzierungen im Sinne von „in welchen gesellschaftshistorischen und -soziologischen Interessekonstellationen, vor allem: In welchen Erkenntnis-, Motivations-, Handlungs- und sozialidentifikativen Zusammenhängen braucht *wer* historische Lexikographie, und zwar *welcher* genauen Ausrichtung? Fragen dieser Art können – wie bereits gesagt – die Rolle von Existenzfragen sprachnational kultureller Art einnehmen; sie verlangen Antworten, die pro Zeit, pro Sozialschicht und -gruppe, speziell pro Bildungsschicht je spezifisch, also je und je anders und oft gegensätzlich ausfallen werden. Mit anderen Worten: Was etwa im 19. Jahrhundert nach Ausweis der Vorrede des *Deutschen Wörterbuches* von Jacob Grimm und Wilhelm Grimm nicht nur für die nationale Bildungsschicht als sinnvoll galt – vor allem mit dem Blick auf die damals noch nicht vorhandene sog. *Reichseinigung* –, kann möglicherweise im 21. Jahrhundert nur noch als Gegenstand einer kleinen und abgehobenen gesellschaftlichen Randgruppe im Bereich akademischer Lexikographie wahrgenommen werden. In dem Maße, in dem Letzteres der Fall ist, wird historische Lexikographie auf Dauer dem Untergang geweiht sein, es sei denn, sie entdeckt in ihrem Gegenstand, also im Wortschatz einer Sprache, eine Perspektive, die ein gesellschaftliches Interesse finden könnte, in dem die nationalpolitische Komponente im Sinne des 19. Jahrhunderts zwar nicht irrelevant, aber doch nur noch reduziert vorhanden wäre und neuen gesellschaftsbezüglichen oder gar gesellschaftsidentifikativen und -konstitutiven Zwecksetzungen weichen würde.

Diese Formulierungen lassen erkennen, dass es ein bleibendes Problem und eine entsprechende Aufgabe sein wird, historische Lexikographie so auszurichten, dass der Interessefunke für sie von den wenigen Lexikographen, die ihre Existenz teils den erstarrten Traditionen der Wissenschaft und selbst der Wissenschaftsförderung verdanken, auf Rezipientengruppen mit einer gewissen sozialen Breite überspringt. Ich mache kein Hehl aus meiner Skepsis, ob dies gelingen wird, und wiederhole nochmals, dass das Problem auch weite Teile der historischen Geisteswissenschaften, und zwar von der Literaturgeschichte bis hin zu den einzelnen Teildisziplinen der Geschichtswissenschaft, betrifft. Letztlich stehen wir also vor einer existentiell entscheidenden Sinn- und Identifikationsfrage, die bis hin zu unserem gesamtgesellschaftlichen Zusammenhalt reichen: Ist eine historische Begründung eines letztlich immer noch national(sprachlich) unterlegten Staates noch möglich? Nach dieser Sicht der Lage, in der sich die historische Lexikographie nach meinem Urteil befindet, komme ich auf die gerade angesprochene Sinn- und Identifikationsfrage zurück.

4 Die übliche Informationsstruktur historischer Wörterbücher

Dazu sei eine kurze Kennzeichnung der generellen Informationsstruktur historischer Wörterbücher vorausgeschickt: Sie sind in aller Regel wortalphabetisch angelegt; sie tendieren dazu, das meist normalisierte Stichwort, also ein Konstrukt, mehr oder weniger umfänglich durch die Angabe z. B. dialektaler, teils auch soziopragmatischer Realisierungen sowie morphologischer Varianten zu belegen, mithin durch Anbindung an tatsächliche Gebräuche zu veranschaulichen, in seiner Zeichengestaltung zu rechtfertigen (usw.). Danach folgen – gemäß der vorgelegten Liste – gewohnheitsmäßig gerne Kurzangaben zur Etymologie, ohne dass deren Funktion im Zusammenhang mit dem je spezifischen Gegenstand und der genauen Bestimmung des Zieles des einzelnen Wörterbuches offengelegt oder auch nur diskutiert würde. Den Mittelpunkt der Behandlung bildet danach die Nennung eines oder mehrerer beschreibungssprachlicher Synonyme, die als Bedeutungserläuterung verstanden werden mögen, aber alle semantischen Nuancen des Stichwortes systematisch einebnen, also z. B. frnhd. *minne*, wenn es denn als 'Liebe' vermittelt sein sollte, zumindest partiell irreführend in Deckungsgleichheit mit nhd. *Liebe* bringen. Das ist zwar nicht gänzlich falsch und wird auch nie gänzlich falsch werden, aber es ist doch so verfälschend, dass es jeden Differenzwert, damit jeden Aufmerksamkeits- und Interessewert tötet. Auf die fälschlich als „Erläuterung“ verstandene Synonymenangabe kann ein Belegblock folgen, der vielfach darauf ausgerichtet ist, die bereits durch die Synonymisierung bewirkte Einebnung geschichtlicher und beschreibungszeitlicher Semantik zu verstärken. Ich gebe zu, dass diese Skizze ein Zerrbild der oft sehr feinfühligen Einzelartikel philologisch und/oder semantisch ausgezeichneten Wörterbücher bildet. In dem Maße aber, in dem das Zerrbild zutrifft, kann das Ergebnis dennoch nur lauten: Die historische Lexikographie gestaltet sich allzu oft als einfache Gebrauchslexikographie für punktuelle Nachschlagezwecke. Speziell ihre alphabetische und zweifellos einzelwortisolierende Anlage schließt ein Verständnis semantischer Differenzen zwischen zeitgenössischem (geschichtlichem) und historisch beschreibungssprachlichem (also je gegenwärtigem) Gebrauch, die das Einzelwort übergreifen, geradezu systematisch aus; und sie schließt – noch kritikwürdiger – vor allem das Verständnis semantischer Zusammenhänge, darunter genereller zeitgenössischer semantischer Prägungen (etwa religiöse, ethische, rechtliche Unterlegungen normalsprachlich profan alltäglicher Wortgebräuche) aus. Sie beschreibt eben nicht systematisch den Wortschatz als Ganzen, gleichsam als umfassendes einzelsprachliches Deutungsnetz von Welt, sondern sie behandelt immer nur isoliert gesehene Einzelwörter. Dabei dienen die etymologischen Angaben – gewollt oder ungewollt – oft lediglich dazu, ein Bewusstsein vom Uraltertum und der Reinheit des Deutschen, speziell seiner sogenannten Stammwörter, letztlich immer noch im Sinne des Patriotismusverständnisses der Barockzeit und dessen Verzerrungen in den nachfolgenden Jahrhunderten hervorzurufen bzw. zu verstärken. Die Funktion der Belege ist meist auf die bloße Veranschaulichung des in der (sog.) Bedeutungserläuterung verallgemeinernd Gesagten ausgerichtet, weniger z. B. auf die Hinführung zu den Texten und Textverbünden, die doch die Vorkommensform von Sprache sind.

Dies alles wird der Funktion des Wortschatzes als Gesamtheit im aktuellen Sprechen und Schreiben nach meinem Urteil nicht hinreichend gerecht. Das sei mit folgenden Aussagen eigens betont:

- Sprache und alle ihre Systemkonstituenten und Realisierungen sind auf allen ihren hierarchischen Ebenen zum Zwecke von Semantik, genauer: zur Semantikkonstitution, da;
- diese erfolgt in Textverbünden und ihren Einzeltexten;
- Texte konstituieren sich über ihre Syntax und diese über die Lexik;
- Lexik ist damit die zentrale hierarchische Ebene des sog Sprachsystems, auf der wir uns die Welt so einrichten, wie wir sie sehen und in ihr handeln;
- das geschieht durch die Nutzung einerseits entlastend vorgegebener fester Einheiten, oft der sog. Simplicia; andererseits bilden diese Einheiten eine nach oben offene (also je nach Situation mittels der Möglichkeiten der Wortbildung) in die Syntax erweiterbare Gesamtheit. Jede dieser Einheiten ist systematisch mehrdeutig, wird also stets pro Einzeltext – jeweils der syntaktischen Aussage und der Textillokution entsprechend – variabel gebraucht. Jedes Wort erfährt folglich in jeder Wortbildung und in jedem Satz und Satzglied des Textes und der Textverbünde eine semantische Nuancierung in Richtung auf die immer einmalige Textillokution.
- Demnach können jedem Wort systematisch mehrere, wortintern zueinander übergängige Bedeutungen, sog. Sememe, zugeschrieben werden; diese können pro angesetzte Einheit in eine jeweils partielle Synonymiebeziehung zu einem der Bedeutungsansätze (Sememe) einer anderen Einheit gesetzt werden (meist also nicht zu der Einheit als ganzer, zum Signifikat, der sog. Gesamtbedeutung, wie es dennoch regelhaft geschieht); Sememsynonymie bildet demnach den Regelfall, nicht Signifikatsynonymie; diese ist ein großenteils außerhalb der sprachlichen Realität liegendes Beschreibungsprodukt.

5 Zentrale Aufgabe historischer Lexikographie

Diese Aussagen, insbesondere letztere, laufen darauf hinaus, dass Sprechen und Schreiben weniger als abbildungstheoretisch verstandene, perspektivisch kaum variante, sondern sichere Bezugnahme auf vorsprachlich und vorkognitiv vorausgesetzte, scharf umgrenzte Gegenstände verstanden werden sollten wie als Gestaltung, Einrichtung unserer Lebenswelt nach je geschichtlich-kulturellen Interessen, ideologischen Leitbildern, sozialen Bedingungen und pragmatischen Perspektiven, zusammengefasst: nach je wechselnden Verhältnissen und gemäß deren je sprachlicher Fassung. Daraus ergibt sich als zentrale Aufgabe historischer Wörterbücher: Sie haben nicht nur zu vermitteln, wie dies pro Wort und Wortgebrauchseinheit (Semem) geschieht, sondern auch, wie dies je nuanciert erfolgt, welche wortinternen und vor allem wortübergreifenden Ähnlichkeiten, vergleichbaren geschichtstypischen semantischen Tendenzen in diesem je spezifischen sprachlichen Handeln und Gestalten erkannt werden können und wie sich eine Gesellschaft in der Gesamtheit solcher semantisierender Tätigkeiten (oft) identifiziert. *Semantisch* ist dabei einmal im kognitiven Sinne zu verstehen, nämlich als Frage: Wie entwerfe/umreiße/ersemantisiere ich z. B. sozio*kognitive* Einheiten wie frnhd. *abenteuer, gewalt, liebe, minne, ordnung, schuld* oder *unzucht* inhaltlich? Es ist zweitens im *handlungs*theoretischen Sinne zu verstehen als Frage: Welche *handlungs*konstitutive Anweisung gebe ich untrennbar verbunden mit dem vorgenommenen *kognitiven* Zuschnitt? Für z. B. *minne* lautet sie anders, wenn ich sie in erster Linie als Seins- und Wesensqualität Gottes bestimme, als wenn ich sie als Möglichkeit und Ergebnis gütlicher Einigung im juristischen Sinn (erkennbar etwa in dem Syntagma bzw. Phrasem „sich in minne schicken") verstehe und damit entsakralisierend/säkularisierend in die Verfügung des Menschen lege. Zum dritten ist das Wort *semantisch* symptomfunktional, d. h. als identifikationsrelevant zu verstehen: Wie gebe ich mich (im hier diskutierten Fall) semantisch als „unterschieden" (von Anderen) zu erkennen?

Mit dem Vorgetragenen unterstelle ich natürlich, historische Lexikographie erstens desto interessefähiger zu machen, je mehr es mir gelingt, sie auf die volle Breite der gerade aufgelisteten Qualitäten der Wortbedeutung, speziell auf ihren kognitiv verstandenen semasiologischen und onomasiologischen Feldcharakter, auf ihre semasiologischen Übergängigkeiten, ihre semantikkonstitutive Leistung, auf die Breite ihrer syntaktischen Gebrauchsmöglichkeiten und auf ihre textillokutive sowie perlokutive Handlungsrolle zu beziehen, sie damit zu soziologisieren und zu pragmatisieren. Historische Lexikographie wird zweitens desto interessefähiger, je mehr man die Handlungsbedeutung und die Symptomwerte herausstellt, ferner auf geschichtliche Besonderheiten bei alledem achtet und außerdem (also drittens) einen erheblichen Anteil des Lexikographen an der Gestaltung der Artikel unterstellt, ihn insofern als Herren seiner Texte (selbst auf der Beschreibungsebene) sieht, diese denn auch gerne als *Metaebene* bezeichnet, damit erhebt und aufwertet. Mit Letzterem meine ich nicht weniger als Folgendes: Der Lexikograph ist nicht nur Beschreibender und vermeintlich objektiv Darstellender einer klar oder gar – wie erläutert – deutlich[5] umrissenen vermeintlich faktischen Vorgabe und sollte sich folglich auch nicht in dieser Weise definieren und dabei Exaktheits-, Richtigkeits- und Vollständigkeitsträumen nachgehen. Letztlich sollte er sich dabei auch nicht in Irrelevanzen aller möglicher, z. B. dialektaler, soziolektaler, etymologischer Art verlieren, sondern seine unhintergehbare hermeneutische Situation nicht erkenntniskritisch (wie allgemein üblich) als objektivitätsstörend, sondern positiv als Bedingung der Möglichkeit zur Benutzeransprache, damit zum Ausdruck eigener Mitteilungsgewichtungen und wiederum damit zu einer Ansprache des Benutzers sehen. Der Lexikograph mutiert auf diese Weise vom historisch ausgerichteten vermeintlich Beschreibenden in einer als sachlich gesehenen Subjekt-Objektposition zur Semantik und Pragmatik schaffenden Kommunizierenden in einer auf wissenschaftlicher Ebene personal ausgerichteten, damit gestaltungs-, von allem interesseoffenen Situation. Bildlich gesprochen: Er schaut nicht rein sachbezogen von oben nach unten auf seine Ausdrücke (wie vermutlich ein Mineraloge auf einen Stein, wobei das Ergebnis seiner Beschreibung den Stein nicht interessiert), sondern er schaut symmetrisch horizontal, also auf gleicher Augenhöhe, auf einen Rezipienten und richtet eine Gegebenheit, die bereits auf objektsprachlicher Ebene durch ihre Fassung als *Stein* (und nicht z. B. als *Wacke*) soziopragmatischer Seinsweise ist, perspektivisch nochmals brechend so ein, dass er seinen Rezipienten damit anzusprechen und zu interessieren vermag. Genau deshalb habe ich vorhin – anlässlich der Aufzählung der Funktionen des Lexikons – auch nicht gesagt: „Jedes Wort *hat* X Bedeutungen“, sondern von *angenommener semantischer Nuancierung, vom Setzen* von Bedeutungen, von der *semantischen Einrichtung der Lebenswelt* usw. gesprochen, also jeweils Formulierungen gebraucht, die einen Sprecher mit Gestaltungsmöglichkeiten und -absichten sowie einen Hörer mit solchen Interessen voraussetzen, die man nach den geltenden gesellschaftlichen Bildungsidealen von ihm erwartet, zu treffen und kommunikativ zu beeinflussen sucht. Begründete Stellung- und Einflussnahme ist damit nicht Parteilichkeit, die unter dem Vorwand der Unhintergehbarkeit zur Entschuldigung[6] aufruft und am besten auszuschalten wäre, sondern die positiv zu sehen ist als Bedingung der Möglichkeit semantik- und pragmatikgeschichtlicher Tätigkeit auch auf der Rezeptionsebene von Lexikographie, dies alles selbstverständlich reflektierter Art. Das Adjektiv *reflektiert* soll dabei nicht ‘unwidersprechbar’ bedeuten, sondern seinerseits zu weiterer Diskussion anregen. Man erkennt: Es gibt keine endgültige Richtigkeit als Ergebnis eines Erkennens von oben nach unten, sondern immer ein

5 Mit der Unterscheidung von *klar* und *deutlich* übernehme ich die entsprechende aufklärerische Unterscheidung der Erkenntnisqualitäten (Genaueres dazu bei Reichmann 1996).

6 Ich beziehe mich hier auf die selbst in hermeneutischen Zusammenhängen begegnende Üblichkeit, Vorprägungen *erklären, entschuldigen, rechtfertigen* zu müssen.

begründetes Semantisieren/Handeln, das auf nur vermeintlich höherer Ebene seinerseits in weitere Semantisierungen/Handlungen mündet. Die gerade angesprochene vermeintlich höhere, üblicherweise als *Metaebene* aufgewertete Beschreibungsebene wird dann ihrerseits zur objektsprachlichen Ebene, auch wenn man sie gerne zur Steigerung der eigenen Würde als *Metametaebene* bezeichnet.

In dem Augenblick, in dem die Aufgabe des Lexikographen so gesehen wird, gewinnt historische Lexikographie neue Funktionen: Die Beschreibungsaufgabe behält natürlich immer einen gewissen Orientierungswert, damit wird auch die punktuell einzelwortbezogene, bloß nachfragebezügliche Lexikographie nicht überflüssig; sie rückt aber gegenüber einer Lexikographie in den Hintergrund, die sich als sowohl hermeneutisch wie pädagogisch und wissenschaftlich gesteuerte Disziplin versteht. *Hermeneutisch* soll dabei heißen: Der Lexikograph hat sich erstens der allgemein gängigen semantischen Vorgaben und Interessevorprägungen der geschichtlichen, je zeitgenössischen Sprachgesellschaft, also z. B. des 16. Jahrhunderts, bewusst zu sein; und zweitens hat er diese Interessen stets in Vergleich mit seinem je eigenen semantischen und pragmatischen Horizont zu bringen. Im ersteren Falle bildeten synchron innerfrühneuhochdeutsche Unterscheidungen den Beschreibungsgegenstand; in letzterem Falle lägen diachrone Unterscheidungen vor, also solche zwischen einer geschichtlichen Sprachstufe und derjenigen Sprachstufe, in der er selbst steht und handelt. Ich nenne letztere *historisch* und unterscheide sie damit von *geschichtlich* im Sinne von *zeitgenössisch. Pädagogisch* soll heißen: Der Lexikograph ist gehalten, das als innergeschichtlich synchron different Erkannte so zu behandeln, dass es den Interessen der Rezeptionsgesellschaft entgegenkommt. Das Verb *entgegenkommen* meint hier Folgendes: Es wird bei historischer Lexikographie und speziell Semantik zwar auch und vielleicht sogar hauptsächlich um „Beschreibung“ im üblichen historischen Sinne gehen, aber es geht nicht nur um Beschreibung. Pure Beschreibung ist wertfrei, es sei denn, sie gewinne ihren Wert im Interesse von Rezipienten. Dieses Interesse anzusprechen oder zu schaffen, ist eine kulturpädagogische Aufgabe hohen, wenn auch allgemein unterschätzten Ranges. Ihre Lösung hat selbstverständlich nach den anerkannten wissenschaftlichen Methoden/Standards zu erfolgen, darunter einer breitest- und tiefstmöglichen einschlägigen Belesenheit des Lexikographen, einer darauf beruhenden qualitativ-inhaltlichen, nicht primär zahlenbestimmten Korpusbegründung,[7] ferner fachmännischer, unter besonderer Gewichtung der Semantik und Pragmatik stehender Exzerption, somit Nachprüfbarkeit der Bedeutungsansätze usw. Mir ist natürlich bewusst, dass jede dieser Forderungen in ihrer Handhabung ihrerseits Spielräumen unterliegt. Gegen diese Spielräume mag und wird man gängige Gegenentwürfe vortragen, z. B. Objektivität, Richtigkeit, Vollständigkeit; es sind bei aller Berechtigung und Notwendigkeit dennoch jeweils unerfüllbare Forderungen, die letztlich dem Wahnsinn (*sit*

7 Ich meine diejenigen (hier nur als Schreckbild dienenden) Begründungen, die selbst bei – sagen wir mal – 3 Milliarden Corpuswörtern noch meinen, das Corpus erweitern zu müssen, damit die bloße Belegdokumentation aufwerten und die zeitaufwendige Tätigkeit eigener semantischer Texterschließung aus den Augen verlieren.

venia verbo) nahekommen und letztlich auf eine Relativierung bis hin zur Verunmöglichung semantikbezüglicher Forschung hinauslaufen.

6 Folgerungen für die Artikelstruktur

Das Vorgetragene verlangt eine Artikelstruktur, die dem allem Rechnung trägt. Das heißt generell: Dem Wörterbuchartikel ist eine Form zu geben, die ihre Verabfassung als soziale, auf Geschichtliches bezogene Verstehenstätigkeit spiegelt (zum mindesten nicht primär also als objektive Beschreibung vermeintlich klar vorgegebener Sachverhalte). Die Bedeutungserläuterung mutiert damit zum gestalterischen, Stellung beziehenden Gesamtwurf eines seinerseits um Verständnis ringenden Lexikographen und insgesamt zum Versuch der kontrollierten Vermittlung der Lebenswelt einer geschichtlichen Epoche. Das Verhältnis zwischen dem Lexikographen und den Benutzern nimmt Züge von Kooperation an.

Dies betrifft alle oben aufgelisteten Beschreibungspositionen des Wörterbuchartikels (und nun werden die einzelnen Informationspositionen erneut aufgerufen): Die gängige alphabetische Anordnung wird dabei aus praktischen Gründen nur als Zugriffsstruktur, nicht etwa als ehrfurchtgebietende Demonstration des alten Copia-Begriffs, fungieren.

- Alle Aufzählungen dialektaler (usw.) Formen und alle etymologischen Angaben werden auf einen bestimmten Zweck hin operationalisierten Umfang bezogen werden können, der in einer hochspracheorientierten Gesellschaft wie der deutschen sicher anders ausfällt als etwa in der stark dialektal, schärfer ausgedrückt, sogar einzeldialektal orientierten schweizerdeutschen Sprechergemeinschaft (nicht dagegen Schreibergemeinschaft).
- Auch die erschöpfende Auflistung von Flexionsformen kann unterschiedlich beurteilt werden: In einer Kleinkorpussprache wie dem Althochdeutschen wird sie aus Dokumentationsgründen so lange als sinnvoll gesehen werden können, wie sie nicht das in den entsprechenden Grammatiken systematisch Aufgeführte nur einzelwortbezogen wiederholt. Das heißt natürlich zugleich, dass man räumlich-typographisch überbordende Auflistungen auf ihren Gebrauchswert und ihren Erkenntnissinn befragen könnte.
- Eine gleichsam in jedem Wörterbuch wiederholte Etymologie wird allerdings generell in Rechtfertigungszwänge geraten. Dem entsprechend verzichtet z. B. das neue MWB auf etymologische Angaben, dies wohl auch deshalb, weil die Etymologie des deutschen Wortschatzes von nicht lösbaren Ausnahmen abgesehen als geklärt gilt (weitgehend schon seit BMZ). Eine ähnliche Lösung verfolgt seit seiner

Konzeption (im Jahre 1974) und seiner Artikelarbeit (seit Mitte der 80er-Jahre) bereits das FWB, indem es für die Simplizia allerdings in Ausnahmefällen kurze etymologische Hinweise gibt und speziell für die Wortbildungen systematisch semantische Motivationen von den Wortbildungsbestandteilen her vorschlägt und sinnvoll auszuführen versucht.[8] Das Schweiz. Id. gibt jeweils ein sog. *Sippenleitwort* mit etymologischen Einordnungen an; vom Leitwort aus werden sodann die Wortbildungen motiviert. Man erkennt: Je nach Gegebenheit verfährt man pragmatisch benutzerbezogen und in der Regel sinnvoll begründbar.
- In den Mittelpunkt des Artikels hat bei alledem die Bedeutungserläuterung, damit die Semantik, zu rücken, und zwar nicht mehr in der Form von Synonymenangaben, sondern in der Form jeweils gezielt umfänglich gestalteter, sog. *phrastischer* Aussagen, denen man das Interesse des Lexikographen durchaus ansehen darf.
- Einen weiteren Zentralteil des Artikels bildet die systematisch zu füllende Position „bedeutungsverwandte Ausdrücke“, die dem Benutzer die Möglichkeit gibt, jeden Ausdruck pro angesetzte Einzelbedeutung (fachsprachlich also pro *Semem*) in ein semantisches Feld und über dieses letztlich in den Gesamtrahmen einzuordnen, in dem eine Sprachgesellschaft eine wie auch immer als realfaktisch vorgegeben gedachte Welt sieht.

Damit ist der Artikel aber noch nicht abgeschlossen: Mit der Angabe bedeutungsverwandter Ausdrücke können nämlich Ausdrücke des jeweiligen semantischen Orientierungsfeldes verbunden sein; außerdem folgen – so jedenfalls im FWB – die sog. Syntagmenangaben, d. h. eine in Kurzform gefasste Auflistung tendenziell aller in den Belegen begegnender syntaktischer Vorkommen.[9] Sie sind nicht primär (aber auch) als fachsyntaktische Angaben im Sinne der üblichen Formulierung „mit Subjekt der Person und Objekt der Sache“ zu verstehen, sondern geben an, *wer* genau es war, der *was* (welche je bestimmte Sache) affiziert oder effiziert hat (usw.). Den Schluss des Artikels bilden die Belege; sie öffnen – wie schon die Syntagmen – dem Wörterbuchbenutzer den Weg in die geschichtlichen Textwelten (so die Belege) bzw. in die volle Breite einzelner Aussagen zu den Gegenständen/Eigenschaften/Handlungen (so in Kurzform die Syntagmen) einer geschichtlichen Zeit.

Inzwischen bin ich zu dem Punkt gekommen, an dem das alles an Beispielen zu erläutern ist. Ich tue dies an Einzelfällen aus dem FWB. Ersterer Fall betrifft das relativ schwach belegte Präfixverb *überformen*: Die Erläuterung lautet (FWB, Bd. 11: 1366):

> ›jn./etw. in Richtung auf ein religiöses Ziel so überbilden, überformen, dass er/es unter Beibehaltung der Form die Seinsweise des Zieles annimmt‹; vgl. *über* (Präp.) 2; 3. Diesem Vorgang liegt das Bild des materialen Überformens eines Gegenstandes mit einem anderen zugrunde; vgl. dazu *über-*

8 Wenn dieses Ziel nicht immer verwirklicht ist, liegt dies an der oft auch ohne Hinweise gegebenen Durchsichtigkeit der Wortbildungen.

9 Im Einzelnen gelten selbstverständlich Sonderregeln.

formieren (erstere Nuance); er findet sich innertrinitarisch auf die menschliche Natur des Sohnes bei gleichzeitiger Göttlichkeit sowie bildhaft auf die Gleichförmigkeit des Menschen mit Gott übertragen; dabei wird *wirdiglichen wandeln* vorausgesetzt; folgende Gegebenheiten müssen von dannen, sterben/vergehen: die *befindlichkeit, eigengeschäftlichkeit, geschäftlichkeit, gedenklichkeit, creatürlichkeit, würklichkeit, grösse, farbe, das kennen/wellen/wissen*; der Zustand der *überformung* erscheint unter sprachlichen Fassungen wie *entsunkenheit, lauterkeit* 2; 3; 4; (auf der Seite des Menschen), *liecht* (*das*) 4, *einfaltige/götliche klarheit, überförmige/einfaltige einigkeit, götliches abgründe, ungeschaffenheit, ungeschaffenes ewiges wort des vaters* (auf der Seite des überformenden Gottes); vgl. *über* (Präp.) *2; 3* (ütr.).

Man beachte: Da steht nicht etwa (wie bei Lexer Bd. 2: 1614) ein zwar treffendes, aber doch schlichtes 'transformare, umgestaltend erheben'; sondern da steht eine längere phrastische Erläuterung, der man gleichsam ansieht, wie der Lexikograph (in diesem Falle ich selbst) um sie gerungen hat. Wie zufrieden oder unzufrieden man mit dem Ergebnis auch sein mag: Man erkennt das Bestreben, das Verb *überformen* als heute nur noch schwer verständliches Kennwort der Mystik herauszustellen und zumindest andeutungsweise deren Denkschema an die möglichen Benutzer des Wörterbuches zu vermitteln. Ergänzend sei hinzugefügt, dass dem zitierten Teil des Artikels noch semantische Kommentare umfänglicher Art folgen können: Ich zitiere für unser Beispiel: „der Zustand der Überformung erscheint unter sprachlichen Fassungen wie *entsunkenheit, lauterkeit* 2; 3; 4 (auf der Seite des Menschen), *liecht* (*das*) 4, *einfältige götliche klarheit, überförmige/einfältige einigkeit, götliches abgründe, ungeschaffenheit, ungeschaffenes ewiges wort des vaters* (auf der Seite des überformenden Gottes)". Sie sind jeweils durch die Belege, die Belegumgebungen, teils auch durch bloße Belegstellenangaben abgedeckt und in Kursive gesetzt.

Außerdem erscheinen zwei bedeutungsverwandte Ausdrücke für *überformen*, nämlich: *überleiben* und *verwaltigen*, und zwar systematisch mit der Angabe des jeweils in Betracht kommenden Semems. Auch wenn diese systematische Absicht für *überleiben* und *verwaltigen* nicht verwirklicht ist,[10] weil beide Basisverben bei der Bearbeitung von *überformen* noch nicht geschrieben waren, ist die prinzipielle Anlage klar: Das FWB ist – soweit ich das überblicke – das bisher einzige Wörterbuch des Deutschen und der umgebenden europäischen Sprachen, das es aufgrund seiner Artikelstruktur erlaubt, die vorhin als semantische Einrichtung der Lebenswelt einer Sprechergruppe charakterisierte Lexik einer geschichtlichen Epoche systematisch als Gesamtbild zu vermitteln, statt sie als weitgehend beziehungslose Menge von rund 100 000 (oder auch mehr) Worteinheiten, genauer gesagt: von einer diese Zahl übersteigenden Menge von Sememen zu präsentieren. Diese Aussage ist zweifellos stark selbstbezüglich und wird als arrogant beurteilt werden. Man wird ihr auch entgegenhalten, dass sich die ohnehin überlange Zeit der Erarbeitung eines Wörterbuches um weitere Jahrzehnte verlängern

10 *leiben* ist inzwischen in Bd. 9: 1727 unter den drei Homonymen *leiben* erschienen; gemeint ist also das drittgenannte mit den zu einander offenen Bedeutungsansätzen 1. 'leben (refl.), einen Leib annehmen' und 2. 'einen Körper mit jm. bilden'; *verwaltigen* ist noch nicht bearbeitet (es folgt 2026/27).

würde, wenn man ihr folgen würde. Dem ist seinerseits zu widersprechen: In dem Augenblick, in dem man über die Belege verfügt, liegen bedeutungsverwandte Ausdrücke, Syntagmen, Wortbildungen, Symptomwertangaben usw. im wahrsten Sinne des Wortes „vor Augen, auf der Hand“ und brauchen nur wahrgenommen zu werden. Natürlich setzt dies einiges an Vorplanungen voraus: Ein neues Wörterbuch sollte nach modernsten lexikographietheoretischen Überzeugungen konzipiert und hinsichtlich seines kulturpädagogischen Zweckes bestimmt sein; vor Aufnahme der Arbeit muss eine dem entsprechende standardisierte Artikelstruktur vorliegen, auch wenn diese sachadäquat (z. B. nach Wortarten, nach Worttypen innerhalb einer Wortart, letztlich auch nach der Spezifik jedes Einzelwortes) modifiziert sein kann. Vorausgesetzt ist weiter eine technisch einfache digitale Erschließung jedes einzelnen Artikels der Druckfassung mittels je bestimmter Auffindestellen (z. B. *Bdv.* hinter der Bedeutungserläuterung) und unter je typographischer Sigle (wiederum z. B. *Bdv.* oder *Synt.*).

Dies alles sei am Beispiel von **ere** im Bedeutungsansatz 3, einem der inzwischen weit über hunderttausend liegenden Sememansätze des FWB (von 100595 bisher bearbeiteten Stichwörtern und 130 515 bearbeiteten Sememen) veranschaulicht:

Das Substantiv/Stichwort/Lemma **ere** (bearbeitet von A. Lobenstein-Reichmann) wurde 11-fach polysem angesetzt. Die unter Nummer 3 formulierte Bedeutungserläuterung lautet, ergänzt durch die Angabe von Phrasemen, bedeutungsverwandten Ausdrücken und Gegensatzwörtern, wie folgt:

Nur dann also, wenn man systematisch eine eigene Beschreibungsposition, in casu eine Position *Bdv.* ‘Bedeutungsverwandte, onomasiologische Angaben’, hat und nur dann, wenn man diese Position an eine fest bestimmte Stelle des Artikelaufbaus setzt und sie digital abgreifbar darbietet, kann sie zu einem Gesamtbild verarbeitet werden. Zur Veranschaulichung sei diese relativ einfachstufige Visualisierung der onomasiologischen Vernetzung für *ere* 3 gezeigt.

Wenn es einfachstufige Bilder gibt, dann muss es auch hier zusammenfassend als *mehr-, viel-, komplexstufige* bezeichnete Bilder geben; diese seien mit folgenden Beispielen dargeboten:

Zur Erläuterung: Die Abbildungen sollen die volle Weite der Vernetzung jedes einzelnen Semems visualisieren, von „einfachstufig“[11] ausgehend in den gesamten Belegraum eines Wortes pro Semem. Die Dichte der Vernetzung erhöht sich auf unterschiedliche Weise. Genannt sei hier nur: Die Kanten/Pfeile, die von einem Ausgangsstichwort (genauer: einem seiner Sememe) auf ein anderes (wiederum pro Semem) verlaufen, können zu einem Bezugswort (pro Semem) zurückverlaufen (wie im Falle *ere* 3 z. B. zu *achtbarkeit, autorität, hochpreisung, reputation*); sie müssen dies aber nicht.[12] Die Gründe dafür

11 Die hier verwendeten Adjektive *einfachstufig, mehrstufig, komplexstufig* usw. werden nicht definiert. Sie repräsentieren lediglich graduierbare Verhältnisse.

12 Man könnte hier natürlich einwenden, dass diese Aussage nicht gilt, wenn man jede Belegung eines Stichwortes in jedem Korpustext in jedem seiner Umfelder in die Bearbeitung eines Semems einbezieht. Dies wäre aber die sicherste Möglichkeit, ein Wörterbuch niemals fertigzustellen.

3. ›zur sozialen Identität e. P. gehörendes gesellschaftlich aushandelbares und ausgehandeltes Ansehen‹ (allgemein); speziell: ›e. P. zugeschriebene Anerkennung in und vor der Welt als soziales Kapital, als ethische, moralische Qualitätszuschreibung, als positives Image‹; ›jm. von der Gesellschaft aufgrund einer besonderen Leistung (z. B. aufgrund von Heldentum, künstlerischer bzw. schriftstellerischer Tätigkeit) zugesprochene Anerkennung, Ruhm, hohes Prestige‹; ›gute Reputation einer Gemeinschaft, seltener einer Institution‹; tropisch: ›Anerkennungsgrad, -status in der Gesellschaft‹; ›soziales Ansehen, Anerkennung einer Handlung‹; in der Dreierformel *leib* bzw. *leben, gut und ere* Existenz, Besitz und Identität eines Menschen anzeigend. Nicht selten wird *ere* auch negativ als vergängliche Einbildung, als Arroganz, Hybris betrachtet, bei der die eigene soziale Identität und das Streben nach einer gehobenen Stellung in der Welt in Relation zu *ere* als sozialem Wert und zur göttlichen Anerkennung im ewigen Leben gering geachtet bzw. geradezu verachtet wird; dann oft mit näherer Kennzeichnung: *weltliche, zeitliche ere*; offen zu 7.

Phraseme (oft in Doppel- und Mehrfachformeln): *geld / gewalt / gut / leben / lob / reichtum und ere*; *zeit hat ere*; *jm. die ere tun* ›etw. zugestehen, anerkennen‹; ⌜*etw. für ere geben, jm. gut für ere geben, etw. um got oder ere willen fürnemen*⌝ ›allein der Anerkennung wegen, ohne materielle Gegenleistung etw. tun‹.

Bedeutungsverwandte: *achtbarkeit*, *ansehen* (*das*) 7, *autorität*, [1]*gunst* 7, *hochpreisung*, [1]*lob* 1, *name* (*der*) 3, [1]*preis* 1, *reputation* 1, *rum* (*der*) 2, *triumph* 1, *würde*, *würdigkeit*; vgl. [1]*acht* 8.

Gegensätze: *laster* 1, *schade* (*der*) 5, *schande* 1, *schmach* 2, *tod* 4; 8, *unere* (*die*) 3, *ungunst* 1.

Abb. 1: Bedeutungserläuterung von *ere* (*die*) 3, wie sie in FWB-online abrufbar ist.

(also für die nicht vorhandene Wechselseitigkeit der Rückläufigkeit im Sinne von 1,1) dafür sind mannigfacher Art. Einmal kann die Belegsituation dies nicht hergeben: Jeder Beleg steht bekanntlich pro Vorkommen in einer einzeltextlich je besonderen Konstellation mit je anderen bedeutungsverwandten Ausdrücken. Es ist also nicht gesagt, dass man, wenn von der Bedeutungsangabe 1 eines Stichwortes a zu einem Sememsynonym eines Stichwortes b kommt, auch rückwärts von b nach a, wohl aber zu vielen anderen Stichwörtern kommt (wodurch sich die Vernetzungsdichte erhöht). Zusätzlich hat der Lexikograph als Herr seines, bzw. in diesem Falle die Lexikographin als Herrin ihres Textes immer die Möglichkeit, einen als bedeutungsverwandt/sememsynonym verdächtigen Bedeutungsansatz im Sinne seines lexiktheoretischen Verständnisses und/oder seiner Beleginterpretation besonders zu gewichten, wie das für den Kultur- und Wertewortschatz des Typs ***ere*** und für deren Verfasserin zweifellos der Fall war. Unmittelbar einsichtig ist auch, dass sich die Komplexität der Bilder des vorgeführten Typs mit dem Bearbeitungsstande eines Wörterbuches immer weiter erhöht.

Abb. 2: *ere* (*die*) 3, mit den relativ *einfachstufig* als bedeutungsverwandt nachgewiesenen Ausdrücken (vgl. FWB Bd. 5: 3209).

Bei weiterer Erhöhung der Komplexität der Vernetzung des Wortschatzes kommt man zu den hier als *Summenbild* bezeichneten Visualisierungen, die selbstverständlich wiederum beliebig stufbar sind. Die höchstmögliche Komplexität ergibt sich dann, wenn man alle Vernetzungen aller Sememe aller bisher behandelten Substantive zusammenstellt. Dieses Bild – arbeitsstellenintern *Milchstraßenbild* genannt – hat folgende Gestalt:

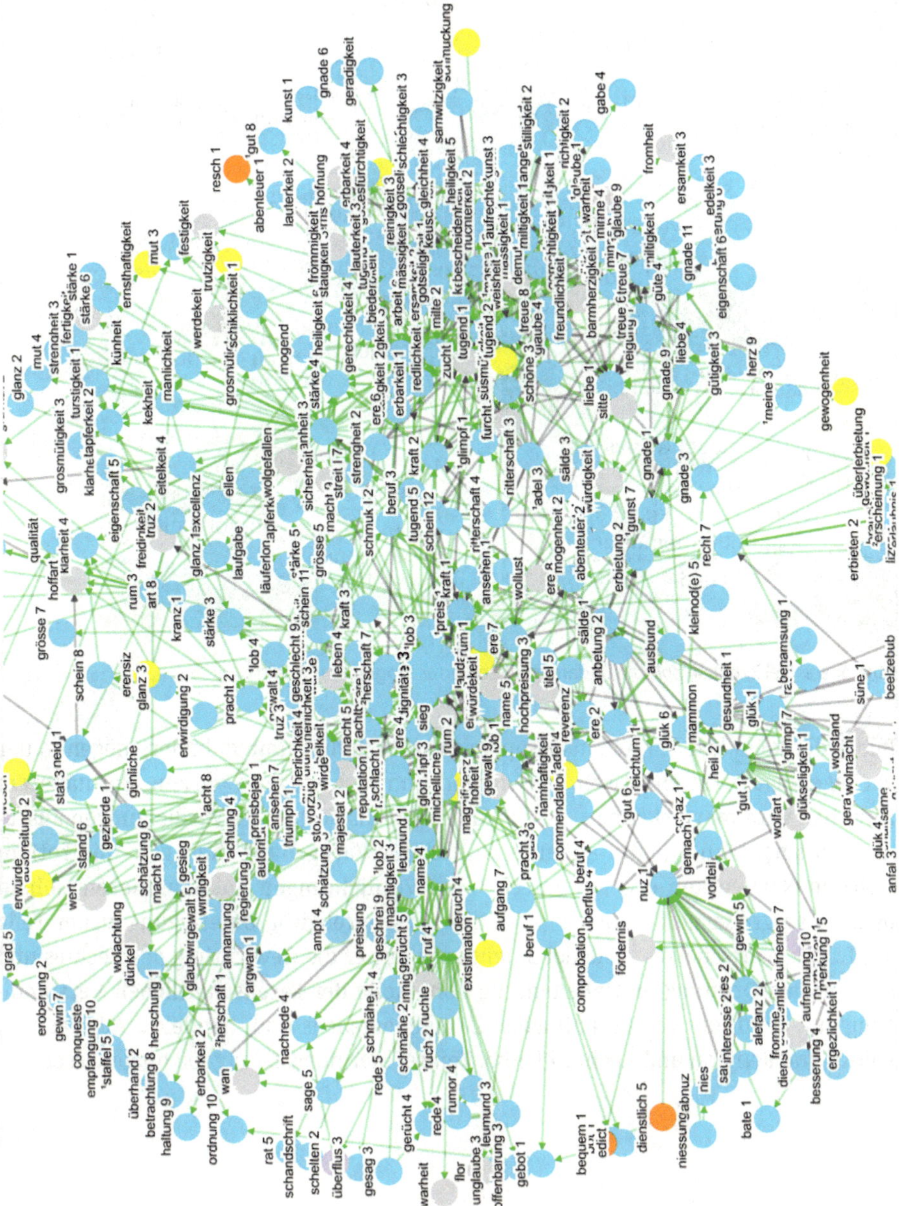

Abb. 3: *ere* (*die*) 3, mit *vielstufiger* onomasiologischer Vernetzung.

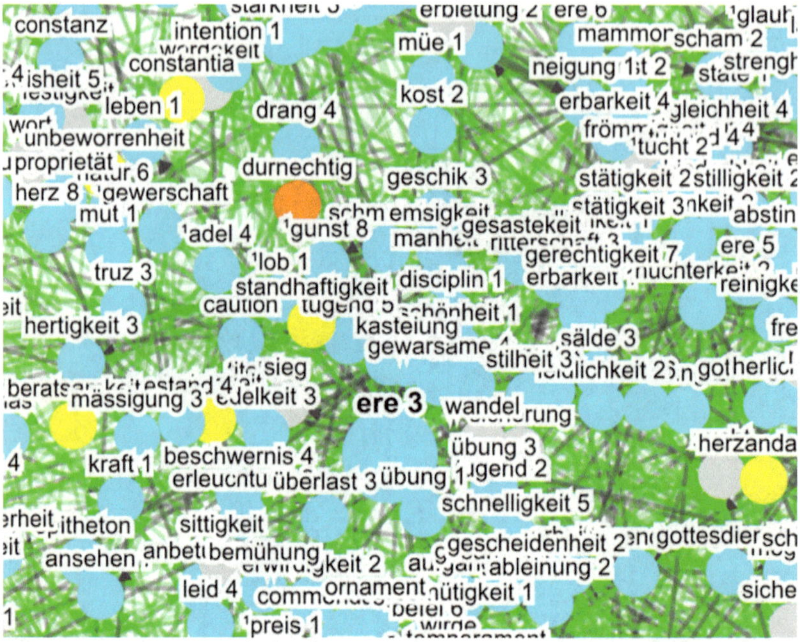

Abb. 4: *ere* (*die*) 3, mit *komplexstufig* dargestellten Vernetzungen (Ausschnitt).

Bilder der komplexeren Art, insbesondere natürlich die Summenbilder, mögen in der vorliegenden Form chaotisch, verwirrend und nichtssagend wirken. Bei näherem Hinsehen wird man erkennen, dass dennoch jeweils bestimmte Verdichtungen auszumachen sind. Man erkennt außerdem durch die Farbgebung (hier gelb und rot), in welchen Netzwerken ***ere*** dominiert. Diese Verdichtungen dokumentieren, sobald man sie vergrößernd heraushebt, z. B. die massive religiöse Unterlegung weiter Teile des frnhd. Wortschatzes;[13] sie dokumentieren ferner die Gewichtung des Rechtes und der sozialen Ordnung, mit alledem die hohe Rolle der gesellschaftlichen Verständigung und damit des gesellschaftlichen Zusammenlebens und -handelns. Auf das Verhältnis von Religion und Recht in frnhd. Zeit sei hier nur als Aufgabe hingewiesen.

13 Ein mediävistischer Niederschlag dieser Gewichtung kann in der immer wieder neu geführten Behandlung der moraltheologischen Werte, speziell des sog. *mittelalterlichen Tugendsystems*, gesehen werden.

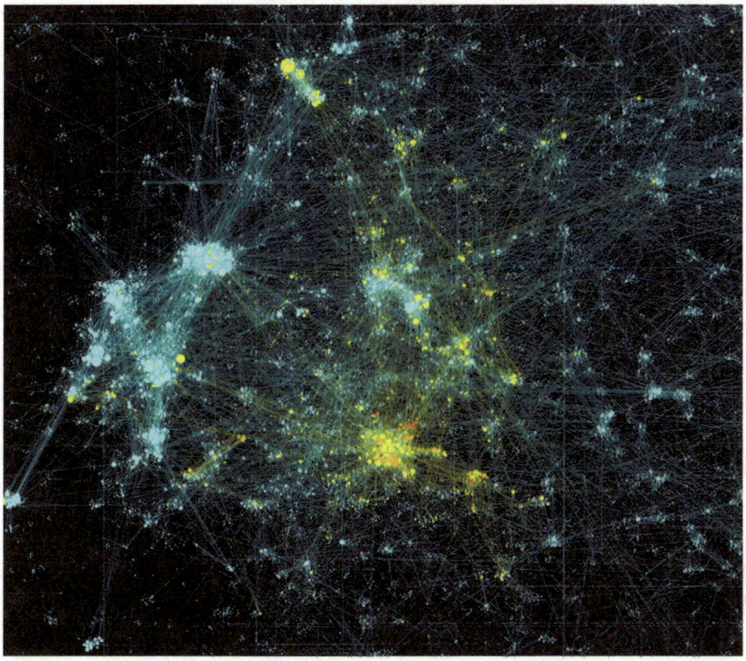

Abb. 5: Summe aller Vernetzungen aller Sememe aller bisher behandelten Stichwörter des FWB (Milchstraßenbild, Ausschnitt).

7 Vision eines Forschungszieles

Ich mache keinen Hehl aus meinem Interesse, diese semantischen Gegebenheiten der sprachlich lexikalischen Fassung/Gestaltung/Fingierung des frühneuzeitlichen deutschsprachigen Raumes, falls sie denn nicht nur als Hypothese gesehen, sondern als geschichtliches Soziofaktum erkannt und vermittelt werden, in Vergleich mit der zeitgleichen Semantik seiner Nachbarsprachen, speziell des Französischen, Niederländischen, Englischen, Dänischen, aber auch z. B. des Polnischen, Tschechischen usw. zu stellen und die Ergebnisse dieses Vergleichs in ein Verhältnis zum Spät- und Mittellateinischen sowie zu den neueren, also neuzeitlichen (aufklärerischen und nachaufklärerischen Epochen) zu bringen. Natürlich ist dies nur eine Vision; und es dürfte so lange eine Vision bleiben, wie die betreffenden Lexikographien eher abbild-, zahlen-, einzelwortbezogen als sozial handlungs-, qualitativ semantik- und gesamtwortschatzbezogen bleiben (wie wohl zu erwarten ist). Immerhin wage ich die Aussage und meine das als Ergebnis des bisher Vorgetragenen, dass historische Lexikographie entscheidend in dem Maße gebraucht wird, in dem es ihr gelingt, die genannten Qualitäten unter Erkenntnisgesichtspunkten als interessantes Vergleichs- und unter symptomwertbezogenen Aspekten als lateineuropäisches Identifikationspotential herauszustellen. Zustandekommen könnte dabei eine allen internen Verschiedenheiten auf spät- und mittellateinischer Grundlage beruhende erstaunlich ähnliche europäische Semantik (quer zur Ausdrucksseite der Lexik). Wenn das gelänge, wäre das ein Grund für die Vision einer lateineuropäischen Semantik; ich meine eine Semantik, die die ausdrucksseitig, grammatisch usw. teils verwandten, aber teils eben auch sehr verschiedenen europäischen Sprachen sprachinhaltlich verbindet. Man könnte der Meinung sein, dies sei eine Begründung der wie auch immer gearteten politischen Einheit Lateineuropas (von Spanien bis ins Baltikum). Hier wird die Semantik direkt politisch: Statt Sprachen als Nationalsprachen auf der Basis ihrer Ausdrucksverschiedenheiten als je besonders zu konstituieren, könnte man sie auch auf der Basis ihrer semantischen Gemeinsamkeiten als ähnlich konstituieren und würde dann zu neuen Gliederungen kommen.

Zuzugeben ist allerdings wiederum, dass genau diese Vision eine gewisse bildungssoziale Gehobenheit auf der Rezeptionsseite der Lexikographie voraussetzt. Man bewegt sich also in einem Wechselverhältnis: Lexikographie setzt bildungssoziale Gehobenheit voraus und untermauert diese. Umgekehrt: Diese Gehobenheit erfordert sie stärkende historisch und nachbarlich orientierte, vergleichende Geisteswissenschaften und damit auch historische Lexikographie. Damit wären wir einerseits beim politischen Aufgabenfeld der Bildung, andererseits bei den fachwissenschaftlichen Aufgaben der Lexikographie. Die Politik steht in der Verantwortung gegenüber der Rezeptionsgesellschaft; und die Lexikographie steht in der Pflicht, der Politik dazu fachlich verlässliche und außerdem verstehbare Vorgaben zu liefern. Auf jeden Fall ist die einzelwortbezogene Beschreibung des Wortschatzes durch eine gesamtwortschatzbezogene und gleichzeitig adressatenorientierte Behandlung zu ersetzen.

Jedes neue Projekt hat sich bei seiner Begründung zu entscheiden: Will man eine letztlich einzelwortbezogene Lexikographie auf der Basis der Interessen des 19. Jahrhunderts oder eine gesamtwortschatzbezogene Lexikographie, wie ich sie meine im FWB realisiert zu haben.

8 Zu den Symptomwertangaben

Zum Abschluss sei ausblickend (in einer Art Anhang) noch auf eine Beschreibungsposition eingegangen, der im FWB ein unübliches Gewicht zukommt. Sie soll auf ihre Attraktion für heutige Interessen befragt werden. Ich meine die sog. *Symptomwertangaben*. Vorausgeschickt sei, dass diese eher für Sprachen mit grammatisch und lexikalisch-semantisch festgelegter und allgemein gültiger Leitvariante (wie wohl für das Neufranzösische) typisch sind als für Sprachen ohne eine solche Variante (wie das zweifellos für das Frühneuhochdeutsche gilt).[14] Gemeint sind Angaben des Typs

14 Es sei allerdings bemerkt, dass die Varianz selbst im Frühneuhochdeutschen, jedenfalls in seinen ja nur geschrieben vorliegenden Texten geringer ist als üblicherweise angenommen.

- räumlich gesehen z. B. „wobd./oobd." (oder je nach Fall variiert, oft komplexer),
- zeitlich gesehen z. B. „älteres und mittleres Frnhd." (oder variiert),
- textsortenbezüglich gesehen z. B. „Texte der Sinnwelt ‚Religion/Didaxe'" (oder variiert).

Angaben dieser Art finden sich in mannigfachen Varianten (oft auch in Kombination) in allen inzwischen erschienenen 12 Bänden des FWB. Sie sind weniger an ein Einzelwort/Stichwort/Lemmazeichen als an eines oder mehrere von dessen Sememen (Bedeutungsansätzen) gebunden, sie erscheinen in einer im Vergleich zu anderen Wörterbüchern auffallenden Gewichtung. Wie dem im Einzelnen auch sei: In vorliegendem Zusammenhang stellt sich die Frage, wie sie im Hinblick auf die Sinnproblematik historischer Lexikographie zu beurteilen sein könnten. Die Antwort lautet entsprechend dem bereits Gesagten: Je mehr sich ein Wörterbuchbenutzer im Wortschatz, damit in der geschichtlichen Semantik der Sprache seiner Gegenwart identifiziert/erkennt, desto wahrscheinlicher wird er sich in den räumlichen, zeitlichen, textsortenbezüglichen Symptomwerten seiner Sprache identifizieren/erkennen, sich vergleichen oder von anderen unterscheiden können.

Der Interessewert der Symptomwertangaben könnte dann steigen, wenn man alle Angaben des genannten Typs zusammenstellt, also zusammenfassende Listen bietet, die z. B. Raumangaben, Zeitangaben, Textsortenangaben auflistet. Solche Listen könnten – nach dem jetzigen Stande der digitalen Erschließung des FWB noch nur hypothetisch (also nicht als Aussage verstanden) – zu Ergebnissen folgenden Typs führen: Das Ostoberdeutsche (also Bairisch-Österreichische) sei in älterer und mittlerer frnhd. Zeit mit vergleichsweise hoher Häufigkeit in Rechtstexten vertreten. Oder: Das Hochalemannische begegne vorwiegend in z. B. Rechts- und Wirtschaftstexten der älteren und mittleren Zeit. Oder: Das Ripuarische sei in jüngerer frnhd. Zeit insgesamt nur schwach als solches belegt. Oder: Das Hochalemannische sei in frnhd. Zeit bereits durch eine Reihe semantischer Besonderheiten gekennzeichnet. Die Arbeit an der digitalen Herstellung von inhaltlich belastbaren Listen dieses Typs ist im Visier der Arbeitsgruppe.

Nach dem bisherigen Bearbeitungsstand des FWB sind Zeit-, Raum- und textsortenbezogene Bilder möglich und jedem Interessierten aus der Digitalfassung (fwb-online.de) des FWB im Handumdrehen erstellbar. Diese Bilder heißen arbeitsstellenintern *Zeitleisten, Raumbilder, Textsortenbilder* und sollen mit je einem Beispiel und nur mit einigen Erläuterungen gezeigt sowie kurz kommentiert werden, teilweise lediglich stichwortartig.

Auffallend ist: Das Gesamtbild[15] (Signifikatbild zum Lemma *ere*) zeigt eine deutliche Verdichtung für das 16. und frühe 17. Jahrhundert. Sich stellende Fragen könnten lauten: Wie erklärt sich diese Verdichtung aus der Geschichte? Kritisch gewendet: Könnte das am Korpus des FWB liegen (dessen Bemessung sich auch aus arbeitszeitlichen Grün-

15 Jede Zeile repräsentiert den Zeitverlauf aller elf angesetzten Einzelbedeutungen. Die oberste Zeile, oben links mittels *gesamt* gekennzeichneter Zeile versteht sich als Summe des Gesamtgebrauchs.

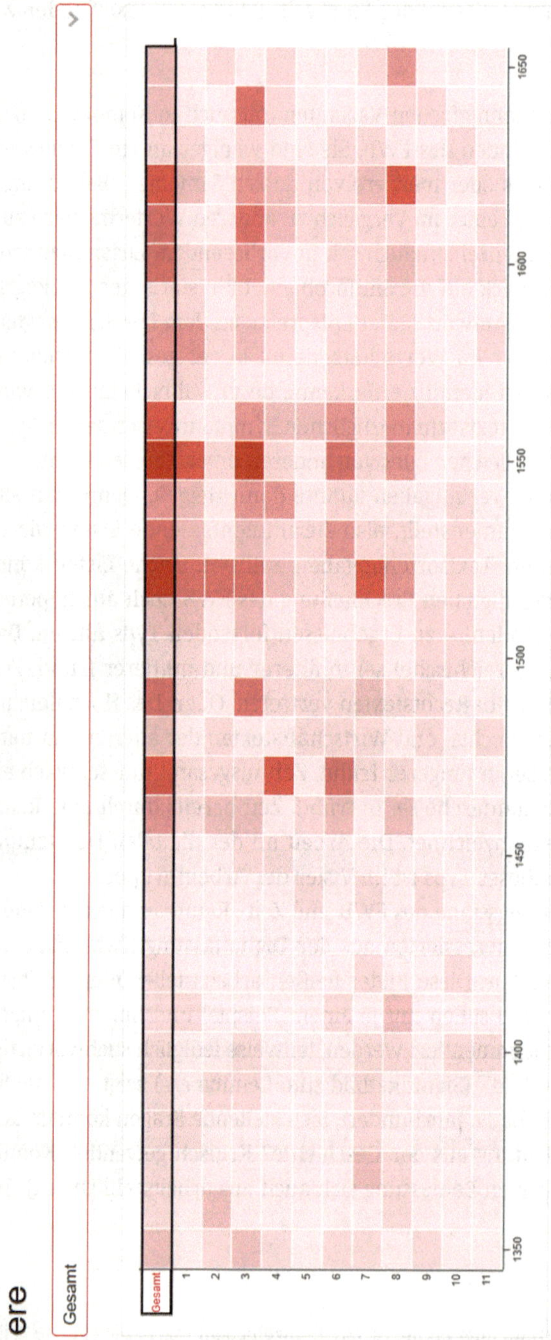

Abb. 6: Zeitleiste zu *ere* in den Bedeutungsansätzen 1–11.

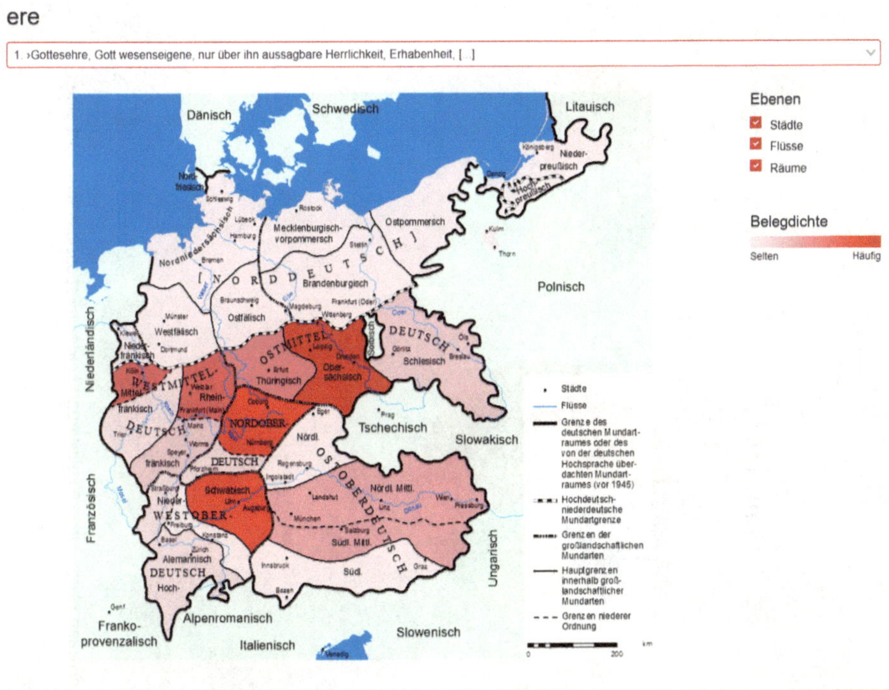

Abb. 7: Raumbild zu *ere* 1 'Gottesehre'.

den ergeben hat und nicht mehr zu ändern ist)? Selbstverständlich gibt es auch Einzelbilder zu ***ere*** 2 bis ***ere*** 11.

Wiederum stellen sich Fragen der Art: Wie erklären sich die Verdichtungen im Mittelbereich des Hochdeutschen, speziell im Ostmitteldeutschen? Offensichtlich ist, dass hier die Gesamtheit von Theologie-, Philosophie-, Geistesgeschichte (weniger von Faktengeschichte) angesprochen ist.

Mögliche Fragen beziehen sich auf textsortenbedingte Verdichtungen. Die Antworten fallen in diesem Fall leichter als für die vorangehenden Bilder. In den gezeigten Bildern wurde das Frühneuhochdeutsche als trotz aller Verdichtungen doch in einem gewissen, wie auch immer bemessbaren Grade als semantische Einheit vorausgesetzt. Dies mag teils berechtigt sein, übergeht aber die auch (in welchem Ausmaß auch immer) vorhandenen räumlichen, zeitlichen und textweltenspezifischen Binnendifferenzierungen innerhalb der Epoche. Dies wiederum bedeutet die zusätzliche Aufgabe, auch den innerfrühneuhochdeutschen Differenzen ihren Darstellungsraum zu geben. Dabei geht es nicht darum, ob man *min niuwe hus* statt *mein neues haus*, sagt und schreibt, sondern vielmehr darum, ob und – falls ja – wo, wann und wie Differenzen im semantischen Gebrauch des (ja normalisierten) Lemmazeichens bestehen: Wer also hat in welchem Zeitabschnitt, in welchem Raum welche Textsorten benutzt,

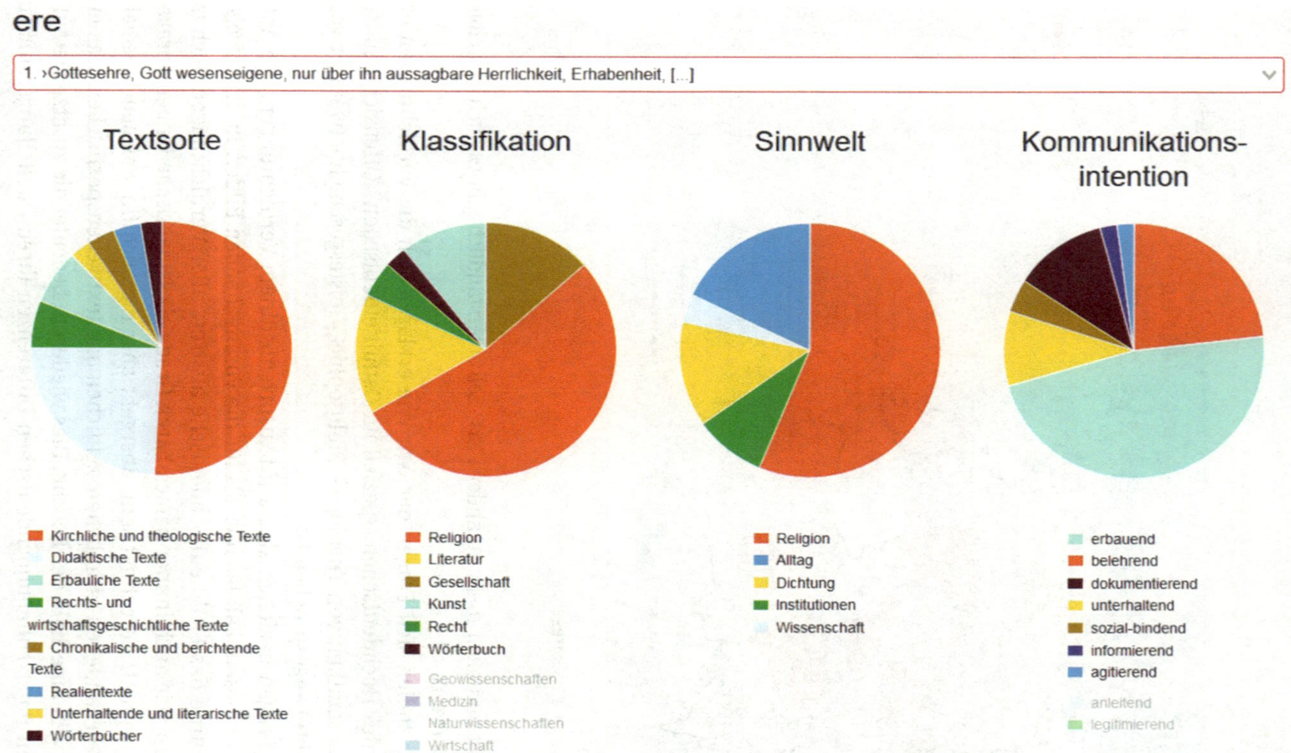

Abb. 8: Textsortenbild zu *ere* 1 (nach Aspekten, die im Bild unter den Ausdrücken *Klassifikation*, *Sinnwelt* und *Kommunikationsintention* erscheinen).

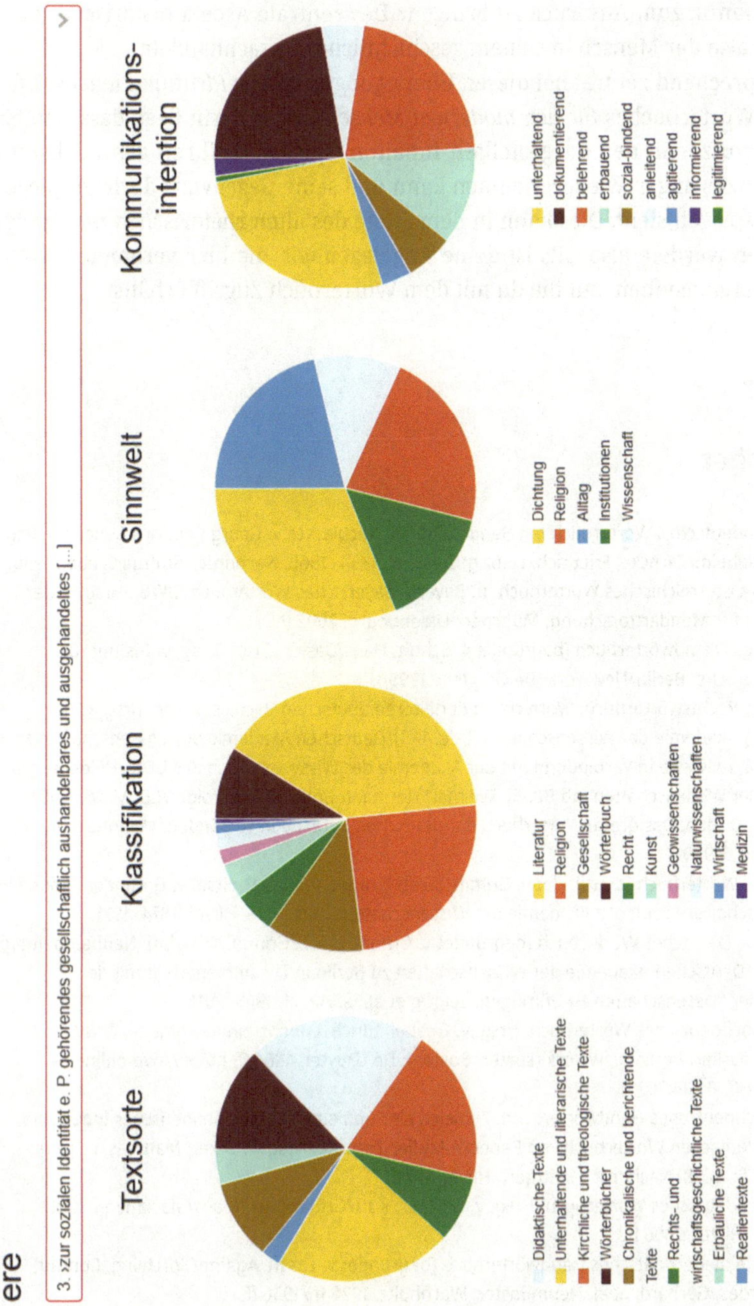

Abb. 9: Textsortenbild zu *ere* 3.

um seine Semantik zum Ausdruck zu bringen? Der zentrale Aspekt historischer Lexikographie ist also der Mensch in seinem geschichtlichen Sprachhandeln.

Dementsprechend zentral bei diesen Überlegungen ist der *Identifikationswert* des historischen Wörterbuches *für den modernen Menschen*, der darin liegt, dass sich ein moderner Benutzer in den dargestellten Inhalten, speziell in ihren gebrauchstypischen Differenzierungen wiedererkennen kann und seine Gegenwart darin gespiegelt oder nicht gespiegelt sieht. Dies kann in dem Sinne des alten rhetorischen *tua res agitur* verstanden werden, also: „Es ist deine Angelegenheit, die hier verhandelt wird". Es ist deine Vergangenheit, auf die du mit dem Wörterbuch Zugriff erhältst.

Literatur

Wörterbücher

BMZ = Mittelhochdeutsches Wörterbuch mit Benutzung des Nachlasses v. Georg Friedrich Benecke. Hrsg. v. Müller, Wilhelm/Zarncke, Friedrich. Leipzig: S. Hirzel, 1854–1866. Nachdruck Stuttgart: ebd., 1990.

BWB = Bayerisch-Österreichisches Wörterbuch. II. Bayern. Bayerisches Wörterbuch (BWB). Hrsg. v. der Kommission für Mundartforschung. München: Oldenbourg, 2002 ff.

DFWB = Deutsches Fremdwörterbuch [begründet v. Schulz, Hans/Basler, Otto]. Hrsg. v. Institut für Deutsche Sprache. Berlin/New York: De Gruyter, ^{2}1995ff.

DRW = Deutsches Rechtswörterbuch. Wörterbuch der älteren deutschen Rechtssprache. Hrsg. v. der Preußischen Akademie der Wissenschaften [Bde. 1–3]/Deutschen Akademie der Wissenschaften zu Berlin [Bd. 4; teilweise in Verbindung mit der Akademie der Wissenschaften der DDR]/Heidelberger Akademie der Wissenschaften [ab Bd. 5]. Weimar: Hermann Böhlaus Nachfolger/J.B. Metzler, 1914 ff.

Duden, Gr. Wb. = Duden. Das große Wörterbuch der deutschen Sprache in 10 Bänden. Mannheim et al.: Dudenverlag, ^{3}1999.

DWB = Deutsches Wörterbuch [begründet v. Grimm, Jacob/Grimm, Wilhelm]. Hrsg. v. Göttinger Akademie der Wissenschaften/Deutsche Akademie der Wissenschaften. Leipzig: S. Hirzel, 1874–1971.

DWB, Neubearb. = Deutsches Wörterbuch [begründet v. Grimm, Jacob/Grimm, Wilhelm]. Neubearbeitung. Hrsg. v. der Deutschen Akademie der Wissenschaften zu Berlin in Zusammenarbeit mit der Akademie der Wissenschaften zu Göttingen. Leipzig et al.: S. Hirzel, 1965–2016.

FWB = Frühneuhochdeutsches Wörterbuch. Hrsg. v. Goebel, Ulrich, Lobenstein-Reichmann, Anja/ Reichmann, Oskar. Berlin/New York (später: Boston): De Gruyter, 1986 ff. https://fwb-online.de (letzter Zugriff: 01.04.2025).

Lexer = Mittelhochdeutsches Handwörterbuch. Zugleich als Supplement und alphabetischer Index zum Mittelhochdeutschen Wörterbuch von Benecke-Müller-Zarncke. Hrsg. v. Lexer, Matthias. Leipzig: S. Hirzel, 1872–1878. Nachdruck Stuttgart: Hirzel, 1979.

MWB = Mittelhochdeutsches Wörterbuch. Hrsg. v. Gärtner, Kurt/Grubmüller, Klaus/Stackmann, Karl. Stuttgart: S. Hirzel, 2006 ff.

Mnd. Hwb. = Mittelniederdeutsches Handwörterbuch [begründet v. Lasch, Agathe/Borchling, Conrad]. Hrsg. v. Cordes, Gerhard, et al. Neumünster: Wachholtz, 1928 ff./1956 ff.

Pfälz. Wb. = Pfälzisches Wörterbuch [begründet v. Christmann, Ernst]. Hrsg. v. Krämer, Julius, et al. Stuttgart: Steiner, 1963–1997. Beiheft 1998.

Preuß. Wb./Z = Preußisches Wörterbuch. Sprache und Volkstum Nordostdeutschlands. [...] Hrsg. v. Ziesemer, Walther. Nachdruck Hildesheim/New York: De Gruyter, 1975.

Rhein. Wb. = Rheinisches Wörterbuch. Hrsg. v. Müller, Josef, et al. Bonn: Klopp, 1928–1971.
Schles. Wb. = Schlesisches Wörterbuch. Hrsg. v. Mitzka, Walther. Berlin: De Gruyter, 1963–1965.
Schwäb. Wb. = Schwäbisches Wörterbuch. Hrsg. v. Fischer, Hermann/Pfleiderer, Wilhelm. Tübingen: Laupp'sche Buchhandlung, 1904–1936.
Schweiz. Id. = Schweizerisches Idiotikon. Wörterbuch der schweizerdeutschen Sprache. Gesammelt auf Veranstaltung der Antiquarischen Gesellschaft in Zürich unter Beihülfe aus allen Kreisen des Schweizervolkes. Hrsg. [mit Unterstützung des Bundes und der Kantone] v. Staub, Friedrich/Tobler, Ludwig/Bachmann, Albert, et al. Frauenfeld: Huber/Basel: Schwabe, 1881 ff.
Shess. Wb. = Südhessisches Wörterbuch [begründet v. Maurer, Friedrich]. Hrsg. v. Mulch, Rudolf/Mulch, Roland. Marburg: N.G. Elwert, 1968–2010.
WBÖ = Wörterbuch der bairischen Mundarten in Österreich (WBÖ). Hrsg. v. Dollmayr, Viktor, et al. Wien: Verlag der Österreichischen Akademie der Wissenschaften, 1963 ff.
WdG = Wörterbuch der deutschen Gegenwartssprache. Hrsg. v. Klappenbach, Ruth/Steinitz, Wolfgang. Berlin: De Gruyter, 1975 [etc.].

Sekundärliteratur

Polenz, Peter von (1999): Deutsche Sprachgeschichte vom Spätmittelalter bis zur Gegenwart. Bd. 3: 19. bis 20. Jahrhundert. Berlin/New York: De Gruyter.
Reichmann, Oskar (2012): Historische Lexikographie. Ideen, Verwirklichungen, Reflexionen an Beispielen des Deutschen, Niederländischen und Englischen. Berlin/Boston: De Gruyter.
Reichmann, Oskar (2018): Das Frühneuhochdeutsche Wörterbuch (= FWB): Von der Entstehung bis zur Digitalisierung. In: Lexicographica 34, 279–357.

Trevor Johnston

Signed language lexicography and the Auslan dictionaries in print and online

Abstract: In this chapter I describe the Auslan (Australian Sign Language) dictionaries and the lexical database they are based on. Since the 1980s, this database has migrated over multiple software platforms as the types of data that could be contained in newer databases (text, graphics, video) improved and increased, enabling the dictionaries to appear in three formats: print, multimedia (CD-ROM), and online. I describe the lexicography underlying these Auslan dictionaries, the lexicology that determines which signs are included, and the types and contents of the data fields used in the database, and how the data is displayed in each edition. I then describe how the entries in the online edition are hyperlinked to attested examples in a corpus of Auslan. I conclude by discussing how the architecture of Auslan Signbank could accommodate data from any signed language and how this can then be used to conduct cross-linguistic investigations of signed language lexicology and phonology.

Keywords: Auslan, Australian Sign Language, deafness, signed language lexicography, signed language lexicology, on-line dictionaries, bilingual dictionaries

Schlagwörter: Auslan, Australische Gebärdensprache, Gehörlosigkeit, Gebärdensprachlexikographie, Gebärdensprachlexikologie, Online-Wörterbücher, zweisprachige Wörterbücher

1 Signed language word lists versus dictionaries

Historically sign(ed)[1] language dictionaries were little more than alphabetical word lists with text describing the production of the sign, or with both text and line drawings or (later) photographs. This was the standard practice for centuries, e.g., records

1 The expression *signed language* is used here to refer to the languages of deaf communities partly because it nicely parallels the expression spoken language, with which they should be compared, and partly because it leaves the older more general term *sign language* to refer to any system of communication that does not use the vocal-auditory channel, is only metaphorically a language (as in *the language of dance*), or is a manual code for a spoken language, from each of which signed languages should be distinguished. However, note that most names for signed languages include *Sign Language* in one of their names, e.g., American Sign Language (otherwise known as ASL).

Trevor Johnston, Monash University, Melbourne; Macquarie University, Sydney,
e-mail: trevor.johnston@monash.edu

https://doi.org/10.1515/9783112216644-006

of the sign language of Cistercian monks (Barakat 1987) or early British Sign Language (Bulwer 1644).

The word in the word list was given as the equivalent of the sign: there was no attempt at a definition apart from the gloss itself and no awareness that deaf signed languages were languages in their own right and not merely visual-gestural systems for representing the words of a spoken language, not unlike writing. Misleading as this practice had been, many word list compilers believed they had faithfully recorded the signs used by deaf people in a particular community. Moreover, most list compilers were teachers of the deaf and believed that the signs used by the deaf were severely limited compared to the ambient spoken and written language. This conclusion was driven by the false belief that there was a one-to-one correspondence between the words of their language and the signs of the local signed language. Thus, the compilers of these word lists not only assigned one single word to each sign, but they also added many invented signs for words of their spoken and written language for which they believed no sign existed. For example, all but one of the signs in Figure 1 are assigned one single translation word, most of which are over-specific or too narrow. Some, like *beetle, beetroot* and *bench* impose an initialization for the letter 'b' (see 3.6) which is taken from the American one-handed alphabet and which is not used in Auslan for 'b'. (Auslan uses a two-handed alphabet.) The contrived signs *began* and *begun*, and *bend* and *bent*, attempt to make a tense distinction which is unnecessary in Auslan.

In English-speaking countries, from about the 1960s, this approach to sign language was often referred to as *Signed English*, and the educational method of aligning signing and speaking at the same time in classroom instruction was often referred to as *Total Communication*. Another aspect of the systematisation of signs vis-à-vis English was sign standardization. Compilers did not document variation that was clearly present in the deaf community because they wanted to achieve standardization through the prescriptive omission of disfavoured forms (Johnston 2003).

Auslan lexicography began in this environment. My aim was to record the language as it was used in the deaf community by deaf people for whom it had been acquired at a very early age as their primary language, and especially by signers from multi-generational deaf families for whom it was clearly a native language. The research program entailed documentary fieldwork, participant observation and elicitation sessions with community members over several years. It also involved working with the deaf community to lobby governments for recognition of the language.

Proper documentation of the language was essential if it was to be recognised as a bona fide language by the wider community, educators and governments as a legitimate language of instruction in schools for the deaf, and in the provision of interpreter services for deaf people funded by governments. One step in recognizing the language of the Australian deaf community involved giving the language a name. In 1982 when I was a young doctoral research student in linguistics doing fieldwork in the Australian deaf community, I coined the name *Auslan* for this language in collaboration with members of the deaf community, some of whom were my deaf relatives.

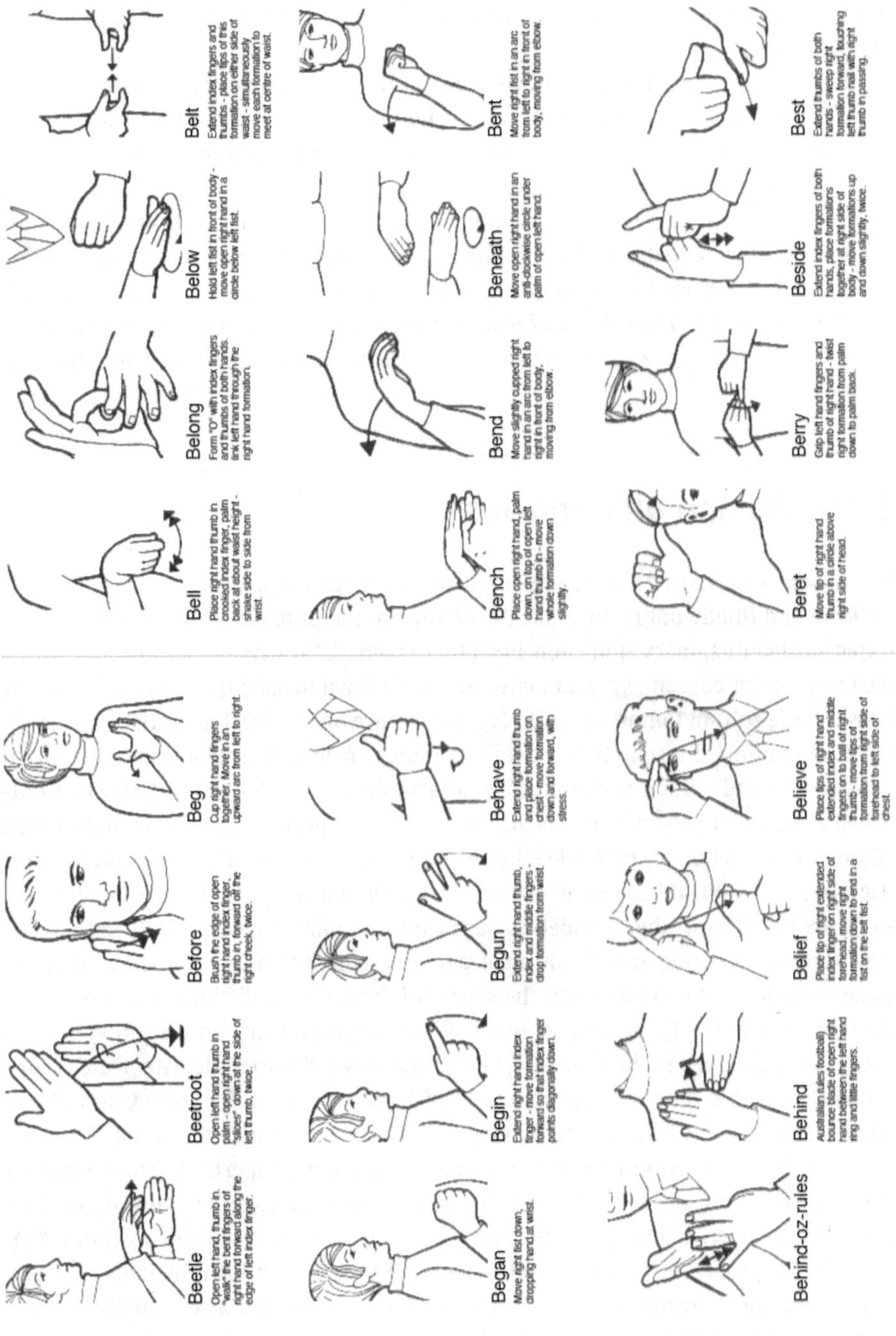

Figure 1: An example of a sign wordlist/dictionary with line drawings (Jeanes et al. 1982).

(I am a hearing person with multiple deaf relatives, including cousins, parents and grandparents.)

Importantly, variation was not ignored but was keenly observed and documented in detail according to its type of variation: phonological, i.e. a common variant in pronunciation, or lexical, i.e., a sign with restricted use according to region (dialect) or employment or specialist use (jargon). Standardization was not the aim, though it was acknowledged that empirical observational data on the language as it was really used would ultimately help the deaf community, in conjunction with educators and governments, to devise acceptable and effective language development strategies and policies. Finally, neither I nor the deaf people involved in the research actively sought to create new signs, but we did embrace lexical innovations we observed within the community.

2 The Auslan dictionaries

The Auslan dictionaries that are the topic of this chapter appeared first in print, then CD-ROM and finally online formats. At the time of the publication of the first unillustrated Auslan dictionary (Johnston 1987) there were 2,736 sign entries and in the first illustrated print edition two years later this had grown to 3,621 (Johnston 1989). In the latest online edition (Johnston/Smith 2024) there are over 7,750, the increase being the result of continued research and deaf community feedback over a thirty-seven-year period. A second edition of the illustrated print dictionary (Johnston 1997a) was published as part of a project that was primarily aimed at producing the first multi-media edition of the dictionary on CD-ROM (Johnston 1997b). The print version had 5,561 entries, but the CD-ROM had fewer entries because it omitted phonological variants and some lexical variants due to video storage capacity limits on early CD-ROMs, and the slow video processing speeds on most personal computers in the 1990s. Using the same reference database that was the source of the previous dictionaries, two smaller dictionaries for specific target audiences of learners, each using only a subset of these data, were published in the following years. One was a children's learner's dictionary, called *Discovering Auslan* (Johnston et al. 2002) and was published as a CD-ROM. The other was an adults' learner's dictionary, call the *Survival Guide to Auslan* (Johnston/Schembri 2003) and was published as a small pocket-sized paperback. These were followed by the first online edition of the Auslan dictionary, called *Auslan Signbank* (Johnston/Catalyst Training Systems 2004). *Auslan Signbank* (henceforth simply *Signbank*) has appeared in two other subsequent editions which have included not only more signs and information about each sign into the site, but also a complete overhaul of the underlying software code of the site to enable new functionality and new data types (Johnston/Cassidy 2008; Johnston/Smith 2024).

2.1 Signs selected for entry in the dictionaries

Most entries in the Auslan dictionaries, like in any dictionary of any language, are lemmas represented by a citation form. Auslan also has lexical and phonological variation, again like any language. Lexical variation is when two or more lemmas have an identical or very similar meanings, but completely different and unrelated forms. They are easily accommodated in the dictionary by creating separate entries for each and describing the distribution of the alternate lemmas at the entry, e.g., as dialectal variants. Phonological variants are also given their own entries and are described as such at the entry and cross-referenced to the citation lemma. The separate entry enables the variants to be sequenced phonologically in the dictionary along with all other sign forms (see 3.3.1). The citation lemma and the phonological variants are tokens of the same lexeme.

Entering phonological variants in dictionaries gives the lexicographer the opportunity to validate the variants (and the learners' experiences because they cannot help but see them in the community) yet enables the lexicographer to refer learners to the most common and even preferred citation sign. Sometimes the choice of which sign form should be considered the citation, and which should be considered the variant, can be difficult to make. This is partly because historically the language has not been well documented, codified or used as a language of instruction in schools, so there can be some uncertainty or even dispute among signers about the status of some variants. Nonetheless, all forms entered in the dictionaries have been confirmed by fieldwork or corpus research and are recognized by signers as occurring in everyday use in at least one region.

Perhaps somewhat surprisingly, invented Signed English signs are also included in the dictionaries because the first Auslan dictionary was created as a reaction to the introduction of Signed English signs in schools for the deaf and its subsequent promotion as a new standardized sign lexicon. At that time, there was confusion in the Australian deaf community and among hearing learners of the signed language used in Australia about their true status. Consequently, a decision was made to include the contrived Signed English vocabulary in the Auslan dictionary because this gave the lexicographer the opportunity to inform readers which signs were artificial Signed English signs and which were Auslan signs. Signed English signs were tagged as *Signed English only* signs (henceforth *SE-only*) if they were inappropriate (because they broke phonological or sign-formation patterns of Auslan) or unnecessary (because the meaning was already adequately covered by a pre-existing Auslan sign, e.g. invented past tense or past participle forms of verbs when Auslan does not morphologically mark tense).

However, part of the confusion about the new signs arose because some of the Signed English lexicon (in Australia) was drawn from genuine Auslan signs, predominantly from the Melbourne dialect, which had been prescriptively defined as the direct equivalent of one and only one English word. Naturally, these signs were already candidates for inclusion in the Auslan dictionaries, so information at the entry made their status clear. Namely, though tagged as also being a Signed English sign, it was evident that the meaning and use of these signs in the Auslan-using community was not that same as claimed in the Signed English word list.

Finally, from the beginning, a small subset of English fingerspelling signs was also included in the Auslan dictionaries. This may appear incongruous if one regards them simply as English words listed in an Auslan dictionary. However, these are actually nativised fingerspellings (as they are known in the signed language linguistics literature), i.e., long-established borrowings from English into the Auslan lexicon. They are conventional symbolic units of Auslan and sometimes their meaning and use is no longer quite the same as their English origin would suggest.

The existence of nativized fingerspellings means there are four major sign types entered in Signbank: citation signs, variant signs, SE-only signs, and English fingerspelling signs. The citation lemma, attested variants, and nativized fingerspellings are *conventional symbolic signs* of Auslan and must be included in a dictionary if it is to be accurate and comprehensive. Even though SE-only signs are not conventionally part of the language, they are entered as a special case, as explained above.

However, there are two other types of manual signs found in Auslan texts collected as a part of fieldwork and corpus analysis that are problematic to list in a dictionary (Johnston/Schembri 1999). The first type can be described as *symbolic indexical units* which point to referents or locations in the co-text or context of utterance, or which are visual representations of the location and/or movement of something. The second type can be described as *non-conventional units* which are enactments of someone doing something or behaving in a certain way (sometimes also to signify an object) or producing gestures of various types. Both types show their meaning in some way and have no real citation form.

The only conventional specifiable aspect of the form of symbolic indexical signs is the handshape—for pointing signs this is usually the extended index finger handshape, and for visual depictions of the movement or location of something this is a small set of meaningful handshapes, e.g., the upright index finger handshape for a person, or a flat hand with the palm facing laterally for a vehicle. The pointing and depicting signs can be represented in the dictionary by placeholder entries even though neither type consists of fully phonologically specified conventional symbolic units of the language. Importantly, the placeholders give the lexicographer the opportunity to describe their use and list the English keywords associated with them so they are discoverable (see also the discussion at Figure 3 and Figure 4).

Non-conventional symbolic units are not language specific because they have no fixed form or context free default meaning. Indeed, non-signers in the same general cultural group are likely to produce similar enactments or gestures as deaf signers do in similar contexts. They are therefore not entered in the dictionary. However, it should be noted that a point, a depicting sign, or an enactment or visualisation can become lexicalized, e.g., pointing to one's ear is the sign HEAR (there is another sign for EAR), a visual depiction of two people approaching each other is the sign MEET, and a stylized and reduced enactment of unscrewing the lid from a container is the sign JAR. Whether or not a highly iconic or mimetic unit is lexicalized in a particular signed language is an empirical fact determined from usage evidence. One cannot prejudge the issue.

Finally, an important early observation during fieldwork and corpus research for the dictionaries was that many manual signs found in a typical Auslan text or given as an Auslan translation for a concept or an English word were actually ad hoc explanations and/or descriptions of a meaning, i.e., different signers produced different strings of signs even if all the signs were conventional. They were not conventional multi-sign lexical units of the language and thus did not warrant entry in the dictionary.

3 The underlying Auslan lexical database

The Auslan lexical database (henceforth ALD) currently has over 7,750 records of which some seventy percent are citation signs and the remainder phonological variants. Each record has scores of fields to store information about the headword (henceforth *headsign*), such as its sign type, its phonology, its morphology, its meaning, its use, and its relationship to other signs. (Not all fields are used in each record.) The fields are for logical, textual, and numerical data or are containers which hold line drawings or videos. These fields are the source of the data displayed in the print and online dictionaries and/or are necessary for the software code underlying the online versions to deliver the appearance and functionality of the sites.

Given the number of fields in each record, the database is designed to be viewed in several layouts that present views of groups of fields related to the different types of information about the sign, such as those described in the following sections.

3.1 Headsign fields

Each record in the database is a headsign, i.e. it is the record in the database (or the lexical entry in a dictionary) that the information in other fields is identifying or describing. It is represented visually by a line-drawing of the sign and a very short video in which the sign is modelled by a deaf signer of Auslan. In the various layouts these visual representations of the headsign always appear so one does not need to know any special phonological script or notation system to know the form of the sign in question—one just views the line-drawing or, preferably, plays the video. These headsign fields are essential for researchers and users to visualize the entry sign and orientate themselves within the database. (Signs are organized visually, according to the phonological features of handshape, location, orientation etc., rather than alphabetically according to gloss, see 3.3.1). If the headsign is tagged as a phonological variant, then a secondary graphic field shows an image of the citation sign of which it is variant.

3.2 Glossing fields

In linguistics, *glossing* means the practice of giving an approximate equivalent of a word in one language using a word of another language. Because the lexicons and the derivational and inflectional systems of any two languages can be so very different, glosses usually identify lemmas.

The ALD glosses not only have this same function, but they are also used to uniquely identify in writing each sign record in the database because there is no widely accepted written form of any signed language. To underline the identifying function of the glosses used in the database they are referred to as *ID-glosses*. Because all signers are bilingual to some extent many signs in Auslan, and most signed languages, are strongly associated with at least one word in the spoken and written language of the surrounding community, even if the two are frequently not simply equivalents. Thus, different Auslan users asked to translate a sign into English will often use the same English word. If possible, this English word is used in the ID-gloss for a sign. However, because each ID-gloss is unique to a form, even in cases where two or more signs could be glossed equally well using the same English word, their ID-glosses will be slightly different in order to keep them distinct.

There are two ID-glossing fields in the ALD. One is used to uniquely name each sign record, and the other is used to uniquely name each sign lemma. The two are not the same because a citation sign and its phonological variants are all entered as separate records in the database, and one needs a unique name for each record. Consequently, signs have their own *record ID-gloss* but share the same *lemma ID-gloss* with any other signs that are phonological variants of the same citation sign. For example, the Auslan sign meaning 'house' has two common forms which are entered in the database and are identified with the record ID-glosses *house1a* and *house1b* respectively: *house1a* is the most common or citation form and *house1b* is a variant made with a different handshape. Both share the same lemma ID-gloss of HOUSE. A sign record in the ALD that has no common phonological variants entered in the database uses the same gloss in both glossing fields, e.g., the sign meaning 'tattoo' has no variants listed and thus has the record ID-gloss *tattoo* and the lemma ID-gloss TATTOO. From these examples one can clearly see that the same English word is used in both glossing fields with the distinction being that lemma ID-glosses are in small caps, as in the convention in linguistics for glossing, while the record ID-gloss is in lower case and, if it is part of an identified lemma that has listed phonological variants, it also has the suffixes of 1a, 1b, and so on.

ID-glossing conventions not only distinguish citation signs and variant signs as described, they also distinguish SE-only signs and fingerspelling-based signs. SE-only glosses are suffixed with _SE (e.g., FLOWN_SE) and fingerspelling-based signs are prefixed with FS_ (e.g., FS_SON). Each record in the ALD is also tagged in a lexical status field as (i) a citation sign, (ii) a variant sign, (iii) a SE-only sign, or (iv) an English fingerspelling entry.

Annotators use lemma ID-glosses in the Expanded Auslan Corpus (Johnston 2024) to identify signs as tokens of sign types. The lemma ID-gloss is labelled the *annotation ID-gloss* in the ALD because its primary purpose is to record how to gloss signs in the corpus, where minor phonological variation is ignored. The annotation ID-gloss names a conventional lexical type (lemma) in the ALD of which an instance in the corpus is a token (Johnston 2001, 2010). In form, the token may be like the basic citation form, one of its common phonological variants, or even one modified for grammatical inflection (Fenlon et al. 2015). For example, the verb GIVE is always assigned the same *lemma ID-gloss* regardless of it being produced with two hands (the citation form) or one hand (a phonological variant), or regardless of how it has been modified to express person, number or aspect (inflected forms). Hence, simply reading the annotation ID-gloss will not tell you if or how the sign varies from the citation form or lemma.

The ID-gloss is simply used to identify the sign uniquely in the database. It serves no other purpose and is not part of the sign definition in the ALD.

3.3 Phonology fields

The phonology fields are used to specify the form of each headsign based on the five main phonemic (or formational) features of a sign in any signed language, namely handshape, orientation, location, movement, and non-manual features (primarily mouth actions and head movements).

For the formational features of handshape, orientation, location and movement there are separate phonology fields, each with their own controlled vocabularies for the possible values of that feature, from which the appropriate phoneme is selected, focussing on the initial phase of the articulation of a sign. Non-manual features are described in a notes text field when necessary. The phonology fields separately code for handshape (e.g., the *flat* hand, the *index* hand, or the *fist* hand, etc., for a complete list see Figure 5), number and type of hands involved (one-handed, two different handshapes, or two identical handshapes), hand arrangement (symmetrical, alternating, parallel, or with only the dominant hand moving), location (primary locations in the head region and the torso region, and secondary locations which are where the right or strong hand contacts or interacts with the left or weak hand (pronated/supinated wrist, palm, back of hand, fingertips), and movement type (none, straight, curved, circular, repeated and so on).

A second phonology field contains a transcription of the articulation of a sign from onset to offset, using a dedicated notation system for signed languages, called HamNoSys (the Hamburg Notation System). The use of HamNoSys for the notation of signs in the Auslan database is a consequence of the historical evolution of the database. When begun in the early 1980s, it was not feasible to store signed language data using existing video technology. A notation system was thus needed to make it possible to record the form rather than the name or meaning of each sign (as in a gloss). However, over the period that the database has evolved, the importance of notation and transcription systems (and the fields that contain this information) has diminished somewhat due to the dramatic improvements in digital video technology and an increase in the storage capacity of the personal computers used by language researchers.

Between the dedicated fields for each sign feature and the transcription strings, the phonological features of each sign are effectively double coded in the ALD, but this is not redundant — each has a different function in the database. The dedicated fields for each phonological feature were created to enable sorting of records according to these features at the onset of each sign (see next section). The transcription strings alone are too complicated to filter and sort in this way because they track the articulation of the sign through time. However, they had the advantage of being readable — without any visual representation of the headsign one can still read the transcription string and 'sign out' the intended sign, much as one might 'sound out' a word in an IPA transcription.

3.3.1 Phonology and the sorting and ordering of database records

Records in databases can be filtered and sorted by different data types (e.g., numerical, textual, logical) in one or more fields in implicational hierarchies determined by the user. (Without being sorted, records simply appear in the order they were created.) The records in the ALD are filtered and sorted according to data in different fields, like the ID-gloss, the handshape used, or the location used. Sorting by ID-glosses alphabetically results in a view of the data which is not unlike the traditional word lists for signed languages described above. One reason for doing this may be to check that ID-glosses are not repeated but always identify unique records or lemmas. However, as a tool for storing and researching the lexicon of Auslan, filtering and sorting records by phonological fields is particularly useful. For example, the lexicologist can filter and sort records by initial handshape, orientation, location and movement features and see if two records with identical forms have been entered with two distinct ID-glosses. This would either be a mistake because there is only one sign that just happens to be glossed by two different English words with similar or related meanings, or it is a genuine case of homophony (the signs have two completely different and unrelated glosses and meanings, and/or the two signs do not have the same underlying iconicity) and thus there are two distinct signs.

The ALD has a default sort order which is based on the values in each of the four phonological feature fields sorted in a specified order, as well as on the controlled vocabulary of possible features in each field which are themselves ordered in a fixed way (often called a value list). For example, records are sorted in a cascading hierarchy starting with the handshape field and a value list that specifies that the index handshape precedes the flat handshape which precedes the spread handshape, and so on. Then, after the handshapes sort, it sorts the location field in which the value list specifies that the forehead location precedes the chin location which precedes the chest location, and so on. Then, after handshapes and locations sort, it sorts the hand orientation field in which the hand oriented up precedes the hand oriented away from the signer which precedes the hand oriented down, and so on. Finally, after handshapes, locations and hand orientations sort, it sorts the movement field in which straight movement precedes curved movement which precedes circular movement, and so on. The way this appears in the print and online versions of the Auslan dictionaries is illustrated in section 4. Indeed, the database allows for the searching, retrieval, cross-referencing and sorting of signs according to any of these criteria, singly or in combination.

3.4 Definition fields

Signs are not defined simply by assigning each one single word (gloss) as an equivalent. Rather they are defined in basic English in dedicated text fields for each grammatical class that applies to the sign: (i) noun, (ii) verb (including predicate adjective and preposition), (iii) modifier (adverb, conjunction, or adjective), (iv) deictic (pronoun, demonstrative, or locative), (v) interrogative, and (vi) interactive (interjection or exclamation).

More than one grammatical class field is required for most sign records because in Auslan, and other signed languages, signs are commonly able to function in more than one grammatical class role without there being any necessary morphological modification of the citation sign which marks this (Johnston 2012, Schwager/Zeshan 2008); thus, the one sign form can have a definition for each grammatical class that applies. Of course, there are also signs whose use is restricted to a single grammatical class and thus only have one grammatical class definition, e.g., BUT (conjunction).

Definitions are written in basic English to capture the general meaning of the sign in one or more of its grammatical class uses and, if one or more English words exist that lexicalizes this same or similar meaning, they are appended to the end of the definition after the expression "English =", as in Figure 2.

The style of the definition in the ALD is adapted from the Cobuild English Learner's Dictionary (Sinclair 1994) restricted vocabulary and serves two purposes. The first

Noun
A small, furry animal with a tail, whiskers, and sharp claws, which is often kept as a pet. English = cat.
Verb
To move your hand slowly and gently over something, such as a small animal, and especially a cat. English = stroke, pat.

(ID-gloss) cat (keywords) cat, stroke, pat

Figure 2: Headsign, definition schema, annotation ID-gloss and keywords.

is to challenge the common assumption that the signs of a signed language simply represent the words of the ambient spoken language by giving more than one keyword, if necessary, and by giving only the definition of each English keyword that is appropriate for each Auslan headsign entry. The second is to make the dictionary useful to deaf users of Auslan, especially deaf school age children, by helping them understand the meaning of English words they do not know by associating them with Auslan signs that they do know. This could help expand their English vocabulary.[2]

The keywords also have an important role in the way users navigate the database using English-based searching, i.e. in addition to searching by formational feature or by ID-gloss. A search for a sign associated with a particular keyword allows for a successful match for some words that have distinct forms in English, but only the one in their ID-gloss, e.g., a search for either ‘introduce’ or ‘introduction’ will match the sign glossed as INTRODUCE which would otherwise fail to match ‘introduction’. Also, one to many relationships can be captured. For example, a search for ‘cat’ matches both CAT and CAT-WHISKERS, both of which share the keyword ‘cat’, but only the former also matches ‘stroke’ and only the latter also matches ‘whiskers’.

In some cases, English does not lexicalize a concept expressed in a single Auslan sign, so given the definition is already stated using English words, a subsequent keyword (or phrase) would essentially be a repetition of the definition and thus be redundant. For example, the sign RECOGNISE-ERROR means ‘the recognition of an error or a mistake’ (noun) or ‘to recognise an error or a mistake’ (verb). Despite this, a keyword or keyword phrase is created in the keyword fields for these types of entry to make them discoverable through a keyword search. In this case, the keyword phrase is *recognise error.*

To make the results of keyword searches more relevant, keywords often carry disambiguating information after them in parentheses. For example, there are several

2 Teachers of the deaf have reported successfully using the Auslan dictionaries in this way. Similarly, deaf teachers of Auslan with hearing students have reported that the presence of more than one keyword, each defined relative to the sign, is helpful in explaining to learners the semantic range of Auslan signs.

signs strongly associated with the keyword *trunk* that are completely different in form to each other and thus have completely different ID-glosses: ELEPHANT, BOOT-HOOD, TRUNK, and BODY. The keywords associated with each have a disambiguation appended to them in parentheses which displays in the found set for a search for 'trunk', thus: *trunk (elephant), trunk (car), trunk (container),* and *trunk (torso)* respectively.

Finally, the high degree of iconicity in Auslan means that lexicalization can be difficult to establish for some signs, or at least be difficult to express without being misleading. For example, some signs can be completely unambiguous when used in context and/or be regularly cited as a translation equivalent for an English word yet lack any genuine language-specific conventionalisation; rather they are iconic or mimetic enactments that tend to be produced in very similar ways by all people, not just signers (Johnston/Schembri 1999). Others are semi-conventional signs called depicting signs (aka classifier signs) which show how something moves or where it is located in a very general way. For these signs, simply providing a definition ending with "English = keyword" would be somewhat misleading. Instead, a general definition field is used to make this clear. Nonetheless one still needs to provide at least one keyword and assign an ID-gloss to the record to make these placeholder signs discoverable in the database (Figure 3).

General

The act of scooping up a soft paste-like substance with something held with your hand, or any thing or any action directly or indirectly associated with this in context.

Noun

A thick, creamy mixture which you can eat by scooping it up with raw vegetables or biscuits. English = dip, savoury dip.

(ID-gloss) savoury-dip (keywords) dip, savoury dip, scoop up

General

An index finger handshape held upright and moved somewhere in the signing space is used to show the direction and path of movement of something. It usually means a person, but it can also mean an animal, a thing or even an abstract entity, depending on the context. The palm can face in different directions and is assumed to represent the front of the thing.

(ID-gloss) pass-in-front-of (keywords) go by, pass by, pass in front of

Figure 3: Two headsigns that use the 'general' definition field.

Yet other signs are deictics which literally point at their referents. In Figure 4, there are ten keywords to cover all possible uses of a point used in the way illustrated.

Pointing sign

1. Used as locative adverbial to refer to a location that is not near either the signer or the person addressed. English = there.
2. Used as a pronoun to refer to something or someone separate and different from the signer and the person they are addressing. If the thing or other person is real and located in the situation, then you point to where it/he/she is located, otherwise you point to where you imagine it/he/she is located. When the pointing sign is made immediately before or after a verb sign, you usually mean that the thing or the other person does the action of the verb or is affected by the action of the verb. English = it (thing); he, him (male); she, her (female); they, them (gender unimportant).
3. When the pointing sign is made immediately before or after a noun sign, the signer usually expects the addressee to know which person or thing they mean because it has already been talked about in the conversation or it is common knowledge. It is very much like an English determiner. When used in this way, the signer is often not thinking of, and not really pointing to, any specific location (so it can point at 'odd' angles). The sign can last for only a very brief time with very little movement. English = the.
4. When the pointing sign is made immediately before or after a noun sign and is made with stress (longer movement, more directed) the signer usually means a particular or special thing or person which has already been talked about in the conversation or which contrasts with something else which has already been mentioned. It is like an English demonstrative. English = this, that.
5. Used as an adverbial of time to refer to a time that is not the present, as if that time is located in a faraway place. English = then.

(ID-gloss)
there-it-the-that1a

(keywords) it, she, he, there, that, the, this, him, her, then

Figure 4: The entry for one of several pointing sign placeholder entries.

3.4.1 Homonym field

It is an unexceptional feature of Auslan that many signs, just like the words of any language, can have several related meanings. The ALD, and dictionaries generally, manage this phenomenon by identifying the various senses of each sign in a principled hierarchy from core to peripheral, metaphorical, and idiomatic senses. The different but related senses of the sign or word at the entry are usually numbered. In some cases, one sense of a sign may emerge over time that is sufficiently distinct from the original core meaning that it is better to treat it as a separate sign that shares the same phonological form, and give it its own entry in the database or dictionary. Two words or signs that share the same form but have two completely different meanings are homonyms. However, in the majority of cases across languages, homonyms also have no apparent historical relationship with each other. They are often found in two dialects of a language, as can happen in Auslan too.

Regardless of how the homonymy arises, when present in Auslan this creates two headsign records in which the phonological specifications are identical, but the definitions, grammatical classes, lexical links and usage information is different for each one. Each member of a homonym set is assigned a separate and sequential number (1, 2, 3, etc., as the case may be) so the user can anticipate while looking at one entry that it has at least one other completely different meaning in the language.

3.5 Lexical links fields

These fields in the database link the headsign to other signs because the meaning of a lexical unit in any language is not fully captured by a definition alone. Words and signs form networks with others and their relationships with each other is also an aspect of their meaning. Definitions in the ALD are thus complemented with fields that cross reference the headsign to other sign records by citing their unique identifying glosses (record ID-gloss). The cross references are of three types: (i) to synonyms or antonyms, which help make the meaning of the sign clearer, e.g. there are at least two signs which share the keyword 'light' in Auslan (LIGHT-WEIGHT and LIGHT-PALE) but the antonym of the first is HEAVY and the antonym of the second is DARK (which also has the synonym ELECTRIC-LIGHT); (ii) to phonological variants, which can be interesting in signed languages because sign phonemes (handshape, movement, etc.) can sometimes carry their own meaning which contributes to the meaning of the overall sign (unlike phonemes in spoken languages which usually do not carry meaning), yet in phonological variants the feature that varies usually makes no difference at all to the meaning of the sign; and (iii) to signs with which the current sign should be compared because of some formational, semantic or usage (e.g., register) characteristic that is important to know to avoid confusion or misuse.

3.6 Morphology fields

The morphology fields describe two aspects of the structure of the headsign—lexical morphology which here means involving fingerspelling or compounding, and inflectional morphology which here means relating to the ability of the sign to undergo types of meaningful grammatical modification involving location in space and/or movement.

Lexical morphology Headsigns involving fingerspelling are tagged in these fields as being a sign for a letter of the alphabet (FS_A = the letter 'a'), an abbreviation (FS_CHQ = CHEQUE), an initialism (FS_DD = DAUGHTER), a nativized fingerspelling (a fingerspelling which has become an Auslan sign, e.g., FS_EGG), or an initialization (a preexisting sign which incorporates a fingerspelling letter to create a new sign, e.g., GROUP + C = CLASS). Headsigns involving two or more signs are described as compounds when there are still two signs evident (e.g., THINK^HOLD = BELIEVE), blends when the two signs have undergone reduction and are merging (RED^BALL = TOMATO), idioms (FINISH TOUCH = 'been there, done that'), or calques of English compounds or multiword expressions.

Inflectional morphology Headsigns are tagged as being directional (able to move in various directions through the signing space), orientating (able to change the orientation and location of the hand in space), or body locating (able to be located on different parts of the signer's body). These inflectional potentials of a sign show how a sign may be modified without the need to list these types of modified forms in the database, just like knowing that a noun in English is a count noun rather than a mass noun means that it can take a modifying plural morpheme 's'.

3.7 Semantic domains fields

The semantic domain fields, of which there are over fifty, tag each headsign for the semantic domain that the sign is related to, e.g., animals, family relationships, numbers, foods, and so on. Naturally, a semantic field network like this knows no real limits, nor will every sign be able to be categorized into at least one of the available semantic domains (unless it includes categories that are so broad as to be of little practical use, e.g., 'thing' and 'action'). Tagging for these semantic fields enables researchers to quickly isolate all signs relevant to major topic areas that they may wish to compare cross-linguistically or to prepare for future fieldwork; or enable teachers accessing the online dictionaries to select vocabulary in thematic areas in lesson preparation.

3.8 Usage fields

The usage fields tag headsigns for sociolinguistic variables such as dialect (in Australia, by region or by state), age (in three bands), sex and sexual orientation, religion and/or school (in Australia, primarily Protestant or Catholic[3]); and also usage, such as

3 For most of the nineteenth century and until the mid-twentieth century, government schools for the deaf were Protestant, i.e., mostly Anglican (Church of England) while private schools were Catholic. This reflected the major British and Irish immigrant groups of the time, and the semi-official status of the Church of England in Australia. This distinction is now only relevant with respect to the origin of some Auslan signs because this religious division in the education of the deaf has no longer been important since the 1970s.

dissemination (marginal), register (formal or casual, polite or offensive), employment or specialist use (jargon), and currency (obsolete).

4 The print dictionaries

Using phonological features coded in the ALD, the first illustrated edition of the Auslan dictionary (Johnston 1989) presented signs that looked very similar to each other together in the same part of the dictionary. These parts of the dictionary were identified by handshape, ordered from the handshape most frequently used in the lexicon to the least frequently used (Figure 5).[4]

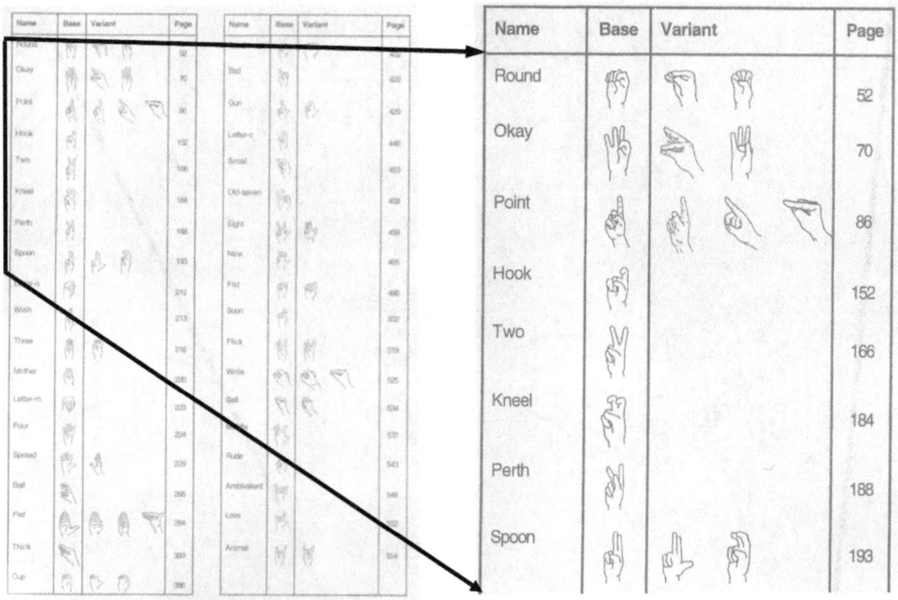

Figure 5: Handshape section order from Johnston (1997a)

Within each handshape section one handed signs were presented before two handed signs, and within each of these two groups, signs were presented from high locations in space or on the body, through middle locations, to low locations. Of course, this

4 For the second edition (Johnston 1997a) the handshape order was changed due to deaf community feedback to a more intuitive handshape order based on a combination of handshapes associated with counting, as well as the number of extended fingers.

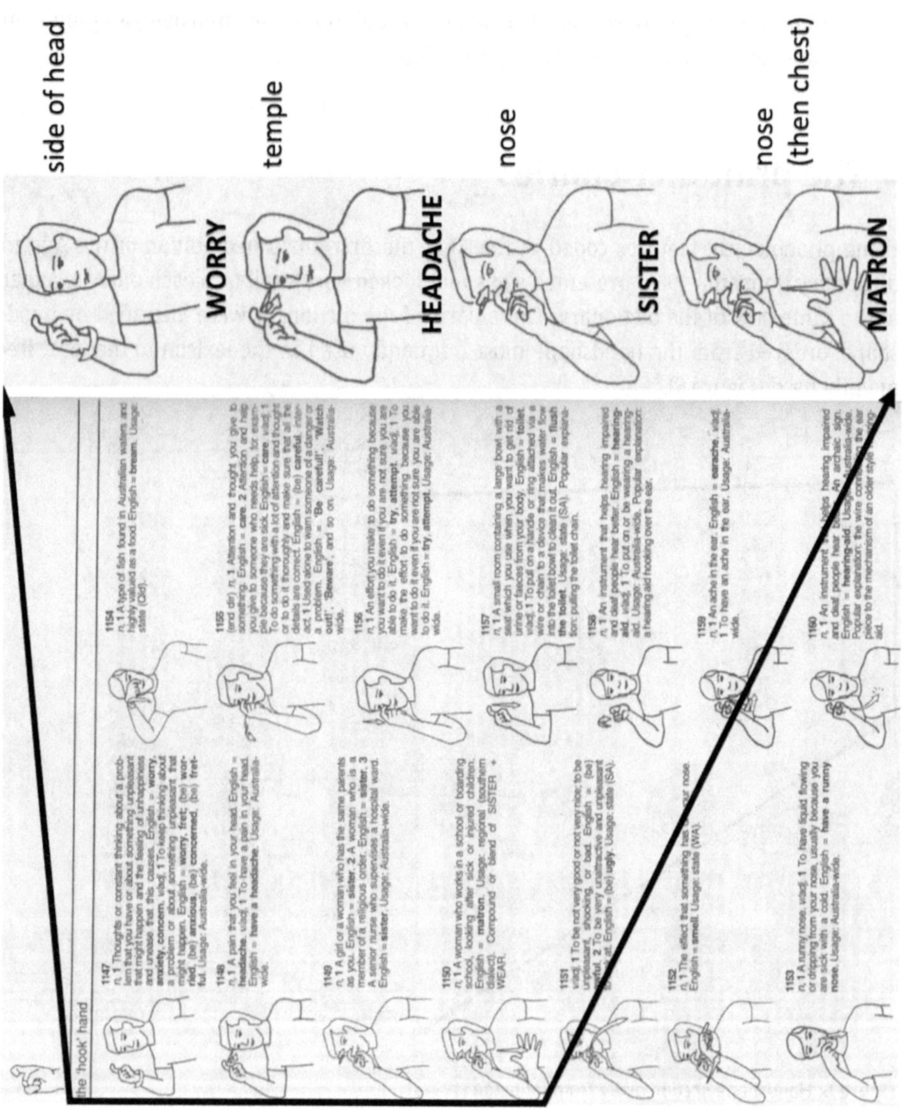

Figure 6: Sample headsign order in the 'hook' hand section from .Johnston (1997a).

meant that entries in the dictionary were not listed alphabetically according to the English translations (keywords) associated with the signs (Figure 6).

This approach was inspired and adapted from the groundbreaking dictionary of American Sign Language (ASL) by William Stokoe and colleagues (Stokoe et al. 1965). In some parts of that dictionary signs were organized according to location and, in another parts, they were organized by handshape. This was partly because the dictionary was unillustrated and entry headsigns were identified in a notation system (called Stokoe notation system) on the basis of which they were then sorted. In the notation system signs that contacted or were very close to body locations (such as cheek, chin, etc.) began with dedicated symbols for the location, while signs that were performed in neutral space had no location symbol but began with a symbol for the handshape used in the sign. In Stokoe notation, almost all handshape symbols were letters of the alphabet or numbers (based on the handshapes used in ASL one-handed fingerspelling or counting) (Figure 7).

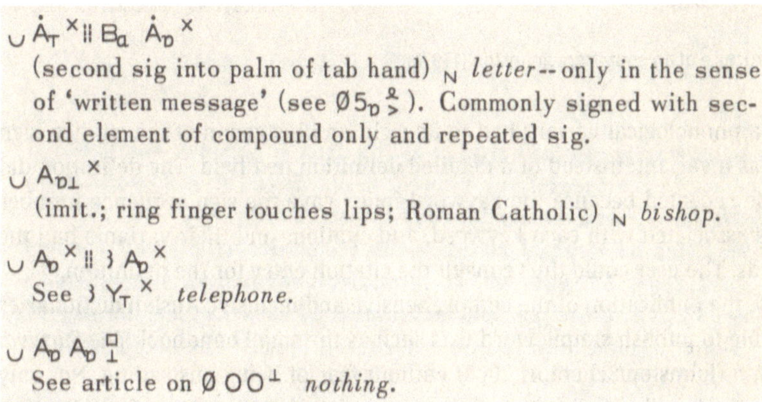
(second sig into palm of tab hand) N *letter*-- only in the sense of 'written message' (see Ø5D). Commonly signed with second element of compound only and repeated sig.

(imit.; ring finger touches lips; Roman Catholic) N *bishop.*

See *telephone.*

See article on Ø OO *nothing.*

Figure 7: Four entries from a page of the ASL dictionary (headsigns in Stokoe notation).

However, the Auslan dictionary was the first signed language dictionary to systematically apply a single phonologically based hierarchy of the most salient formational features of each sign to sequence all entries. There were thus two ways to consult the dictionary. The first involved familiarizing oneself with the organizing principles of the dictionary, described in the introduction to the dictionary, and scanning or browsing the entries according to formational features to locate a sign one may have seen, but whose meaning one did not know. The second involved consulting the index of English keywords which listed the relevant sequence order number of each sign in the dictionary for any given keyword. The user could then go and view that sign and its full definition.

Entries were created by exporting information stored for each sign record in the ALD into text files which were then semi-automatically formatted into a single text field to the right of an illustration of the headsign. The structure of entries was consciously modelled on typical dictionary entries for spoken languages to reinforce to the user that Auslan was a real language and different to English in a number of ways, even if the two languages were related (Figure 8).

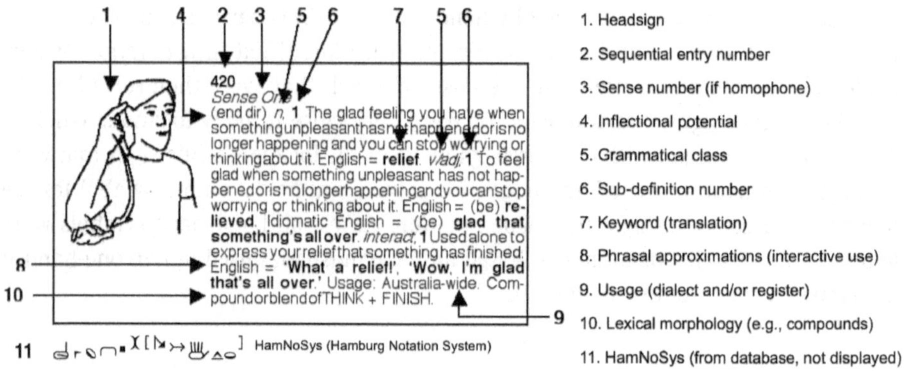

Figure 8: The structure of an entry from .Johnston (1997a).

An entry for a phonological variant had to its right an illustration of the citation sign of which it was a variant, instead of a detailed definition text field. The definition did not need to be repeated because the keyword index gave the sign sequence number for all entries associated with each keyword, and citations and their variants had the same keywords. The user could thus consult the citation entry for the definition.

Ironically, the publication of the comprehensive and inclusive Auslan dictionaries made it possible to publish simple word lists such as the small handbook *The Survival Guide to Auslan* (Johnston/Schembri 2003) without fear of being misleading. Not only were users of the handbook directed to the comprehensive dictionary for full information about each sign, but the keywords by which the entries were sorted alphabetically were disambiguated with a second keyword or by parenthetical information where necessary (Figure 9).

Finally, the Auslan dictionaries also influenced other signed language dictionaries. After the publication of the Auslan dictionary, dictionaries of British Sign Language and New Zealand Sign Language were published that adopted and adapted the model set by the comprehensive Auslan dictionaries (Brien 1992; Kennedy et al. 1997).

5 The multimedia CD-ROM dictionary

By the late 1990s, improved personal computer processing power and the increased data capacity of CD-ROM technology enabled video to be included in dedicated applications which could be run on personal computers.

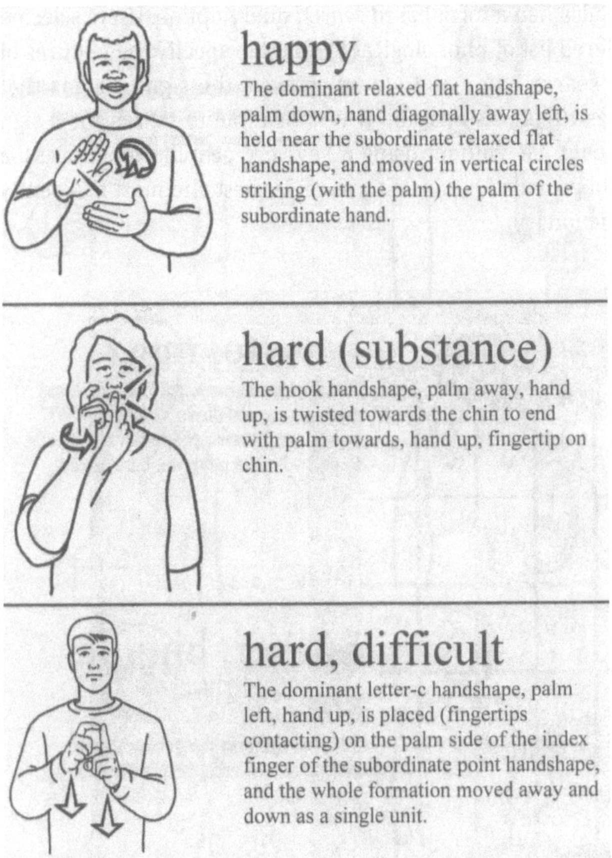

happy

The dominant relaxed flat handshape, palm down, hand diagonally away left, is held near the subordinate relaxed flat handshape, and moved in vertical circles striking (with the palm) the palm of the subordinate hand.

hard (substance)

The hook handshape, palm away, hand up, is twisted towards the chin to end with palm towards, hand up, fingertip on chin.

hard, difficult

The dominant letter-c handshape, palm left, hand up, is placed (fingertips contacting) on the palm side of the index finger of the subordinate point handshape, and the whole formation moved away and down as a single unit.

Figure 9: A page of the Survival Guide.

In the CD-ROM application the individual line-drawing graphics stored in the ALD were replaced by newly created digital video clips of each sign modelled by a deaf signer. Each video clip was retrieved and played whenever its record on the CD-ROM was accessed, and could be replayed in repeat, slow, or frame by frame modes by clicking on video control icons. Rather than seeing sign entries in a vertical list, users were able to scroll through the dictionary viewing signs in their phonological sequence order one after another, i.e. one entry displayed per screen view.

Software developers wrote the program that ran the CD-ROM on Windows and Macintosh personal computers. The program had a unique user interface to navigate through the database which exploited the thousands of phonological tags, keywords, and cross references based on record ID-glosses between signs in the database, such as synonyms, antonyms, and variants. At each sign entry page synonym, antonym and variant buttons were active if they existed for the sign. They would take the user directly to the entry for the related sign which could be viewed before returning to the starting point. The interface also had a form-based search query option. Users selected from a hierarchical and ordered list of phonological features to specify the features of a possible target sign. The search command would retrieve the sign or signs that matched the criteria (Figures 10–12). As a result, it was possible to search for a sign without knowing what it meant, i.e. without using a keyword search. Nonetheless, a keyword search field was still provided because it was the easiest and most frequently used way of searching the dictionary.

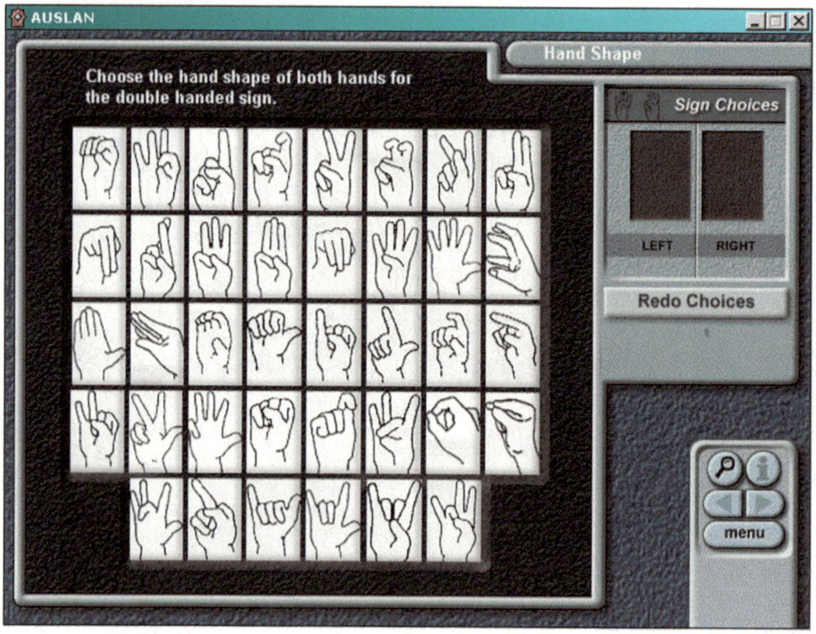

Figure 10: Search page specifying handshape(s) and hands.

The era of the CD-ROM was short-lived. The programming behind the CD-ROMs needed to be updated and the disc itself re-pressed with every new operating system, so that users needed to purchase replacement disks. This was expensive for both the publisher and the consumer. The problem was solved by the rapid and spectacular growth of the internet and the increase in the speed and volume of data that could be transmitted, making CD-ROMs themselves no longer viable.

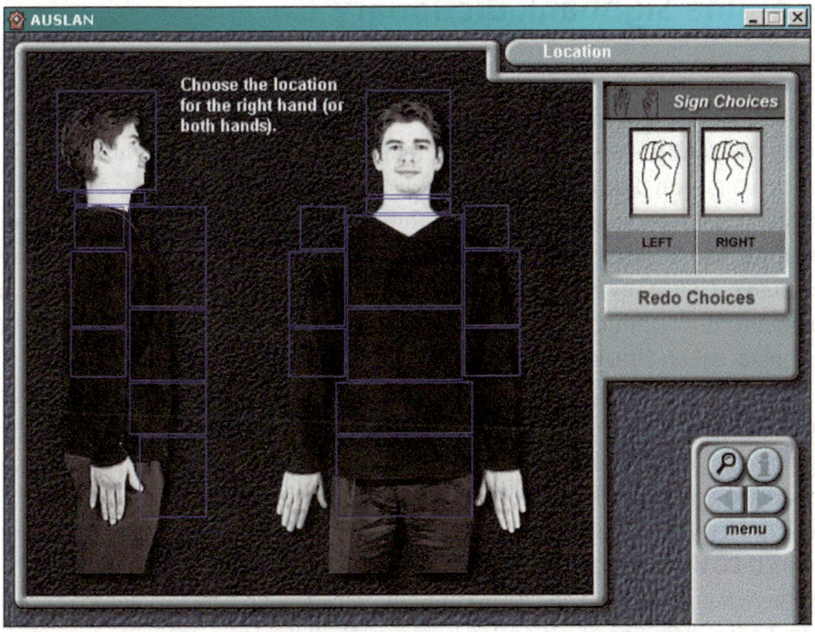

Figure 11: Search page specifying major body locations.

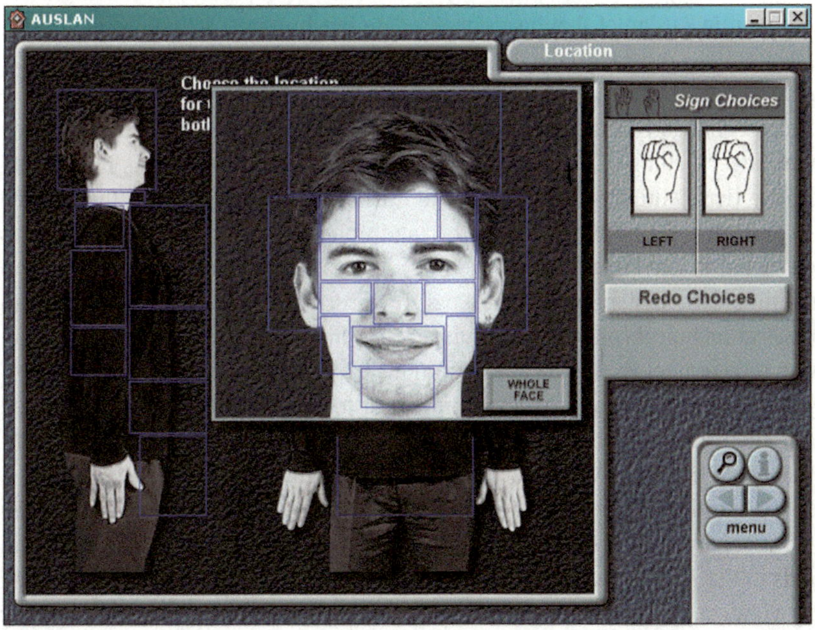

Figure 12: Search page specifying finer locations on the head and face.

6 The online Signbank dictionary

Signbank is designed to enable continuous editing without the need for the discrete editions that the print and CD-ROM publications demanded. Changes to Signbank are informed by on-going linguistic and lexicographic research, input from Auslan teachers or interpreters, and deaf community feedback.

Signbank has appeared in three editions, the first in 2004. The general layout and interface of Signbank combined elements of the print and CD-ROM editions already described above. One innovation in the 2004 edition was a feedback page where users could comment on definitions or missing signs and upload videos. This information could then be acted on after consultation with other signers.

The second 2008 edition greatly expanded the information from the ALD stored or displayed on the site. However, it moved some information on sign phonology and the phonology-based query field, both of which were visible on the public user pages, to two private restricted access pages for which the user had editorial privileges (See 'Go to Detailed View' in Figure 13). (Searching by phonology had proven to be rarely used by most users of the CD-ROM. It was something that mostly interested teachers and researchers.)

Two other changes to Signbank occurred in the 2008 edition. The first added a video field for an Auslan definition of the Auslan headsign. Until this innovation, all signed language dictionaries were bilingual and sometimes bi-directional (in the Australian context, English to Auslan, or Auslan to English). Now it was possible to have a monolingual route through the dictionary: search by phonological features, view an Auslan headsign and view a definition in Auslan of that headsign. To date five-hundred definitions have been used in slightly more records (some definition videos are used more than once). Auslan definitions are gradually being added to records as resources become available.

The second change was the creation of English entries in which the headsign video is a manual fingerspelling of an English word. These entries are tagged as English entries and have two definition field types—the Auslan definition field and the already existing English text definition fields. As the tag implies, these are not Auslan entries but were created at the request of teachers of the deaf and their deaf students, who wanted definitions in Auslan for difficult English words such as the vocabulary used in trade courses at technical colleges, or in subjects like mathematics and science. In addition, Auslan interpreters wanted to see definitions in Auslan for medical and legal terminology to give interpreters ideas about how best to provide circumlocutions, based on the definitions, in their work. In both cases, there was no common or accepted Auslan sign that could be listed. All are clearly marked as English entries.

In the 2024 edition of Signbank (Figure 14), the ALD and Signbank have essentially merged, so a separate ALD database is no longer needed. That is, all the data and media fields in the ALD appear somewhere in the Signbank site—some on the regular dictionary view, some on the detailed linguistic view, and some on the non-public and/or non-published view. To achieve this, the software underlying Signbank has been completely re-written to make it easier for editors to edit any of the data fields,

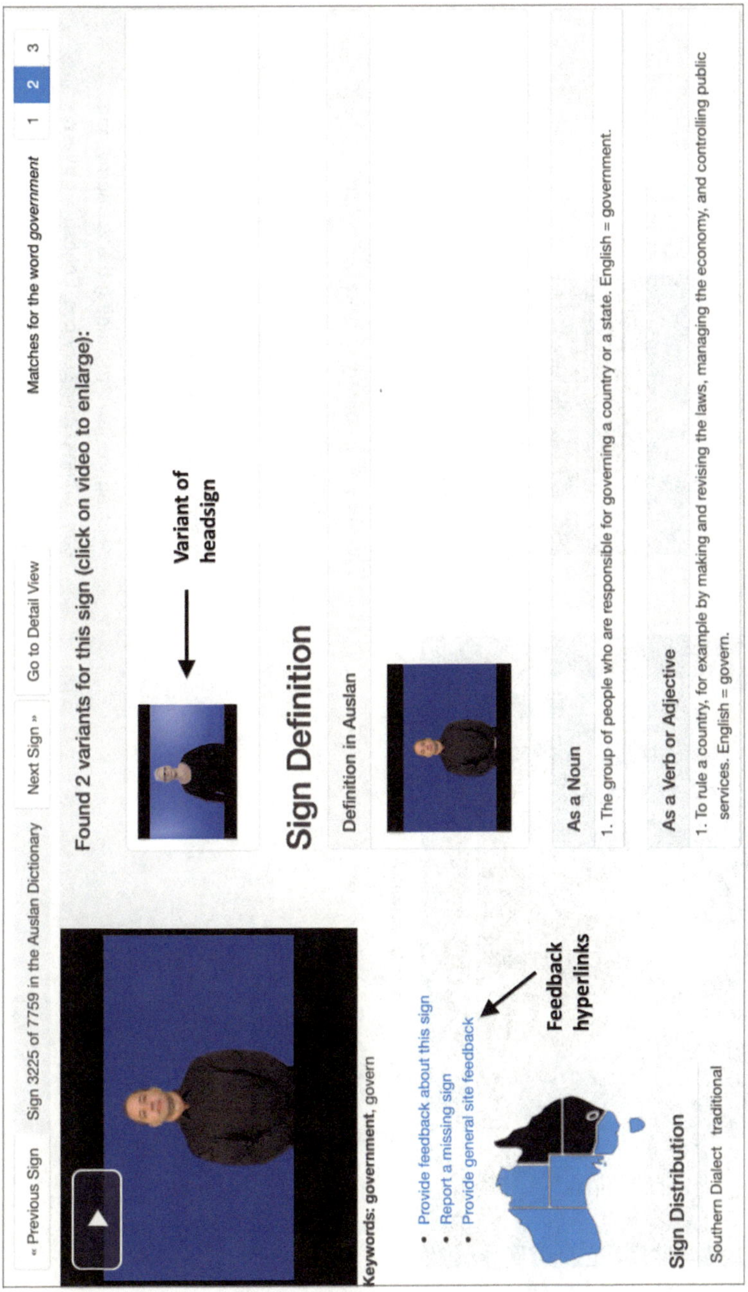

Figure 13: The simple dictionary view in Signbank 2008.

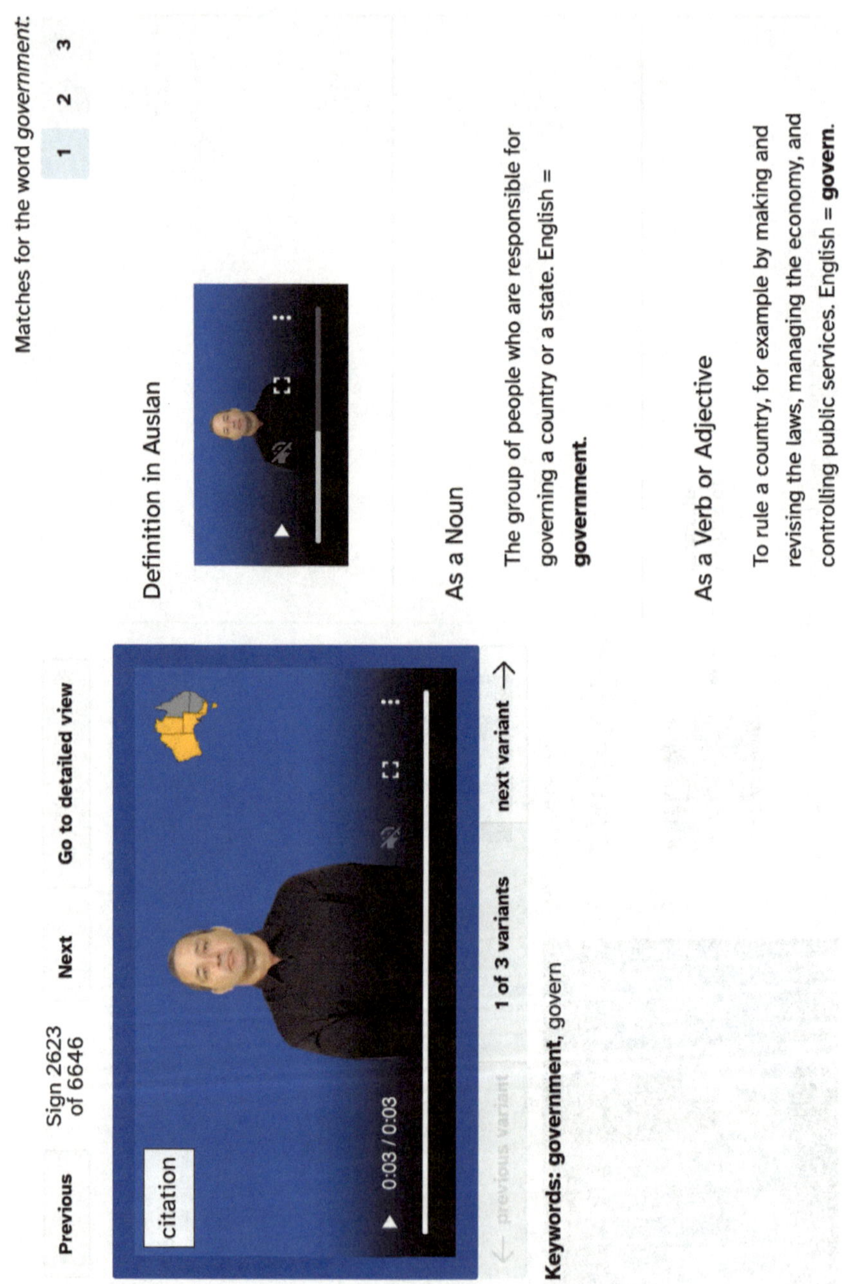

Figure 14: The simple dictionary view in Signbank 2024.

and for software developers to alter the placement and visibility of different types of data anywhere on the site. No longer are most data entered, corrected, deleted or updated in the ALD and then imported into Signbank. It is all done in Signbank.

Also in the latest edition, instead of variant videos being displayed separately on the citation sign page as in the two previous editions, they are now stacked under the headsign citation video and viewed by clicking an arrow. Another difference in the latest edition is that the feedback link (now on the landing page) is intended only for general feedback on, or issues with, the site itself, not for corrections to entries or suggestions for new entries. The use of social media by the deaf community has grown enormously since 2004 and 2008 and Auslan lexicographers can now consult or engage with Auslan users on several deaf community groups on social media apps where the meaning and use of Auslan signs are regularly discussed.

Another innovation in this edition is the colour coding of the four types of entries (citation, variant, SE-only, and English entry) to assist users navigating Signbank. Though the four types do have distinct glossing conventions (cf. 3.2), the ID-glosses are not visible on the regular dictionary view page where most users interact with the dictionary, so the four colour coded borders around the headsign video help distinguish them (Figures 15–18).

After the 2008 edition of Signbank great interest was shown by other signed language researchers in adopting and adapting the architecture of the online dictionary for other signed languages. I have long maintained that the ALD could be populated with signs from any signed language (Johnston 2001). It was not Auslan specific, though language specific adaptations would be necessary, e.g., adding or subtracting language specific phonological values, such a handshape, to implement this. To facilitate this, the software and coding underlying the Auslan Signbank site was shared on

Figure 15: The blue coloured frame for a *citation* sign entry.

Figure 16: The light blue coloured frame for a *variant* sign entry.

Figure 17: The red-ochre coloured frame for a *SE-only* sign entry.

GitHub, an online software sharing and development platform. Several other Signbanks soon appeared, e.g., of Signed Language of the Netherlands (NGT Signbank),[5] and of British Sign Language (BSL Signbank).[6]

5 https://signbank.cls.ru.nl/datasets/NGT (last access: 25 April 2025).
6 https://bslsignbank.ucl.ac.uk/ (last access: 25 April 2025).

Keywords: anaemia

Figure 18: The orange-yellow coloured frame for a *fingerspelled* sign entry.

A final innovation in the 2024 edition of Signbank will be the hyperlinking of dictionary lemma ID-glosses with another online language resource: the Expanded Auslan Corpus (Johnston 2024). The corpus contains 150 hours of digital video recordings of 100 deaf Auslan signers which have been segmented into about 1,000 individual task clips suitable for annotation. Of these, approximately one third have been annotated using time aligned multimedia annotation software using the lemma or annotation ID-glosses from Signbank. Work is currently in progress to link Signbank entries to attested examples in the corpus via the matching of lemma ID-glosses in each resource. The links will work in both directions not only allowing dictionary users to see real-life examples of the sign used in context, but also, for those viewing the corpus, easy access to the dictionary entry for a sign.

The linking of the dictionary to the corpus will unlock the full potential of both resources in the teaching and learning of Auslan. Users will be better able to see the ways the production of a sign can vary from its citation form due to (i) phonological processes found in continuous signing, and (ii) morphological processes that change the shape of signs in systematic ways to express various meanings. Linking will also have practical advantages for Auslan researchers. Annotation fields that contain a glossed sign can be checked against phonological, lexical and grammatical information in the dictionary to ensure the correct ID-gloss has been chosen; in new annotation fields, the appropriate ID-gloss can be located by searching the dictionary by ID-gloss, keyword, or phonological feature(s), to find the correct match. The accuracy of the dictionary and the speed of annotating the corpus will be enhanced, as will the integrity of research based on both.

7 Towards a universal database of sign forms

Auslan Signbank and the Expanded Auslan Corpus are key components of the Gesture and Sign Corpus of Australia (GeSCA) repository at Monash University. The GeSCA is a repository for multi-modal video-based annotated corpora collected in Australia or the Asia Pacific region—both for signed languages and for spoken languages where multimodal features have been annotated (Smith et al. 2022, Willoughby et al. 2024). The GeSCA was created as part of the Language Data Commons of Australia (LDaCA) which aims to secure and make discoverable fragmented and vulnerable digital language resources in Australia, and to open up future possibilities for language research using these resources.[7]

The structure of Signbank means that signs from other signed languages or citable gestures identified in co-speech gesture can also be entered into it. Regardless of its provenance, all one needs to do is tag any new entry for a new sign form for its formational features for it to appear in the default form-based sign sequence. It automatically appears next to others that look very similar to, or even exactly like, the new entry. The form and meaning of neighbouring entries can then be easily compared. Of course, records can also be filtered by any other formational feature that is the focus of research attention, not just in the default sort order. An open-ended or universal Signbank such as this allows one to display the following types of signs and gestures in distinctive ways or to filter them out completely: (i) conventional lexical signs of Auslan, (ii) citable gestures and emblems used by both deaf Auslan-users and hearing Australian English speakers; (iii) conventional signs of the signed languages of Indigenous Australia; and (iv) conventional signs found in other deaf communities.

The potential for this type of open-ended database of sign forms has long been recognized by some signed language researchers (Crasborn et al. 2001; Johnston, 2001) and at least one such online database of this kind has already been established, called Global Signbank[8] (Crasborn et al. 2024) which grew out of NGT Signbank, which was itself modelled on Auslan Signbank, as mentioned earlier. The 2024 edition of Signbank is thus another potential universal database of sign forms, but initially it will be based on signs and citable gestures from Australia and the Asia Pacific.

7 The GeSCA has benefited from the Language Data Commons of Australia Data Partnerships (LDaCA-DP) and the Language Data Commons of Australia Research Data Commons (LDaCA-RDC) (https://doi.org/10.47486/HIR001), each of which has received investment from the Australian Research Data Commons (ARDC). The ARDC is funded by the National Collaborative Research Infrastructure Strategy (NCRIS).

8 https://signbank.cls.ru.nl/ (last access: 25 April 2025).

Bibliography

Barakat, Robert (1987): Cistercian Sign Language. In: Sebeok, Thomas A./Umiker-Sebeok, Jean. (eds.): Monastic Sign Languages. Berlin/New York: Mouton de Gruyter, 67–322.
Brien, David (1992) (ed.): Dictionary of British Sign Language/English. London: Faber & Faber.
Bulwer, John (1644): Chirologia, or The Natural Language of the Hand.
Crasborn, Onno/van der Hulst, Harry/van der Kooij, Els (2001): SignPhon: A phonological database for sign languages. Sign Language & Linguistics 4, 1–2: 215–228. https://doi.org/10.1075/sll.4.12.15cra.
Crasborn, Onno/Zwitserlood, Inge/van der Kooij, Els/Ormel, Ellen (2024): Global Signbank manual, version 3. 10.13140/RG.2.2.16320.92166.
Fenlon, Jordan/Schembri, Adam/Johnston, Trevor/Cormier, Kearsy (2015): Documentary and Corpus Approaches to Sign Language Research. In: Orfanidou, Eleni/Woll, Bencie/Morgan, Gary (eds.): Research Methods in Sign Language Studies: A Practical Guide. Hoboken: John Wiley & Sons, 157–169.
Jeanes, R. C./Reynolds, B. E. (1982): Dictionary of Australasian signs for communication with the deaf. Melbourne: Victorian School for Deaf Children.
Johnston, Trevor (1987): A preliminary signing dictionary of Australian Sign Language (Auslan). Adelaide: TAFE National Centre for Research and Development.
Johnston, Trevor (1989): Auslan Dictionary: A dictionary of the sign language of the Australian deaf community. Sydney: Deafness Resources Australia.
Johnston, Trevor (2001): The lexical database of Auslan (Australian Sign Language). Sign Language & Linguistics 4(1/2): 145–169. doi: 10.1075/sll.4.12.11joh.
Johnston, Trevor (2003): Language standardization and signed language dictionaries. Sign Language Studies 3(4): 431–468. doi:10.1353/sls.2003.0012.
Johnston, Trevor (2010): From archive to corpus: transcription and annotation in the creation of signed language corpora. International Journal of Corpus Linguistics 15(1): 104–129. DOI: 10.1075/ijcl.1015.1071.1005joh.
Johnston, Trevor (2012): Lexical Frequency in Sign Languages. Journal of Deaf Studies and Deaf Education 17(2): 163–193. doi:10.1093/deafed/enr036.
Johnston, Trevor (ed. 1997a): Signs of Australia: A new dictionary of Auslan. Sydney: North Rocks Press.
Johnston, Trevor (ed. 1997b): Signs of Australia: A new dictionary of Auslan [CD-ROM]. Sydney: North Rocks Press.
Johnston, Trevor (ed. 2024): The Expanded Auslan Corpus. Melbourne: Monash University. https://doi.org/10.26180/26053972.
Johnston, Trevor/Cassidy, S. (2008): Auslan Signbank (http://www.auslan.org.au). Sydney: Macquarie University.
Johnston, Trevor/Catalyst Training Systems (2004): Auslan Signbank (http://www.auslan.org.au). Sydney: Royal Institute for Deaf and Blind Children.
Johnston, Trevor/Schembri, A. (1999): On defining lexeme in a sign language. Sign Language & Linguistics 2, 2, 115–185. DOI:10.1075/sll.2.2.03joh.
Johnston, Trevor/Schembri, A. (eds. 2003): The Survival Guide to Auslan: a beginner's pocket dictionary of Australian Sign Language. Sydney: North Rocks Press.
Johnston, Trevor/Smith, River Tae (2024): Auslan Signbank (http://www.auslan.org.au). Melbourne: Monash University.
Johnston, Trevor/Thornton, Darlene/Napier, Jemina (2002): Discovering Auslan: A beginner's dictionary of Australian Sign Language. [CD-ROM]. Sydney: North Rocks Press.
Kennedy, Graham/Arnold, Richard/Dugdale, Pat/Fahey, Shaun/Moskovitz, David (eds. 1997): A dictionary of New Zealand Sign Language. Auckland: Auckland University Press with Bridget Williams Books.

Schwager, Waldemar/Zeshan, Ulrike (2008): Word classes in sign languages: Criteria and classifications. Studies in Language 32, 3, 509–545. doi: 10.1075/sl.1032.1073.1003sch.
Sinclair, J. (ed. 1994): Collins Cobuild English Learner's Dictionary. London: Harper Collins.
Smith, Garth/Kentwell, Ann/Dyson, Ross (1975): Let's Talk with Our Hands: NSW Dictionary of Fingerspelling & Signs for Communication with Deaf Children. Sydney, North Rocks Central School for Deaf Children, NSW.
Smith, River Tae/Willoughby, Louisa/Johnston, Trevor (2022): Integrating Auslan Resources into the Language Data Commons of Australia. Proceedings of the 10th Workshop on the Representation and Processing of Sign Languages, Language Resources and Evaluation Conference (LREC2022), Marseille, 20–25 June 2022.
Stokoe, William/Casterline, Dorothy/Croneberg, Carl (1965): A Dictionary of American Sign Language on Linguistic Principles. Washington, DC: Gallaudet College Press.
Willoughby, Louisa/Smith, River Tae/Johnston, Trevor (2024): The GeSCA repository: Gesture and Sign Corpus of Australia, Australian Journal of Linguistics. DOI:10.1080/07268602.2024.2380672.

Pius ten Hacken

Terminology from a lexicographic perspective

Abstract: Wüster's *Allgemeine Terminologielehre* was the first general theory of terminology. Despite numerous attacks, it continues to be dominant in guiding the work of standardization institutions. In this paper, it is evaluated to what extent this dominance can be explained from a lexicographic perspective. The challenges discussed are based on corpus-based terminology work, terminological work in the service of language preservation, and the relationship between precisely delimited terms and prototype semantics. Also a recent proposal by San Martín (2022) is discussed, which implies the replacement of definitions consisting of necessary and sufficient conditions by a more flexible selection of information. It is argued that a user-oriented lexicographic evaluation of terminological resources should admit that Wüster's theory serves an important user category, that of the domain experts.

Keywords: definition, necessary and sufficient conditions, homonymy, polysemy, Wüster

Schlagwörter: Definition, notwendige und hinreichende Bedingungen, Homonymie, Polysemie, Wüster

For a long time, the field of terminology has been dominated by Wüster's (1979) ATL. From the 1990s, this theory has been challenged from different angles. What these challenges have in common is that they want to introduce methods and considerations that are typical of lexicography. Here I will present the ensuing debate and evaluate to what extent these challenges undermine the value of ATL. I start by explaining the position of ATL in the field of terminology in section 1. Then section 2 presents the basic assumptions of this theory. In section 3, three types of challenge are discussed, corpus-based terminology, language policy and prototype semantics. Section 4 presents a more radical attack on ATL based on the idea that its approach to definitions is not adequate. In section 5, I use criteria based on the evaluation of lexicographic resources to determine to what extent ATL is still valid.

Pius ten Hacken, University of Innsbruck. Institut für Translationswissenschaft, Herzog-Siegmund-Ufer 15, 6020 Innsbruck, Austria, e-mail: pius.ten-hacken@uibk.ac.at

https://doi.org/10.1515/9783112216644-007

1 The position of Wüster's ATL in terminology

As a field of study, terminology is relatively young. This is not to say that no terminology was used until relatively recently, but that terminology was not considered a field of study of its own. Crosland (2006) discusses the development of technical language in the second half of the 18th century. Characteristic of terminology in this period is the work of Antoine de Lavoisier (1743–1794). Together with three colleagues, he published a *Méthode de nomenclature chimique* in 1787. This nomenclature can be seen as the watershed between alchemy and modern chemistry (cf. Bensaude-Vincent/Stengers 1995: 116–121).

In alchemy, experiments were carried out in a pursuit of personal knowledge and knowledge transfer took place only in passing on experience and results to apprentices. Written notes served to support memory, but often used idiosyncratic expressions and symbols. In chemistry, experiments are described and published in such a way that they can be reproduced on the basis of the description. Public discussion and exchange of ideas are central in the development of the field.

The chemical nomenclature was a crucial component of this development, because it imposed a standard on the use of terminology. The publication of the standard enabled anyone with sufficient background knowledge to use the terminology in a generally accepted way. However, the system underlying the chemical nomenclature is dependent on properties of chemistry that are not found in other fields. Therefore, it does not embody a transferrable methodology for achieving a terminological standard in a given domain.

Wüster (1979) presents an *Allgemeine Terminologielehre* (ATL), a general theory of terminology. ATL proposes a methodology for establishing and describing terminology that can be applied generally. It does not depend on particular properties of the field. As described by Lang (1998), ATL is the outcome of Eugen Wüster's (1898–1977) long engagement with terminology in various fields. In particular, Wüster was involved in TC 37, the technical committee for terminology, from its foundation in 1936 as a committee of ISA and chaired it after its revival as ISO/TC 37 from 1952 to 1971. The presentation in Wüster (1979) is based on the manuscript used for his lectures taught at the University of Vienna between 1972 and 1975 and was published posthumously.

Because of his work in ISO/TC 37, Wüster had on one hand a strong practical basis in the development of his theory and on the other an influence on its use in standardization efforts. His experience in working with terminology and its standardization gave him an unmatched authority in national and international organizations.

2 ATL as a theory of terminology

A central assumption of ATL is formulated by Wüster (1979: 1) in (1).

(1) a. Jede Terminologiearbeit geht von den *Begriffen* aus.
    b. Sie zielt auf scharfe Abgrenzung zwischen den Begriffen.[1]

In (1a), *Terminologiearbeit* has a characteristic ambiguity. *Arbeit* ('work') can be interpreted as the process of working and as the result of this process. *Begriff* is used here as a concept, a unit of meaning. Although (1a) mentions the concept as the point of departure, it implies that we are dealing with a particular domain. Wüster does not say much about the delimitation of the domain, perhaps because in the context of ISO, the domain is given. Standards in ISO are developed in working groups (ISO, 2024). These working groups are set up by a Technical Committee, when there is a request from within the field. This means that from the perspective of the working group, the domain has been determined at the point when it starts working.

The emphasis in (1a) is on the direction of work. Taking the concept as the starting point stands in opposition to linguistic description, which takes the explanation of linguistic expressions as its basis. ATL has an onomasiological approach to terminology. In (1b), a central concern of terminology work is identified. In order to use terms consistently, it is necessary to establish precise boundaries between the concepts.

In ten Hacken (2022), I propose the terminological triangle in Figure 1 as a representation of a term.

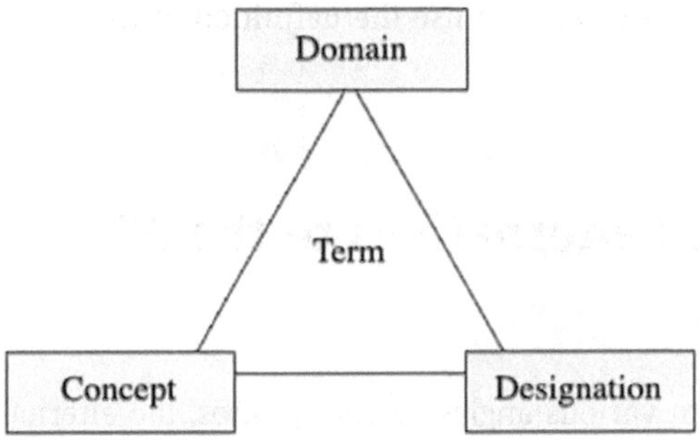

Figure 1: Terminological triangle.

1 'Every undertaking in terminology starts from the concepts. It aims to achieve sharp boundaries between concepts.' My translation, PtH. Emphasis as in the original. The division in *a* and *b* was added for convenience of reference.

In Figure 1, the *Term* is a combination of a concept, a designation and a domain. The concept and the designation correspond to the meaning and form of the term. They are similar to the two sides of the linguistic sign adopted by Saussure (1916). The domain specification distinguishes terms from general words.

In ATL, (1a) specifies the concept as the starting point. However, the concept is taken from a domain. For each concept, there are three tasks, which can be directly related to the three angles of the triangle in Figure 1. They are listed in (2).

(2) a. Definition: determining the boundaries of the concept
b. Naming: selecting a designation for the concept
c. Positioning in the domain: specifying the relationships to other terms

The task in (2a) corresponds to the goal formulated in (1b). The onomasiological direction of work specified in (1a) does not mean that (2a) should be treated first. The three tasks in (2) are in principle not ordered with respect to each other. Each task may be used to support the others, but none of them requires another one to have been completed. The onomasiological approach to terminology is implied in (2b), because only after the concept has been identified, a name is chosen. Identifying a concept and defining it are different tasks. For the identification of a concept, it is only necessary to establish which concept one is talking about. Names for terms are ideally motivated by the concept they designate, but the need to distinguish the term from related terms may also help in the selection of a good designation.[2] The task in (2c), when carried out for all terms in a domain, leads to an ontology. For an individual term, it implies determining where in the ontology the term is located. The relationship to other terms may be used in the definition, but we can also use the definition to find relationships to other terms.

3 Lexicographically based alternatives to the ATL model

The ATL model has been criticized from various angles. In many cases, the alternatives proposed are based on ideas that are common in lexicography. Here I will present three of these ideas. First, corpus-based terminology challenges the way terms are selected. Then, language policy introduces other concerns about the choice of a desig-

2 Wüster (1979: 29) states in this respect that for a "zweckmäßige Benennung" ('effective designation'), it is necessary that the concept has first been "geklärt und definiert" ('clarified and defined'). I would argue that the latter should be taken in the sense of 'identified', not as (2a). It is not necessary to determine whether Pluto is a planet before selecting a name for the concept *planet*. See also the discussion in section 3.3 below.

nation than the purely communicative ones in ATL. Finally, prototype semantics challenges the feasibility and usefulness of determining precise boundaries between concepts. As can be seen, each of these three ideas starts from a different angle in the triangle of Figure 1. Term selection addresses the treatment of the domain, language policy in particular the designation and prototype semantics the concept.

3.1 Corpus-based terminology

Wüster (1979) does not mention corpora as a tool for terminology. This is not surprising, because large electronic corpora were not available at the time. Twenty years after Wüster's death, Pearson (1998: 43) writes that "corpus linguistics is a relatively new field of enquiry". For special purpose corpora, she assumes that a reasonable size is one million words (1998: 56). It is therefore remarkable that Sager (1990: 130) makes the observation in (3).

(3) Systematic terminology compilation is now firmly corpus-based, i.e. terminology is no longer extracted from previous lists or by individual searches but from a corpus of material.

The step addressed in (3) is the preliminary step in ATL, the work that has to be done before (1a). For Wüster, this step is not particularly noteworthy. His idea is based on the working practice at ISO. When experts meet, it is not a problem to come up with a list of the most relevant concepts in their field of expertise. Typically, in advance of the meeting someone will prepare a base list which will then be extended or modified as needed.

The situation is very different for general vocabulary. It is not useful to sit down as a group to brainstorm about the words one knows. Preparing for such a meeting by letting someone compile a list does not help very much. In lexicography, corpora have been used long before they were available in an electronic format. The system of citation slips used for the first edition of the *Oxford English Dictionary*, as described by Gilliver (2016), is a particularly advanced version of analogue corpus management.

In the field of lexicography, using earlier dictionaries as a source of the word list is a well-known phenomenon, especially in the period that no electronic corpora were available. This explains the mention of "previous lists" in (3). The mention of "individual searches" is probably a reference to the way terminology is usually handled in translation. A translator will spend some time with research about terms they come across in a translation and record the results of this research to make them available for later use.

Clearly, using previous lists to come up with a list of terms is not a good solution, if only because it requires someone to have compiled that list. Individual searches of the type carried out by translators do not result in a systematic coverage of a domain.

Expert groups producing not just a list, but a structure of the domain based on relationships between terms constitute a solution that Sager does not take into account in (3).

When we consider the implementation of a corpus-based approach to terminology, we can still use the triangle in Figure 1, but the trajectory is different. Starting from the domain, a corpus is compiled for term extraction. It should be noted, however, that *term* in *term extraction* is not the same as *term* as used in Figure 1. In Figure 1, *term* refers to the combination of a concept and a designation in a domain. In *term extraction*, what is extracted is a set of designations. The *term* in Figure 1 needs to be constructed. The designation must be interpreted in order to come up with a concept. Its relations to other concepts must be retrieved to come up with a structure of the domain. This means that domain expertise remains the basis for constructing a term, once the designation has been identified in a corpus.

Three complications need to be mentioned in this context. First, a corpus of specialized texts from a particular domain does not only contain terms from that domain. Texts from, for instance, cardiology may contain terms from other medical fields, e.g. hospital care, and from fields outside medicine, e.g. insurance law. This means that not all terms in the corpus belong to the relevant domain. The terminologist has to recognize which terms are relevant.

Secondly, a corpus of specialized texts from a particular domain may contain terms that do not fit within the same theoretical framework. A domain where this is well documented is syntactic theory. When we compile a corpus of texts from syntactic theory, some texts may contain terms that are, for instance, based on Chomsky's Minimalist Program and other texts terms based on Cognitive Grammar. Even within different versions of Chomsky's theory, developed by himself or by other researchers, incompatible terms may be used, sometimes with the same designations. In such a field, the terminologist has to recognize which terms fit together theoretically.

Whereas the first two problems are caused by the fact that terms in the corpus do not fit into the same ontology, the third problem is of the opposite nature. In a domain, not all concepts are equally discussed. Some concepts are rarely mentioned, not because they are of marginal interest, but because they do not raise any controversy and can simply be presupposed. This means that in a corpus, they will be rare and can easily be missed out. Terminologists should in such cases supplement the data they find in their corpora on the basis of the domain structure they are building up.

The three complications mentioned here for corpus-based terminology do not occur in a context of a group of domain experts sitting together to compile a list of key concepts for the domain. They will not go outside their domain and will approach the domain on the basis of shared domain knowledge, so that theoretical inconsistencies are immediately noted. The gaps in corpora will not occur as a problem, because they approach the domain systematically.

This is not to say that corpus-based terminology is methodologically inferior. In fact, nowadays (though perhaps not so much in 1990) experts do use corpora as part of their regular working practice, as a supplement to what comes to mind on the basis of their domain knowledge. The statement in (3), however, may be taken to suggest that their work as domain experts is worth less than what terminologists without domain knowledge can extract from corpora. This is not true.

Corpora are used in terminology as a source of knowledge about the actual use of terms. This includes, for instance, collocations and syntactic constructions. They are also used as a resource for normative decisions. Establishing standards is guided by a sense of what is correct usage. Actual use is an important source in such decisions, because, as argued by Wright (2006), the closer a norm is to established usage, the easier it is to accept it.

3.2 Terminology and language policy

Wüster was active in the Esperanto movement (cf. Lang 1998: 23–24) and his multi-volume Esperanto-German dictionary is still the most extensive bilingual dictionary for this language pair. His attitude to multilingualism shows the influence of the Esperanto movement. He considered different languages first of all as an obstacle to successful communication. In practice, the idea in ATL is that terms are established language-independently and only task (2b), the selection of a name, is repeated for each language. In this way, the impact of different languages on terminology work is minimized.

From the perspective of the protection of minority languages and small languages, such an attitude to multilingualism has been rejected. Cabré (1999) proposes that a Spanish terminology database with translations of designations into Catalan is not a bilingual terminology database, but only a monolingual database with translations. In order for a terminology database to be truly bilingual, she proposes that the compilation work should be repeated for Catalan, so that there are two monolingual terminology databases, and followed by the compilation of a database of correspondence records. A correspondence record contains the conditions under which a particular Spanish term and a particular Catalan term correspond.

A first observation about Cabré's proposal is that in a multilingual environment this leads to an explosion of the number of databases. In the EU, with 24 official languages (not including Catalan), there would have to be 24 monolingual and 276 correspondence databases, i.e. 300 databases. For practical reasons, a simplification is necessary.

A second point is that in many cases, we do not want to have different concepts in different languages. In 2006, the International Astronomic Union adopted a new definition of *planet*. This definition and the designation *planet* have been translated into many different languages. However, the extension of the concept designated by *planet* in English, *pianeta* in Italian, and *planète* in French should be the same. The decision whether Pluto is a planet should not depend on the language. In many fields, the ATL assumption of cross-linguistic equivalence reflects the requirements of domain specialists.

At the same time, there are two valid points of concern that evolve from Cabré's proposal. One point is that the formation of terms should keep up with the developments in the field so that domains are not lost for a smaller or minority language. For most languages, the main risk is that in certain domains, it will no longer be possible to communicate using this language because no terminology is available. Terminology is first determined in English and in the absence of a corresponding term in the smaller language, domain specialists will have to switch to English.

Another point is that not all domains behave like astronomy. A good example is the domain of meat processing. In Britain, cows are carved up in a different way to the way they are in Germany. This means that for some pieces, e.g. *silverside*, there is no direct German equivalent. German has *Hüfte*, but this includes the *topside*, the *silverside*, and part of the *rump*. This type of information can be usefully covered in a correspondence record. Domains of this type are typically those where international communication is less prominent than national or regional cultural factors. Needless to say, terminologists should always be attentive to the possibility of such cross-linguistic conceptual mismatches.

3.3 Terms and prototypes

In the formal analysis of word meaning, componential analysis has been an important tool since the 1920s, in particular in the European tradition of the study of lexical semantics. Lyons (1977: 317–335) describes the historical background. The binary nature of features, comparable to the elaboration of phonological features by Trubetzkoy (1958 [1939]), may suggest that the meaning of a lexical expression can be delimited precisely. In describing concepts, Wüster (1979: 7) refers to this tradition in (4).

(4) Unter dem Inhalt eines Begriffes versteht man, wie gesagt, die Gesamtheit seiner Merkmale.[3]

The statement in (4) summarizes a discussion of the relationship between *Begriff* and *Begriffsinhalt*. The latter concept is at the basis of intensional definitions. Wüster (1979: 30–31) takes *Inhaltsdefinitionen* ('intensional definitions') as the crucial tool to achieve the goal in (1b).

Rosch (1973) and Labov (1973) challenge the view of meaning as described in binary features. They show that natural concepts, i.e. concepts as they are stored in the

3 The content of a concept is understood as the full set of its features, as mentioned above. My translation, PtH.

mental lexicon, do not have sharp boundaries. Labov (1973) used an experiment in which people were asked whether a particular object is a cup and found that judgements formed a continuum from clear cups to clear non-cups without any natural boundary. Rosch (1973) proposed that concepts in the mental lexicon have a prototype structure. At the centre, we find prototypical examples of the concept and as we move further away from the prototype, examples become less and less typical. For a concept such as *bird*, the prototype may be *robin*. *Chicken* is further away from the prototype and *penguin* is more marginal.

Temmerman (2000) takes prototype semantics to be in conflict with ATL. She interprets what she calls the "Vienna School" of terminology, i.e. ATL, as making the claim that a concept is clear-cut (2000: 16). When we look at (1b), however, Wüster presents the idea of a sharp boundary as a goal, not as a claim. In ten Hacken (2015; 2018), I develop the idea that the degree to which a sharp boundary is required depends on the way the term is used. Ten Hacken (2015) makes a distinction between terms in the narrow sense (TiNS) and specialized vocabulary. For *bird* as a concept in zoology, we need to be able to determine exactly whether a particular species belongs to it or not. In specifying a set of criteria that serve as a definition, we replace the prototype structure of the concept by a much simpler one, determined exclusively by its boundary. Zoologically, a robin is not a better example of a bird than a penguin. The only distinction that counts is the one between birds and non-birds.

Ten Hacken (2018) proposes a further distinction within TiNS, depending on the reason why precise boundaries are required. The two classes that are distinguished are labelled *scientific* and *legal* (2018: 75). Whereas for scientific terms, the boundary is used to evaluate theoretical claims, for legal terms, the purpose of the definition is to impose sanctions when rules are not kept. *Bird* is an example of a scientific term. Its definition is necessary for the evaluation of claims such as (5).

(5) Birds first appeared in the Early Cretaceous.

For an evaluation of (5), it is not sufficient to determine whether a species is similar to the robin. Zoologists have to agree on the set of properties that are crucial for a species to be a bird. As long as there is no agreement, there is no generally accepted evaluation of claims such as (5). However, only criteria with a strong enough theoretical foundation are accepted. If we do not have them, more research is necessary and we suspend judgement.

An example of a legal term is *moped*. The introduction of bicycles with a small motor as a special category of vehicles with special rights and obligations presupposes that it is determined exactly for which vehicles these rules are valid. Here we cannot suspend judgement until we have a good reason for the criteria, but we also do not have to base these criteria on a theoretical foundation. The Vienna Convention on Road Traffic (2022) specifies in Article 1(m) the definition as in (6).

(6) "Moped" means any two-wheeled or three-wheeled vehicle which is fitted with an internal combustion engine having a cylinder capacity not exceeding 50 cc and a maximum design speed not exceeding 50 km (30 miles) per hour.

In (6), the boundaries of 50cc and 50 km per hour are necessary to determine whether a particular vehicle falls within the scope of the rules pertaining to mopeds. They are arbitrary in the sense that they could have been set at different points of the scale, e.g. 40 cc and 40 km per hour, and there is no logical or theoretical argument for one point or the other. They have practical value in the sense that they influence the world. There are many vehicles which satisfy (6) by having a cylinder capacity between 49 and 50 cc on the market, but very few (if any) vehicles with a cylinder capacity between 50.1 and 55 cc.

For specialized vocabulary, it is not necessary to have a sharp boundary. In many contexts in which tools are used to achieve something, we encounter terms that belong to specialized vocabulary. Ten Hacken (2018: 66–68) gives the example of *bridge* in violin making. COED (2011: *bridge*[6]) defines the relevant sense in (7).

(7) the part on a stringed instrument over which the strings are stretched.

There is no need to know exactly what still can be counted as an instance of *bridge* and what not, because the aim is to make good violins. A bridge is typically made of wood and is a piece with a specific height and thickness. Its shape is similar to what in Italian is named a *ponticello,* the type of ornamental bridge used in designing parks. Whereas for mopeds, the incentive is to increase cylinder capacity in order to increase the performance, for a violin maker, the prototypical instance of a bridge serves as a model. There is no prohibition against experimenting with the shape, size or material, but the experimental bridge would have to compete with a long tradition that resulted in this prototype. Therefore, there is no need to define *bridge* more precisely.

In evaluating the impact of prototype semantics on terminology, it is important to see the difference between TiNS and specialized vocabulary. ATL makes the general claim in (1b), but it is a declaration of the goal of terminology, not a claim on what terms are. The need for a boundary stems from the way the concept is used. In specialized vocabulary, it is sufficient to avoid confusion with other concepts, but no definition with necessary and sufficient conditions is required. For TiNS, the nature of the conditions and the tolerance for suspending a decision depend on the question whether the definition is used to evaluate theoretical claims or to enforce rules.

3.4 ATL and lexicographic concerns

In ATL, it is presupposed that a group of domain experts gathers to determine the terminology of a domain. This is the practice in the context of ISO and other organizations geared towards the development of standards. The lexicographic concerns discussed in this section add considerations that do not necessarily come up in such a context. This is not to say that they are not relevant.

Corpus-based terminology highlights the importance of the analysis of language use in developing a standard. The availability of electronic corpora makes it possible for terminologists and domain specialists to use evidence of actual communication directly. The domain specialists' knowledge reflects the use of terms in their experience of domain-specific communication, but corpora can supplement this. Decisions still have to be taken by terminologists and domain specialists. They cannot be derived automatically from corpus data.

Considerations of the protection of languages were not on Wüster's mind when he developed ATL. That the availability of good terminology is a strong tool for the protection and revival of languages is beyond doubt. There is a trade-off between the effort involved in repeating terminological groundwork for each language and the effect on actual communication. The outcome is not the same in all domains. In fields characterized by the prevalence of international communication and internationally unified concepts, it is rather the selection of good designations that is required. A more detailed language-specific study of the nature of the concepts and of the relations between them is useful when the nature of the field leaves the speech community the freedom to vary them.

The challenge of prototype semantics resides in the interaction of standardized terminology with the mental lexicon of the speakers in the speech community. The approach proposed in ATL should be interpreted more strictly for TiNS, but can be relaxed somewhat for specialized vocabulary.

4 The nature and use of definitions

Formulating definitions is one of the key tasks both of terminology and of lexicography. Hanks (2016) gives an overview from the lexicographic perspective, treating approaches ranging from Leibniz and Aristotle to prototype and frame semantics. Löckinger et al. (2015) give an overview from a terminological perspective, focusing more narrowly on intensional definitions. About the function of definitions, there are two main contrasting views, listed in (8).

(8) a. A definition of X characterizes the meaning of X.
    b. A definition of X delimits the extension of X.

In (8), it is not stated what X stands for. In (8a), we can take X to be an expression, because expressions have a meaning. In (8b), X is rather a concept, because concepts have an extension. If we take Figure 1 to represent the structure of a term, this leads us to the conclusion that (8b) is the correct interpretation for terminology and (8a) is only adequate for lexicography.

However, the discussion of prototype semantics in section 3.3 challenges this conclusion. It showed the need for a distinction between TiNS and specialized vocabulary. For TiNS, there is a demand for a precise delimitation of the extension of the concept, so that a definition should be of the type in (8b). For specialized vocabulary, there is no demand for such a delimitation, so we might use (8a) as a starting point. However, an item of specialized vocabulary is still a term, i.e. an item with the structure in Figure 1. For all terms, a definition should be a characterization of the concept, not an explanation of the designation.

Against this background, we can consider San Martín's (2022) proposal to take a more flexible approach to terminological definitions. Two statements (2022: 56) characterizing his approach are given in (9).

(9) a. Terms do not possess meaning in themselves.
b. Since meaning is context-dependent (. . .), it is only possible to talk of semantic potential, in other words, all the knowledge that a term can invoke (Allwood 2003; Evans 2009).

The statement in (9a) is the first sentence of a new section. It is presented as a common background. However, it is incompatible with the representation of terms in Figure 1. In (9a), *term* is not used as a triple of a concept, a designation and a domain, because for such a triple, "possess[ing] meaning" is not a possible property. Words have a meaning, but terms consist of a concept and a designation in a domain. In (9b), it is significant that the two sources that are indicated do not refer to terms, but to words. The meaning of a word depends on the interpretation of its reference in context. However, the definition of a term should identify its concept.

It is well known that in some cases, the same expression can refer to different concepts. A common approach in terminology is to treat these as homonyms. This means that the fact that they have the same form is taken to be accidental. An example is *game*. Wittgenstein (1953) discusses the problems of defining the word *game*. As a term, *game* occurs in several fields, e.g. chess, tennis, hunting, and game theory. The terms in these domains have the same designation, but different concepts. From a terminological point of view, they are unrelated. In hunting, *game* refers to a category of animals. In chess, tennis, and game theory, it is an event, but the event is defined by means of properties that depend on the particular domain. Therefore, in the case of *game*, a treatment as homonyms is adequate.

As an argument against generalizing this approach, San Martín (2022: 59) presents the example of *methane*. He distinguishes four meanings that arise in different domains, quoted in (10).

(10) a. *methane* in Waste Management, defined as a gas emitted by the decomposition of organic waste;
b. *methane* in Water Treatment and Supply, defined as a by-product of wastewater treatment;
c. *methane* in Air Quality Management, defined as a greenhouse gas;
d. *methane* in Energy Engineering, defined as a fuel.

Whereas *game* is a different concept in chess and in tennis, *methane* is the same concept in all domains listed in (10). Therefore, treating *methane* as four homonyms, i.e. as four separate concepts, in the domains in (10) is unsatisfactory.

The key to understanding *methane* as a single term used in different domains is to decode San Martín's use of "defined as" in (10). If we take, for instance, (10b) as a definition, it does not comply with the requirement that a definition should be sufficient. As Wüster (1979: 30–31) emphasizes, we should be able to reverse a definition to end up with the concept defined. However, not every by-product of wastewater management is methane. In the case of (10d), we could say that "a fuel" is a hyperonym and the only thing we have to do to complete the definition is to add necessary conditions that exclude co-hyponyms. By contrast, in (10b), it is not a hyperonym, but a description that is given. San Martín uses "defined as" in the sense of (8a).

The fact that we are dealing with the same concept in all four cases of (10) gives a clue as to how to proceed. The question to be asked is how we determine that *methane* designates the same concept in each case. How can we determine that methane as a fuel is the same substance as methane as a greenhouse gas? We also have to ask the question of how to evaluate a claim such as (11).

(11) Methane has been detected on Mars.

In order to evaluate (11), *methane* has to be treated as a TiNS. This means that it should have a definition satisfying (8b). Such a definition can be seen as an algorithm in which necessary conditions are applied to determine whether something is an instance of the concept that is defined. For *methane*, such a definition might be (12).

(12) a. Methane is a chemical compound
b. with the composition CH_4

In (12a), I propose a hyperonym that applies to all uses in (10). A further condition is the chemical composition in (12b). The definition in (12) enables us to verify that we are dealing with methane, independently of the context. We can use it to evaluate (11) and to identify methane in each of the contexts in (10).

While the definition in (12) serves as a delimitation of the concept, it does not capture the information expressed in (10). This information should be expressed in the specification of the ontology of the relevant domains. The most attractive way of encoding it is to specify it by means of relations between two terms. In ten Hacken/Resi (2024), it is proposed that for a precise and flexible expression of relations between terms in an ontology, the nature of the relation should be expressed as the value of a feature, not as an attribute. For (10b), we can use the feature combination in (13).

(13) a. Base term: wastewater treatment
b. Nature of the relation: leads to the formation of
c. Target term: methane

In (13a), the base term is the term for which the information is specified. In a terminological database, it is essential for maintenance and consistency that each relation in the ontology is specified exactly once. This is not a limitation of the retrievability, because any proper query system makes it possible to find the information on the basis of any combination of features. Therefore, we can use the specification in (13) to retrieve the relation as one of the relations pointing to the record for methane. In (13b-c), the specification of the relation is broken down into two parts. In this way, we do not have to pressure the exact nature of the relation into a mould prescribed by the available attributes, but can describe the relation in detail. Formally, (13b) and (13c) each specify a feature in the term record indicated by (13a).

It is interesting to consider the treatment of the information in (10c) and (10d), because in these statements, it seems that different hyperonyms are used. On closer inspection, however, it turns out that they are not adequate as hyperonyms in a terminological definition. When we try to add further conditions to distinguish methane from co-hyponyms, we end up with the information in (12). Therefore, a more systematic approach encodes the information in (10c) and (10d) as a relation between two terms rather than as a definition. Following the pattern in (13), we can use (14) and (15), respectively.

(14) a. Base term: methane
b. Nature of the relation: has the effect of
c. Target term: greenhouse gas

(15) a. Base term: methane
b. Nature of the relation: can be used as
c. Target term: fuel

The problem that methane can be both a greenhouse gas and a fuel is solved by specifying the nature of the relation more precisely. Whereas in (14) the effect is the focus, in (15) it is the use. Both are specified as properties of methane, because in both cases, methane is an example of the substances that have this relation to the target term.

When San Martín (2022) proposes to treat the information in (10) as an argument to formulate four different definitions, he assumes that a definition of a term should specify all relevant information. It is on this basis that he advocates "creating a set of contextualized definitions for the same concept" (2022: 61). If definitions are treated as a delimitation of the concept, it is more appropriate to distribute the information. Instead of a holistic approach throwing together all information in a definition of the type (8a), I therefore propose an analytic approach with a definition of the type (8b) supplemented by relations to other concepts in the domain as illustrated in (13–15).

5 A lexicographic evaluation of terminological resources

The traditional view of a dictionary is that it is a description of the vocabulary of a language. Ten Hacken (2012) describes how the OED struggled with this requirement. For the evaluation of a dictionary, there are in principle three sources of criteria. They can be summarized as in (16).

(16) a. A dictionary should reflect the usage of the language.
b. A dictionary should reflect a native speaker's knowledge of the language.
c. A dictionary should reflect the norm of the language as it is accepted in the speech community.

Criteria based on (16a) use a corpus as a starting point. This is a common view among lexicographers, but it has the problem that a corpus contains errors. COCA (2020) contains 35 instances of *langauge*. That this is a typo rather than a rare word can only be determined by someone who knows the language. This points to criteria based on (16b). However, native speakers differ in their knowledge of the language. In many cases, especially those where their judgement is required, speakers disagree. A dictionary is not meant to describe the knowledge of a particular native speaker. Among non-specialist users of dictionaries, (16c) is a common view. However, the norm is not an empirical entity.

In view of the problems with all of the criteria in (16), ten Hacken (2009) proposes that a dictionary should rather be seen as a tool than as a description. A dictionary is a tool for its users to help them solve lexical problems. This is in line with the functional theory of lexicography proposed by Tarp (2008).

When we consider terminological resources from the perspective of a tool, it is necessary to specify the type of user. This is in no way different from the evaluation of general language dictionaries. A historical dictionary such as OED (2000–2024) is intended for a different type of user than a learner's dictionary such as COBUILD (2021), so that different criteria should be used for their evaluation.

Wüster's (1979) ATL is directed at the needs of domain specialists. These are the users of the standards produced by ISO. These standards reflect the norms, not as an empirical entity, but as an entity created by a group of domain specialists with the authority to set up the norm. Wüster (1979: 2) distinguishes *Ist-Norm*, reflecting actual usage, and *Soll-Norm*, reflecting agreed standards. As he notes, in terminological domains, *Soll-Norms* will generally become *Ist-Norms*.

The considerations discussed in section 3 are relevant to such groups of domain specialists. Corpus use can ensure that the *Soll-Norm* is close to the existing *Ist-Norm* so that it is more easily accepted. The availability of terms in their own language will facilitate communication among domain specialists. Classification problems will in general be limited to TiNS. For a TiNS, the definition should provide the information about the current state of knowledge as approved by the relevant authority. In this way, the domain specialist consulting the terminological resource can take a decision reflecting the current norm.

The considerations discussed in section 4 are of a different kind. San Martín (2022: 54) claims that definitions of the type in (12) "[do] not help non-specialist users to understand the concept and its relevance". This is not an argument against the use of terminological resources containing such definitions, but an argument that some users need resources of a different kind. Such resources may be lexicographic or encyclopedic, but they are not terminological in the sense of ATL.

In conclusion, we can say that lexicographic considerations can be used to improve terminological practice, but that there is a genuine need for terminological resources that give definitions of concepts with necessary and sufficient conditions. From the perspective of lexicography as the production of problem-solving tools, such terminological resources are what is necessary for domain specialists. We should therefore not stop making them. At the same time, we can think of other ways to serve different users. These are not a single category. As an example, translators have different needs to monolingual users. More studies are needed on how different categories of users use terminological resources, how successful they are and which features of the representation and content determine the degree of success. Educating users is a good starting point for increasing this degree of success. One aspect that needs to be emphasized in this effort is that definitions in terminology have a specific function. They are not the repositories of all relevant information about the concept, but only delimit it. Terminological databases should contain a description of their contents in a way parallel to the preface in a dictionary, so that users may find all categories of information they provide.

Bibliography

Allwood, Jens (2003): Meaning potentials and context: Some consequences for the analysis of variation in meaning. In: Cuyckens, Hubert/Dirven, René/Taylor, John R. (eds.), Cognitive Approaches to Lexical Semantics. Berlin/New York: Mouton de Gruyter, 29–65.

Bensaude-Vincent, Bernadette/Stengers, Isabelle (1995): Histoire de la chimie, Paris: La Découverte.

Cabré, M. Teresa (1999): Terminology: Theory, methods and applications. Translated by Janet Ann DeCesaris. Edited by Juan C. Sager. Amsterdam: Benjamins.

COBUILD (2021): Collins COBUILD Advanced Learner's Dictionary. New York: HarperCollins.

COCA (2008–2020): The Corpus of Contemporary American English. Edited by Mark Davies. http://corpus.byu.edu/coca/ (last access: 25 April 2025).

COED (^{12}2011): Concise Oxford English Dictionary. Edited by Angus Stevenson and Maurice Waite. Oxford: Oxford University Press.

Crosland, Maurice (2006): The Language of Science: From the Vernacular to the Technical. Cambridge: Lutterworth.

Evans, Vyvyan (2009): How Words Mean: Lexical Concepts, Cognitive Models, and Meaning Construction. Oxford: Oxford University Press.

Gilliver, Peter (2016): The Making of the Oxford English Dictionary. Oxford: Oxford University Press.

ten Hacken, Pius (2009): What is a Dictionary? A View from Chomskyan Linguistics. In: International Journal of Lexicography 22, 399–421.

ten Hacken, Pius (2012): In what sense is the OED the definitive record of the English language? In: Fjeld, Ruth V./Torjusen, Julie M. (eds.): Proceedings of the 15th EURALEX International Congress. Oslo: Dept. of Linguistics, 834–845.

ten Hacken, Pius (2015): Terms and Specialized Vocabulary: Taming the Prototypes. In: Kockaert, Hendrik J./Steurs, Frieda (eds.): Handbook of Terminology. Vol. 1, Amsterdam: Benjamins, 3–13.

ten Hacken, Pius (2018): Terms between Standardization and the Mental Lexicon. In: Roczniki Humanistyczne 66, 11, 59–77.

ten Hacken, Pius (2022): Warum Termini? Warum Definitionen? Kommunikative und translatorische Überlegungen. In: Hebenstreit, Gernot/Hofeneder, Philipp (eds.): Translation im Wandel: Gesellschaftliche, konzeptuelle und didaktische Perspektiven. Berlin: Frank & Timme, 93–112.

ten Hacken, Pius/Resi, Rossella: Concept Systems and Frames in Terminology. In: Applied Ontology 19, 1–5.

Hanks, Patrick (2016): Definition. In: Durkin, Philip (ed.): The Oxford Handbook of Lexicography. Oxford: Oxford University Press, 94–122.

ISO (2024): Developing Standards. Geneva: ISO. https://www.iso.org/developing-standards.html (last access: 25 April 2025).

Labov, William (1973): The Boundaries of Words and Their Meanings. In: Bailey, C.-J.N./Shuy, R.W. (eds.): New Ways of Analyzing Variation in English. Washington DC: Georgetown University Press, 340–373.

Lang, Friedrich (1998): Eugen Wüster – His Life and Work until 1963. In: Oeser, Erhard/Galinski Christian, (1998) (eds.): Eugen Wüster (1898–1977): Leben und Werk – Ein österreichischer Pionier der Informationsgesellschaft. Wien: TermNet, 13–26.

Löckinger, Georg/Kockaert, Hendrick J./Budin, Gerhard (2015): Intensional definitions. In: Kockaert, Hendrik J./Steurs, Frieda (eds.): Handbook of Terminology. Vol. 1, Amsterdam: Benjamins, 60–81.

Lyons, John (1977): Semantics. Cambridge: Cambridge University Press.

OED (^{3}2000–2024): Oxford English Dictionary. Edited by John Simpson and Michael Proffitt. Oxford: Oxford University Press. www.oed.com (last access: 25 April 2025).

Pearson, Jennifer (1998): Terms in Context. Amsterdam: Benjamins.

Rosch, Eleanor H. (1973): On the internal structure of perceptual and semantic categories. In: Moore, Timothy E. (ed.): Cognitive Development and the Acquisition of Language. New York: Academic Press, 111–144.

Sager, Juan Carlos (1990): A Practical Course in Terminology Processing. Amsterdam: Benjamins.

San Martín, Antonio (2022); A flexible approach to terminological definitions: Representing thematic variation. In: International Journal of Lexicography 35, 53–74.

Saussure, Ferdinand de (1916): Cours de linguistique générale. Edité par Charles Bally et Albert Sechehaye. Édition critique préparée par Tullio de Mauro. Paris: Payot, 1981.

Temmerman, Rita (2000): Towards New Ways of Terminology Description: The Sociocognitive Approach. Amsterdam: Benjamins.

Trubetzkoy, Nikolaj S. (1958): Grundzüge der Phonologie. Göttingen: Vandenhoeck & Ruprecht, orig. Travaux du Cercle Linguistique de Prague 7, 1939.

Vienna Convention on Road Traffic (2022). New York & Genève: United Nations Economic and Social Council, https://en.wikisource.org/wiki/Vienna_Convention_on_Road_Traffic_(2022) (last access: 26 May 2024).

Wittgenstein, Ludwig (1953): Philosophische Untersuchungen – Philosophical Investigations. Translated by G.E.M. Anscombe. Oxford: Blackwell.

Wright, Sue Ellen (2006): Terminology Standards for the Language Industry. In: ten Hacken, Pius (ed.): Terminology, Computing and Translation. Tübingen: Narr, 19–39.

Wüster, Eugen (1979): Einführung in die allgemeine Terminologielehre und terminologische Lexikographie. Edited by L. Bauer. Wien: Springer.

Pam Peters

Online terminography for Indigenous Australians

Abstract: This paper presents an initiative in applying user-based lexicography principles to online terminography. It discusses ways of designing an online termbank of terms in Australian Family Law to make content accessible to Indigenous users with low literacy. It requires rethinking of all the verbal demands in the semasiological design of dictionaries and termbanks. Instead it uses an onomasiological design, foregrounding the conceptual structure of the resource for users. The termbank's structure is vested in a set of keywords as in a thesaurus, coupled with iconic images as in the "easy-read" approach. It provides audio support in voiceovers for each keyword as the cursor runs over them, and for all subsidiary terms. Recordings of definitions of each word/term are linked to each termpage, to assist those with low reading skills. Thus the online termbank makes use of multiple media (graphic, audio, verbal), to facilitate users' access to unfamiliar words and concepts in family law.

Keywords: online terminography, low-literacy users, Indigenous needs, onomasiological design, easy-read approach, multimedia

Schlagwörter: Online-Terminographie, Benutzer*innen mit niedriger Bildung, Bedarf der Eingeborenen, onomasiologischer Entwurf, Methode des leichten Lesens, Multimedia

1 Introduction: user-based lexicography

Recent decades have seen a marked shift away from the customary approach in monolingual dictionary-making as creating repositories of lexical information. It foregrounded their content, with users taken for granted – essentially the native- or near-native-speaker fully literate in the dominant language. The seismic shift in English lexicography, to take account of the needs of dictionary-users began after WWII with A.S. Hornby's *Oxford Advanced Learners Dictionary of English* (1948). It was designed on pedagogical principles for ESL students, with words included in its macrostructure by reference to their frequency, and supplementary information on "word patterns"

Pam Peters, Department of Linguistics, Macquarie University, Australia, e-mail: pam.peters@mq.edu.au

https://doi.org/10.1515/9783112216644-008

to detail their grammar and idiomatic combinations.[1] His pioneering approach was taken up in 1970s/80s by British publishers Collins and Longman, with their respective "learners dictionaries" developed in tandem with other educational materials, and with inputs from educators in applied linguistics (Peters/Fernandez 2017). The high tide of English learners dictionaries was seen in the mid-1990s, in the publication of the "big four", with revised editions by Longman, Collins and Oxford UP, as well as an "international" learners dictionary by Cambridge University Press.[2] There was thus strong competition in the marketplace for English language learners to select the dictionary best suited to their needs. All four were substantially different from the traditional "concise" dictionaries, because of their radical reduction in the dictionary's macrostructure (i.e. the number of words included), and substantial enrichment of the microstructure of individual entries, with attention to the grammatical, semantic and combinatorial aspects of each word – for the benefit of non-native-speakers.

Against this backdrop of the development of learners dictionaries, pedagogical and "user-based" lexicography emerge as elements of the "functional" theory of lexicography (Tarp, 2009). For them the enrichment of the microstructure with information about the meanings and combinations of words ensured more accurate encoding of the most frequent words of the other language. Yet other categories of dictionary user are identified in Kwary (2018), by reference to 14 user variables. The dictionary needs of translators are naturally of a different order from language learners, especially in relation to specialized language (Tarp 2013). Translators as encoders and/or decoders of texts in another language require more detailing of the microstructure and/or a greatly enlarged macrostructure to cope with highly specialized texts. Specialized dictionaries of such proportions are only possible in C21 in the online medium (Fuertes-Olivera/Tarp 2014). The open-endedness of digital space allows specialized lexicographers/terminographers to meet the challenges of the ever-expanding terminology of new scientific disciplines – environmental science, sociology, human sciences such as psychology. The macrostructure of online dictionaries can be updated continuously, while serving the perennial need for enriched microstructure of the key terminology of the discipline.

1 A.S.Hornby compiled his dictionary on the strength of long experience of teaching English in Japan in the 1930s. He was in contact with contemporary American lexicologists (Edward Thorndike and Irving Lorge), who pioneered research on word frequencies, published in the *Teachers Word Book of 30,000 Words* (1944).

2 Their full titles are: *Longman Dictionary of Contemporary English* (3rd ed.), *Collins Cobuild Advanced Learners Dictionary of English, Oxford Advanced Learners Dictionary* (5th ed.), *Cambridge International Dictionary of English.*

2 User-oriented terminography

Terminography as a new arena for specialized lexicography is a product of late C20 shifts in thinking about terminology (Alberts 2001). The word captures the growing interest in a descriptive approach to terminology, as distinguished from the traditional approach in the "hard sciences" (physics, chemistry) and engineering, where univocity (one-for-one correspondence between word and concept) could be expected, with no variation in meaning. Yet terms in the biomedical sciences are typically polysemous (e.g. *screening*) by virtue of their applications in different contexts, and require some verbal description to account for their usage. The seminal treatise on terminographic methods can be found in Temmerman's *Towards New Ways of Terminology Description* (2000). Growing recognition of this new frontier in terminology is visible in occasional uses of *terminography* during 1990s, and the first occurrences of *terminographer*, as in Meyer/Mackintosh (1996).

Like general lexicography, terminography is increasingly associated with online projects (Fuertes-Olivera/Tarp 2014), demanding fresh consideration of user needs in terms of their language proficiency as well as their level of knowledge in the specialized field of the dictionary. Users' access to technical information depends firstly on their ability to decode the explanatory language of the online resource. The tendency to overestimate the dictionary users' language skills was tellingly demonstrated by De Schryver/Prinsloo (2011) in a study of Dutch dictionaries designed for primary and secondary school learners. They used survey techniques to investigate the users' views on the complexity of language in its definitions, finding that at both junior and senior levels, the language was pitched about two grades above them.

The need to ensure the readability of dictionary language has been embraced in pedagogical lexicography by those such as the English Collins and Longman's dictionaries, with their creation of "controlled" vocabularies of 3000 words/lemmas to be used in all definitions. This is more easily said than done, depending on the size of the macrostructure of the dictionary, and the range of words to be defined. With less common and more specialized words, lexicographers are obliged to deploy words outside the controlled vocabulary in order to explain their meanings and make the definitions precise. It can hardly be avoided in specialized lexicography if it is to do justice to the complex ontologies of technical terms. This issue sits alongside the lexicographer's common challenge of making the explanatory language accessible to the intended users with greater or lesser proficiency in reading the dictionary's content, as with school dictionaries.

Specialized dictionaries and termbanks have multiple challenges to meet in relation to the language proficiency of their users. They may have to provide for adults with low reading skills in the dictionary's explanatory language, i.e. their needs as first- or second-language readers. Almost all the known readability scales base their metrics on the norms for first-language school students, rather than factoring in adult or second-language readers (Peters/Kruger 2021). They take no account of sentence structure (Collins-Thompson 2014) or matters of cohesion within and across sentences (McNamara et al. 2014). The dictionary users' prior knowledge of the area must also be factored in (McNamara/Kinsch 1996).

These different competencies in language and knowledge of the discipline are recognized in lexicographic research (Fuertes-Olivera/Arribas-Bano 2008) and by Kwary (2018) as existing on separate scales for individual users. But their stages are not likely to be exactly aligned, despite broad similarities in their progression. Language acquisition and proficiency can be formally defined in stages as in the CEFR scale (Common European Framework Reference) shown below. Whereas those for specialized disciplinary knowledge sit on a continuous scale representing incremental growth in a person's understanding of and expertise in a specialized field (from beginner to expert). See Figure 1 below.

Termbank user resources						
*Language (L2) proficiency	A1	A2	B1	B2	C1	C2
*Specialized knowledge	novice/ trainee	>>	>> intermediate	>>	>>	>> advanced

Figure 1: Twin scales of language proficiency and content knowledge in termbank users.

As indicated, the individual user's resources on the two spectrums (reading proficiency, knowledge of the discipline) cannot be lined up exactly. While the user's reading skills may be benchmarked by standard testing, there is nothing comparable for the spread of background knowledge to be expected among users of a termbank. For beginners it may include some basic cultural knowledge (Mateo 2017), while others depend on formally acquired knowledge. Developing graduated knowledge content to meet the needs of the user range from novice to expert is probably unachievable, and perhaps unnecessary since experts are least likely to consult the dictionary (Humbley 2017). Terminographers typically focus on the novice to intermediate range of specialized vocabulary, as a practical and inclusive solution.

Apart from the user variables to be considered in a termbank's design, there are open questions as to what range of terms used in the discipline are to be included in it (Landau 2001: 356–359). A specialized reference must include the terminology that represents the central concepts of the discipline, especially those uniquely associated with it. But it raises questions about the less-specialized terms to be included, such as include general terms that may be deemed peripheral. These may be *subtechnical* terms (Davies/Smith 2018), i.e. words taken over from general language usage and given specialized meanings within the discipline, such as *party* in legal usage. The difference between the specialized and non-specialized meanings of such words are usually known by L1 users, but may be missed or mistaken by L2 users. Other candidates for inclusion are the *semi-technical* terms of the discipline (Davies/Smith 2018). These are terms that are widely used across scientific and other disciplines that use scientific methodologies, e.g. *sample, variable.* For users whose scientific education was acquired in west European languages, these terms are familiar enough, but not so for those whose science education was gained in an Asian language medium. Feedback from Chinese users of an Australian termbank highlighted the need for more such *semitechnical* terms to be included in a medical termbank (Ding/Peters/Smith 2015).

Designing a user-friendly termbank thus involves decisions about the range of more and less specialized terms to include. Terms representing the essential disciplinary concepts must be included, but key subtechnical terms and a certain number of semitechnical terms from legal practice are also necessary to meet the needs of novices. They may be all equally foreign for second-language users. But for those with some (intermediate) knowledge of the discipline, rather more specialized terms would be desirable, e.g. those which are hyponyms of the core terms, and common heteronyms, e.g. *kidnapping* as a synonym for *abduction.* The termbank can thus help L2 users to recognise some terms as belonging to hyponymic structures where they exist, and others which are simply alternatives.

3 Explanatory strategies

Essential support for dictionary users lies in the explanatory language by which to accessing information in a lexicographic source. This includes the use of plain English or plain language definitions, bilingualization, and easy-read, discussed in turn below.

3.1 Plain English and plain language

The use of Plain English to reduce the amount of difficult language in government documents has been advocated in many countries since the first public campaigns in the UK and Canada in 1960s. It was upheld as a way of combating impenetrable bureaucratic and legal language that obstructed people's ability to access necessary information, most critically in multilingual countries such as South Africa, where the English-using community consists of both L1 and many L2 users from multiple language backgrounds. Plain English was signed into American law by President Obama in 2010. Its scope has since widened internationally as "plain language" in non-English -speaking countries where the language of law and government is not understood by many of its citizens. The need for Plain English in legal and government documents was recognized from the 1980s, with the Australian government signing its commitment to the international plain language agreement in 2020.

Despite the language focus in the terms "Plain English" and "plain language", both address aspects of document design, structure and formatting, as important in facilitating access to information. These aspects of usability are further articulated in standards for online users' access to information in the Web Content Accessibility Guidelines (WCAG) compiled and updated by the WorldWideWeb consortium.[3] The WCAG guidelines present broader issues than language that affect user's access to online information, such as the operability of the online system, which are thrown into relief by comparison with access to the printed dictionary.

An outstanding application of plain language in print lexicography can be found in the *Plain English Legal Dictionary: Northern Territory Criminal Law* (online 2015). It was developed in collaboration with multilingual fieldworkers and case managers working with Indigenous clients, as well as legal advisers. Two sample definitions from it are shown below:

> **bail** n. *Bail is the law that says if a defendant will wait in jail or if he will wait out of jail while waiting to come back to court. When a defendant gets bail, he will wait outside of jail for his court case. When a defendant does not get bail, he will wait in jail for his court case.*

The words of the entry for "bail" are almost all monosyllabic, apart from "defendant", which requires some explaining (provided in a separate entry in the *Dictionary*). The three complex sentences consist of short subordinate clauses which mirror each other in structure and wording to some extent. Their transparency is intended to reflect the syntactic structure of Indigenous languages, making them relatively easy for interpreters to translate for Indigenous clients before the court. Yet the hypothetical subordinator "if", and abstract uses of "when" are not so easily rendered in Indigenous languages. (See the Introduction to the *Dictionary* for modal features of English which Indigenous languages lack.)

> **aggravated** adj. *Aggravated is a word used to talk about charges. When a charge is 'aggravated', it is worse. It is more serious, that is, the law says there is a bigger punishment (sentence) for that charge. Many charges might be aggravated. For example, aggravated assault or aggravated robbery.*

This entry for "aggravated" strives for simplicity to explain the relative nature of the crime it refers too, and the *charge* attached to it. It uses comparative expressions ("worse", "more serious") to convey the relativity, but without expressing the *comparandum* (point of comparison). In discussing "aggravated" with clients, it would need to have the different points of comparison spelled out in "aggravated assault" or "aggravated robbery". Again it shows where the role of the supporting lawyer and social workers come in to mediate the concept to the person they are assisting. Part of their role is to address the general lack of "legal literacy" in Indigenous communities

3 Its website is at https://www.w3.org/WAI/standards-guidelines/wcag/ (last access: 28 April 2025).

(Family Law Council Report 2012); and unfamiliarity with the workings of Australian law.

The use of plain language can be unpopular with some readers when it changes the register of the text, and seems to be talking down to them. Its use in specialized writing (as in law or science) tends to suggest it's intended for the general reader rather than other professionals, who may therefore react negatively to it (see further under 3.3 below). A different issue arises with using Plain English in letters from government: plainer language may give them a friendly, neighborly voice, when an authoritarian voice is needed to express the urgent need for compliance. Writers have to consider the essential purpose of the letter, and how strongly worded it should be to persuade their readers to a given course of action.

3.2 Bilingualization of dictionary entries

The use of bilingualization in learners dictionaries was advocated during the1990s (Marello 1998) to support L2 language learners, rather than have them turn to bilingual dictionaries for explanations of the new terms. The insertion of bilingual (translation material) into the dominant (L2) language of the learners dictionary provides them with L1 help to understand the concepts represented in the dictionary. The extent of bilingualization varies with the dictionary, often just headword and the definition, but may also be applied to examples (Marello 1998). A prime example is the *Oxford Advanced Learner's English-Chinese Dictionary* (4th ed. 2004) with Chinese bilingualization of definitions, examples and the keywords in longer entries. Though intended for Chinese learners of English, its high degree of bilingualization could well help English-speakers to learn some Chinese (McArthur 2005).

Bilingualized dictionaries are by nature confined to a single other language for the anticipated L2 learner, which limits their marketability to learners with other L2s. There is little chance of creating multilingualized dictionaries in print, because the format for accommodating interlinear translation in an entry can hardly be stretched to include translations from more than one language.

An online solution is to present the translation equivalents in separately translated versions of the headword and other key elements of each term's page, which can be called up by clicking on the name of the language. Each translation set is based directly on the original English source, avoiding the problem of progressive distance from the source word(s) – as happens in some multilingual glossaries laid out in parallel columns. But an online multilingual termbank such as the LawTermFinder shown below can provide accurate translations in quite a few languages, each one rendering the English directly. See the list in Figure 2. It serves as a multilingual reference for the speakers of the largest groups of heritage languages used among first-generation immigrants in the Australian community.

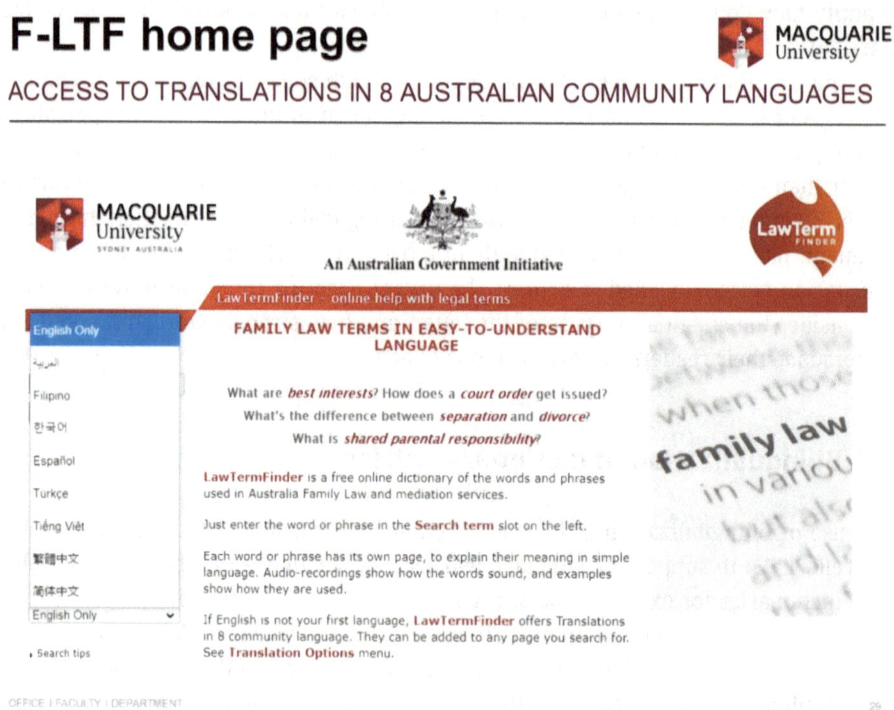

Figure 2: Australian community languages accessible in multilingual versions of Family-LawTermFinder (F-LTF).

Selections from the list of target languages, including both forms of Chinese (Mandarin and Cantonese) are shown on the left-hand-side, linking users to translated versions of each page. It provides a solution to the practical and theoretical problems in multilingualizing a dictionary or online termbank. Yet it relies on the assumption that users are able to read the English and/or the target language of their family's heritage in accessing information in the termbank. Where the user's literacy in either or both languages is very limited, an alternative solution must be found.

3.3 Easy-read information delivery online

During the period of the Covid pandemic, health authorities round the world were suddenly faced with the responsibility of ensuring that crucial health practices were understood and maintained among citizens with all degrees of literacy and understandings of the health issues that were at stake. In Germany, authorities used Easy-read ('leichte Sprache') in public health messaging, often with accompanying graphics. Research into their effectiveness by Hansen-Schirra et al. (2020) found that the visualisations were "quite important" in illuminating the message, but with the caveat that some were "neither precise nor equivalent to the term they were intended to elucidate".

The relationship between a graphic and the accompanying text is all the more uneven when used in a sequence. A fragment of Australian health messaging from the first year of Covid, is projected in easy-read format below (Figure 3).

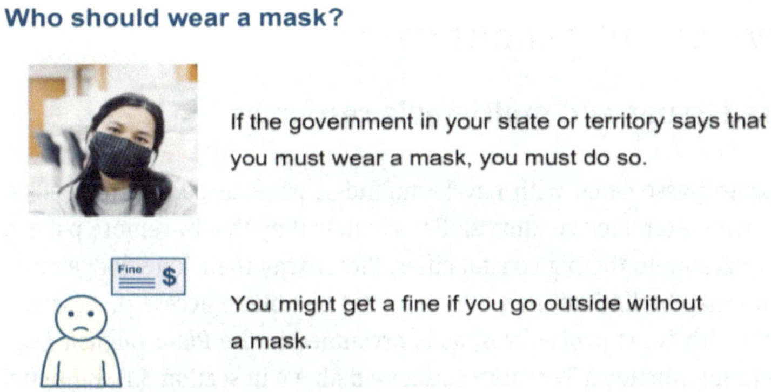

Figure 3: Easy-read information on a health practice to be maintained, with legal enforcement.

In pioneering examples of *easy-read* information delivery like this, adhoc images had to be found, often dissimilar in their style of representation, as in this sequence of a photo followed by a line drawing. In general, the photo is more effective in being attached to reality, but a line drawing can be more informative (Landau 2001). The communicative impact of the two in Figure 3 is starkly different. The photo presents a lifelike person wearing a face-mask, while the drawing tries to connect a token human figure without any mask and the fine to be imposed for it. The two images seem unrelated since the photo shows a young woman (not a young man) wearing a mask, while the drawing is non-gender-specific. Such issues are of course inherent in most kinds of imagery, whether photographic or quasi-iconic.

The direct address of the text of the accompanying text is clearly expressed in plain language to interpret each image for users. One residual issue lies in the sequence of image + text, if the "you" attached to the first image is connected only with women's obligation to wear masks, in line with strict gender-specific dress codes for women in some cultures. It probably needs to be explained (verbally) in the accompanying text as an obligation on everyone for which non-compliance may incur a fine. Thus the implied narrative from one image to the next needs careful management.

In Germany, the use of Easy-read ('leichte Sprache') is mandated by law in several German states for public communication, especially for those with communicative or cognitive disabilities. Research focusing on its effectiveness has found that those with such disabilities typically gained from easy-read messaging. Unfortunately they also found some negative reactions to its use, especially by those whose faculties are "unimpaired" (Hansen-Schirra/Maass 2020), although it was not intended for them. The researchers thought that this negativity impacted also on those who really need and benefit from its use, though more research is needed.

4 Designing an online termbank in Australian Family law for Indigenous users

4.1 User-focused issues and multimedia resources

In the easy-read project associated with LawTermFinder, we focused on the needs of Indigenous people who often lack reading skills, whether they live in remote parts of Australia or have migrated to the big coastal cities. Either way their knowledge of the English legal system may be limited; and they may not be able to access professional help needed to deal with court procedures, as is presumed in the *Plain English Legal Dictionary* for use in the Northern Territory (discussed above in section 3.1). Bilingualization *or multilingualization* was not considered an option for the termbank, because very few of the 300+ Indigenous languages recorded have communities with cross-generational use of the language to maintain them.[4] Even those who speak their local Indigenous languages may not be able to read them. If they have some ability to read English, it is as L2 users rather than L1.

These circumstances made it necessary to use a form of Aboriginal English (a contact-based form used widely by Indigenous people) for the target language of the termbank, and to render it in easy-read form with images as far as possible. The value of images in illuminating concepts has been tested and consistently affirmed in multiple genres of writing: especially in the illustrations used in educational and instructional texts (Lemke 1998), and as diagrams or photos in scientific articles or newspaper articles (Parkinson et al. 2023). Visualizations are thought to help readers cope with new information by using more than one "code"[5] of communication, provided they are distinct enough from each other (Sweller 2002). Research on the use of illustrations in online dictionaries found they were faster to process than the equivalent text (Lew 2015), and more easily remembered (Parkinson et al. 2023). They are valued especially by L2 users (Lew 2015), and "quite important" for L1 readers (Hansen-Schirra et al. 2020).

4 There are less than 18 according to the latest (3rd) National Survey of Indigenous Languages (2020).

5 "Code" and "mode" are to be distinguished (Kroger 2020) in that "code" refers to different forms of communication (such as images v. text); whereas "mode" captures the sensory channel by which those forms are processed. Thus images and text are both visual *modes*, whereas sound recordings are aural mode.

Audio recordings also have a very important place in supporting those with low literacy in the written code, and as a key resource in audiovisual media (Maass/Hernandez Garrido 2020). They provide an alternative code and mode for communicating the written word, and used as an auxiliary medium in audio-descriptions of what's on screen for the blind. They pick up the needs of L2 viewers in dubbed television programs, and in voiceovers embedded with information provided on some websites. In an early evaluation of our Easy-read LawTermFinder, it was suggested that voiceovers for the individual terms be presented onscreen, and they were then built into the platform. We thus harnessed both audio and visual modes for delivering essential information, and alternative visual codes (textual, graphic) for detailing information.

4.2 Accessing an online termbank

A dictionary-like reference depends on recognizing words or terms in their written form, and as access to its lemma (Gouws 2017). Without that initial recognition, the user cannot advance into typically dense, information-rich microstructure, however carefully designed. Thus the conventional semasiological access to the termbank had to be redesigned along onomasiological lines, i.e. by foregrounding a single key word a small set of core concepts, like the key word in a thesaurus with which other terms and concepts can be associated.

In the Easy-read Family Law termbank, the eight core terms/concepts are presented on individual "cards"[6] with the term and a sketch image for each of them. Apart from this graphic support for recognizing each term, there are voiceovers on every card as the user runs the cursor over it.[7] With this additional aural cue to connect the sound of the term with its spelling and meaning, the Easy-read termbank uses both visual and audio modes with alternative distinct codes of communication to connect users with the key word/term through multiple cognitive channels (Sweller 2002). The keycard terms indicate the broad scope of family law as a concept, while detailing its important facets for Indigenous purposes.

The eight core terms/concepts are presented to the termbank user as a set of cards with voice-overs on the homepage, as shown below in Figure 4.

There are two kinds of audio features in the Easy-read termbank. Running the cursor over any of the keycards activates the voiceover to help users to identify the word. Clicking on any of the keycards takes them to a subsidiary set of semantically related termcards (from 12 to 25) with explanatory text on the meaning of each term and its application for the user. The termbank thus expands the conceptualization of the keycard to

6 See below, section 5, for this use of "card" to refer to individual terms and their termpages.
7 Visit the Easy-read LawTermFinder website at LawTermFinder.mq.edu.au to hear the audio features.

Figure 4: The set of eight core cards/concepts used to access the termbank.

embrace related others, and acts as a cognitive anchor for it. On both keycards and every subsidiary card, the text containing the definition/explanation is supported by a full audio-recording of the explanation, activated by clicking on the Listen link on each term-card. The selection of voices recorded for the audios on each of the Easy-read cards is discussed below in section 5.3.

For the keyterm *court people,* some of the subsidiary cards to which it provides access are illustrated below. They are of two types, as explained in the two sentences shown on the keycard, helping to scope the core concept of the set. It identifies two aspects of it: terms referring to the professionals who work there, and those used for the roles of the people who are participating in the court case under discussion.

The terms featured in Figure 5 are not strictly "terms" in family law, but rather *semitechnical* ones shared by other fields of law that involve litigation. Such terms may not be familiar to those with low legal literacy, including Indigenous people needing to understand the functions of the different kinds of officials and professionals they meet at court. The legal roles that they themselves take up in a court case also need explaining, hence the card for "party", a puzzling subtechnical term for either of the two sides in a court case, entirely different from its meaning in everyday language. Other complex terms in need of explanation for those unfamiliar with court cases are *applicant* and *respondent,*

Figure 5: A subset of the 12 termcards attached to the keycard *Court People.*

applied to the person who has taken the case to court, and the one who is required to answer to it, respectively.

The family law terms associated with each of the keyterms in this termbank do not form strict ontologies. The selection is essentially pragmatic, designed to demystify the legal processes in family law, and to explain where help can be found for those faced with challenging family issues. Yet in some areas, terminology has expanded noticeably in current Australian practice to produce a new hyponymic set, as with "family violence" shown in Figure 6. Its various forms, now recognized as grounds for litigation, are articulated in the text attached to the keycard and a sample of its subsidiary cards for "physical" and "sexual" violence, as well as "emotional abuse" and other forms of verbal violence in "harass" and "threats and intimidation".

Figure 6: The *Family Violence* card and some of its subsidiaries.

The illustrations on these subsidiary cards (8 out of 18 of the subtechnical terms in family violence) help to concretize different types of aggressive behavior that represent violence against other adults or children. Neglect of vulnerable children is also presented as a kind of family violence punishable by law.

Legal remedies against family violence can be sought in particular "Orders & Rules", as detailed by some of its subsidiary cards in Figure 7 below. It includes mini-ontologies of terms that stand for different kinds of judicial *orders*, enforceable by law, which are intended to protect the family from violent or threatening behavior.

Collectively they are explained on the core card (not shown) as "The things a judge decides for your family. What must be done to deal with the family problems and keep everyone safe."

The terms on the *Orders & Rules* cards are a mix of legal terms for the actions prescribed, and everyday expressions for the prohibition, provision or agreement they represent. A key order is the comprehensive "violence order" (known in other Australian states as a "restraining order"), and enforceable by law. It signals that the person named in it must stay away from another person or persons, their home or workplace, find another place to live, and not expose children to violence. Some of these prohibitions are spelled out in separate cards, as in the one for "stay away from some people". "No humbugging" is a colloquial term used in Aboriginal English to refer to pestering another family person for money.

Other kinds of prohibition orders are designed to protect women from the more remote forms of molestation facilitated by mobile phones. Their intention cannot be

Figure 7: Some subsidiary cards (12/23) for *Orders and Rules.*

mistaken in straightforwardly worded cards such as "no sexy photos", "no trouble online".

Some legal orders and rules relate to the sharing of children after a family has split up. The relevant legal principle is that children should spend "substantial and significant time" with both parents, a legal term/concept illustrated in the red card with mother and father having equal numbers of days with the child. In practice the child will spend more time with one parent (the one they "live with" shown as pregnant mother and child under the same roof), but is encouraged to "spend time with" the other as a regular visitor (shown as kicking ball towards another adult). These phraseologies are relatively new terms of law, now used in Australia instead of "residence" and "contact" or "custody" and "access", the older legal terms. The fact that many contemporary terms used in Australian family law are subtechnical means they can be recognized (if not fully understood) through everyday language, and are not masked in unfamiliar latinate vocabulary.

Clusters of subsidiary terms in sets like those in Figures 5, 6 and 7 form the internal structure of the termbank, accessed through one of the eight keywords as the initial point of access. They are intended to enlarge the user's conception of relevant facets of family law, while meeting them at their point of need, in the specifics of their individual circumstances.

5 Source materials for the Indigenous termbank

The raw material of the Indigenous termbank (image and text for each card) was developed in a frontier project titled *Blurred Borders,*[8] established by Legal Aid-Western Australia in 2016. The project involved fieldworkers and linguists working with Indigenous people on the remote borders of Western Australia (WA) and the Northern Territory (NT). Family law there comes under different jurisdictions: the NT side is under Australian Federal Law, while on the WA side it is an independent court system; and differences in the related criminal law on either side of the border result in practical issues for people living and moving on both sides. The first crossborder issues addressed were bail and restraining orders, and then family violence, with child protection as a further focus. The *Blurred Borders* staff worked to produce sets of printed materials with images and text on the areas of concern, in the form of A4-sized discussion cards that were revised and enhanced in consultation with Indigenous groups. The project principal at Legal Aid (WA) gave Macquarie University researchers permission to use these cards (both images and the accompanying text) in developing an interactive online termbank for use by Indigenous people on the East Coast of Australia. The number of Indigenous people now living in Sydney is estimated to be

8 Its website is at https://blurredborders.legalaid.wa.gov.au (last access: 28 April 2025).

300,000, the largest community in Australia, though they maintain ties with their rural relatives in central and northwestern New South Wales (particularly Wiradjuri and Gomeroi/Kamilaroi country).

5.1 The Blurred Borders images

The images used in Easy-read termbank were created by a Northern Territory artist for the Blurred Borders project. They capture the meanings of the key terms in law from the human perspective, focusing on people wherever possible. They form an artistically consistent set, unlike the mix used in public information on Covid practices shown above (section 3.3). The images present iconic figures of individuals, in pairs (mother and child) or groups (the extended family) that represent social relationships. Professional persons are indicated by their standard equipment: the court's family consultant carrying a batch of files, the psychologist taking notes, the medical worker with stethoscope. The images thus help to identify the different kinds of people that Indigenous people may encounter in the legal procedures of family law, or by way of social support. There is minimal representation of the built environment, apart from the home (or angled home roof) used to symbolize shelter – except when its integrity is violated. The locations of the images are non-specific, applicable to Indigenous people living in either remote or urban settings. Images of furniture are used sparingly, to represent the roles of professional players in the processes of family law, such as the judge's desk, the witness box in court, and armchairs for consultation with the psychologist or counsellor. The generic design of the images facilitates their use in different parts of Australia, with different communities of Indigenous people. Their emphasis on human relations and family structures is essential to their culture wherever they live. The images allude to traditional ways of living even for Indigenous people in urban contexts, tapping into their often-expressed aspirations to "return to country", meaning the outback environments from which they emigrated to the city.

The images created by Blurred Borders cover terms for the most serious matters impacting on Indigenous people everywhere, i.e. family violence and child protection. To them we added some others to represent the terminology of different Australian states, for example the names of legal orders that differ from state to state, and varying nomenclature for child protection authorities. Research showed that terms relating to divorce and property settlements in family law rarely come before the courts with Indigenous people, so there was no need to add them to the set of terms already identified.

5.2 Using the Blurred Borders texts

The Blurred Borders cards came with texts written in plain language, like that of the Northern Territory *Plain English Legal Dictionary* introduced above (section 3.1). But Blurred Borders cards go much further in terms of simplicity of language and using the interactive grammar of spoken English. A key point is their use of the second person pronoun *"you"* instead of a strictly third person style with "he"/ "she"/ "it", "they". Using *"you"* provides a simple reference point for information, instead of the more abstract use of referential pronouns *"it"* and *"he"/"him"/"his"* as the notional person in the examples quoted above in section 3.1. The use of subordination in Blurred Borders texts is more straightforward, avoiding hypothetical subclauses with "when" and "if", and the modal verb "might", which are known to lack equivalents in Indigenous languages. Their uses of subordination are transparent, as in the relative clauses used to define the two kinds of terms on the card for the core card "court people": those for the professionals who work there, and those for the roles taken up by people in legal proceedings (see above, Figure 5). Subordinate clauses in the example below use "when" and "where" in their concrete meanings in the wording of the text attached to the figure.

Bail is the law that says where you will wait for your next court date.

When a judge or police officer decides to give you bail, you will sign a paper called a bail undertaking or bail paper.

This means you agree to come back to court on the day written on the bail paper, and to follow all of the rules written on the bail paper.

Explanatory text attached to Bail Undertaking (Figure 8).

The wording here lays out the significance of the term "bail-undertaking" for the Indigenous person. *Bail* is one of the most difficult terms to define, as shown in the strictly legal definition from the *Plain English Dictionary* discussed above in section 3.2. Definitions often suffer from "semantic fragmentation" within them (Lew 2015), and are thus challenging to L2 readers with limited vocabularies. The text shown here in Figure 8 shifts the focus onto the person impacted and implications for them, i.e. *you*: where you will continue to live, when you must return to the court, and the behavioral obligations you are accepting by signing the "bail undertaking" form. These points articulated in the original Blurred Borders text are thus part definition of the term, part explanation of its impacts. The explanatory language takes the user's point of view fully into account – especially their need to understand the agreement that they are entering into.

All these features of the texts in the Blurred Borders material were well-judged and required little adaptation. Some of the information regarding child protection did need to be paraphrased for use on the east coast to reflect the different agencies involved. Some explanations were too long for presentation in the online frames of the Easy-read termbank, and were trimmed down. Overly solid paragraphs were broken

Figure 8: Easy-read card for *Bail Undertaking.*

up so as to space out the different issues they address, often creating one-sentence paragraphs, as in the layout of information for "bail undertaking" in the text for Figure 8. This separate paragraphing of pieces of information is designed to mitigate the intimidating impact of solid paragraphs on unskilled readers – and to avoid the rather dense appearance of conventional dictionary entries.

Exceptions to the one-sentence paragraph policy was made for some terms with several important aspects to be explained. One such is the complex role of the professional psychologist in relation to family law clients. Two-sentence paragraphs are used in the text attached to Figure 9 to explain that the psychologist will be a sympathetic listener as well as asking strategic questions in the discussion. Likewise the fourth paragraph juxtaposes the important fact that topics discussed with the psychologist are kept confidential – except when they have serious implications that should be communicated with legal authorities.

A worker with training to understand the way that people think and act.

Your psychologist will help you to understand your feelings, like when you are really sad or angry. They will talk with you and ask you questions about your worries.

Your psychologist will help you become strong in your thinking and become a better mum or dad.

Psychologists keep most of the things people tell them secret. But sometimes they must tell the judge or child protection service.

Explanatory text attached to Figure 9.

Figure 9: Easy-read card for *Psychologist.*

The spacing between one-sentence paragraphs is important in enhancing the overall legibility of the text online – while maintaining the coherence of the overall narrative which is crucial to effective communication with Indigenous readers. For them the use of continuous narrative or "story" is the customary mode of exposition for all kinds of information exchange (Cooke 1998; Eades 2013). Narrative text is recommended for use in conveying medical information to Indigenous readers, for example, in areas of public health. Health information that is written around the person affected by ill health makes a coherent message, and interconnected stages of their experience can be understood as relevant aspects. The impersonal language of expository health information doesn't form coherent discourse for them. In the text attached Figure 9, the primary information focus in all four paragraphs is on the psychologist, but connected with Indigenous readers through upfront use of "your" in the two middle paragraphs. The legal information on Easy-read termpages is mediated in interpersonal language, and giving agency to the Indigenous reader in subject roles as far as possible.

5.3 Addition of audios to easy-read termpages

The addition of voiceovers and audio-recordings of the texts was an opportunity to employ Indigenous voice actors as authentic presenters of family law information to others in their communities. It raised sociolinguistic questions as to the balance of male and female voices to use in the termbank, since family law matters are raised by women in the great majority of court cases. But using female voices with most or all of the termpages could deter Indigenous men from accessing the termbank, and undermine its value for them. To avoid this we allocated equal numbers of male and female voices to all 8 keyterms and their subsidiary termpages. Within this overall distribution, we also took care to allocate female voices to terms involving women as victims of family violence, and male voices to the terms for serious legal matters, such as "bail undertaking", "exclusion order", and "lockup/jail/prison", to add the weight of a male voice to their implications.

The age of the voices was also a consideration in selecting the voice actors. Within Indigenous communities there is great respect for certain elders, known to all as "Uncle" or "Aunty", who gain those titles by virtue of their knowledge of Indigenous culture and traditions, as well as their contribution to Indigenous welfare. Their voices would therefore carry weight with the termbank users. On the other hand, we were advised that the demographic of those most in need of family law help, both women and men, was adults in the 20s-to-late-30s age bracket. So voices from that age bracket would come across as peers dealing with the same kinds of contemporary lived experience, and able to identify with users and counsel them appropriately. The voice (male or female) selected for the voiceover on each card was used also for the audio-recording of the text, to provide aural cohesion between the two.

6 Evaluation

The materials used in the Indigenous Easy-read termbank have been evaluated at several stages along the way. The Blurred Borders story cards were extensively and very positively reviewed during their development with field workers and Indigenous people in northern West Australia. An evaluation framework was put in place involving legal professionals, social service organizations and government departments.[9] On the east coast of Australia, and in conjunction with developing the Easy-read LawTermFinder termbank, the Blurred Borders cards were adapted in consultation with Legal Aid-NSW, with changes made especially in relation to legal procedures and the social service authorities in that state. The Indigenous termbank has been included as a resource on the Legal Aid-NSW website.

At Macquarie University we consulted further with staff at Wallumattagal legal office about the suitability of the Easy-Read termbank for their clients. They applauded the look and feel of the material as fit for purpose with Indigenous users, apart from the possibly negative reaction by some more advantaged Indigenous peo-

9 Details are provided at https://blurredborders.legalaid.wa.gov.au/evaluation (last access: 28 April 2025).

ple in the city, who felt that the simplified language of the text was beneath them. (Cf. the response to easy-read materials by some German respondents above, reported in section 3.3). An Indigenous teacher/researcher at Macquarie University pinpointed the lookup problem for Indigenous users with very limited reading skills, prompting the addition of voice-overs to each card. Further consultation will be undertaken with Indigenous teaching staff and students in different faculties of Macquarie University, to discuss extending the range of terms included in the termbank.

7 Implications for lexicography and terminography, and conclusions

The research and development project in user-based terminography discussed above has addressed a fundamental issue in accessing lexical information online. Users have to recognize and understand the entry term in its written form, and then be able to construct its meaning through connections with other written words (Gouws 2017). This demands more than minimum levels of reading proficiency from users of the matrix language, and alienates those without it – especially the most disadvantaged Indigenous citizens. The strategy used in the Easy-read LawTermFinder project is to prioritize a small number of keyterms with recognizable images and audio support, so as to establish the core concepts. They are then expanded through links with other related terms and concepts which users may encounter. The termbank provides users with an onomasiological way into its internal structures, and bypasses the upfront lexical demands of semasiologically structured lexicons.

All this is possible in online terminography, with all the digital media available: audio, verbal, graphic that facilitate access to specialized concepts for those with limited reading skills. In this project multimedia resources have been harnessed to meet the particular needs of Indigenous users. They would be available for use or adaptation to the needs of other disadvantaged groups with low levels of literacy – such as those with special communication needs or other physical or cognitive disabilities.

This Easy-read project has also shown the value of including subtechnical and semitechnical terms, especially those that use everyday language to express core legal terms and concepts (e.g. "stay away from" for "exclusion order"). Subtechnical terminology has a crucial role to play in expanding the conceptualizations of terms for those with minimal literacy and/or legal literacy. It affirms the value of an inclusive approach to the question of what count as terms in terminography.

Bibliography

Alberts, Marietta (2001): Lexicography versus terminology. In: Lexikos 11 (AFRILEX-reeks/series 11: 2001), 71–84.
Collins-Thompson, Kevyn (2014): Computational assessment of text readability. In: International Journal of Applied Linguistics 165, 97–135.
Cooke, Michael (1998): Aboriginal evidence in the cross-cultural court room. In: Eades, Diana (ed.): Language in evidence. Sydney: University of New South Wales Press, 55–96.
De Schryver, Gilles-Maurice/Prinsloo, Daniël (2011): Do dictionaries define on the level of their target users? In: International Journal of Lexicography 24:1, 5–28.
Ding, Jun/Peters, Pam/Smith, Adam (2015): The construction of online HealthTermFinder and its English-Chinese bilingualization. In: Proceedings of the Elex Conference 123–135.
Eades, Diana (2013): Aboriginal ways of using English. Canberra: Aboriginal Studies Press.
Family Law Council Report on Improving the Family Law System for Aboriginal and Torres Strait Islander Australians. (2012). Australian Government.
Fuertes-Olivera, Pedro/Arribas-Bano, Ascension (2008): Pedagogical specialised lexicography: the representation of meaning in English and Spanish business dictionaries. Amsterdam: John Benjamins
Fuertes-Olivera, Pedro/Tarp, Sven (2014): Theory and practice of online specialized dictionaries. Amsterdam: John Benjamins
Gouws, Rufus (2017). Dictionaries and access. In: Fuertes-Olivera, Pedro (ed.): The Routledge Handbook of Lexicography. London/New York: Routledge, 43–58.
Hansen-Schirra, Silvia, et al. (2020): Technologies for the translation of specialized texts into easy language. In: Hansen-Schirra, Silvia/Maass, Christiane (eds.): Introduction: Easy language research: text and user perspectives. Easy – Plain – Accessible, vol. 2. Berlin: Frank & Timme, 99–127.
Hansen-Schirra, Silvia/Maass, Christiane (2020) (eds.): Introduction: Easy language research: text and user perspectives. Easy – Plain – Accessible, vol. 2. Berlin: Frank & Timme.
Humbley, John (2017): Specialised dictionaries. In: Fuertes-Olivera, Pedro (ed.): The Routledge Handbook of Lexicography. London/New York: Routledge, 317–334.
Kröger, Janina (2020). Communicative barriers and cultural participation: a visit to a wildlife park as a multicodal accessible text. In: Hansen-Schirra, Silvia/Maass, Christiane (eds.): Introduction: Easy language research: text and user perspectives. Easy – Plain – Accessible, vol. 2. Berlin: Frank & Timme, 179–193.
Kwary, Deny (2018): The variables for drawing up the profile of dictionary users. In: Lexicography 4:2, 105–118.
Landau, Sidney (^{2}2001). Dictionaries: The art and craft of lexicography. Cambridge: Cambridge University Press.
Lemke, Jay (1998): Multiplying meaning: visual and verbal semiotics in scientific text. In: Martin, James/ Veel, Robert (eds.): Reading science: critical and functional perspectives on discourses of science. London et al.: Routledge, 1–19.
Lew, Robert (2015): Research into the use of online dictionaries. In: International Journal of Lexicography 28:2, 232–253.
Marello, Carla (1998): Hornby's bilingualized dictionaries. In: International Journal of Lexicography 11:4, 292–314.
Maass, Christiane/Hernandez-Garrido, Sergio (2020): Easy and plain language in audiovisual translation. In: Hansen-Schirra, Silvia/ Maass, Christiane (eds.): Introduction: Easy language research: text and user perspectives. Easy – Plain – Accessible, vol. 2. Berlin: Frank & Timme, 131–162.
Mateo, Jose (2017): The Alicante dictionaries. In Fuertes-Olivera, Pedro (ed): The Routledge Handbook of Lexicography. London/New York: Routledge, 421–437.

McArthur, Tom (2005): The first English learners dictionary: the Chinese dimension. In: English Today 21:1, 60–64.

Meyer, Ingrid/Mackintosh, Kristen (1996): Refining the terminographer's concept analysis methods. In: Terminology 3:1, 1–26.

McNamara, Danielle/Kinsch, Walter (1996): Learning from text: effects from prior knowledge and text coherence. In: Discourse Processes 22:3, 247–288.

McNamara, Danielle, et al. (2014): Automatic evaluation of text and discourse with Coh-Metrix. Cambridge: Cambridge University Press.

Oxford Advanced Learner's English-Chinese Dictionary = *OALDCE4* (2004). Oxford: Oxford University Press.

Parkinson, J., et al. (2023): Visual recontextualisation of meaning in science research articles and news-and -views articles. In: Iberica 48, 97–127.

Peters, Pam/Fernandez, Trinidad (2013): The lexical needs of ESP students in a professional field. In: Journal of English for Specific Purposes 32, 236–247.

Peters, Pam/Fernandez, Trinidad (2017): Lexicography and applied linguistics. In: Fuertes-Olivera, Pedro (ed.): Routledge Handbook of Lexicography. London/New York: Routledge, 105–122.

Peters, Pam/Kruger, Jan-Louis (2021): Readability of online health information for L1 and L2 Australians. In: Text and Talk 41:5–6, 787–812.

Plain English Legal Dictionary: Northern Territory Criminal Law. (2015). Aboriginal Resource and Development Services (ARDS) https://www.ards.com.au/resources-2/p/legal-dictionary-plain-english (last access: 28 April 2025).

Smith, Adam/Davis, Aleisha (2018): Disambiguating the use of common terms across related medical fields. In: Lexicography 4:1, 63–80.

Sweller, John (2002): Visualisation and instructional design. In: Science and Education Open Access, 1501–1510.

Tarp, Sven (2009): Reflections on lexicographical user research. In: Lexikos 19: 275–296.

Tarp, Sven (2013): What should we demand from an online dictionary for specialised translation? In: Lexicographica 29: 146–162.

Temmerman, Rita (2000): Towards new ways of terminology description. Amsterdam: John Benjamins.

Lauren W. Reed, Alison L. Mount, Alexandra Marley, Kira Davey, Mahesh White-Radhakrishnan, Grace Smith, Kaitlyn Lodewikus, Tamarind Meara

The AIATSIS Dictionaries Program: Supporting the strengthening of Australian Indigenous Languages

Abstract: In this paper, we describe the Australian Institute of Aboriginal and Torres Strait Islander Studies (AIATSIS) Dictionaries Program, which is part of the Australian government's effort to strengthen Aboriginal and Torres Strait Islander languages. We begin by situating the history of Aboriginal and Torres Strait Islander languages in Australia. This is followed by a description of the program's history, and a discussion of some challenges of dictionary making given the linguistic features of Aboriginal and Torres Strait Islander languages. We then take a deep dive into three dictionaries published via our program, focusing on a strong language, an endangered language, and a reawakening language.

Keywords: lexicography, Australian Aboriginal languages, Torres Strait Islander languages, dictionaries, language endangerment

Schlagwörter: Lexikographie, australische eingeborene Sprachen, Torres Strait Islander Sprachen, Wörterbücher, Sprachengefährdung

Lauren W. Reed, Australian Institute of Aboriginal and Torres Strait Islander Studies (AIATSIS) and Australian National University, Canberra, Australia, e-mail: lauren.reed@aiatsis.gov.au/lauren.reed@anu.edu.au

Alison L. Mount, Australian Institute of Aboriginal and Torres Strait Islander Studies (AIATSIS), Canberra, Australia

Alexandra Marley, Australian Institute of Aboriginal and Torres Strait Islander Studies (AIATSIS), Canberra, Australia

Kira Davey, e-mail: kira.davey@anu.edu.au

Mahesh White-Radhakrishnan, Sydney Conservatorium of Music, The University of Sydney, Australia

Grace Smith, Australian Institute of Aboriginal and Torres Strait Islander Studies (AIATSIS), Canberra, Australia

Kaitlyn Lodewikus, Australian Institute of Aboriginal and Torres Strait Islander Studies (AIATSIS), Canberra, Australia

Tamarind Meara, Australian Institute of Aboriginal and Torres Strait Islander Studies (AIATSIS), Canberra, Australia

https://doi.org/10.1515/9783112216644-009

1 A brief introduction to Aboriginal and Torres Strait Islander languages

Australia is home to a stunning amount of Indigenous linguistic diversity. The most commonly quoted figure for discrete languages at the time of British colonisation is more than 250 languages. This is a number based on the notion of a "language" as defined and distinguished by its mutual non-intelligibility from another. Another perspective is to consider the linguistic varieties that were salient to communities and thus often named, even if these were mutually intelligible. If counting known named varieties such as these, then the figure is usually posited closer to 600–800 (Koch/ Nordlinger 2014; Bowern 2023). These linguistic varieties include not just regionally delineated dialects but also codes that are indexed by social and cultural factors such as clan, gender, moiety or kinship.

Most Aboriginal and Torres Strait Islander spoken languages had small speaker populations; Simpson and Wigglesworth (2019) estimate that speaker numbers varied between 1,000 and 3,000. However, some languages may have been considerably smaller. Kayardild, spoken on Bentick Island and today with around 43 elderly speakers (Australian Bureau of Statistics 2021), likely never had more than around 150 speakers at its peak (Evans 2009). One of the current-day largest speaker populations is Bininj Kunwok, which has a relatively large speaker base of around 2,200 speakers (Australian Bureau of Statistics 2021).[1] This is bolstered by the variety's history of being a regional lingua franca (Evans 2003).

Estimating historic speaker population is difficult due to the high degree of multilingualism in Aboriginal and Torres Strait Islander populations. There was a high degree of multilingualism amongst Aboriginal and Torres Strait Islander peoples; this is still the case among people who speak their traditional language. People traditionally acquired the languages bequeathed to them via their matri- and patri-lineages, from exogamous marriages, through ties to country or clan-estates, and from interactions with neighbouring peoples. Traditions of exogamy and a prevailing ideology of viewing languages as being embedded in the land created the conditions for stable and extensive multilingualism (Evans 2009; Rumsey 1993). Further nurturing multilingualism is the ideologically-entrenched practice of continuing to acquire languages throughout one's life, with some linguistic varieties (particularly restricted respect registers such as "mother-in-law languages"[2]) not being mastered until well into adulthood (Evans 2003).

1 There are some significant limitations regarding Census data as it pertains to measuring language vitality and intergenerational transmission of Indigenous Australian languages. This issue is considered in the National Indigenous Languages Report (Commonwealth of Australia 2020) and Simpson et al. (2018).

2 Aboriginal and Torres Strait Islander communities often consider the relationship between a man and his mother-in-law (or a woman and her son-in-law) as particularly sensitive or taboo and contact between the two should be kept to a minimum. In instances where they need to refer to one another

In addition to spoken language diversity, Indigenous Australia is host to a significant degree of signed language diversity (Kendon 1988; Green 2023). Here, the distinction between an "alternate" and a "primary" sign language is relevant (as conceived by Kendon 1988: 4). A primary sign language is one that is used primarily by deaf people as their sole or main means of communication. An alternate sign language is one that is used mainly by hearing people as an alternative to speech; other alternate sign language examples worldwide include Plains Indian Sign Language (Davis 2010), Sawmill Sign Language (Meissner et al. 1975) and Monastic sign languages (Quay 2015). In Aboriginal and Torres Strait Islander communities, alternate sign languages were and are used for functions such as hunting, in ceremony, for politeness purposes, in avoidance relationships such as with one's mother- or son-in-law, or (in some communities) by widows observing a traditional period of silence during mourning. Alternate sign languages varied in complexity, with the most elaborate being found in Central Australia and Cape York (Kendon 1988; Green 2023). In some cases, such as among Yolngu people, alternate sign languages are used as the primary sign languages of deaf people in those communities (Maypilama/Adone 2013; Bauer 2014). For more information on Indigenous sign languages, see Ellis et al. (2018), Green/Wilkins (2014), Jorgensen/Green/Bauer (2021); for information on sign languages of the Torres Strait, see Reed (in press).

There is currently no identifiable linguistic family connection between Aboriginal and Torres Strait Islander languages and neighbouring languages of the Pacific or Asia; the only exception is Meriam Mir, a language of the eastern Torres Strait, which is a Trans-Fly language of Papua New Guinea. There are around 25 Aboriginal and Torres Strait Islander language families, with the distribution of these families quite geographically uneven (the classification of and number of languages in the non-Pama-Nyungan (nPN) bloc are debated). One of these families, Pama-Nyungan (PN), spans around seven-eighths of the continent, stretching from the Torres Strait south to Victoria and west to Western Australia (see Figure 1). The remaining 24-odd language families, often referred to as nPN, are found in the north-west of the continent. Linguists have been consumed by the quest to account for this intriguing distribution, and there is growing evidence that all the Australian languages are related at some point in the distant past (Evans 2020). The most recent attempt at reconstructing an ancestral language – Proto-Australian – by Harvey and Mailhammer (2024) puts the likely home region of this language somewhere in the "Top End" (see red boxed area in Figure 1).

or the other is within earshot, a special avoidance register is employed. This register often differs only in the lexical domain, with a one-to-one correspondence between everyday terms and respect terms (Walsh 2023). In Indigenous Australian alternate sign languages, "ordinary" signs may be modified in respectful contexts (Green/Wilkins 2014; Green 2019).

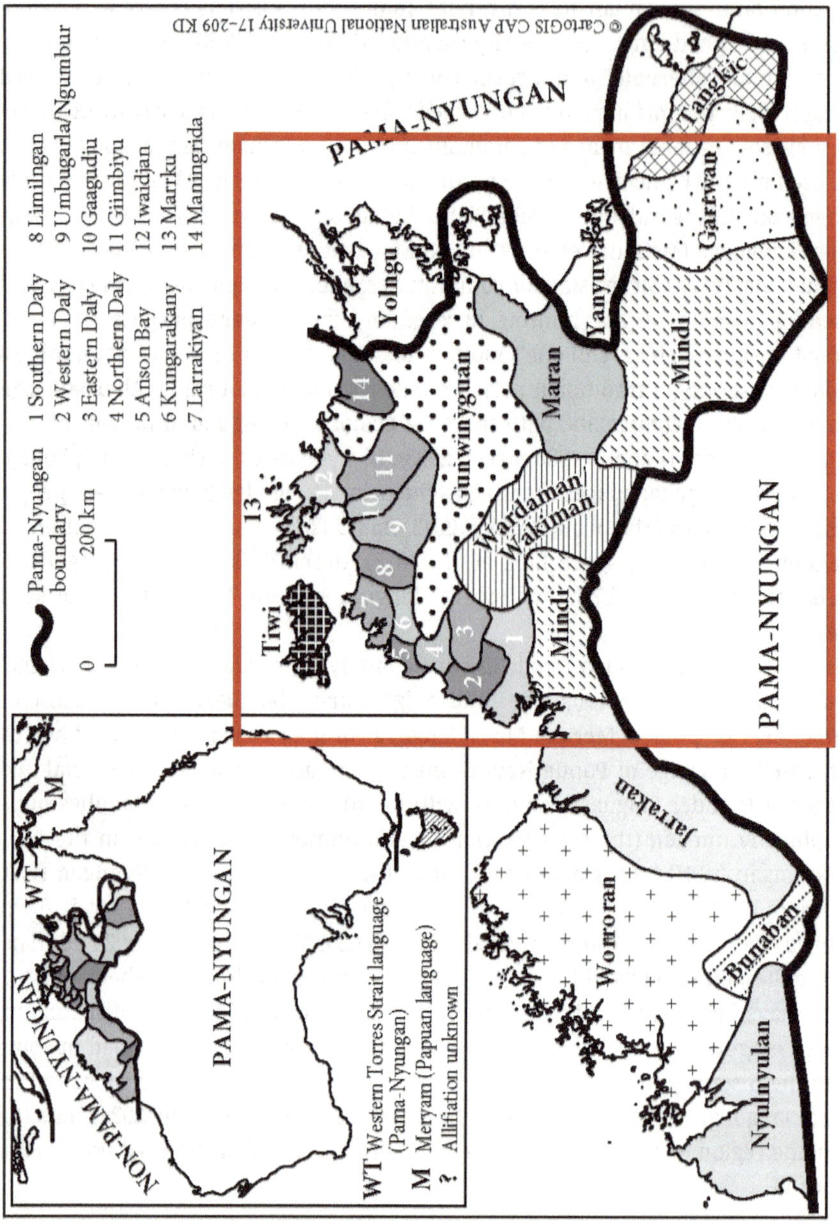

Figure 1: Map of non Pama-Nyungan languages and Pama-Nyungan languages. Adapted from Evans (2020: 119).

One group of languages that is still to be classified are the languages of lutruwita[3]/Tasmania. The exact number of languages spoken on the island is unknown, but estimates range from between 8 to 14 languages (Crowley/Dixon 1981; Bowern 2012). Our understanding of these languages is limited due to the forced relocation of Tasmanian Aboriginal people to missions and internment camps far from their traditional homelands, which resulted in major disruption to language transmission. The fragments of languages found in a handful of wordlists, songs and phrases jotted in colonisers' journals have unfortunately been insufficient to reconstruct any of the languages, but separate comparisons over the years of this data have all arrived at the same conclusion that Tasmanian languages are not related to the PN or nPN languages of the mainland (Crowley/Dixon 1981; Bowern 2012; Harvey/Mailhammer 2024). Furthermore, there is no evidence that these languages formed a single family (Bowern 2012), leaving us with a linguistic mystery that is unlikely to ever be solved. There are extensive and ongoing efforts to develop a new language of lutruwita, called palawa kani, which is derived from all the knowledge of the languages of the island (Reynolds/Sainty 2023).

One of the core functions of the Australian Institute of Aboriginal and Torres Strait Islander Studies (AIATSIS) is to report regularly to the Australian Government on the situation and status of Aboriginal and Torres Strait Islander culture and heritage. One way the Institute does this is by regularly carrying out the National Indigenous Languages Survey (or NILS). The NILS provides up-to-date information about the language vitality of Aboriginal and Torres Strait Islander languages. The most recent 2018–2019 NILS ("NILS3") found that only 123 of the more than 250 original languages are still being spoken (Commonwealth of Australia 2020). Of these, the vast majority are only spoken by older people; only 12 traditional languages are still being learned by children as a first language (Commonwealth of Australia 2020: 9). Intergenerational transmission is widely cited as the most crucial factor in ensuring a language is strong into the future (Fishman 1991; UNESCO Culture Sector 2011; Lee/Van Way 2016). By this measure, the vast majority of Aboriginal and Torres Strait Islander languages are in a devastating situation where, without major action, they will no longer be passed on to the next generation. As a result, Australia now has the "dubious distinction" (Meakins 2021 as cited in ANU 2021) of one of the highest rates of language loss in the world (Bromham et al. 2022; Simons 2019).

The decline of Indigenous languages is sometimes described as "loss". However, the use of this term minimises the deliberate silencing of Aboriginal and Torres Strait Islander languages as either a directly intended consequence or seemingly unintentional byproduct of government actions and policies. It is more accurate to say that Aboriginal and Torres Strait Islander peoples were dispossessed of their languages, or as Kevin O'Keefe (1992: 53–54) puts it, that their languages were stolen:

3 There is a convention of not capitalising words in palawa kani, the reconstructed language of lutruwita, with exception of names of people, tribes, spirit entities, and cultural objects (Reynolds/Sainty 2023).

> Now some white people will try to tell you that you haven't got language – that you've lost your language. Well we didn't lose our languages; they got taken off us. Hundreds of them – stolen.

In the next section, we give a brief overview of the contextual history that has led to the current state.

2 Contextual history of the current situation

British colonisation of Australia commenced in 1788. At first, the official attitude towards Australia's Indigenous peoples was relatively benign. Governor Arthur Phillip (1787 in Watson 1914), the first Governor of the new State of New South Wales (NSW), gave official orders that:

> You are to endeavour by every possible means to open an Intercourse with the ~~Savages~~ Natives and to conciliate their affections, enjoining all Our Subjects to live in amity and kindness with them. And if any of Our Subjects shall wantonly destroy them, or give them any unnecessary Interruption in the exercise of their several occupations . . . It is our Will and Pleasure that you do cause such offenders to be brought to punishment according to the degree of the Offence.

However, as British settlement began to expand past Sydney Cove and skirmishes ensued, the colonial administration took a more aggressive attitude towards Aboriginal and Torres Strait Islander peoples across Australia. The expansion of pastoral settlement led to Aboriginal and Torres Strait Islander peoples being either forced off or forcibly removed from their traditional Countries, or in other cases, massacred. This period between 1788 and the 1920s is known as the "Frontier Wars" and was characterised by co-ordinated resistance from Aboriginal peoples to the British invasion.[4] There is scarce information about any language exchange during the Frontier War period but it was likely to be unequal and sporadic as the decimation and dispersion of Aboriginal communities and culture would have been accompanied by shifts towards English as the language of power, and the emergence of contact varieties (see, e.g., Troy 1990).

From 1814, missions began to be established across Australia. German missionaries established some of the earliest in Australia, including Wellington Valley (north-west of Sydney) in 1832, Piltawodli in current-day Adelaide in 1838, and Zion Hill near Brisbane, also in 1838 (Ganter 2018). Some missionaries took an interest in learning languages, particularly as a means of communicating the Gospel. At the Piltawodli "Native Location", missionaries from the Dresden Mission Society established Australia's first monolingual Aboriginal language school (Amery 2018). Kaurna children were instructed in their own language, and hymns and Bible passages were translated into

---

4 For more on the Frontier Wars, see Connor (2010), Watson (1982) and the Colonial Frontier Massacres in Australia, 1788 to 1930 map (Ryan et al. 2017–2022).

Kaurna. The mission closed in 1845 and subsequent government policies led to Kaurna people being dispossessed of their language, but language documentation from this period (chiefly that recorded by Teichelmann and Schurmann [1840]) has formed the basis for today's Kaurna language revival.

By 1911, all Australian states and territories apart from Tasmania had some form of Aboriginal "protection act". These were laws ostensibly aimed at protecting the welfare of Aboriginal peoples but in practice, the laws controlled their movements, freedoms and resources. Arguably, Tasmania did not have need for a specific act, because by that time, colonisation of Tasmania had thoroughly devastated the Indigenous population and by the late 1870s, Tasmanian Aboriginal peoples had been installed on a single government reserve at Cape Barren Island. These "protection" acts included the power to compel Aboriginal peoples to move onto missions and reserves. These institutions controlled the lives of the Aboriginal peoples living there, such as their movement in and out of the reserve, their ability to gain employment, and even their ability to marry. In many cases, the reserves included dormitories where parents were encouraged or forced to place their children. In some cases, the mission manager would be the legal guardian of the children on the mission, not their own parents living on the mission (AIATSIS 2022). In Queensland, Western Australia (WA), South Australia (SA) and the Northern Territory (NT), laws were passed that made the "Chief Protector" the legal guardian of every Aboriginal child in their state or territory – not their parents (Human Rights and Equal Opportunities Commission 1997).

In some cases, language use was encouraged on missions. At Ernabella Mission in the A̲nangu Pitjantjatjara and Yankunytjatjara Lands, Dr Charles Duguid demanded that "There was to be no compulsion nor imposition of our way of life . . . nor deliberate interference with tribal custom . . . [Mission staff] must learn the tribal language . . . and all teaching for the first years should be in Pitjantjatjara tongue" (Duguid 1972: 115–116).[5] At many missions, however, the use of language was actively discouraged and/or punished. Dickson (2006) recounts an experience told to him by a Ngandi speaker in Arnhem Land (northern Australia):

> He told me that one time, his teacher heard him speaking his language, Ngandi. His teacher took him into the store room, got a stick and belted him 15 times. After that, his teacher made him write lines. He had to write 50 times, "I must not speak Language at school." He reckons he was about 8 or 10 years old at the time . . .

Abuse for speaking one's traditional language(s) was widespread across Australia. In his biography, Muruwari man Jimmie Barker (1977: 123) recounted the effect verbal abuse had on the use of Muruwari and Ngemba languages at Brewarrina Mission in northern NSW:

5 The second author is the great-grandchild of Dr Duguid.

> I have noticed that when people were talking to one another in Muruwari or Ngemba the white man who heard them would immediately jeer at "old Jacky-Jacky speaking in his dirty lingo".[6] On many occasions I have noticed that the dark people would just stop talking when a white person approached, as they did not want to appear foolish.

At the Roper River Mission, children living in the mission dormitories shifted to an English-lexified contact variety, which would later go on to be called Roper River Kriol. While their parents had been traditionally multilingual in several local languages, the children had not yet had the ability to become so (Harris 1993). The need to communicate with one another, as well as the punishment if they were heard speaking any Aboriginal language (as mentioned above by Dickson), led to children being dispossessed of their traditional languages (see also Rhydwen 1993; Dickson 2015).

Another shocking and devastating period in which government policies decimated Aboriginal and Torres Strait Islander languages was what is known as the Stolen Generations. From the mid-1800s to as late as the 1970s, various government policies authorised the removal of Aboriginal children from their parents. The children who were most targeted were those of mixed Indigenous and non-Indigenous heritage. Children were placed in institutions ("children's homes") where they were subject to physical, sexual and emotional abuse. They were also actively prevented from speaking their own languages:

> Y'know, I can remember we used to just talk lingo. [In the Home] they used to tell us not to talk that language, that it's devil's language. And they'd wash our mouths with soap. We sorta had to sit down with Bible language all the time. So it sorta wiped out all our language that we knew (Confidential evidence 170 in Human Rights and Equal Opportunity Commission [1997])

The Stolen Generations era had a devastating impact on intergenerational transmission of languages. This was due to the "brute force" of removing children from their parents, but also the inculcation in stolen children that Indigenous ways were inferior, and should be left behind in order to assimilate and become a "proper Australian".

Even in situations where Aboriginal people were not removed from their country and families were not broken up, people were punished for speaking language. Wiradjuri Elder Stan Grant Senior recalls this example (as told to the New York Times):

> "My grandfather [Mr. Johnson] was a Wiradjuri elder," he said, and was anxious to pass along the culture. "But he was arrested after he called to me in Wiradjuri to come home from the park. 'Barray yanha, barray yanha,' 'Come quickly,' he called out" . . . After the arrest, Mr. Johnson, who spoke seven languages, refused to speak Wiradjuri in public. "He was a linguist with enormous respect for his own people and culture," said Mr. Grant . . . "But he told me, 'Things are different now.' He would only speak his language in the bush. (Grant 2016, as cited in Innis 2016)

6 "Lingo" is an Aboriginal English term that refers to traditional Aboriginal languages. Aboriginal English is a cover term for a range of acrolectal, English-lexified contact languages.

This kind of treatment led to many parents and grandparents consciously or unconsciously ceasing transmission of language to children in an effort to improve their prospects and experiences in the majority and power-wielding white society. In some cases, however, recognising the loss of intergenerational transmission of their language, speakers went to great lengths to document their own language for the sake of future generations, with little resources to support them and often in the face of enormous threats of violence (Baird 1959; Barker 1968; Lazarus 2022; Oates 1990; Wafer/Turpin 2017 inter alia). In a further devastating blow to Indigenous Australian languages, in 2008, the NT government effectively dismantled bilingual education in the Territory (Simpson et al. 2009). This has led to a loss of both domains of use and prestige for Aboriginal languages in Central and Northern Australia, with an associated decline in their rates of intergenerational transmission.

Even while dispossession was ongoing, various significant events starting from the 1960s began to change the future for Australian Indigenous languages. The Australian Institute of Aboriginal Studies (AIAS) (now the AIATSIS) was established in 1964 with an aim to record Aboriginal and Torres Strait Islander culture and heritage. This reflected the Australian government's burgeoning interest in acknowledging and caring for Indigenous heritage, although the focus of the AIAS was at the time to record only "traditional" cultures before they "perished", and for Indigenous people to be positioned as "informants" rather than participants or contributors to the research (AIATSIS n.d.). Over the intervening 60 years, the Institute now known as AIATSIS has majority Indigenous control via its senior leadership and Council (Lambert 2011). The Institute is now focused on creating a world in which Aboriginal and Torres Strait Islander peoples' rights, knowledge, cultures, and stories are recognised, respected, celebrated, and valued.

The civil rights movement in the 1960s and 1970s saw significant gains for Aboriginal and Torres Strait Islander peoples, including the land rights movement which saw much traditional lands handed back to Indigenous people. This culminated in the 1992 Mabo Decision, which overturned the concept of *terra nullius* in Australia, the legal term that had been used to fictitiously claim that the land belonged to no one before the arrival of the British colony. The Court also determined that all Indigenous people in Australia had lived with rights to their land with their own laws and customs prior to colonisation and thus had prior rights to the land, which led to the encoding of "native title" into Australian law. This allowed many Aboriginal and Torres Strait Islander people to practice self-determination for the first time since colonisation began.

The first "language centre", the Kimberley Language Resource Centre, was established in 1984. As of September 2024, there are 25 federally funded language centres across Australia, all of which support one or more languages local to their area (Indigenous Languages and Arts 2024). In some parts of Australia, Indigenous communities have supported their own language work for decades (or supplemented the support received from governments), in many cases dedicating personal or business funds or using resources related to native title claims, such as royalty agreements with mining companies and income from land use agreements and cultural heritage surveys. For example, the Warlpiri Education Training Trust was set up in 2005 using royalties from the Newmont Tanami gold mine. It supports bilingual education and produces Warlpiri language resources, among other educational outcomes (Commonwealth of Australia 2024). On the east coast, the Giingana Gumbaynggirr Freedom school is partly funded by philanthropic sources and partly funded by an eco-tourism enterprise run by Bularri Muurlay Nyanggan Aboriginal Corporation (Naylor 2024).

Beginning in the 1970s, many Aboriginal communities who had been dispossessed of their languages began to embark on a process of language revitalisation (Hobson 2018; Gale 2023). The Ngarrindjeri community of SA began their language revival journey in 1985. For them, many people on Raukkan Mission still remembered significant amounts of language and spoke this intermingled with their local variety of Aboriginal English (Gale 2020). There are now several Ngarrindjeri dictionaries (the second and third editions published with support of AIATSIS) as well as learning resources. The language is taught at primary and high schools in SA both as the selected "Language Other Than English" (LOTE) and in other mother tongue or Aboriginal Studies programs (Gale n.d.).

The Ngunnawal people of Canberra commenced their language revival journey in earnest in 2014, supported by AIATSIS, whose main offices are on Ngunnawal country. Unlike the Ngarrindjeri, the Ngunnawal had only little recollection of language words (although after language work began, they did realise that they recalled more language than they had thought). As such, Ngunnawal language revival has mainly been carried out by reviewing historical texts where Ngunnawal language had been recorded and reconstructing the language from these sources. By 2019, AIATSIS' third NILS found that there were at least 31 communities actively engaged in language reawakening practices and at least 123 Aboriginal and Torres Strait Islander language varieties that are in use or being revitalised (Commonwealth of Australia 2020: 9).

The *Our Land Our Languages* report was commissioned by the Australian government and released in 2012. The report included several recommendations concerned with Aboriginal and Torres Strait Islander languages, including that there be an increase in funding for languages, that bilingual education be supported, and that a National Indigenous Interpreter Service be established (Commonwealth of Australia 2012). Although not all the recommendations have been taken up at the time of writing, this still represented a huge about-face considering policies just 50 years earlier had been focused on assimilating Aboriginal and Torres Strait Islander peoples to a European, Anglophone, homogenised "Australian" culture.

In 2016, AIATSIS was approached by Prime Minister Malcolm Turnbull to deliver an Acknowledgement of Country when handing down the 2016 *Closing the Gap Report.*[7]

7 "Closing the Gap" refers to a suite of government responses aimed at closing the many gaps between Indigenous and non-Indigenous Australians, such as in measures of disadvantage including incarceration rates and birth weights.

After training by the Ngunnawal community and AIATSIS and with the appropriate cultural permissions, Prime Minister Malcolm Turnbull delivered an Acknowledgment of Country in Ngunnawal on February 10, 2016 (Gordon 2016). This represented the first time a Prime Minister had spoken an Indigenous Australian language in a parliamentary speech (Battin 2020). In a further positive development, in 2017, the NSW Government established the NSW Aboriginal Languages Trust with the objective of providing a "focused, coordinated and sustained effort in relation to Aboriginal language activities at local, regional and State levels". To date (October 2024), this is the only legislation in Australia that "acknowledge[s] that Aboriginal people are the custodians of Aboriginal languages and have the right to control their growth and nurturing", and that "as a result of past Government decisions Aboriginal languages were almost lost, but they were spoken in secret and passed on through Aboriginal families and communities" (*Aboriginal Languages Act 2017 No 51* [NSW]).

In response to the United Nations International Decade of Indigenous Languages (IDIL, 2022–2032), the Australian government established an Indigenous "Directions Group" to provide guidance on Australia's activities in response to the Decade. This culminated in the production of *Voices of Country* (First Languages Australia and Commonwealth of Australia 2023), Australia's action plan for IDIL. Most recently, the new National Agreement on Closing the Gap includes a target that is specifically dedicated to supporting the strengthening of Australian Indigenous languages. The Australian government has established a Languages Policy Partnership (the "LPP") made up of five Indigenous peak organisations, five independent Aboriginal and Torres Strait Islander members and nine representatives from federal, state and territory governments. The LPP is responsible for driving new language-related policy and legislation. There is still much progress to be made in terms of the Australian government's commitment to changing the story for Indigenous Australian languages, but in many areas, the tide seems to indeed be turning.

3 The AIATSIS Dictionaries Program

The AIATSIS is the only national Australian institution exclusively focused on preserving and promoting Aboriginal and Torres Strait Islander cultural heritage. The AIATSIS delivers a range of programs and services in service of these functions. The Institute cares for a collection of more than one million items of Aboriginal and Torres Strait Islander culture and heritage including books, audio, photographs, manuscripts, moving image, and art and object material. It also has a publishing arm, Aboriginal Studies Press (ASP), which publishes scholarly works, children's books, biographies, general interest books on topics relating to Australia's first peoples, and dictionaries.

The AIATSIS Dictionaries Program is a key activity through which the Institute supports the strengthening of Aboriginal and Torres Strait Islander languages. The AIATSIS first supported a dictionary project between 1987 to 1989 (the "AIAS National Lexicography Project"). This project was funded by the Australian Bicentennial Authority and had two aims: to support the production of dictionaries and to establish an archive of machine-readable data files (MRDFs) of language materials. Primary outputs included the digitisation and compilation of various lexical material collected in Western Australia, the compilation of a Kukatja dictionary, and the scanning of the translated Diyari dictionary (Nash/Simpson 1989). At the conclusion of the project, AIAS held over 40 megabytes of MRDFs of language materials, including wordlists in over 100 languages, texts in 10 languages, grammars and grammatical sketches of 10 languages, and substantial dictionaries for 24 languages (see Nash/Simpson 1989). A subsequent 1992–1994 "AIATSIS Aboriginal Dictionaries Project" supported lexicographical work on 52 languages. A condition of the 1992–1994 project was that primary data must be accessioned into the AIATSIS Aboriginal Studies Electronic Data Archive (ASEDA) so that files could be accessed and reused in the future (Thieberger 1995). Dictionaries published via the program include *The Sydney Language* by Ngarigu linguist Prof. Jakelin Troy (1993).

In between established programs, AIATSIS has supported the production of dictionaries via philanthropic support through the AIATSIS Foundation Dictionaries Fund (the AIATSIS Foundation being a registered charity established in 2014). In 2016, the AIATSIS Foundation supported an update and reprint for Troy's *The Sydney Language,* in part thanks to a donation from the Preatures music group (AIATSIS 2019). Following the success of the Sydney dictionary reprint, the AIATSIS Foundation continued to work to attract further funding. Around 2017, the Foundation secured funding for the publication of a Warlpiri dictionary, which would be the culmination of some 60 years of work on the language, incorporating the contributions of many hundreds of speakers and work by celebrated American linguist Prof. Ken Hale (see Laughren, this volume).[8]

Since 2018, the National Indigenous Australians Agency has funded what was known as the "Indigenous Languages Preservation: Dictionaries Project". The project has been extended twice and current funding runs to 2025; at the time of publication, negotiations are proceeding for an extension to 2027. In 2024, the project was renamed the "AIATSIS Dictionaries Program" to appropriately reflect the program's success and longevity. So far, the program has published 22 dictionaries from 21 diverse language contexts (including languages in revival, and languages still acquired by children as a first language) and from a vast spread of geographic locations (see Figure 2). As of August 2025, four dictionaries are in press or negotiating funding agreements.

8 The authors thank Rita Metzenrath, AIATSIS, for valuable discussions to inform this section.

Unlike the earlier two dictionaries programs, which supported the linguistic labour required to build lexical databases which could eventually become dictionaries, the AIATSIS Dictionaries Program recognises that in many cases, a community has an extensive language database (perhaps stored in a text file, Microsoft Excel, FieldWorks Language Explorer [SIL 2022], or another software) but does not have funding to turn the database into a physical publication. In other cases, a dictionary may exist, but it has gone out of print and there are no funds to re-publish the work (let alone update it). As such, the program supplies funds for publishing costs, including copy-editing, proofreading, indexing, design and typesetting, artwork licenses, map production, printing and distribution. Applicants do not need to publish through ASP; they are free to nominate their publisher of choice. AIATSIS also does not seek copyright of the resulting dictionary. To be accepted into the program, compilers must demonstrate community support for and involvement in the dictionary, most usually by letters of support from Aboriginal or Torres Strait Islander community-controlled organisations from the relevant language group. The program allows for a generous number of free copies to be produced and made available to local schools, libraries, and other community groups. The AIATSIS also supports a community launch event.

Each dictionary is assessed against two major criteria: (1) quality and (2) significance. A dictionary's quality is demonstrated by factors such as richness of entries (such as inclusion of scientific names of plants and animals, archival source, or speaker), number of entries, ease of use, and adequacy of front matter. However, as we will see in Section 5, quality is assessed relative to the amount of language material a community has at its disposal. A dictionary's significance is demonstrated by its ability to endure, its completeness, and its level of community support and engagement. Dictionary applications are assessed by an internal panel made up of members of the AIATSIS Centre for Australian Languages (ACAL), and then by two external expert assessors who are members of the AIATSIS Languages Advisory Committee (LAC) (an internal committee which provides strategic advice to the AIATSIS Chief Executive Officer on language matters). For dictionaries published by ASP, once a final manuscript is submitted to the publisher, the time to publication is often around 18 months. This is because the copyediting, indexing and typesetting for dictionaries are complex and there is a limited number of copyeditors, indexers and typesetters in Australia with experience in publishing dictionaries and appropriate knowledge of Australian languages. Two copies of the published dictionary are archived in the AIATSIS collection.

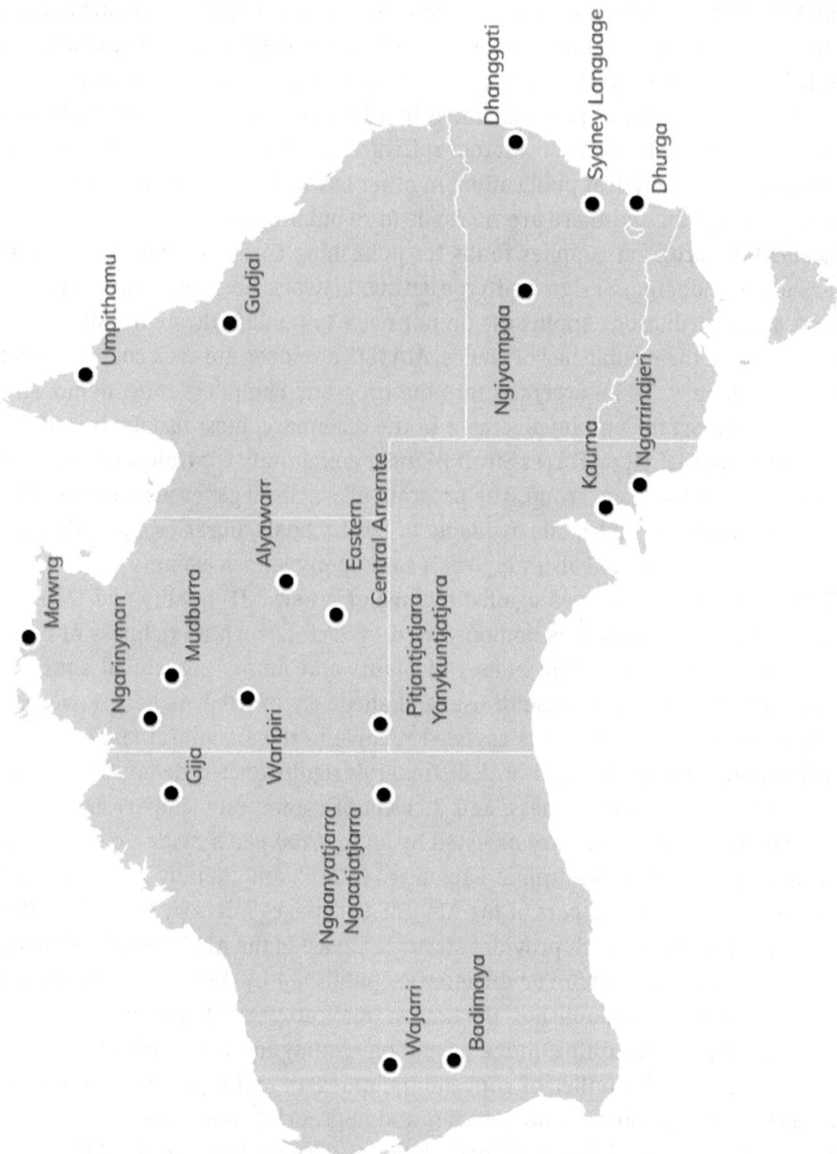

Figure 2: 22 dictionaries in 21 languages have been published through the AIATSIS Dictionaries Program (2018–2025) (Morrobolam and Ngardi not shown on map). Two dictionaries have been published for the Ngarrindjeri language: a 'concise' and a 'complete' dictionary.

4 Writing dictionaries of Aboriginal and Torres Strait Islander languages

In addition to securing funding, there are a number of challenges to surmount when creating dictionaries for Aboriginal and Torres Strait Islander languages, many of which have been detailed in Thieberger (2015). Many Australian languages are agglutinating or, in the case of some nPN languages, polysynthetic. Consider the following word from Kundjeyhmi (a variety of Bininj Kunwok): *Abanyawoyhwarrkahmarne-kanjkinjeng*. We can analyse it like so:

(1) *Aban-yawoyh-warrkah-marne-kanj-kinje-ng*
1m>3pl-again-wrong-BEN-meat-cook-PP
'I cooked the wrong meat for them again'
(Evans 2003: 1)

Here, three arguments are marked on the verb stem, *-kinje*, including an incorporated noun ("meat"), as well as modifiers "again" and "wrong". Deciding on a head word in such instances is a challenge for lexicographers, especially when speakers may not find uninflected entries intuitive or comprehensible. The Mawng dictionary (Singer et al. 2021), published as part of the AIATSIS Dictionaries Program, tackles complex verbal morphology by presenting headword verbs complete with the present tense third person masculine gender subject and object prefix:

(2) *Kini-wu-n*
3MA>3MA-hit-NP
'He hits him'
(Singer et al. 2021: 2)

Another very common feature of Aboriginal and Torres Strait Islander languages that complicates dictionary making is the compound verb. A compound verb typically consists of a "coverb", which contains the semantic information, followed by a "light verb" which takes on the grammatical information. In the following example from the Gija dictionary, the coverb *berdij* combines with the light verb *-ni* to mean "get up":

(3) *Berdij ngini-ni*
Get.up 3MA.PAST-say/do
'He got up'
(Kofod et al. 2022: 68)

A single coverb may combine with a number of light verbs (often a limited set of broad actions such as "put", "come/go", "bring/take", "be/become") to yield slightly different meanings. The Gija dictionary has addressed this feature by listing every coverb + light verb combination in English under separate coverb headwords. For example, *berdij* is repeated as a headword five times for each of the five light verbs with which it combines (see Section 5.2 for more on the Gija dictionary).

Representing linguistic variation is another hurdle for dictionary makers in Australia. The Warlpiri Encyclopaedic Dictionary aims to be as comprehensive as possible to account for the variation in dialects, registers and the language background of the user (see Laughren, this volume). One way the dictionary accounts for this variation is by including variants from different dialects as headwords and indicating the communalect of origin in the entry (Laughren 2022). While all languages have variation, the difficulty in Australia is that it is often the "dialectal" variety that is named and culturally salient to Aboriginal and Torres Strait Islander communities, not the broader language to which their variety belongs. This means dictionary creators need to decide whether to create a pan-dialectal dictionary under an exonymic umbrella title or to centre community perspectives on language and focus on just one or a group of varieties for their dictionary.

Finally, we must consider whom the dictionaries are for. From the start, the first vocabularies in Australia were bilingual, typically between an Aboriginal and Torres Strait Islander language and English,[9] with the language of explanation being in the European language, not the Indigenous one. These first wordlists and vocabularies made were usually produced by Christian missionaries to aid their work in translating the Bible and converting local communities (Simpson 1993). The focus, therefore, was on ensuring that Western concepts could be expressed in Aboriginal and Torres Strait Islander languages, rather than attempting to explore and document the rich cultural nuances and ecological expertise that arose after millennia of living on this land. The rise in interest in historical linguistics in the 19th century was another reason for making wordlists and vocabularies, with philologists searching for cognates in order to demonstrate a common heritage of Australian languages (Koch 1983; Simpson 1993).

Over the decades, dictionary-making has moved towards development by and for the community (see the examples in Sections 5.1–5.3). Recent Indigenous language dictionaries provide a more culturally sensitive and reliable account of the language and culture by now referring to natural example sentences rather than contrived ones from Biblical translations; including multimodal practices such as 'hand signs' or lip-pointing; representing Indigenous epistemologies of the natural world rather than relying on western taxonomic concepts (e.g. McConvell/Day/Black 1983 and the classification of fish in the Meriam Mir dictionary); and describing important cultural systems via, for example, inclusion of kinship and moiety charts. Appreciating systems like these is crucial to navigating elements of a language, such as dyadic kin terms, and knowing when to employ a certain register with restricted kin.

9 Sometimes the translated language was German, e.g. Diyari-German dictionary by J.G. Reuther (see Austin 2024) and the Arrernte-German dictionary by Carl Strehlow (see Kenny 2018).

On a final note, the advancement of technology has meant that print dictionaries can link to online audiovisual material including archival audio recordings of now deceased fluent speakers (where culturally appropriate) or new audiovisual material produced to support language learning in a revival context (see *Yaru!* in Section 5.3). For dictionaries of languages which are no longer spoken fluently, this is of great value to community members who may be concerned about mispronunciations deriving from the misinterpretation from the written word (see Mount et al. 2024). In other cases, QR codes link to video recordings which can inform users on non-spoken elements of language such as sign, gesture, gaze and lip-pointing. The *Mudburra to English Dictionary* (Green/Green/Hamilton-Holloway/Meakins/Osgarby/Pensalfini 2019), published by the AIATSIS Dictionaries Program, provides QR codes that link to videos of community members producing traditional "hand signs".

5 Three case studies of dictionaries supported by the AIATSIS Dictionaries Program

5.1 Pitjantjatjara/Yankunytjatjara to English Dictionary

Pitjantjatjara and Yankunytjatjara are two closely related dialects of a language which has the largest geographical reach in Australia. That language has no single endonym but is called the "Western Desert Language" by linguists (Douglas 1964; Miller 1971 inter alia). It is a PN language (see Section 1). The Western Desert language is spoken in a huge geographical region in the arid lands in the central west of Australia, spanning, together with the Warnman language, some 600,000 square kilometres (Babinski/Rojas-Berscia/Bowern 2023: 893). It is one of the strongest Indigenous languages in Australia today, with several thousand speakers. Children are still robustly acquiring Western Desert varieties as their first language. The Western Desert language is spoken in three Australian states. Much educational policy is set at a state level and as such the amount of bilingual education in Western Desert languages differs between those states. Pitjantjatjara and Yankunytjatjara are spoken either side of the NT/SA border, to its westernmost side. Many Aboriginal people in this region live in remote or very remote towns, while many also live in one of Australia's largest regional towns, Mparntwe (Alice Springs).

This dictionary is the fourth edition of sorts, although it is technically referred to as the "revised second edition, updated". The compilation is by Prof. Cliff Goddard, who compiled the original dictionary in 1987, and has been updated by Dr Rebecca Defina. Both are non-Indigenous linguists with longstanding connections with Yankunytjatjara (Goddard) and Pitjantjatjara (Defina) communities. The dictionary is published by the Institute for Aboriginal Development (IAD) Press. IAD is based in Mparntwe (Alice Springs) and has a long history of supporting Aboriginal and Torres

Strait Islander language work, as well as the training of Aboriginal and Torres Strait Islander peoples as language teachers. Yami Lester acted as consultant for the dictionary. Yami was blinded by nuclear fallout as a result of nuclear bomb testing conducted by the British and Australian governments on Yankunytjatjara lands. He went on to become a prominent advocate for his people and an anti-nuclear advocate (see Lester 1993). His daughter, Karina Lester, is a member of the LPP through her responsibilities as co-manager of the Mobile Language Team (one of two federally funded language centres in SA) (see Section 2).

Interestingly, the dictionary has very little front matter when compared to the other dictionaries profiled below. Overall, the dictionaries published by the AIATSIS Dictionaries Program that have the most front matter tend to be dictionaries for languages which are in a revival context; that is, where people are learning to speak the language again after a period of not having been used for some time. That extensive front matter often includes notes on grammar, as well as songs and maps. The purpose of the Pitjantjatjara/Yankunytjatjara dictionary may be somewhat different, in that it primarily supports children's acquisition of literacy in their language/s. That is, children who have acquired Pitjantjatjara/Yankunytjatjara as a first language do not need to be instructed in the grammar of their language, but they (and their teachers) do require a dictionary as a resource for the accurate spelling of words. Separate published learner's guides also exist, rather than the grammar needing to be included in the dictionary itself (e.g. Eckert/Hudson 1988; 2010).

In the reproduction of the preface to the original 1987 edition, Goddard states that:

> . . . this is an attempt at a true dictionary of Pitjantjatjara and Yankunytjatjara. It is not merely a 'word list', but attempts to set out the full range of meanings that a word or expression may have, along with grammatical, cultural and usage information. (Goddard/Defina 2020: viii)

Accordingly, the dictionary entries are significantly rich. Each head word has a part of speech. This may seem trivial but is often not possible in the case of Aboriginal languages in a state of revival (see Section 5.3 on *Yaru!* below). The entries include dialectal variants (if these exist), synonyms, and a definition. Example sentences are given, which have been drawn from Goddard's fieldnotes and recordings, as well as from "oral literature" and newspapers published in Pitjantjatjara/Yankunytjatjara country (Goddard/Defina 2006: ix). Like many Western Desert languages, Pitjantjatjara and Yankunytjatjara have ceremonial registers (Kral et al. 2019), which are only used in closely guarded cultural contexts and not included in the dictionary. Other entries are marked with an '[?]', presumably to indicate they should be checked or reconfirmed. Figure 3 shows sample entries from the Pitjantjatjara/Yankunytjatjara dictionary.

Browsing the dictionary gives insight into the Pitjantjatjara and Yankunytjatjara lifeworlds. For example, *ulpuru* denotes both "dust" and "a good spot for kangaroos, a local habitat of the kind favoured by kangaroos, an open plain with plenty of grass and no spinifex [a sharp-leafed plant] or prickles". *Nuunpunganyi* is a verb meaning

people as well.

mar̲u-mar̲u (Y) *noun*
inland pigweed (*Portulaca oleracea*). The plants are uprooted and allowed to dry to release the tiny black poppy-like seeds, which are winnowed, yandied and ground to a paste from which small cakes are made.
= **wakati**

mar̲un̲i *transitive verb (l)*
blacken, make black: Likara nyangatja kutjar̲a mar̲ur̲ampa, ul̲upungkulampa . . . *This bark — you blacken it by burning, make it into a powder . . .*

matjanya (Y) *noun*
a kind of dangerous, venomous snake, or possibly a cover term for venomous snakes [?].

matjar̲amilan̲i *transitive verb (l)*
muster, round up (from English 'muster'): Wati panya tjut̲angku mungartji puluka matjar̲amilan̲ingi. *The blokes were mustering cattle yesterday.*

matji *noun*
match (from English).

mat̲u (Y) *adverb*
true, genuine, serious, real.
= (P) **mulapa**, (Y) **mula**, (Y) **munytjur**

Figure 3: Example of entries from the Pitjantjatjara-Yankunytjatjara dictionary (Goddard/Defina 2020: 88).

to twitch, but more specifically, to experience telaesthesia, which is when a certain body part tingles. This is understood to mean that a particular relative is thinking about you. Relatives are mapped to particular body parts (see Douglas 1990). The dictionary includes some words of English origin which have been adopted into the Pitjantjatjara and Yankunytjatjara phonological system, such as *ruuta* ("road") and *ulkumunu* ("old woman").

Some of the dictionary entries are accompanied by black-and-white line-drawn illustrations. Many are now part of *Arkleny map-akert* or the Australian Indigenous Languages Image Bank (AILIB) (Kral/Disbray/Green 2022). *Arkleny map-akert* means "having many designs/pictures" in Anmatyerr language. AILIB is an open-access bank of over 1,300 illustrations by artists Faye Alexander, Christine Bruderlin, Jennifer Green, Julie Jones, David Le May, Jenny Taylor and Brenda Thornley. AILIB has been deposited in the Pacific and Regional Archive for Digital Sources in Endangered Cultures (PARADISEC) with permission from the individual illustrators, with reuse permissions for non-commercial learning resources and reference materials. The images in AILIB are found in many Australian Aboriginal dictionaries, and as such, these publications form a network or web as such; for an Australian linguist, the AILIB images stir a sense of familiarity, connectedness and community, recurring as they do in so many publications (see Figure 4).

Finally, the cover of the dictionary includes colourful images of people, animals, things and places from Pitjantjatjara and Yankunytjatjara country. In a nod to the intimacy and small scale of Australian linguistics, the car featured on the back of the volume is that once owned by Dr Doug Marmion PSM, founder and former Director of the ACAL. Similarly, the young girl featured on the front is a former student of Doug's. The cover illustration was by Christine Bruderlin, who is also one of the illustrators to feature in AILIB.

Figure 4: Illustrations by Christine Bruderlin (2022) from the AILIB collection (Kral/Disbray/Green 2022). From left: 'wallaby' [AILIB-ANIMAL_038-00], 'blow [fire]' [AILIB-ACTION_083-00], 'net bag [string bag]' [AILIB-ARTEFACT_029-00].

5.2 Gija Dictionary

The Gija Dictionary was published in 2022 by ASP. While Pitjantjatjara and Yankunytjatjara represent what is known as a "strong" language ecology, where children are still acquiring those languages as their mother tongue, Gija is now spoken only by elderly people. Younger people in Gija country have shifted to Kimberley Kriol, a basilectal English-lexified contact variety (de Dear et al. 2020). Gija country is in northwest Australia. Like Pitjantjatjara and Yankunytjatjara country, it is remote; the major centres are the small communities of Warmun and Halls Creek, which are several hours drive from Kununurra (the largest regional town, albeit home to only around 5,000 people). Gija is a nPN language (see Section 5.1).

The authors of the Gija dictionary are Frances Kofod, Eileen Bray, Rusty Peters, Prof. Joe Blythe and Anna Crane. Frances Kofod is a linguist who has worked with Aboriginal people of the East Kimberley for over 40 years, including on Gija and Miriwoong language projects. Eileen Bray and Rusty Peters are the main Gija consultants who provided input on the latest draft version of the dictionary. The dictionary contains data from over 56 named Gija speakers, which reflects the strong community investment in the project. Prof. Joe Blythe has worked with Gija people for the past 25 years, first publishing a Gija language phrasebook with the Kimberley Language Resource Centre, Australia's first language centre (see Section 2). Anna Crane did work to update the finder list, as well as proofreading.

The front matter of the dictionary is quite extensive. The preface and acknowledgements detail the history of the book at hand, growing from a 900-item word list recorded by Dr Patrick McConvell in 1987 at the Ngalangangpum School. This school was established in 1979 with a two-way curriculum, which taught Gija language and culture alongside subjects typically taught in Western education. Painting, art and cultural items were used as didactic tools for transferring cultural and language knowledge (Massola 2011). Reading the front matter, what is salient is the variety of different grants and schemes that have supported the dictionary development down the years, including from the Hans Rausing Endangered Languages Project (administered by the School of Oriental and African Studies, London), the West Australian state government, various universities, and the AIATSIS. This highlights the precariousness of language work in Australia; much work is not securely funded and relies on a continual effort to secure grant funding through various means.

The dictionary also includes an extensive discussion of Gija "skin names" or, in anthropological parlance, subsections. The skin system governs relationships in Gija society, including delineating who are preferred marriage partners, and which relations are in an avoidance relationship to one another. As detailed in Section 3.4 of the dictionary, Gija "dreamtime" animals also all have skin names (the "dreamtime" or "dreaming" being the mythological past and present of Aboriginal spirituality).

The dictionary also includes an extensive grammar section which covers many aspects of grammar, as well as the "coverb" class, which is found in Gija and other nPN languages of Australia (see Section 4). The dictionary entries themselves are rich, featuring a headword and its part of speech. Many of the Gija coverbs have multiple entries because they have different meanings depending on the inflecting verb with which they are combined (see Section 4). As noted earlier, this highlights a challenge of lexicography for nPN languages, and perhaps for other languages (such as Papuan languages) that use serial verb constructions. Dictionary entries also include a definition, example sentences and a translation. Most of the translations are in English, but some are in Kriol, the lingua franca of the Kimberley. Latin names of plants and animals are included. Figure 5 shows some sample entries in the Gija dictionary.

nyinge-nyingeg *coverb.* annoy. • **Ragim nyinge-nyingeg-ayi, berde-werdij woomberramande-birri . . .** *Ants were annoying them like that, climbing all over them . . .*

nyinggelarre *noun.* snot. • **Berrema nyinggelarre-ningi nyoomboorroo.** *This snot is dripping from his nose.*

nyingginy *noun masculine.* hairy caterpillar, itchy grub. *Euproctis lutea.* [NOTE: also recorded meaning 'scabies', *Sarcoptes scabiei*]

nyingginy, nyinggil, nyinggim *noun.* people in avoidance or restricted relationship. • **Ngoowan garij joonbimnha thamboorroom, ngajim, nyinggim damga.** *Don't say the names of mothers-in-law or sisters, it is forbidden, they*

nyinjinybany *coverb+GET.* start forgetting. • **Nyinjinybany-ngarri yamberramenya thoowiyanyji.** *When we start forgetting anything (due to old age).*

nyin'ge *coverb+HIT.* make deaf, make someone forget. • **Berremawa yardem nyin'ge ngenayidji.** *This (bad cold) made me deaf then.*

nyiny *coverb+SAY/DO.* blow nose. • **Nyiny nginini.** *He blew his nose.* SEE: **nyoony**.

nyinya *verb.* she IS, she is STAYING.

nyinyande *verb.* she IS, she keeps on STAYING.

nyinyil; niyinyil *noun.* zebra finch. *Taeniopygia guttata.* [NOTE: stole fire in the dreamtime; word used for all other finches as well]

nyireg REDUP: **nyire-nyireg**. *coverb+SAY/DO.* be quiet (e.g. when game is sighted). • **Nyireg-**

Figure 5: Example of entries from the Gija dictionary (Kofod/Bray/Peters/Blythe/Crane 2022: 253).

The dictionary includes photographs of people, places and animals on Gija country. The photographs of people are captioned with the Gija person's name; that is, the caption is not merely the headword that is being referred to. Rather, the extensive captions which include the names of people serve to ground both the language and the dictionary in Gija country and society. In this way, the dictionary is something of a community photo album and illustrates the diversity of form and function for dictionaries within an Australian context. Like the Pitjantjatjara/Yankunytjatjara dictionary, the Gija dictionary includes a sparse English-to-Gija finder list at the back of the book.

The front cover art is an excerpt of a painting by Gija custodian Hector Jandany featuring two local hills. These are said to be two men who were respectively speakers of Gija and a neighbouring language, Miriwoong. Figure 6 shows a cake which in turn represents the cover art of the dictionary, and/or the original artwork. This, then, is a traditional spiritual story which has been rendered into an artwork, which has been licensed with adaptation for a dictionary cover, and then re-created by a local baker as cake icing to celebrate the dictionary launch (Figure 7). This fluidity and metamorphosis highlight the resilience, flexibility, and enduring nature of Aboriginal cultures in Australia.

Figure 6: Celebratory cake at the launch of the Gija Dictionary.

Figure 7: Joonba' dancers at the launch of the Gija Dictionary, 2023.

5.3 *Yaru!* Gudjal Learner's Guide and Dictionary

The *Yaru! Gudjal Learner's Guide and Dictionary* is considerably different to both the Pitjantjatjara/Yankunytjatjara and Gija dictionaries, for reasons we will explore. Gudjal is the language of the region around current-day Charters Towers, an inland town in far north Queensland. The post-colonial history of Gudjal people and their language is detailed on page 6 of the dictionary. From 1860–1890, Gudjal people were violently assaulted by pastoralists as well as by the Native Mounted Police, specialised units of Aboriginal troopers led by white officers used to patrol colonial outposts, conduct raids and deal out retribution.[10] By the 1890s, many Gudjal people lived on the edges of cattle stations where they worked for low or no wages. Many were removed to missions and settlements far away including Palm Island, Yarrabah, Cherbourg and Woorabinda. The state of Queensland moved Aboriginal people across the state to these missions, which led to a particular dissolution of traditional languages, as the people living in these far-flung settlements had no traditional history of multilingualism in each other's tongues. By the 1970s, only a handful of Gudjal people still recalled the language as they had learned it in childhood. Linguists Peter Sutton, Tasaku Tsunoda and Gavan Breen recorded four older Gudjal men speaking the language: Fred

10 For more on the Native Mounted Police, see Richards (2008) and Wallis et al. (2017).

Toomba, George Reid, Harry Bunn and Ranji Pope. These recordings are now stored at the AIATSIS. The history of displacement meant that younger Gudjal people had shifted to Aboriginal English.

Yaru! is the work of four authors: William Santo, Alex Anderson, Cassy Nancarrow and Myfany Turpin. Santo is a Gudjal Elder. He recalls as a child growing up hearing old people speaking in a language he did not understand. He was unsure if this was Gudjal or another language (Santo/Anderson/Nancarrow/Turpin 2023: vii); the displacement of people throughout Queensland meant the speakers may have been living many miles from their traditional lands. Santo has worked for decades to piece his language back together, working from diaries written by non-Indigenous cattle station owners on Gudjal country who had made records of local people's language; from the recordings of Toomba, Reid, Bunn and Pope held at AIATSIS; and with careful comparison with grammatical work done on related languages Warrongo and Gugu-Badhan. His first dictionary of Gudjal was published in 2006 (Santo 2006) and this second book in 2023.

What is striking about *Yaru!* is that two-thirds of the book is what could be conceived of as front matter. The dictionary proper is only 16 pages. This represents the sum total vocabulary that exists in the records for Gudjal. When compared to the mammoth size of the Warlpiri dictionary (Laughren, this volume), and bearing in mind that Gudjal was a language no less complex than Warlpiri (or, indeed, any human language), this gives a sense of the utter decimation of the Gudjal language. Those 16 pages represent the entirety of what is known of the vocabulary of Gudjal. The lion's share of the volume is a learner's guide. This begins with a section on "language learning tips". It then steps through Gudjal grammar in a very user-friendly manner, accessible to a layperson. Like the Gija dictionary, the Gudjal dictionary includes a section on the Gudjal "skin system". The book also includes songs composed in blends of English and Gudjal, including to the tune of familiar Anglophone songs (such as "Hush Little Baby").

A "Welcome to Country" entirely in Gudjal is also included in the book. The Welcome to Country is an Australian Indigenous tradition, which involves the Traditional Owners of a particular country formally welcoming visitors to their lands. This tradition has been incorporated into many meeting protocols in Australia (such as at the opening of an academic or industry conference, at a local council's Annual General Meeting, at a community event such as a local community sports day, and so on). "Visitors" to a Country comprise both non-Indigenous peoples and Indigenous peoples of other Aboriginal or Torres Strait Islander nations visiting or living on that country. A Welcome to Country can only be delivered by Traditional Owners of that particular Country. If they are not in attendance, then an "Acknowledgment of Country" will be delivered by non-Indigenous people or Indigenous people not hailing from that Country. This will be a shorter, more formulaic acknowledgement of the lands upon which a meeting is being held.

The dictionary entries themselves are sparse. In a sense, the dictionary section is more of a wordlist. Each entry contains a headword, an English translation, and the speaker/s from whom that word was recorded, by including the initials of the speaker/s after each entry. There are no parts of speech, likely because there is not enough recorded Gudjal to be able to confidently posit word classes. Some example sentences are included; again, the speaker who uttered that sentence has their initials recorded after each. Figure 8 shows some sample entries from the Gudjal dictionary.

gara (GR, HB) ~ **garra** (RP)
no, don't.
• *Gara nhagay.* I don't see. (GR)

gari (FT, HS) ~ **garri** (HB, RP)
sun.
• *Gari yinda-ya guwa.* The sun sets in the west. (FT)

garingga (HB, RP)
morning.

garra (FT)
probably, maybe.
• *Yanga-wu garra yani-na.* He probably went (looking) for his mother. (FT)

garra (RP) ~ **gara** (GR, HB)
no, don't.
• *Gara nhagay.* I don't see. (GR)

gaybal (RP)
1. fire.
• *Gaybal-du ngaya nyinana.* I'm sitting next to a fire. (RP)
2. firestick.

gaygara (BD, FT, HS) ~ **gaygarra** (HB, RP)
wallaroo, old man kangaroo.
• *Gaygara nhaga-na ngali, yara yani-na mudhara-ngga.* We saw a wallaroo, and a man went into the scrub (after him). (FT)

gayimbula (HB) ~ **gayambula** (RP)
cockatoo.

gayinmadhara- (FT)
to play.

gayu (HB) ~ **gayun** (HS)
Aboriginal woman.

Figure 8: Example of entries from the Gudjal dictionary (Santo/Anderson/Nancarrow/Turpin 2023 86).

Page 14 describes the authors' mindful approach to example sentences. In the learner's guide, as many example sentences as possible have been included from the original recordings. Reading the original example sentences likely helps Gudjal people feel a connection with the Elders whose language is featured in *Yaru!*. Similarly, it gives a level of confidence that the language being presented is authentic, given it hails directly from the source. The authors have included some constructed examples based on their current understanding of Gudjal grammar and have marked these with "(New example)". Finally, the Gudjal dictionary employs QR codes to great effect. The QR codes link to archival recordings as well as new audiovisual material produced to support language revival, including songs.

6 Conclusion

The colonisation of Australia by European settlers had a devasting impact on Aboriginal and Torres Strait Islander languages and cultures. There has been a recent shift in cultural and societal attitudes within Australia towards a respect and recognition for Aboriginal and Torres Strait Islander identity and support for self-determination. Now, thanks to the efforts of Aboriginal and Torres Strait Islander Traditional Owners, knowledge holders and language custodians, and to the changing Australian government response, the future is looking brighter. Dr Alitya Rigney of the Kaurna Plains School commented that:

> Have you ever seen a kid's face when they learn the language of their people and country and see the joy, the pride and the identity that comes from that and the wonder that will take them into the future? It is absolutely magic. (House of Representatives Standing Committee on Aboriginal and Torres Strait Islander Affairs 2012: 14)

The AIATSIS Dictionaries Program helps to make this magic happen by supporting the publication of Aboriginal and Torres Strait Islander language dictionaries. These help to support education, interpreting and other practical pursuits. They are also tangible vehicles of cultural pride.

Appendix 1

Gloss abbreviations

MA	Masculine
3	3rd person
NP	NON-PAST
PP	PAST-PERFECT
BEN	Benefactive
M	minimal
≥	indicates compound pronoun comprised of subject (first element) acting on (>) object (second element)

Bibliography

Aboriginal languages act 2017 no 51 (NSW). https://legislation.nsw.gov.au/view/whole/html/inforce/current/act-2017-051 (last access: 4 November 2024).

Australian Institute of Aboriginal and Torres Strait Islander Studies (AIATSIS) (n.d.): The AIATSIS journey. https://aiatsis.gov.au/aiatsis-journey (last access: 29 October 2024).

AIATSIS (2019): The Sydney Language now available to a new generation. AIATSIS. https://aiatsis.gov.au/whats-new/news/sydney-language-now-available-new-generation (last access: 23 October 2024).

AIATSIS (2022): Missions, stations and reserves. Australian Institute of Aboriginal and Torres Strait Islander Studies. https://aiatsis.gov.au/explore/missions-stations-and-reserves (last access: 22 October 2024).

Amery, Robert (2018): Piltawodli Native Location (1838–1845). In: Ganter, Regina (ed.): German Missionaries in Australia – a web-directory of intercultural encounters. http://missionaries.griffith.edu.au/mission/piltawodli-native-location-1838–1845 (last access: 4 November 2024).

ANU (2021): 1,500 endangered languages at high risk. Australian National University. https://www.anu.edu.au/news/all-news/1500-endangered-languages-at-high-risk (last access: 22 October 2024).

Austin, Peter Kenneth (2024): Reuther's Diyari dictionary. https://diyari.org/resources/reuther-dictionary (last access: 5 November 2024).
Australian Bureau of Statistics (2021): Table 1.3.4 Aboriginal and Torres Strait Islander persons who spoke an Aboriginal or Torres Strait Islander language at home by age [data set]. https://www.abs.gov.au/statistics/people/aboriginal-and-torres-strait-islander-peoples/language-statistics-aboriginal-and-torres-strait-islander-peoples/2021/Language%20speakers.xlsx (last access: 10 October 2024).
Babinski, Sarah/Rojas-Berscia, Luis-Miguel/Bowern, Claire (2023): The Wati (Western Desert) subgroup of Pama-Nyungan. In: Bowern, Claire (ed.): The Oxford guide to Australian languages. Oxford: Oxford University Press, 893–917.
Baird, Norman (1959): Gugu-Yalanji wordlist: given to W.J. and L. Oates [manuscript]. AIATSIS call number PMS 2515.
Barker, Jimmie (1968): Marawari word list and discussion [audiotape reels]. AIATSIS call number BARKER_J03.
Barker, Jimmie (1977): The two worlds of Jimmie Barker. The life of an Australian Aboriginal, 1900–1972 as told to Janet Mathews. Canberra: Australian Institute of Aboriginal Studies.
Battin, Jacqueline (2020, March 18): Indigenous languages in Australian parliaments. AIATSIS. https://aiatsis.gov.au/blog/indigenous-languages-australian-parliaments (last access: 4 November 2024).
Bauer, Anastasia (2014): The use of signing space in a shared sign language of Australia. Berlin/Nijmegen: De Gruyter/Ishara Press.
Bowern, Claire (2012): The riddle of Tasmanian languages. In: Proceedings of the Royal Society 279, 4590–4595.
Bowern, Claire (2023): How many languages are and were spoken in Australia? In: Bowern, Claire (ed.): The Oxford guide to Australian languages. Oxford: Oxford University Press, 56–64.
Bromham, Lindell, et al. (2022): Global predictors of language endangerment and the future of linguistic diversity. In: Nature ecology & evolution 6, 163–173.
Bruderlin, Christine (2022): AILIB-ACTION_083, AILIB-ARTEFACT_029-00, AILIB-ANIMAL_038-00. In: Kral, Inge/Disbray, Samantha/Green, Jennifer (compilers): Arlkeny map-akert / Australian Indigenous languages image bank 'AILIB'. Collection AILIB at catalog.paradisec.org.au [Open Access]. https://dx.doi.org/10.26278/GY4E-MH93 (last access: 4 November 2024).
Commonwealth of Australia (2012): Our land our languages. Language learning in Indigenous communities. https://aphref.aph.gov.au/house/committee/atsia/languages/report/full_report.pdf (last access: 23 October 2024).
Commonwealth of Australia (2020): National Indigenous languages report. https://www.arts.gov.au/what-we-do/indigenous-arts-and-languages/indigenous-languages-and-arts-program/national-indigenous-languages-report (last access: 4 November 2024).
Commonwealth of Australia (2024): Warlpiri Education and Training Trust. NAIDOC. https://www.naidoc.org.au/awards/winner-profiles/warlpiri-education-and-training-trust (last access: 23 October 2024).
Connor, John (2010): The frontier that never was. In: Stockings, Craig (ed.): Zombie myths of Australian military history. Sydney: University of New South Wales Press, 10–28.
Crowley, Terry/Dixon, Robert Malcolm Ward (1981): Tasmanian. In: Dixon, Robert Malcolm Ward/Blake, Barry John (eds.): Handbook of Australian languages. Canberra: ANU Press, 395–421.
Davis, Jeffrey Edward (2010): Hand talk. Sign Language Among American Indian Nations. Cambridge, UK: Cambridge University Press.
de Dear, Caroline/Possemato, Francesco/Blythe, Joe (2020): Gija (East Kimberley, Western Australia) – Language Snapshot. In: Language documentation and description 17, 131–141.
Dickson, Greg (2006, May 17): ai bin gulijap krai. That Munanga linguist. https://munanga.blogspot.com/2006/05/ai-bin-gulijap-krai.html (last access: 4 November 2024).

Dixon, Robert Malcolm Ward ([1]2002): Australian languages. Their nature and development. Cambridge: Cambridge University Press.
Douglas, Wilfred (1964): An introduction to the Western Desert language. Sydney: Oceania Linguistic Monographs.
Douglas 1990 = Illustrated topical dictionary of the Western Desert language. Revised and enlarged. Kalgoorlie: Kalgoorlie College Press. [3]1990 [[1]1959].
Duguid, Charles (1972): Doctor and the Aborigines. Adelaide: Rigby.
Eckert, Paul/Hudson, Joyce (2010): Wangka wiru. A handbook for the Pitjantjatjara language learner. St Marys, SA: Mirrabooka Press [original edn. 1988].
Ellis, Elizabeth Marrkilyi/Green, Jennifer/Kral, Inge/Reed, Lauren W (2019): 'Mara yurriku'. Western Desert sign languages. In: Australian Aboriginal Studies 2, 89–111.
Evans, Nicholas (2003): Bininj Gun-wok. A pan-dialectal grammar of Mayali, Kunwinjku and Kune. Canberra: Pacific Linguistics.
Evans, Nicholas (2009): Dying words. Endangered languages and what they have to tell us. Chichester: Wiley-Blackwell.
Evans, Nicholas (2020): Time, diversification, and dispersal on the Australian continent. Three enigmas of linguistic prehistory. In: Crevels, Mily/Muysken, Pieter (eds.): Language dispersal, diversification, and contact. Oxford: Oxford University Press, 116–141.
First Languages Australia and Commonwealth of Australia (2023): Voices of Country – Australia's action plan for the International Decade of Indigenous Languages 2022–2032. https://www.firstlanguages.org.au/voices-of-country (last access: 4 November 2024).
Fishman, Joshua Aaron (1991): Reversing language shift. Theoretical and empirical foundations of assistance to threatened languages. Clevedon: Multilingual Matters
Gale [20]20 = Ngarrindjeri Dictionary. Compiled by Gale, Mary-Anne/Williams, Phyllis/the Ngarrindjeri Elders and community. MIPAAC (Miwi-inyeri Pelepi-ambi Aboriginal Corporation). [3]2020.
Gale, Mary-Anne (2023): Language revival. In: Bowern, Claire (ed.): The Oxford Guide to Australian Languages. Oxford: Oxford University Press, 738–753.
Gale, Mary-Anne (n.d.): Ngarrindjeri language resources. Mobile Language Team https://mobilelanguageteam.com.au/languages/Ngarrindjeri (last access: 23 October 2024).
Ganter, Regina (2018): German Missionaries in Australia – a web-directory of intercultural encounters. https://missionaries.griffith.edu.au/ (last access: 28 October 2024).
Goddard/Defina 2006 = Pitjantjatjarra/Yankunytjatjarra to English Dictionary. Compiled by Goddard, Cliff. Updated by Defina, Rebecca. Alice Springs: IAD Press, 2nd rev. edn. [[1]1996].
Goodwin, Timothy/Murphy, Julian (2019, May 15): Raised voices. *Parliamentary debate in Indigenous languages.* Australian Public Law. https://www.auspublaw.org/blog/2019/05/raised-voices-parliamentary-debate-in-indigenous-languages (last access: 4 November 2024).
Gordon, Michael (2016, February 12): Closing the gap and learning the language. Sydney Morning Herald. https://www.smh.com.au/opinion/turnbulls-address-to-parliament-mark-of-respect-for-ngunawals-rediscovery-of-collective-soul-20160212-gmsanf.html (last access: 4 November 2024).
Green, Jennifer/Wilkins, David (2014): With or without speech. Arandic Sign Language from Central Australia. In: Australian Journal of Linguistics 34, 2, 234–261.
Green, Jennifer (2019): Embodying kin-based respect in speech, sign, and gesture. In: Gesture 18, 366–391.
Green, Jennifer (2023): Australian Indigenous sign languages. In: Bowern, Claire (ed.): The Oxford guide to Australian languages. Oxford: Oxford University Press, 612–627.
Green/Green/Hamilton-Holloway/Meakins/Osgarby/Pensalfini 2019 = Mudburra to English dictionary. Green, Rebecca/Green, Jennifer/Hamilton–Holloway, Amanda/Meakins, Felicity/Osgarby, David/ Pensalfini, Rob. Canberra: Aboriginal Studies Press.

Harris, John (1993): Losing and gaining a language. The story of Kriol in the Northern Territory. In: Walsh, Michael/Yallop, Colin (eds.): Language and culture in Aboriginal Australia. Canberra: Aboriginal Studies Press, 145–154.

Harvey, Mark/Mailhammer, Robert (2024): Proto-Australian. Reconstruction of a common ancestor language. Berlin/Boston: De Gruyter.

Hobson, John (2018): Language revival in Australia. In: Hinton, Leanne/Huss, Leena/Roche, Gerald (eds.): The Routledge handbook of language revitalization. New York: Routledge, 320–329.

House of Representatives Standing Committee on Aboriginal and Torres Strait Islander Affairs (2012): Our land our languages. Language learning in Indigenous communities. Parliament of the Commonwealth of Australia.

Human Rights and Equal Opportunities Commission (1997): Bringing them home. Report of the national inquiry into the separation of Aboriginal and Torres Strait Islander children from their families. Commonwealth of Australia. https://humanrights.gov.au/our-work/projects/bringing-them-home-report-1997 (last access: 4 November 2024).

Human Rights Commission (n.d.): Historical context. The Stolen Generations. Australian Human Rights Commission. https://bth.humanrights.gov.au/significance/historical-context-the-stolen-generations (last access: 22 October 2024).

Indigenous Languages and Arts (2024): Indigenous Languages and Arts program – language centre's [sic] List. https://www.arts.gov.au/sites/default/files/documents/indigenous-languages-and-arts-program-language-centres-list-september2024.pdf (last access: 4 November 2024).

Innis, Michelle (2016): An heir to a tribe's culture ensures its language is not forgotten. The New York Times. https://www.nytimes.com/2016/04/09/world/asia/australia-aboriginal-tribe-wiradjuri.html (last access: 4 November 2024).

Jorgensen, Eleanor/Green, Jennifer/Bauer, Anastasia (2021): Exploring phonological aspects of Australian Indigenous sign languages. In: Languages 6, 2, 81.

Keeffe, Kevin (1992): From the centre to the city. Aboriginal education, culture and power. Canberra: Aboriginal Studies Press.

Kendon, Adam (1988): Sign languages of Aboriginal Australia. Cultural, semiotic and communicative perspectives. Cambridge: Cambridge University Press.

Kenny 2018 = Carl Strehlow's 1909 comparative heritage dictionary: an Aranda, German, Loritja and Dieri to English dictionary with introductory essays. Ed. by Kenny, Anna. Acton: ANU, 2018.

Koch, Harold (1983): Etymology and dictionary-making for Australian languages (with examples from Kaytej). In: Pacific linguistics, Series A, Occasional papers 66, 149–173.

Koch, Harold/Nordlinger, Rachel (2014): The languages of Australia in linguistic research. Context and issues. In: Koch, Harold/Nordlinger, Rachel (eds.): The languages and linguistics of Australia. A comprehensive guide. Berlin/Boston: De Gruyter, 3–21.

Kofod/Bray/Peters/Blythe/Crane 2022 = Gija Dictionary. Kofod, Frances/Bray, Eileen/Peters, Rusty/Blythe, Joe/Crane, Anna. Canberra: Aboriginal Studies Press, 2022.

Kral, Inge/Green, Jennifer/Ellis, Elizabeth Marrkilyi (2019): Wangkarra. Communication and the verbal arts of Australia's Western Desert. In: International journal of intangible heritage 14, 33–47.

Kral, Inge/Disbray, Samantha/Green, Jennifer (Compilers) (2022): Arlkeny map-akert / Australian Indigenous Languages Image Bank 'AILIB'. Collection AILIB at catalog.paradisec.org.au [Open Access]. https://dx.doi.org/10.26278/GY4E-MH93 (last access: 4 November 2024).

Lambert, Jacqueline (2011): A history of the Australian Institute of Aboriginal Studies 1959–1989. An analysis of how Aboriginal and Torres Strait Islander people achieved control of a national research institute [Doctoral Thesis]. Australian National University.

Laughren 2022 = Warlpiri encyclopaedic dictionary. Ed. by Laughren, Mary. Canberra: Aboriginal Studies Press, 2022.

Laughren, Mary (this volume): Encyclopaedic lexicography. The Warlpiri Encyclopaedic Dictionary.

Lazarus, Robert (2022): Circulating cassettes of ceremony. Indigenous peer-to-peer networks in Arnhem Land. In: Media, culture & society 44, 1, 141–160.
Lee, Nala/Van Way, John (2016): Assessing levels of endangerment in the Catalogue of Endangered Languages (ELCat) using the Language Endangerment Index (LEI). In: Language in society 45, 271–202.
Ryan, Lyndall et al. (2017–2022): Colonial frontier massacres in Australia, 1788–193. Newcastle: University of Newcastle. https://c21ch.newcastle.edu.au/colonialmassacres/ (last access: 28 October 2024).
Lester, Yami (1993): Yami. The autobiography of Yami Lester. Alice Springs: IAD Press.
Massola, Cate (2011): Why is there a donkey in that painting? In: Artlink 31, 2, 126–129.
Maypilama, Elaine/Adone, Dany (2013): Yolngu Sign Language. An undocumented language of Arnhem Land. In: Learning communities, International journal of learning in social contexts 13, 37–44.
Meissner, Martin/Philpott, Stuart B./Philpott, Diana (1975): The sign language of sawmill workers in British Columbia. In: Sign Language Studies 9, 291–308.
McConvell, Patrick/Day, Ron/Black, Paul (1983): Making a Meriam Mir dictionary. In: Papers in Australian linguistics no. 15, Australian Aboriginal lexicography. Canberra: Pacific Linguistics, 19–30.
Miller, Wick R. (1971): Dialect differentiation in the western desert language. In: Anthropological forum 3, 1, 61–78.
Mount, Alison Louise, et al. (2024): The Jimmie Barker corpus. A Muruwari man's documentation of Aboriginal languages, history and culture between 1968 and 1972. In: Australian Journal of Linguistics 44, 2–3, 104–126.
Nash, David/Simpson, Jane (1989): AIAS National Lexicography Project: final report, AIATSIS call number PMS 4646.
Naylor, Catherine (2024): They'd be so proud. The 10-year-olds accepting challenge laid for them 40 years ago. Sydney Morning Herald. https://www.smh.com.au/national/nsw/they-d-be-so-proud-the-10-year-olds-accepting-challenge-laid-for-them-40-years-ago-20240306-p5fafr.html (last access: 23 October 2024).
Oates, Lynette Frances (1990): Aboriginal recording of Aboriginal language. In: Austin, Peter, et al. (eds.): Language and history in honour of Luise A. Hercus. Canberra: Pacific Linguistics, 221–232.
Quay, Suzanne (2015): Sign language from medieval to modern times. In: Jepsen, Julie Bakken, et al. (eds.): Sign languages of the world. A comparative handbook. Berlin/München/Boston: De Gruyter Mouton, 871–900.
Reed, Lauren Wambach (in press). Sign languages of the Papuasphere. In: Evans, Nicholas/Fedden, Sebastian (eds.): The Oxford guide to the Papuan languages. Oxford: Oxford University Press.
Reed, Lauren Wambach/Mount, Alison Louise (2023): The Language revival index. Presentation to the Australian Linguistics Society Conference. University of Sydney. https://www.academia.edu/117204756/Reed_and_Mount_2023_The_Language_Revival_Index_presentation_to_Australian_Linguistic_Society (last access: 4 November 2024).
Reynolds, Annie/Sainty, Theresa (2023): The revitalization of the sleeping Tasmanian Aboriginal languages. In: Bowern, Claire (ed.): The Oxford guide to Australian languages. Oxford: Oxford University Press, 950–957.
Richards, Jonathan (2008): The secret war. A true history of Queensland's native police. St Lucia: University of Queensland Press.
Rumsey, Alan (1993): Language and territoriality. In: Walsh, Michael/Yallop, Colin (eds.): Language and culture in Aboriginal Australia. Canberra: Aboriginal Studies Press, 191–206.
Santo 2006 = Gudjal language pocket dictionary. Compiled by Santo, William Charles. Thuringowa, Queensland: Black Ink Press, 2006.
Santo/Anderson/Nancarrow/Turpin 2023 = Yaru! Gudjal learner's guide and dictionary. Ed. by Santo, William/Anderson, Alex/Nancarrow, Cassy/Turpin, Myfany. Canberra: Aboriginal Studies Press, 2023.

SIL (2022): FieldWorks Language Explorer. https://software.sil.org/fieldworks/ (last access: 5 November 2024).
Simons, Gary (2019): Two centuries of spreading language loss. In: Proceedings of the Linguistic Society of America 4, 1, 27:1–12.
Simpson, Jane (1993): Making dictionaries. In: Walsh, Michael/Yallop, Colin (eds.): Language and culture in Aboriginal Australia. Canberra: Aboriginal Studies Press, 123–144.
Simpson, Jane/Caffery, Jo/McConvell, Patrick (2009): Gaps in Australia's Indigenous language policy: dismantling bilingual education in the Northern Territory. AIATSIS discussion paper (24). https://aiatsis.gov.au/sites/default/files/research_pub/simpson-caffery-mcconvell-dp24-indigenous-language-policy_0_3.pdf (last access: 5 November 2024).
Simpson, Jane Helen, et al. (2018): Census data on Australian languages. In: Drude, Sebastian/Ostler, Nicholas/Moser, Marielle (eds.): 22nd annual conference of the Foundation for Endangered Languages. United Kingdom: FEL & EL Publishing, 115–120.
Simpson, Jane/Wigglesworth, Gillian (2019): Language diversity in Indigenous Australia in the 21st century. In: Current issues in language planning 20, 1, 67–80.
Singer et al. 2021 = Mawng to English Dictionary. Ed. by Singer, Ruth/Garidjalalug, Nita/Urabadi, Rosemary/Hewett, Heather/Mirwuma, Peggy/Ambidjambidj, Philip/Fabricius, Anne. Canberra: Aboriginal Studies Press, 2021.
Teichelmann, Christian Gottlieb/Schürmann, Clamor Wilhelm (1840): Outlines of a grammar, vocabulary and phraseology, of the Aboriginal language of South Australia, spoken by the Natives in and for some distance Around Adelaide. Adelaide: Published by the authors, at the "Native location".
Thieberger, Nicholas (1993): Dictionaries project. In: Australian Aboriginal studies 2, 120–123.
Thieberger, Nicholas (1994): Report on the AIATSIS visiting research fellowship, Aboriginal Studies Electronic Data Archive. A report to AIATSIS Council on the conclusion of the Visiting Research Fellowship. AIATSIS call number MS 3346.
Thieberger, Nicholas (1995): The Aboriginal Studies Electronic Data Archive (ASEDA). In: News. In: International journal of the sociology of language 113, 147–150.
Thieberger, Nick (2015): The lexicography of indigenous languages in Australia and the Pacific. In: Hanks, Patrick/de Schryver, Gilles-Maurice (eds.): International handbook of modern lexis and lexicography. Berlin: Springer, 1–16.
Triple J (2017): The Preatures release new music. ABC News. https://www.abc.net.au/triplej/news/the-preatures/8771564 (last access: 23 October 2024).
Troy, Jakelin (1993): The Sydney Language. Canberra: Aboriginal Studies Press.
Troy, Jakelin (1990): Australian Aboriginal contact with the English language in New South Wales, 1788 to 1845. Canberra: Pacific Linguistics.
UNESCO Culture Sector (2011): UNESCO's language vitality and endangerment methodological guideline: Review of application and feedback since 2003. Background paper prepared by UNESCO's Culture Sector for expert meeting "Towards UNESCO guidelines on language policies: a tool for language assessment and planning", 30 May–1 June 2011. https://www.academia.edu/35753965/UNESCOs_Language_Vitality_and_Endangerment_Methodological_Guideline_Review_of_Application_and_Feedback_since_2003 (last access: 5 November 2024).
Wallis, Lynley, et al. (2017): Rewriting the history of the Native Mounted Police in Queensland (Nulungu Insights 3). Nulungu Research Institute. https://researchonline.nd.edu.au/nulungu_insights/3/ (last access: 5 November 2024).
Walsh, Michael (2023): Restricted respect registers and auxiliary languages. In: Bowern, Claire (ed.): The Oxford guide to Australian languages. Oxford: Oxford University Press, 689–696.

Wafer, Jim/Turpin, Myfany (2017) (eds.): Recirculating songs. Revitalising the singing practices of Indigenous Australia. Canberra: Asia-Pacific Linguistics.
Watson, Frederick (1914) (ed.): Historical records of Australia: Series 1, vol. 1 (1788–1796). Sydney: Library Committee of the Commonwealth Parliament. http://nla.gov.au/nla.obj-442186184 (last access: 5 November 2024).
Watson, Don (1982): The war on Australia's frontier. In: Meanjin quarterly 41, 1, 138–146.

Mary Laughren

Encyclopaedic lexicography: The Warlpiri Encyclopaedic Dictionary

Abstract: The Warlpiri Encyclopaedic Dictionary is the outcome of a collaborative enterprise started in 1978 between Warlpiri speakers, linguists and many others who contributed their particular knowledge and skills. Its form and contents were determined to a great extent by the linguistic, historical and social context that is described in this chapter. The role of the bilingual education programs established from 1973 in Warlpiri community schools is shown to be a crucial factor while the brilliant documentation of Warlpiri language carried out by linguist Professor Ken Hale starting in 1959 provided rich and reliable data to seed the dictionary. The rationale for including encyclopaedic content, rather than limiting the dictionary to the purely linguistic (if that is even possible) and some of the presentational issues that arise especially where the languages and cultures diverge are addressed.

Keywords: Australian languages, Pama-Nyungan, Ngumpin-Yapa, Warlpiri, lexicography, dictionaries

Schlagwörter: Australische Sprachen, Pama-Nyungan, Ngumpin-Yapa, Warlpiri, Lexikographie, Wörterbücher

1 Introduction

The Warlpiri Encyclopaedic Dictionary (henceforth WED) is bilingual (Warlpiri-English) and attempts to provide a broad and detailed record of the Warlpiri lexicon supplemented by grammatical information. It also aims to present the environment and culture of traditional Warlpiri-speaking people conveyed in their own words. This article sets out the context in which the dictionary was compiled, the reasons for compiling a bilingual encyclopaedic dictionary, and gives information about the compilers and other contributors. Some areas in which textual description is best supplemented by visual aids are also covered.

Note: My thanks to the organisers, especially Pam Peters, and participants at the EMLEX conference *Lexicography at Large* held at Macquarie University 25–26 March, 2024, for their feedback on an earlier version of this paper.

Mary Laughren, Honorary Senior Research Fellow, School of Languages and Cultures, The University of Queensland, St Lucia QLD 4072, Australia, e-mail: m.laughren@uq.edu.au

https://doi.org/10.1515/9783112216644-010

1.1 Warlpiri country and people

Warlpiri country, which covers approximately 140,000 km^2, is largely semi-desert with almost no permanent surface water. It supports a variety of vegetation types including open spinifex grass plains, sand dunes, and wooded areas dominated by eucalypts and acacias. Survival in Warlpiri country depended on many factors, among which the following were crucial:
- thinly distributed population over a very large area (shown in Figure 1)
- an intimate knowledge of country and its resources
- expert hunting and food gathering skills
- minimal multi-functional toolkit
- strong intra- and inter-family allegiance and cooperation
- good relationships with non-Warlpiri neighbours
- shared spiritual beliefs that legitimate occupation and use of land
- shared language and sense of shared identity

1.2 Warlpiri language

The Warlpiri language is spoken as a first language by approximately 3000 people and by many others as a second language.[1] Despite the large area occupied by Warlpiri speaking people, and the distances between the main villages where people were settled after 1946, the language is relatively uniform, although regional dialects reflect contact with the different neighbouring languages, especially in their lexicon. Warlpiri is the southern-most language in the Ngumpin-Yapa (NGY) group of Pama-Nyungan languages (McConvell/Laughren 2004) as shown on the map in Figure 1.

The Ngumpin languages include Ngarinyman, Bilinarra, Mudburra, Gurindji, Ngardi and Walmajarri. In recent years these NGY languages have been well documented in dictionaries and grammatical descriptions (see Meakins *et al.* 2023). Neighbouring languages of the Arandic group spoken to the east of Warlpiri and Western Desert languages spoken to the west and south of Warlpiri have also been documented in dictionaries and grammatical descriptions (see Figure 2).

2 Historical context

During the 19th century Warlpiri people's contact with Europeans was very rare. These contacts were restricted mainly to small parties of explorers and prospectors. However some indirect effects of the encroaching European presence were experi-

1 According to the 2016 Australian Census 2,276 people indicated that they speak Warlpiri at home.

Figure 1: Warlpiri and neighbours (map drawn by Brenda Thornley).

enced including from the construction and operation of the overland telegraph line from Adelaide to Darwin (completed in 1872), the establishment of pastoral leases on Arrernte land in the 1870s, and the establishment of the Lutheran Mission at Hermannsburg in Arrernte country in 1877.

Figure 2: WED and some neighbouring language dictionaries and grammars.

The 20th century saw increased contact with Europeans which intensified after World War 1, as mining operations were started on Warlpiri land to obtain gold, wolfram/tungsten and tin. Europeans established cattle stations on Warlpiri country taking up the best watered country. Consequently Warlpiri were drawn into European occupied and controlled places including mines and pastoral properties for work and to receive government rations. Some men worked for the army during World War 2 when the European population of the Northern Territory soared.

It was after World War 2 that the government moved most Warlpiri people into settlements it established on or near Warlpiri traditional country: at Phillip Creek in 1945 to the east, at Yuendumu in 1946 in the south, at Lajamanu (formerly Hooker Creek) in 1949 to the north, and at Alekarenge (formerly Warrabri) in 1956 to the east of Warlpiri country. Relatively few families continued living on pastoral stations such as Willowra (now Wirliyajarrayi). Although there continued to be movement of people between these settlements, one of the results of sedendarisation was dialect and language mixing, combined with new contact influences which resulted in the creation of distinctive communilects. It was only in the 1950s that schools (primary level only) were established on settlements with instruction in English, although Warlpiri teaching assistants who spoke to the children in their own language were employed in some schools.

2.1 Bilingual education

From 1973 bilingual education programs were introduced into schools on Warlpiri communities, with instruction given in both English and Warlpiri with initial literacy focused on Warlpiri (Hoogenraad 2001). Lothar Jagst, a linguist stationed at Lajamanu employed by the Summer Institute of Linguistics, developed a standard Warlpiri orthography. The American linguist, Professor Ken Hale from the Massachusetts Institute of Technology (MIT), who had documented the Warlpiri language starting in 1959, was invited to instruct Warlpiri adults in the new orthography in a series of workshops in Warlpiri communities. He also compiled a basic bilingual dictionary/ glossary, and an illustrated syllabary. He created children's songs and other pedagogic material aimed at supporting the bilingual school programs. Collaboration between Ken Hale and Warlpiri people continued until his death in 2001.[2]

Members of early generations of school graduates literate in English and Warlpiri were employed as teaching assistants to give formal instruction in Warlpiri literacy. Others were engaged as Warlpiri literacy workers to write and illustrate books and other pedagogical materials in their own language.[3]

Linguists were engaged by the Department of Education to support the teaching programs in bilingual schools. In August 1975 Laughren took up one of these positions at Yuendumu to assist the Warlpiri program. Printing facilities were set up at Yuendumu School in 1976 to produce books for the schools running bilingual programs in Warlpiri communities: Yuendumu, Lajamanu and Willowra. One of the tasks assumed by Laughren from 1978 onwards was the compilation of a Warlpiri dictionary.

2.2 Why a bilingual encyclopaedic dictionary

In this education context there was a need for the dictionary to be of use to Warlpiri speakers as well as the many non-Warlpiri people working in Warlpiri communities as teachers, administrators, nurses, police, shopkeepers, clergy and others. The dictionary also needed to serve as a reference for linguists and other researchers. Given the range of users, the dictionary needed to be bilingual (Warlpiri-English), and to be as comprehensive as possible. It had to include all dialects of Warlpiri, and as many words as possible along with their full range of meanings, idiomatic usages, register variation and possible English glosses as determined by context. It also needed to include grammatical information, especially for non-Warlpiri users.

2 Hale supervised PhD students David Nash and Jane Simpson, co-compilers of the WED and obtained funding from the National Science Foundation and other sources to support the WED project.

3 These can be viewed at https://indigenous.pub/ (last access: 2 August 2024).

It was also evident that the dictionary should reflect speakers' knowledge of the traditional Warlpiri world, including its physical, social and intellectual aspects. The school programs aspired to be not only bilingual but bicultural, so an encyclopaedic dictionary was required to support them. Furthermore, in the 1970s when the dictionary project commenced, the linguist had access to rich data: linguistic, cultural, about Warlpiri land, its flora and fauna, the traditional hunter-gatherer life, social organisation and was able to observe the day-to-day life of Warlpiri people which was still influenced by pre-settlement culture. However life style changes due to sedentarisation were being observed; these were thought likely to result in a loss of the knowledge that underpinned traditional Warlpiri life. Warlpiri elders wanted the young to be taught traditional language and about traditional life, as well as to learn English and obtain the "new" knowledge.

2.3 Language sources

The dictionary draws on a wide range of Warlpiri language sources both oral and written. These include the audio recordings of Warlpiri speakers representing three distinct regional dialects and transcription notes made by linguist Ken Hale on field trips in1959–60, 1966–7, and 1980, in addition to audio and video recordings made by other linguists and researchers, teachers, and Warlpiri people themselves. These recordings contain elicited explanations of word meanings and examples of typical word usage as well as spontaneous speech including conversations, sermons, addresses to formal meetings.

Hale's recordings, and others made principally between the 1970s and early 2000s, were made with people who had lived a relatively traditional life on Warlpiri country and/or who had been raised by parents and grandparents who had done so. Their world view was that of traditional Warlpiri people familiar with their land and its relationship to people, art and ceremony.

The written language sources drawn on in compiling the dictionary also include transcriptions of recorded speech edited by Warlpiri literacy workers, the contents of books (stories, poems, songs, instructional) written (and illustrated) by Warlpiri people. Warlpiri co-compilers, Jeannie Egan Nungarrayi at Yuendumu and Paddy Patrick Jangala at Lajamanu wrote hundreds of the definitions of word meaning and examples of word usage in the WED.

The dictionary compilation has been a collaborative enterprise involving Warlpiri people, linguists, anthropologists, musicologists, teachers, wildlife researchers, computer scientists and others. No one person has the knowledge and expertise to undertake the compilation of an encyclopaedic dictionary alone.

3 Compiling and managing lexical data

The processes involved in managing the data evolved over time.[4] In the pre-computer years (1978 to 1983) data was written on a series of A5 cards arranged in alphabetical order and stored in shoeboxes. Information about each word (also suffixes and enclitics) was written on a single card or group of cards. This information included the word, its meaning and grammatical properties, usage examples, translations, sources, related words, usage in fixed expressions or idioms, comments on usage, on dialect and register, and any other relevant information.

From 1983 onwards, the handwritten data was transitioned to electronic files and David Nash initiated the on-lining of the Warlpiri corpus at MIT and later at Yuendumu. Dictionary entries were converted into structured text files with the start and end of data fields marked by backslash codes or other identifiers as shown in the partial entry for *jilja* in Figure 3.[5]

```
\me jilja (N):
\dm topography: walya: \edm
\gl sandhill, sand ridge, dune \egl
\eg
\wed Jilja karnalu ngarrirni – tiri-tiri walya. Purlu-piya. Wiri-yijala ka parntarri jiljaji. \[hn:185]
\et <Jilja> is what we call the very red earth (formed) like a rocky hill. Sandhills are also big (like rocky hills). \ewed
\wed Jilja ka pirli-piya parntarrinja-yani – kulalpa murdukayi jiljangka yantarla, lawa – kalaka yukami. \[hn]
\et A sandhill stretches out like a rocky hill – a car cannot go over a sandhill – it's likely to get stuck in it. \ewed
\eeg
\alt jitja \ealt
\cf manangkarra, manja, pamarrpa, pirli \ecf
\syn ngalyarrpa, yilyampuru \esyn
\eme
\sse jilja-marra-marra (N):
\gl multiple ^[sandhill]sandhills, ^[sand ridge]sand ridges, ^sandhill ^country, rows of ^sandhills \egl
\eg
\we Yirlangkurrunyu karnalu watiyakari ngarrirni yika...
```

Figure 3: Partial database entry for *jilja* 'sandhill'.

3.1 Contents of the Warlpiri Encylopaedic Dictionary

The dictionary entries, both Warlpiri to English and English to Warlpiri sections, constitute the heart of the dictionary. Preceding them is various forematter:

- Preface, acknowledgements, contributors
- Brief introduction to Warlpiri people, land and language

4 See Nash (2022) for a detailed chronology of the making of the Warlpiri Encyclopaedic Dictionary.

5 Different text editors were used over time starting with EMACS at MIT in 1983, and then QUED/M and finally TextWrangler on Apple computers. The marking of distinct fields within lexical databases followed the practice initiated by linguists from the Summer Institute of Linguistics (SIL).

- Overview of language structure: phonology, orthography, grammar (by Jane Simpson)
- How to use the dictionary; contents & structure of dictionary entries (by Jane Simpson)

Following the dictionary entries is a series of appendices:
- Lists of flora, fauna, fungi: Latin names, Warlpiri names and English common names
- Kin terms: family relations and "skin" names
- Lists of suffixes and enclitics
- Chronology and list of reference works (by David Nash)

The dictionary also contains maps, photos, line drawings, and graphics which illustrate and supplement the information given in word entries.

3.2 From database to printed dictionary

The structured data base was the source of three sections of the dictionary:
- Warlpiri to English entries
- English to Warlpiri word finder list
- Flora, fauna, fungi lists (alphabetised by Latin genus and species name) in Appendix 1

This transformation was enabled by the computational routines authored by computational linguists Nay San and Ellison Luk.[6] These check the validity of the data structure and export the data in xml-formatted files. Nay had previously set up routines for allowing multi-person data entry and assuring master file control. Christine Bruderlin at Aboriginal Studies Press, Canberra, did the final layout using Adobe InDesign. The transformation from backslash structured database to dictionary layout is illustrated by comparing Figures 3 and 4.

3.3 A picture is worth a thousand words

The principal concern of an encyclopaedic dictionary is to present unfamiliar knowledge to the reader in a way that can be as immediately and as accurately understood as possible. It is especially those semantic domains where each language structures information in different ways that are the most challenging for both dictionary com-

6 See <https://coedl.github.io/yinarlingi> and <https://coedl.github.io/tidylex> (last access: 29 April 2025).

jilja (N): sandhill, sand ridge, dune. PHOTO: p. A4. ♦Jilja karnalu ngarrirni – tiri-tiri walya. Purlu-piya. Wiri-yijala ka parntarri jiljaji. Jilja *is what we call the very red earth (formed) like a rocky hill. Sandhills are also big (like rocky hills).* ♦Jilja ka pirli-piya parntarrinja-yani – kulalpa murdukayi jiljangka yantarla, lawa – kalaka yukami. *A sandhill stretches out like a rocky hill – a car cannot go over a sandhill – it's likely to get stuck in it.* VARIANT: **jitja.** SEE ALSO: **manangkarra, manja, pamarrpa, pirli.** SAME AS: **ngalyarrpa, yilyampuru.**

jilja-marra-marra (N): multiple sandhills, sand ridges, sandhill country, rows of sandhills. ♦Yirlangkurrunyu karnalu watiyakari ngarrirni yika

Figure 4: Partial dictionary entry for *jilja* 'sandhill'.

piler and dictionary user. Text-based descriptions can provide rich and useful information but in some cases these fall short of allowing the reader to capture in their mind's eye or to fully fathom fine nuances of meaning, or to see the significance of a given word relative to others in its particular semantic domain.

3.3.1 Artefacts

Entries where a visual illustration is useful include the range of manufactured articles and artefacts, such as tools, weapons, body decorations, and shelters all of which have a distinctive Warlpiri "style". This also applies to aspects of Warlpiri country, such as its land forms, water sources, flora and fauna and also to methods of food preparation. The interplay between textual explanation and graphic illustration enables the user to construct a truer perception of what the vocabulary in these areas refers to. Elements of how the word *pikirri* 'spearthrower' is presented to the dictionary reader, shown in Figure 5, illustrate this point.

Pikirri ngulaji yangka watiya pilirri-pilirri manu narnngu-kurlu manu rdakurlpa kirrirdimpayi, kurlarda kijirninja-kurlangu manu wiral-pinja-kurlangu -- *pikirri*ji.

A *spearthrower* (pikirri) is a thin curved thing make of wood with a hook and a long concave section. It is for throwing spears and launching them.

Pikirri, wardiji wiri, watiya -- rdilyki-pakarni karnalu, ngulanya karnalu pampi tiirl-pakarni. Ngurrju-mani karnalu, rdukulku-manilki karnalu -- nyanunguju pikirri, witarralku mani karnalu yangka wakirdi -- ngula karnalu yali-kirra narra yirrarni. Palya karnalurla yirrarni, wawirrirli karnalu wirlingki wayirni narraji. Yangka jatarla-kurraji nyanunguju pikirri palyanya kalurla yirrarni.

A *spearthrower* (*pikirri*) is made from a big section of mulga wood that we chop down and we split into two. We make them (from it). We hollow it out -- the *spearthrower* that is -- and then we taper it down to a narrow end that we attach the hook to. We put spinifex wax on it, and we tie the hook on with kangaroo leg sinew. It is on the handle of the *spearthrower* that we put spinifex wax.

Figure 5: Definitions and illustrations of *pikirri* 'spearthrower'.

3.3.2 Flora and fauna

Given the many published works on the flora and fauna of central Australia, photographic images were mostly restricted to the lesser known food sources such as the insect galls which form on Bloodwood (*Corymbia terminalis)* trees shown in Figure 6.

Those galls which are on the bloodwood trees, they split them open to eat the insect larvae (*warnparnpi*) inside. From these larvae, they are nymphs first, they all turn into winged insects. We call *wangarla* those small things like mosquitoes, which have two wings and which originate from *warnparnpi* insects, inside the bloodwood gall. When the tree dies, when the galls all dry up, then the dried galls all crack and all those *wangarla* insects like mosquitoes fly out. We are not describing those big *wangarla* , the feathered *wangarla* ('crows'), which are birds, but rather the little insects like mosquitoes that live in the bloodwood galls.

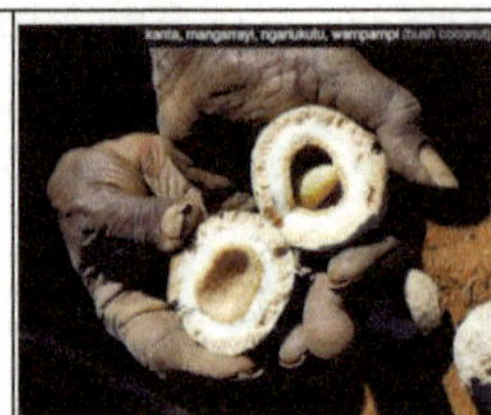

Figure 6: Translation of definition of *kanta* 'Bloodwood gall' with photograph.

A vegetable staple following good rains are yams (*Ipomoeia costata*) such as those described and shown in Figure 7. These plants produce three distinct tubers, each with its own names, coming from different parts of the plant.

People used to dig up piles of yams. The earth would swell up as a result of the presence of the bush potato below.

The surface runners spread out from the bush potato plant in different directions. They go down into the earth. They send roots down into the earth. Then the actual edible tubers form down in the ground -- what we call *ngamarna*. They come from the plant and form an edible tuber.

Figure 7: Definitions of *ngamarna* 'bush potatoes' with photographs.

3.3.3 Water sources

Given the scarcity of surface water in Warlpiri country, knowledge of the location of subterranean sources (wells, springs), especially permanent ones, and of where to find ephemeral surface waters (rockholes, swamps, creeks, claypans) was crucial to assure survival. Each water source is named, features in ancestral stories and is celebrated in song. Recall that people only moved about their country on foot. Some of the named water sources are shown on the map in Figure 8. Water-related vocabulary is rich as each type of water source is distinguished in the lexicon.

The dictionary entries distinguish formal definitions from examples in which the featured word is used. In Figure 9 the English translation of one definition of *warnirri* 'rockhole' (rain water captured in rock cavity) is given along with photographs of each type referred to in the definition, one showing how people drank from a rockhole.

3.3.4 Kin relations

Other domains are more abstract and they pose different challenges. There is almost no one-to-one match between Warlpiri and English kin terms, as illustrated in Figure 10. Furthermore, the relationships between *all* Warlpiri people (and others in their social orbit) can be referred to by kin terms. Kin terminology reflects a complex network of relationships based on the contrast between paternal and maternal relations (Laughren 1982).

Furthermore the principles that underlie words that designate the eight Warlpiri social classes known colloquially as "skins" (*subsections* in the anthropological literature), are even more foreign to non-Aboriginal English speakers, as are the ways in which society can be viewed as made up of complementary halfs (or *moieties*). The "skin names" which designate the class to which a person belongs are commonly used to address and refer to people where use of their personal name is inappropriate. The graphic representation of words in this domain which models the overall system of

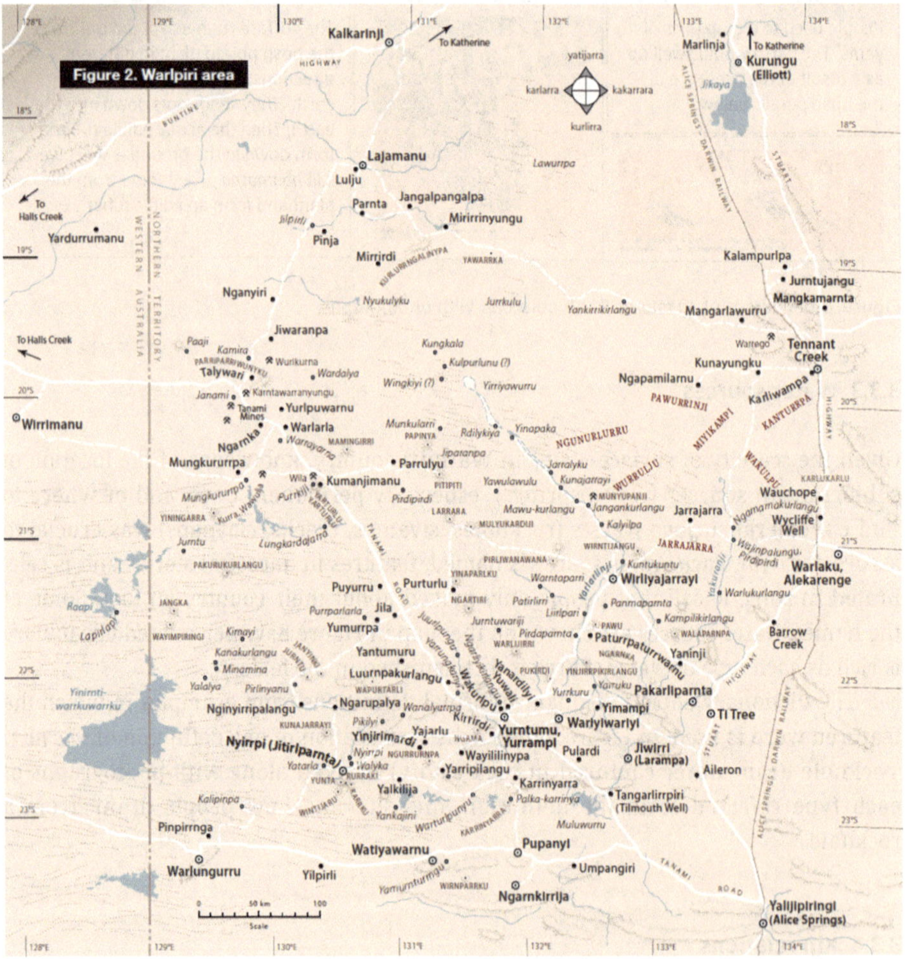

Figure 8: Named locations of water sources (map by Brenda Thornley).

A rockhole (*warnirri*) is what lies like on a big rocky hill, on the side of it, on up on top, on the surface. You can't see one on the ground, find a rockhole there. If you see some whitewoods, or mulga trees, or a clump of conkerberry bushes, there may be what is also called a rockhole there on some flat rock. The rockhole might lie there just on the rocky surface. You can find one in a clump of mulga trees, you can find a rockhole there, if it's lying there on an expanse of flat rock – not up on a rocky hill – that's how a rockhole that is down on ground level is. That's a rockhole.

Figure 9: Definition of *warnirri* 'rockhole' and photographic images.

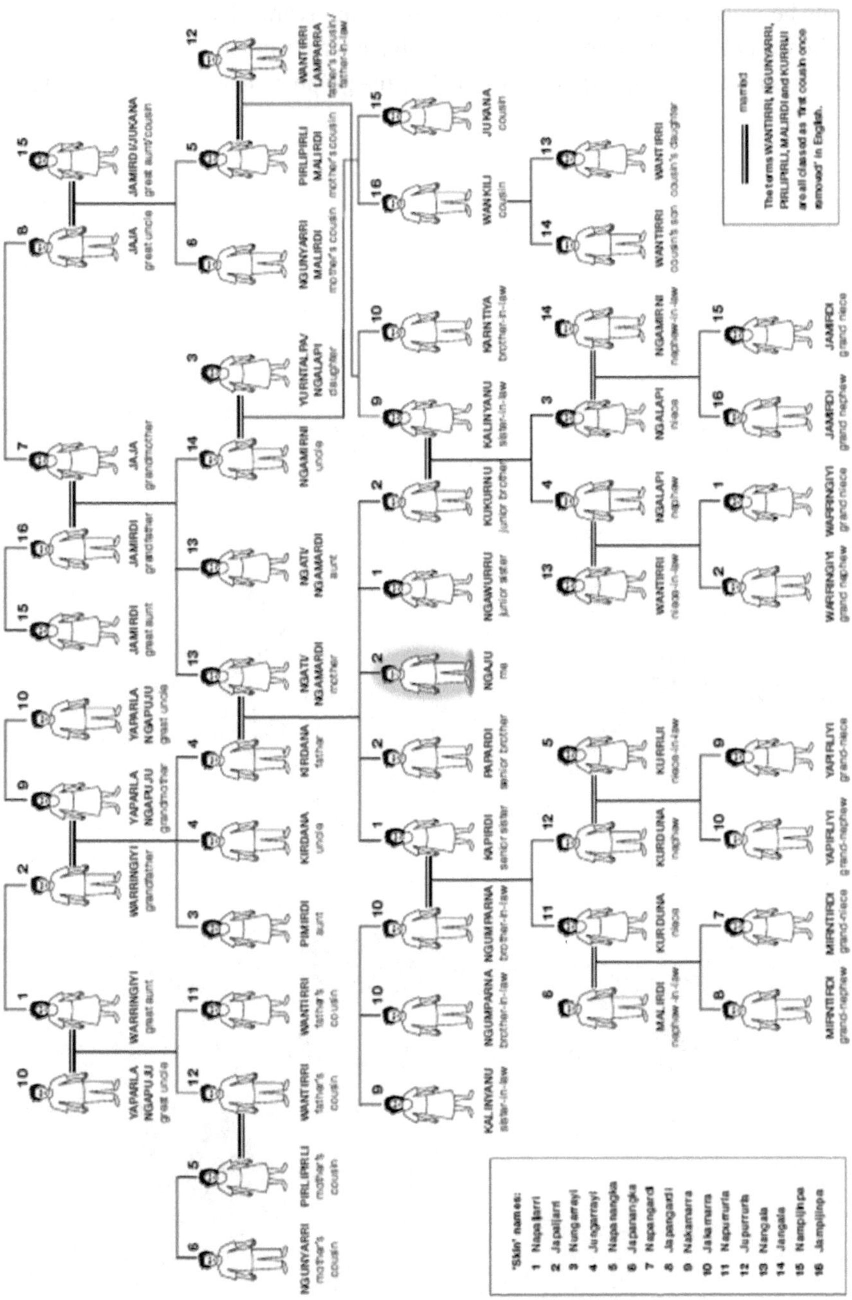

Figure 10: Warlpiri words for a male speaker's kin folk.

relations between these named classes reveals to the reader how the "skin" system works in a way that a written definition of a single term cannot, although definitions usefully supplement the information carried by the graphic model shown in Figure 11.

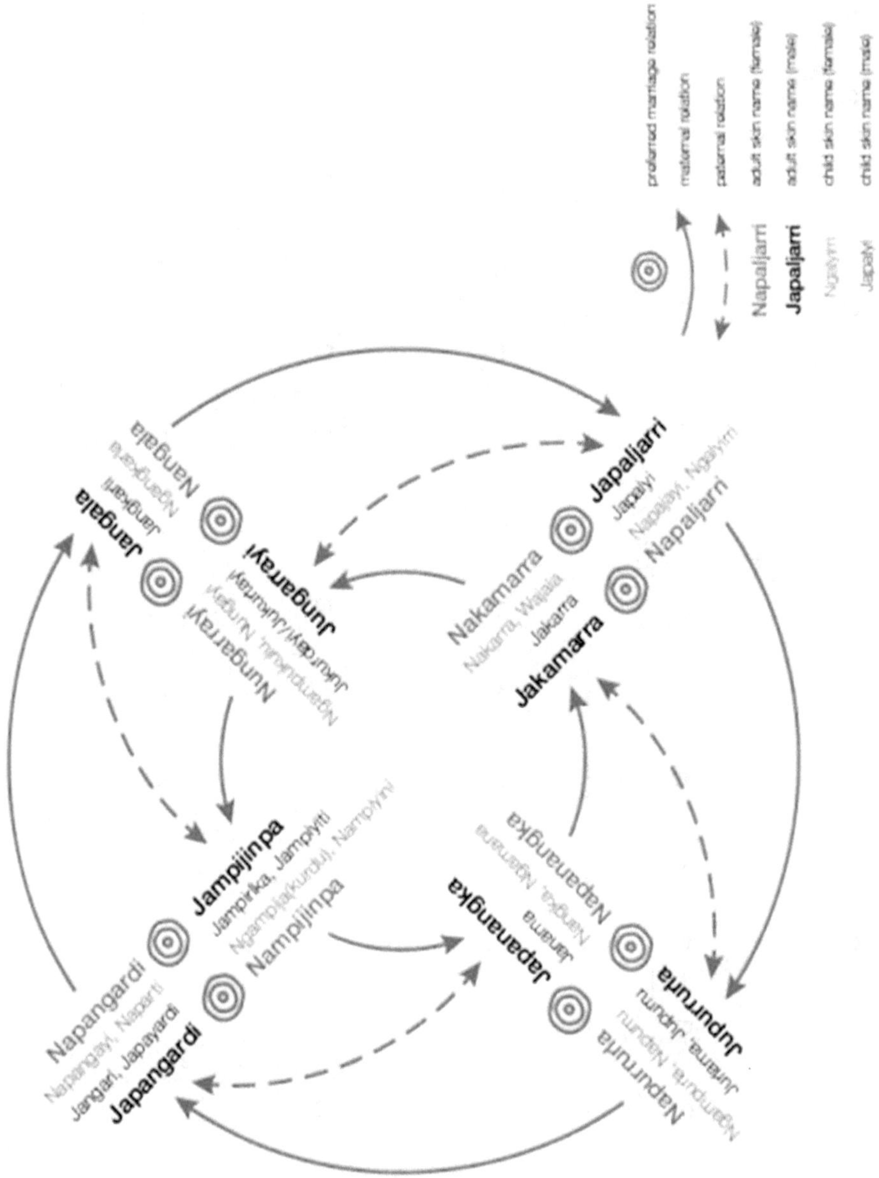

Figure 11: Warlpiri "skin" names.

Warlpiri also use "trirelational" kin terms which encode the relationship between the speaker, and the two people (or groups of people) referred to by a kin term. For example, while the word for speaker's own mother (or mother of speaker's sibling) is *ngati* or *ngamardi* (depending on dialect), when referring to the mother of a non-sibling, other words must be used. This principle is totally foreign to English speakers, so the textual explanations and examples of usage in the dictionary entries for these words are usefully complemented by a graphic representation as shown by comparing the information in Figures 12 with the dictionary entry for one of these 'mother' words part of which is shown in Figure 13.

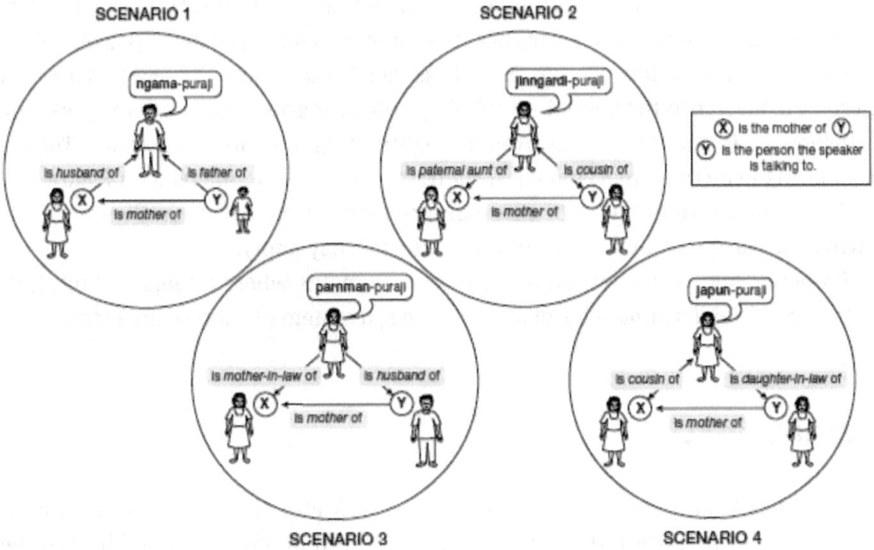

Figure 12: Model of "trirelational" kin term usage.

From dictionary entry for *jinngardi*
Kajilparla wangkami Napaljarri -rlangu nyanunguku purdangkaku jukanaku, kajika payirni Nampijinpa,
jukana-nyanu, Napaljarrirliji. "Nyarrpara -kurra kanpa yani? *Jinngardi* -puraji-kirlangu-kurra mayi?
Nungarrayi-kirlangu-kurra?" "Yuwayi, *ngati*-kirlangu-kurra karna yani waja."
If Napaljarri for example is talking to her cousin then she might ask Nampijinpa, her cousin, "Where are
you going? To your *mother*'s place? To Nungarrayi's place?" "Yes, I am going to my *mother*'s."

Figure 13: From dictionary entry for *jinngardi* (mother of cross-cousin and paternal aunt of speaker).

Kin terms also constitute a subcategory of nominals which host a distinctive set of suffixes which mark deictic features of the people referred to as a function of their kin relationship. This is another characteristic of kin terms. While each of these has its own dictionary entry, they are also shown in the tables of kin terms in Appendix 3 and are again listed in Appendix 4 along with all suffixes and enclitics.

3.3.5 Directions

Another semantic domain characterised by specific morphology where each member is best understood as an element in an overall system is that of cardinal (horizontal) and vertical directions. These terms are used in many contexts where speakers of European languages would use terms such as "left" and "right" or even "here" and "there". Furthermore the special morphology which marks these words express fine distinctions that can only be conveyed in English by multi-word expressions. The distinctions made by these morphological contrasts are shown in the table in Figure 14.

A graphic representation of cardinal direction terms, shown in Figure 15, was drawn by a Warlpiri man to show how these terms may apply.

Pronouns and verb conjugations are other domains where understanding single forms depends on locating their place in an overall system of contrasting forms.

4 What next?

The WED has been published as a hard cover book and also as an ebook. Modern technology allows more interactive behaviour within an electronic publication between media and file types and also between a Dictionary and its users. We aim to include other media into the data base including sound files, video and film clips as well as additional images and graphics. The planned electronic version of the dictionary would be interrogated via the *Kirrkirr* interface created by Kevin Jansz, Christopher Manning and Nitin Indurkhya which also allows the user to "create" their own version of the dictionary by deciding on the information fields to be displayed, and the search type (literal or fuzzy) and search fields, and it allows them to add their own notes and to play a series of word games generated from the dictionary contents.[7]

7 Information about *Kirrkirr* can be accessed at https://nlp.stanford.edu/kirrkirr/ (last access: 2 August 2024).

	north	east	south	west	up	down
to X	yatijarra	kakarrara	kurlirra *or* kurlarra	karlarra	kankarlarra	kaninjarra
towards X	yatijarra-purda	kakarrara-purda	kurlirra-purda	karlarra-purda	kankarlarra-purda	kaninjarra-purda
X-wards	yatijarra-kari	kakarrara-kari	kurlirra-kari	karlarra-kari	kankarlarra-kari	kaninjarra-kari
from X	yatijarni	kakarrarni	kurlarni	karlarni	kankarlarni	kaninjarni
on X side of	yatijarni-nginti	kakarrarni-nginti	kurlarni-nginti	karlarni-nginti	kankarlarni-nginti	kaninjarni-nginti
just to X of	yatuju	kakarru	kurlulu	karlu	kankarlu	kanunju
in X direction	yatuju-kari	kakarru-kari	kurlulu-kari	karlu-kari	kankarlu-kari	kanunju-kari
across X side of	yatujumparra	kakarrumparra	kurlaminyarra	karlumparra	kankarlumparra	kanunjumparra
along X side of	yatujumparrarnu	kakarrumparrarnu	kurlaminyarrarnu	karlumparrarnu	kankarlumparrarnu	kanunjumparrarnu
having crossed on X side	yatujumparra-warnu	kakarrumparra-warnu	kurlaminyarra-warnu	karlumparra-warnu	kankarlumparra-warnu	kanunjumparra-warnu
far to X	yatujumpayi	kakarrumpayi	kurlulumpayi	karlumpayi	kankarlumpayi	kanunjumpayi

Figure 14: Warlpiri cardinal direction and “up-down” words.

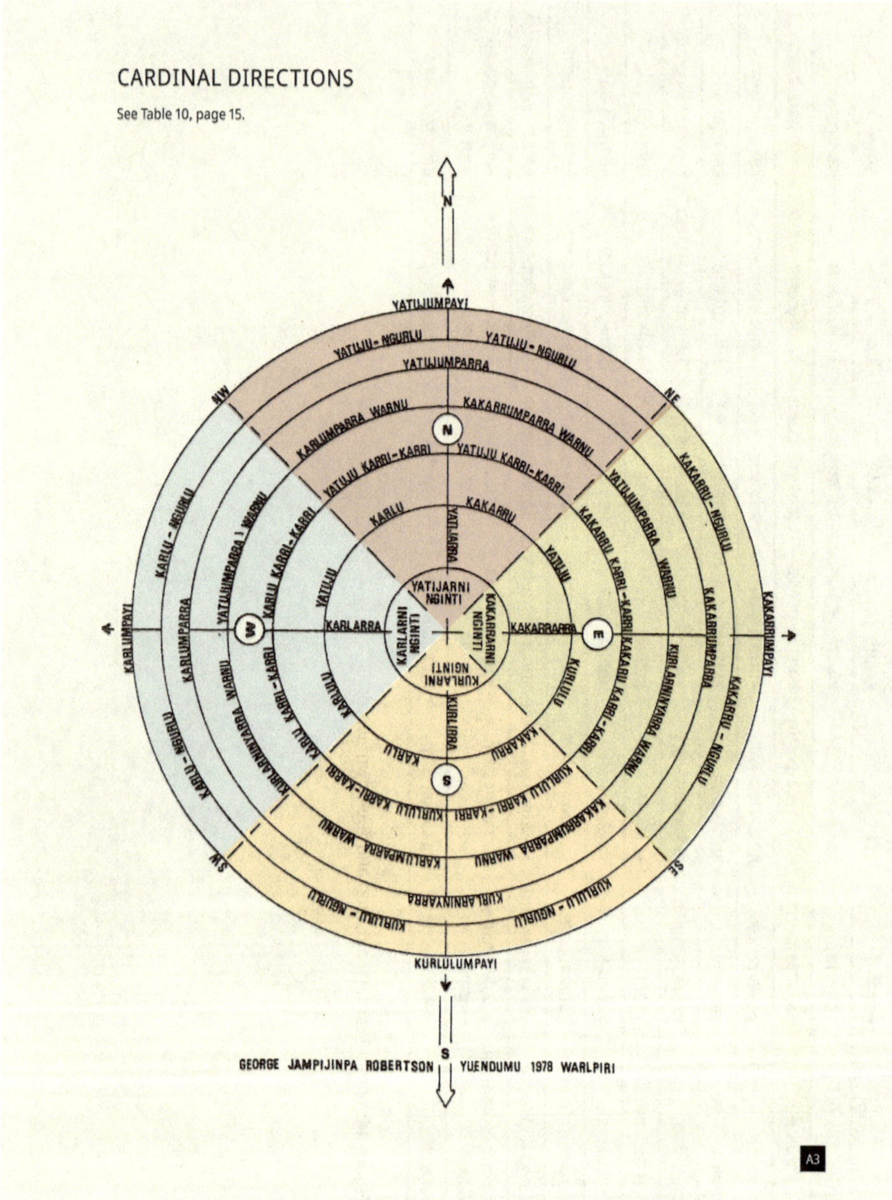

Figure 15: Warlpiri cardinal direction terms.

Bibliography

Edited volumes, and chapters in edited volumes

Hoogenraad, Robert (2001): Critical reflections on the history of bilingual education in Central Australia. In: Simpson, Jane/Nash, David/Laughren, Mary/Austin, Peter/Alpher, Barry (eds.): Forty years on: Ken Hale and Australian languages. Canberra: Pacific Linguists, ANU Press, 123–150.

Laughren, Mary (1982): Warlpiri kinship structure. In: Heath, Jeffrey/Merlan, Francesca/Rumsey, Alan (eds.): Languages of Kinship in Aboriginal Australia. Sydney: University of Sydney, 72–85.

McConvell, Patrick/Laughren, Mary (2004): The Ngumpin-Yapa Subgroup. In: Bowern, Claire/Koch, Harold (eds.): Australian Languages: Classification and the comparative method. Amsterdam: Benjamins, 151–178.

Meakins, Felicity Ennever, Thomas/Osgarby, David/Browne, Mitch/Hamilton-Hollaway, Amanda (2023): Ngumpin-Yapa languages. In: Bowern, Claire (ed.): The Oxford guide to Australian languages. Oxford: Oxford University Press, 918–932.

Nash, David (2022): The emergence of the Warlpiri Encyclopaedic Dictionary: a chronological account. In: WED. Appendix 6, 1380–1388.

Dictionary

WED = Warlpiri Encyclopaedic Dictionary: Warlpiri yimi-kirli manu jaru-kurlu. Compiled by Laughren, Mary (chief compiler)/Hale, Kenneth/Egan, Jeannie Nungarrayi/Patrick, Marlurrku Paddy Jangala/Hoogenraad Robert/Nash, David/Simpson, Jane. Canberra: Aboriginal Studies Press, 2022.

Kate Burridge and Howard Manns

Behind the lingo – slang and the dictionary

Abstract: This paper examines the complexities of slang, focusing on its ephemeral nature, unpredictable evolution and challenges in lexicographical documentation. Using Australian slang as a case study, the discussion spans historical examples such as James Hardy Vaux's 19th-century convict glossary, modern slang innovations, as well as the results from a 2021 survey of 2,848 participants on "Aussie" terms. By analyzing linguistic survivors and fleeting trends, the paper highlights cultural, sociohistorical and linguistic forces shaping slang's lifecycle. Technology, globalization and Australia's embrace of informality further complicate the task of tracing and defining slang. As an embodiment of linguistic creativity, slang exemplifies the interplay between formal and informal language, reflecting a dynamic, ever-changing lexicon that lexicographers must navigate with increasing complexity.

Keywords: slang, etymology, etymythology, phonesthemes, sound symbolism, language change

Schlagwörter: Slang, Etymologie, Etymythologie, Phonästhems, Lautsymbolik, Sprachwandel

1 Introduction

The focus of this paper is on slang expressions – the loose cannons of the linguistic world. Their unruly nature, and in particular the many diverse and unpredictable forces that shape their evolution, present a number of challenges for the makers of our dictionaries. The first challenge revolves around the shelf-life of slang terms – most are spectacularly short-lived, but a number last for centuries, sometimes even retaining their playful and casual character. The second is a related challenge that centres on the difficulty of documenting the etymology of these terms.

To delve into both these issues, we present examples of success stories and lost causes within slanguage, particularly Australian slanguage, old and modern. The historical examples that form the backdrop of our discussion are among the survivors in James Hardy Vaux's 19th century glossary of convict slang; a few modern innovations and surprising survivors; and a selection of modern examples from the findings of a 2021 survey, in which 2,848 participants were called on to supply their favourite "Aus-

Kate Burridge, Howard Manns, School of Languages, Literatures, Cultures and Linguistics, Clayton Campus, Monash University, Australia 3800.

https://doi.org/10.1515/9783112216644-011

sie" slang terms[1]. Drawing on insights from Vaux, our survey and these prominent slangy innovations and survivors, the paper highlights the complex of cultural, socio-historical and linguistic drivers of lexical change in an attempt to uncover the factors that account for why some expressions have staying power beyond a fleeting craze.

Of course the evolution of all words, not just slang, is shaped by this interplay of pressures, and life-cycle and etymology are already well recognized lexicographical challenges. But, slang, "the pulsing life of language" (Partridge 1933: 19), epitomizes linguistic creativity and dynamism, and keeping pace with its constant evolution takes the challenges to another level. Moreover, fresh complexities have been introduced by the fact that slang has now well and truly escaped its informal boundaries. Technology and globalization have been accelerating change by contributing to shifting the dynamics between private and public domains – pinning down slang terms now requires navigating not only rapid changes, but also new tensions between formal and informal language. In this regard, Australia is slightly unusual. The country's love of informality has always given slang and swearing free rein (and this is very evident in the public life of these words, something that is often remarked upon by overseas visitors to Australia; see Schweinberger/Burridge 2025). This deep national attachment to the vernacular dates back to the original mix of slang, dialect and underworld jargon that gave rise to Australian English – shaped by a spirit of anti-authoritarianism, colloquial speech grew into a defining marker of identity providing additional conundrums for lexicographers.

2 Defining slang and "Australian slang"

Definitions of slang can be elusive. Some works operationalise and use the term slang but do not define it (e.g., Djenar/Ewing/Manns 2018), while others go to great lengths to define slang and why what they are writing about is indeed slang (e.g., Reyes 2005). In a sea of contested and under-defined meanings, long-time slang scholars like Julie Coleman (2014) and Connie Eble (1994) provide a useful starting point for understanding "slang". Julie Coleman (2014: 7) writes that slang is:

> informal, non-technical language that often seems novel to the user and/or listener, and that challenges a social or linguistic norm. It can also imply complicity in value judgements and thus play a performative role in defining personal or group identity.

1 This survey was conducted by the members of the research group "Metaphors and identities in the Australian vernacular", a project that has been supported by the Australian Research Council under the scheme Special Research Initiatives 2020 (SR200200350), see https://auslanguage.net (last access: 29 April 2025). There were 2,848 responses to the first prompt of the survey ('very good'); the figure then dropped to 2,372 by the third prompt ('stupid').

Eble's (1994) earlier take on slang largely overlaps with this definition, but she also adds the importance of "flippancy" or playful humour to slang. Eble (1994) also highlights the "short-lived" nature of slang expressions. However, as we show below, "short-lived" creates some thorny issues. For those examining slang, there is a tricky distinction to be made between "slang" and "colloquial language". The distinction is not always clear. The difference between slang and colloquial language is often presented as a matter of degree (Blake 2010: 200–211). In fact, the Oxford English Dictionary (OED) and Blake (2010: 200) share an assessment of slang as words and phrases that are "very colloquial".

Modern views and approaches to slang can be traced to the 19th century. This was an era of rapid vocabulary expansion in English, due to migration and scientific and technological advances (Bailey 1996). During this time, there was a proliferation of works on "correct" words and "right" ways of speaking, but also works on the "secret" and "curious" language of criminal and street types. Some writers – like Charles Dickens – began to integrate the slangy words of the poor, criminal and street types into their works. Slang was varyingly viewed as an object of fascination but also "bad" language that needed to be stamped out. In contemporary social terms, slang remains a lightning rod for controversy. For some, it is "the people's poetry" (Adams 2009) but for others it is "dustbin language" (Burchfield 1989). Writing of "slangery", John Badcock (1823, under the pen name John Bee), says, "[w]hat a host of enemies will not this one little word engender? How will every repetition and inflection of *slang* raise the ire, expand the nostrils, and redden the frothy muns . . ." (p. iv). Slang, especially youth slang, is often in the crosshairs of media, schools and adults. Because slang challenges popular notions of "good" speaking, it is often described as "linguistic mayhem" and its users as "inarticulate" (Kiesling 2004: 281).

Of course, modern language scholars and dictionary-makers take a more nuanced approach to slang. Burridge (2023) points out that "new language" (like slang) might more aptly be viewed in terms of metaphors of "dirt" and "taboo". Drawing on anthropologist Mary Douglas (1966), she argues that "dirt" is merely "matter out of place", and the public's negative view of slang is a reaction to the dirtying of those "tidy classification systems" humans rely on (p. 249). Yet, dirt is in the eye of the beholder and, while "the urge to cleanse and control will remain constant, definitions of dirt will shift with time" (p. 259). Language scholars know that slang normally takes one of three paths. First, most slang will fade away with time. While there was a moral and linguistic panic about "bodgie" youth slang in Australia in the 1940s/1950s, bodgie slang faded when the bodgies became adults. We no longer hear about the *royal smooch* 'girlfriend' and her penchant for *etching the edges* 'applying lipstick'. Second, however, some slang survives and rises to the level of respectability. Words like *banter, hoax, mob, shabby* and *tandem* could have easily gone the way of the *royal smooch*, but didn't (see Blake 2010: 206). We use them as part of our everyday English. But thirdly and lastly, there is a special category of slang that maintains its slangy edge. The word *cool* is somehow still *cool* after decades. It's not been consigned to the dustbin of history, but it's also not gained that kind of respectability that goes with words like *shabby* or *tandem* (Moore 2004).

The Australian lexicon presents an interesting conundrum when it comes to the latter pathway – these slangy words that somehow stay slang. Many Australians refer to their cherished lexicon as "Australian slang". However, the most core aspects of this lexicon – so-called Australian slang – are more than 100 years old. Moore (2008) has flagged a series of words that encapsulate Australian identity and social values (key aspects of slang, as noted by Coleman 2014 and Eble 1994). But in each case, the longevity of these words raises sticky theoretical issues for Australian slang's status as a slang – *mate* (first attested in 1842); *wowser* (1879); *larrikin* (1891); *dinkum* (1894); *battler* (1896); *bludger* (1899); *ocker* (1916); *rort* (1919). Moore (2014: 175) flags this creates a serious issue for Australian dictionary-makers: "we have a seeming paradox: for mainstream Australian lexicography there is no Australian slang; for popular Australian lexicography, Australian English is full of slang". There are clear tensions between the way "Australian slang" functions in the wider community, but how language scholars view the term. In the strictest scholarly terms, Australian slang meets most but not all of the criteria for slang as per Coleman (2014) and Eble (1994) above (see Manns et al. 2024, for an extended discussion of this point). However, Australians do cherish their "slang" and this makes it a useful focus for understanding the issues that dictionary-makers face, but also many of the issues of longevity that word-watchers seek to understand.

3 Slangy words that stay slang – some early examples

A work such as James Hardy Vaux's *New and Comprehensive Vocabulary of the Flash Language* confirms, the shelf-life of slang can vary unexpectedly.[2] Vaux was a convict, transported to Australia on three separate occasions during his "checkered and eventful life" (his words); in 1812 he compiled a collection of *flash language* (which he defined as "the cant language used by the family"); all entries follow one of the three paths just identified for slang. The majority of his 771 entries are "the mayflies of language", as J.M. Wattie poetically put it back in 1930 – vibrant but short-lived (e.g. *barnacles* 'spectacles'), but around 20% persist today.[3] Most have lost their vitality and become part of the mainstream (e.g. *patter* 'talk'), showing the usual progression for

2 Vaux's dictionary appeared in Volume 2 of *Memoirs of James Hardy Vaux, Written by himself* printed (1819) in London by W. Clowes (https://babel.hathitrust.org/cgi/pt?id=nyp.33433082394838, last access: 29 April 2025).

3 Many thanks to Dylan Hughes for compiling a spreadsheet of Vaux's entries, and a special thanks to Keith Allan for doing the hard work of determining the survivors.

language change (as language evolution shows, yesterday's informal usage becomes tomorrow's formal usage; see Bauer 1994: 17; 144). However, a baffling few have not only survived, they have remained freshly slangy (e.g. *croak* 'to die'; *grub* 'food'). As just flagged, their survival is the challenge to unravel.

The table 1 below is a sample of just 20 of the survivors, selected because of their frequency in general usage – all expressions are still part of informal vocabulary, and some have distinctively Australian uses (e.g. *swag, plant*).[4] The dates given in the table show the first appearances as provided by the *OED*. Pinpointing first sightings of words is notoriously difficult of course, especially for slang which even today can live and breathe in speech long before it is documented and (possibly) placed in a dictionary. Nevertheless, even these provisional dates emphasize the remarkable longevity of this group of words (and the other survivors).

Table 1: A selection of 20 survivors from Vaux's glossary of slang (1819).

Less colloquial	More colloquial
bolt 'run away suddenly' (1522)	*chum* 'a fellow prisoner' (1684)
bring to light 'reveal [booty]' (1526)	*croak* 'die' (1819)
dues 'what's owing' (1423)	*dicky* 'inferior' (1788)
frisk 'search [stolen goods]' (1789)	*duds* 'apparel' (1567)
grab 'seize, apprehend' (1589)	*flash* 'smart', 'to reveal' (1785)
job 'work [arranged crime]' (1557)	*grub* 'victuals of any kind' (1659)
patter 'to talk' (1450)	*mug* 'face' (1708)
plant 'hide; conceal' (1610)	*pigs* 'police runners' (1811)
swag 'booty' (1794)	*pins* 'legs' (1515)
toddle 'walk slowly' (1590)	*weed* 'tobacco' (1600)

Items in the right column have been labelled "colloquial" in The Macquarie Dictionary (MD); they represent the more slangy end of a register continuum, though as earlier described this distinction is not clear-cut, especially for Australian English. While the MD describes colloquialisms as "words and phrases which most commonly suggest a relaxed and easy attitude to things [. . .] all share the quality of being inappropriate for use in serious or formal situations", tellingly, the Australian National Dictionary (AND) omits labels such as "colloquial" from these words. From the beginning these editors have argued that this kind of sensitive handling is "overrestrictive" for Australian English, a variety that has always allowed "easy movement between formal and informal usage" (Introduction, 1st ed. *AND*; see Laugesen

4 According to the *OED*'s frequency values, all 40 terms are at least Band 4 (so "likely be used unproblematically in fiction or journalism"); admittedly, this is a rough approximation since frequency bands do not capture slang sub-usages (and of course words of Australian significance, such as *swag* and *plant*, could potentially show higher frequency levels).

2024).[5] The AND's approach contrasts starkly with the good etiquette gauge used by other mainstream dictionaries to determine whether words are "slang", "colloquial", "slang", "vulgar" and so on without reference to context.

A number of expressions in Vaux's collection have shifted completely in meaning (*swag* originally 'stolen plunder' is now more usually 'a camper's bed-roll'), and many like *chum* have shed their criminal senses; however, most meanings have remained fairly stable (e.g. *grab*). Some expressions in the left column (e.g. *grab* and *toddle*) have more colloquial uses in other phrases (e.g. *how does that grab you* and *toddle off*), but for the most part they fall into standard everyday vocabulary. In fact, all expressions in this column (with the exception of *patter*) started life as general terms, but Vaux's often lengthy explanations show that they were pressed into a specialist criminal service within the cant and slang of the day; for example, the entry for *bolt* describes a thief responding to an alarm; *dues* refers to punishment; *job* is defined as a "concerted robbery" (see Coleman's 2004 account of 19th-century cant). The survival of these terms is not probably surprising, given they always had a life outside of these slangy uses.

More interesting are the colloquial survivors in the right-hand column, which have followed the last of the three trajectories typically taken by slang. Not only have they endured, they are still slangy after centuries – contemporary-sounding, even a little "disgraceful", as Vaux originally described them. What has kept *pins* 'legs' alive and relevant, but not *stamps* (used for legs and shoes)? How can we explain its longevity?

4 Opening the door to slang in the dictionary

In 1989, Robert Burchfield, the editor of the OED at the time, wrote of the impossibility of stopping continuity and change in language: "No form of linguistic engineering and no amount of linguistic legislation will prevent the cycles of change that lie ahead" (1989: 173). Words and their meanings, more than other areas of the linguistic system, are constantly on the move, and dictionary compilers are always having to redraw the admission and exclusion boundaries for marginal vocabulary items. Reference materials that fail to reflect current usage, lose their relevance and usually their readership (cf. Stockwell/Minkova 2001: 191–192) – and yet paradoxically, efforts by lexicographers and style guide authors to embrace language trends can provoke concerns about falling standards in language and education (e.g. the regular controversies around updates to the official Scrabble dictionary).

5 This tradition continues with the second edition (2016), although some words (especially racist terms) are branded if they are judged to be offensive.

With the current tilt towards casual language, however, these objections have become fewer and quieter. The increasing informality of communication and behavioural norms has for some time now been driving a preference for more conversational, relaxed and accessible forms of expression – and the public airing of these colloquial features has been blurring the already blurry lines between informal and formal, speech and writing and private and public (see Mair's 2024 reflections on the four related "-izations" (colloquialization, conversationalization, informalization and democratization for corpus-informed research across languages); also Biber/Finegan's 1988 early account of the evolution of writing styles and the "drift" towards orality). The cultural, social and of course technological shifts that have been steering these changes have elevated the vernacular and given it a new prestige – features once condemned as ignorance and corruption are now viewed with pride (as already highlighted, Australia's cultural affection for slang has always ensured its place as a cherished form of expression).

People's preference for informal lexis is not surprisingly reflected in recent dictionary updates. The Australian English contributions to the OED's July 2024 updates, for example, includes a hotchpotch of boisterous slang among their new entries: *alco* ('an alcoholic'), *bizzo* ('a thingummy'; from *business*), *pash rash* ('a rash or inflammation around the mouth resulting from passionate kissing'), *to strain the potatoes* ('to urinate'), *to grog on* ('to drink alcohol over an extended period'), *no wuckers* and *no wucking furries* (an assurance that all is fine, or to express one's agreement or acquiescence; from 'no fucking worries').[6] The expressions appear so casual, some even so newly minted, that readers might wonder at the wisdom of editors to include them at all. But we know they have been scrutinized within an inch of their lives and would not be there unless they showed signs of durability; in other words, staying power or the ability to succeed and develop over time. However, determining durability is no straightforward matter.

There is a sense in which mainstream dictionary-making was more straightforward for early lexicographers. New entries were sourced almost exclusively from books, and dictionaries were largely repositories of respectable words – anything else that managed to sneak through would be branded (originally with symbols such as the dagger (†), the double dagger (‡), the asterisk (*), even the fleur-de-lis (⚜), and later with more precise usage labels such as "low", "(im)proper", "ludicrous", "barbarous", "vulgar", as appeared in Samuel Johnson's 1755 dictionary (e.g. *shabby* which he defined as "a word that has crept into conversation and low writing; but ought not to be admitted into the language"; see Burridge 2019). These days, it is very different. The digital revolution, combined with the democratic and descriptive nature of modern dictionaries, means that lexicographers cast their nets wide to capture diverse

6 https://www.oed.com/discover/aussieness-new-australian-english-additions-to-the-oed/ (last access: 29 April 2025).

kinds of texts. These can be newspapers, magazines, pamphlets, menus, memos, TV and radio broadcasts and, of course, emails, chat-room discussions blogs and so on – all generating a never-ending pool of slang creators and a bounty of fresh vocabulary each year for lexicographers to track (the Global Language Monitor estimates that these days new words are created every 98 minutes[7]).

As a recent slang word that emerged from internet culture, *skibidi* highlights the two dictionary-related challenges described earlier. *Skibidi* has no inherent meaning but is often used as a part of gaming culture. It might be shouted in frustration, to say something is "cool", and so on. The first dictionary-related challenge is will *skibidi* endure long-term? As we go on to discuss, a concurrence of factors might create the perfect set of conditions to launch the career of a word, but the prospects for lasting success are unclear. *Skibidi* has risen quickly, but it might fizzle out just as fast, or it might gain widespread use and remain enduringly popular. So how do lexicographers determine if an expression has lasting relevance and the potential to stick around – in other words, does it have a place in mainstream dictionaries?

The second challenge involves its creative etymology. Modern slang such as *skibidi* demonstrates the layered and often chaotic influences that are at play in lexical evolution and that make dating and untangling the nuances of colloquial expressions so difficult at times. In the etymological notes to accompany the September updates of the OED, Philip Durkin (the deputy chief editor) explained that "even for quite common words, we sometimes have to state quite honestly that we do not have a clear etymology".[8] The word *skibidi* is widely believed to have originated from a viral song but, as outlined in online discussions, its popularity benefited considerably from additional sources, including a rush of meme off-spring and, most notably, a surreal YouTube series *Skibidi Toilet* created by Alexey Gerasimov in February 2023 (featuring toilets with human heads). How much of this detail belongs in the etymological accounts of *skibidi*? Popular myths or "folk etymology" are thought to obscure a word's true origin – they are misconceptions that lexicographers must navigate in order to provide accurate accounts in their entries. However, as we demonstrate, when it comes to successful slang terms, there is usually no single "aha" starting point, but rather a conflation of influences (including anecdotes about their origins) that shape their meaning and their likelihood of success. While recent etymological accounts acknowledge lexical disorderliness, some even challenging the idea of the lexicon as a set of distinct words, each with a single, true etymon, they have done little to incorporate the untidy truths behind word histories.

7 https://languagemonitor.com/number-of-words-in-english/no-of-words/ (last access: 29 April 2025).
8 https://www.oed.com/information/updates/september-2024/ (last access: 29 April 2025).

4.1 Take off – the "perfect lexicographical storm"

To illustrate the challenges slang presents for dictionary compilation, let us examine a recent term that has gained remarkable popularity, yet has an unpredictable future: *twerk* ('to dance in a low squatting stance'). In his description of the overnight success of this word, Zimmer (2013) draws on the apt metaphor of the "perfect lexicographical storm". *Twerk*, both noun and verb, emerged in the 1990s (as part of the "bounce-music" scene of New Orleans), but it took two colliding doses of high-profile backing to shoot it to stardom in 2013 – a twerking Miley Cyrus coinciding with the inclusion of *twerk* in the quarterly new words update of Oxford Dictionaries and the predictable knock-on publicity (Is *twerk* a real word? Why are the Oxford's lexicographers fixated on trendy adolescent lingo? Is Miley Cyrus the reason *twerk* is in the dictionary? Do you know how to twerk? and so on). Advertising initiatives leave us in no doubt about the power of "celebrity" to attract attention to brands, products and services, and we see similar effects when lexical innovations are hitched to known names. Clearly social media has a big role in spreading these linguistic cults and trends – within a matter of hours, expressions can have a worldwide following (a recent example is *rizz* 'charm' (short for *charisma*); when (Spider-Man) actor Tom Holland used it five times in a short Buzzfeed interview, his remarks ignited a global flurry of meme creativity, and shortly after *rizz* was crowned the Oxford Word of the Year 2023).[9]

Filling a need is another important component of this lexicographical storm – *twerk* names a popular dance move and plugs a semantic gap, at least for the moment (dance moves come in and out of fashion). Certainly, Grieve's research involving internet slang lends statistical support to the importance of communicative usefulness as a predictor of survival, at least a broader perspective of this concept (see Grieve et al. 2016; Grieve 2018a; 2018b). In his study of Twitter words, Grieve expands the idea to include "words that express unique meanings, that are more efficient, and that can be used across a wide range of communicative contexts" (Grieve 2018a: 5). It stands to reason that filling a need in this way is an important aspect of survival; however, pinpointing what "usefulness" means is difficult, especially in the context of most slang. The simple fact is the majority of slang expressions are colloquial synonyms for already existing words, and in many semantic fields (such as sex, food, bawdy body parts and drink), we are looking at a revolving door of literally hundreds of words (Allan/Burridge 1991; 2006). Only a fraction of expressions ever survive, and many of the survivors do not remedy any obvious semantic shortfall. Clearly, usefulness is not simply a matter of functional gaps in the lexicon, but encompasses social meaning and cultural significance. As Enfield concludes in his wide-ranging account of "the utility of meaning", to properly grasp the meaning of words, we must under-

---

9 https://www.youtube.com/watch?v=ITvNeFBSpEs (last access: 29 April 2025).

stand people's reasons for using them (2015: 176), and in the next section we explore the idea of saliency to intergenerational identity and the role it plays in survival.

Additional factors have contributed to the success of *twerk*. Among modern methods of creating words, blending has emerged as a leading trendsetter, especially in slang; moreover they have become funnier (or 'punnier') and more memorable (see Lignos/Prichard 2015).[10] Most wordsmiths assume *twerk* to be a portmanteau. However, what exactly is being blended here? Oxford Dictionaries suggest it is a contraction "to work (it)" (Martin 2013), as do many twerkers themselves (*t'work* then spelled *twerk* to better reflect pronunciation; Gaunt 2015: 247). Tweeters have suggested compacted forms of *footwork* or *boot work* (i.e. working the booty), and even German *Gesamtkunstwerk* "the fusion of all the arts into a single medium of dramatic expression"[11]. Others have proposed a variety of different ingredients for blended *twerk* including *twitch, twat* and even *berk* (< *Berkley Hunt* 'cunt'). Multiple origins include these sorts of creation stories that speakers attach to their much-loved slang expressions; they may not carry the lexicographers' stamp of approval, but these creation myths indicate and bolster success. For the OED, the word *twerk* is "of uncertain origin", though "perhaps a blend of *twitch* (or perhaps *twist*) and *jerk* (or perhaps *quirk*)". English is awash with *tw-* words that relate to turning or distorting. *Twist, twitch, twirl, tweak, twiddle, twizzle, twistle*, and even the rare 16th-century verb *twirk* 'twirl [e.g. a moustache]' are just some. Any one of them – or perhaps all of them – could have inspired *twerk*. As we go on to illustrate, phonesthetic phenomena in English word formation are common to many success stories in the evolution of slang.

4.2 Survival – the making of an international lexical megastar

> For every international lexical megastar like "cool" which makes it, there are thousands of items being used in unusual ways, which just don't make it – the equivalent of bands which play a single gig and are forgotten forever. We hardly notice the slightly unusual uses, we don't copy them, and they don't make it into general consciousness nor into the linguistics literature. (Greville Corbett, p.c.,13 May 2016)

We now move to a much older success story, *OK* (*okay*), a word that not only took off in usage, it transcended its roots to become a truly global term. Now one of Corbett's "international lexical megastars", *OK* (*okay*) offers insights into the key elements that drive and sustain success over the long term. As our account of *twerk* has suggested, beyond high-profile endorsements and usefulness, there are two additional (inter-

10 Algeo's (1991) study of neologisms over a 50-year period (1941–91) showed blends counting for only 5% of new words; compare this to the roughly 34% blends in Tony Thorne's (2020) impressive online collection of over 100 COVID-related terms (and the figure increases to more than 40% if we consider only slang; see Burridge and Manns 2020).

11 https://twitter.com/blue439/status/372256656144338944 (last access: 29 April 2025).

twined) factors behind a word's rise to prominence: multiple origins and aesthetics. Both demonstrate the poetic inventiveness of ordinary people, and they reveal a folk culture that has been paid too little attention by lexicographers and linguists alike.

As Read originally documented in a series of articles in *American Speech* (e.g. Read 1963), *OK* first appeared in 1839 as an abbreviation of *Orl Korrekt*. It was one of a number of faddish abbreviations for jokey misspellings that included *OW* for *Orl Wright* (all right) and *KG* for *Know Go* (no go). None of these other comical abbreviations endured, but a concurrence of factors created the necessary lexical tempest that propelled *OK* into the limelight and maintained its continued prominence. Celebrity endorsement came from the Democratic candidate Martin Van Buren. Born in Kinderhook (New York State), he acquired the nickname "Old Kinderhook", and his supporters at the time (1840s) adopted this as an election slogan to raise money for campaigns. As Read (1963) emphasized, "Vote for OK" and the "OK Club" were certainly catchier than rallying cries using his Dutch name, or even his nickname Old Kinderhook. Expressions can take off in this way and even flourish, but this still does not guarantee they will be long-lasting. Just as politicians come and go, so too do their slogans. Other contributing factors ensured that *OK* was more than a temporary fixture in the public eye.

OK is handy – as a functional and adaptable discourse marker, it is widely used in lingua franca interactions and of paramount importance in facilitating communication in a globalized society (Sabbah-Taylor/Jenks 2024). Nevertheless, there's a lot of heavy lifting involved in making a linguistic innovation "stick" and become part of our everyday language. Young people often bear the brunt of this heavy lifting, as well as aggressive criticism, through their use of slang. For instance, to give a non-*OK* example, the youthful use of *like* as either a discourse/focus marker or intensifier (e.g. *it was like so difficult*) or quotative (e.g. *I was like, "gag me with a spoon"*) has been in the crosshairs of proscriptivists for decades. Marker/intensifier *like* has been around since the 1950s and quotative *like* since the 1970s (its spread usually associated with Valley Girls). In the 1990s, a high school teacher of one of the authors frequently and scornfully tapped a sign in his classroom with *like* in a red circle, crossed out. And yet, despite the pushback young people have faced for using this feature, it persists across generations – marker/intensifier *like* appears in 87% of first-language Englishes (Kortmann, 2020: 261). One part of this story is functionality, adaptability and filling a niche – discourse markers are a particularly salient place where this sort of innovation takes place. Quotative *like* has arguably survived because it is a useful way to mark a reduced commitment to what's been said (e.g. *I said, "gag me with a spoon"* = I definitely said it like this; *I was like, "gag me with a spoon"* = I might not have said it this way exactly, but this was the vibe of what I said) (see Tagliamonte and Hudson 1999). However, utility isn't necessarily enough and it sometimes takes some heavy lifting to keep these innovations alive across generations.

Returning to *OK*, as noted earlier, there is no "big bang" etymology for many slang terms, but rather a complex pattern of mutual influences, including those from popular etymologies – all coincide, not just to establish the form and its meaning, but also to contribute to its success. *OK* is a stellar illustration of what Oxford etymologist Durkin (2016: 252) has described as "the complex and often messy realities of the histories of words". What helped to popularize *OK* was the fact that it was also used as an abbreviation for other misspelled catch phrases such as *Out of Kash* (cash), *Oll Koming* and *Oll Konfirmed.* Many other competing theories relating to the origin of *OK* have been in evidence since its earliest appearances, and an extraordinary array of nearly 40 imaginative etymologies now form part of the support network that keeps this expression going. These include alternative English initialisms such as *Open Key* (the telegraph signal), *Orrin Kendall* (the purveyor of quality biscuits) and the boxing term *KO* (or *kayo*), an abbreviation for "knock out" – if the boxer wasn't *kayoed*, he was *OK*. Other sources draw from languages around the world and include Latin, Greek, Choctaw, Finnish, German and French.[12] There is scant support for most of these stories, and often the chronology does not align (boxing *kayo*, for example, appeared nearly 100 years after *OK*). However, a crucial facet of language change is "evaluation"; in other words, how a speech community reacts to a linguistic shift, and the ways in which these reactions affect its evolution (part of Weinreich et al.'s 1968 "actuation" problem). In the context of lexical change, group scrutiny can have a crucial effect on the propagation and integration of individual expressions, especially because they are more conspicuous than changes elsewhere. Lexicographers and linguists might throw wet blankets over "folk etymologies" in the form of cautious disclaimers such as "of uncertain origin" or "etymology unknown", yet people's creation myths, along with their puns and wordplay, indicate and also bolster the success of expressions like *OK*, and, much like threads in a cloth, they create the complete history of the word.

Folk etymology contributes to another facet of language change, namely "embedding"; in other words, when people reframe expressions in this way, this indicates they have taken hold within the language (see Weinreich et al. 1968). Only a small number of neologisms become sufficiently implanted in the social and linguistic system to convert to lasting change; successful slang expressions continue to resonate with the ethos of speakers and, when widely adopted within the community, this can trigger innovation around the terms. The success of *OK* is demonstrated by the extent to which it has entrenched itself in the lexicon, and this also includes the creative spin-offs it has inspired; e.g. *okey doke; okey-dokey, A-OK, M'kay* (popularized by South Park) and *okily dokily* (the Simpson's). Even how you write the word has become significant, with different forms conveying different emotional tones – longer versions (like *okay*) are generally warmer and more thoughtful (though when paired with a full-stop it can come across as cold), while shorter ones (like *k* or *kk*) can feel

12 A Wiki entry outlines language, context and supporting notes for the various etymologies: https://en.wikipedia.org/wiki/List_of_proposed_etymologies_of_OK (last access: 29 April 2025).

dismissive or curt[13]. Being caught up in other word formation patterns in this way has helped to secure a place in the linguistic system.

These adaptions of *OK* highlight the creativity in slang's morphological patterns, a creativity that is often overlooked in the evolutionary battle. As Charles Darwin observed in his *Descent of Man* (1872: 93), humans have a deep-seated craving for novelty and expressiveness, and they are constantly reimagining and adapting the aesthetics of their expressions. This dimension of slang encompasses overlapping elements of both structural design and artistic appeal and is instrumental in helping to sustain the relevance and appeal of phrases. Aesthetic pleasure bears a decidedly understated role in the survival of lexical items. As Australian cartoonist and poet Michael Leunig (2024: xiii) observed about the "folk poetry" he grew up with as a child: "Its rhymes and rhythms, brevity, emotion and naughtiness held it together and ensured its survival".

Structural elements of the aesthetic experience can involve word formation processes; as just described, blending has become a standout performer among the modern word formation techniques. *OK*, however, started life as an abbreviation, another popular method of creating words (the first letters of the phrase *Orl Korrekt*), but the letters combine into a word that can be spoken as a easily pronounceable acronym (*okay*). Length is another contributing factor that adds to the appeal of an expression. Shorter words tend to be more successful over time (and this is again backed up by evidence from Grieve's 2018 internet findings). Shortenings generally have a longstanding reputation for fostering a sense of belonging within a group and signalling informality and closeness – both the hallmarks of slang (as described earlier)[14]. The fact that *OK* is clearly shorter and snappier than *OW* would have had a role in its success. However, brevity is also a by-product of popularity, because *length* of words is tangled up with frequency effects. It is a simple fact of linguistic life that frequently used expressions (such as discourse markers) will shrink (e.g. *OK* reducing to *K*), making shortenings a predicted fall-out of success[15].

---

13 https://www.insidehook.com/article/advice/the-difference-between-texting-k-ok-kk-explained (last access: 29 April 2025).

14 Clear examples are Australian English "-o/-ie shortenings" such as *arvo* 'afternoon' and *compo* 'compensation'; *Chrissie* 'Christmas' and *mozzie* 'mosquito' (see Kidd et al. 2016; Manns 2020; Wierzbicka 1992 on the social functions of these shortened forms). Other interesting examples of the compact nature of slanguage are doublets such as *daft/daff; dirk/dick, arse/ass; curse/cuss; girl/gal; burst/bust; baby-bubby; saucy/sassy; teat/tit* and even *pater/patter* — here the less colloquial member has a long tense vowel and its more colloquial partner a short lax vowel; see Allan (2001: 167) for a longer list of these doublets.

15 Reduction results from the repetition of articulatory movements; when gestures of articulation become automatic, this triggers a reduction in the timing and magnitude of these gestures. The transition between sounds becomes more fluent, and the movements might even overlap — in other words, the expressions shorten (see Bybee 2001 on the phonological effects of repetition; Lindblom 1990 and Zipf 1936 on the dueling forces of "economy of gesture" and the imperative of comprehensibility).

The artistic aspects of slang (both the auditory experience and the imagery) are instrumental in helping to sustain the relevance and appeal of phrases such as *OK*. Life is full of examples where sound influences our preferences, and the vowel-consonant arrangement of *OK* has a balance and pleasing rhythm that none of the other faddish shortenings displayed (cp. OW for "orl wright" (all right); KY for "know yuse" (no use), NC for "nuff ced" (enough said) etc.). Whether for stylistic, emotional or sensory reasons, people opt for something on the basis of how it sounds – the piano over the fortepiano, church bells over electronic chimes and so on. Why should it not be the same for language? It stands to reason that measures of lexical success must also include the crafting and enjoyment of the sensory qualities of language – both conceptual and phonological aspects are central to the way people use language every day (see Benczes 2019 for a comprehensive account of phonologically motivated phenomena in English word-formation). Powerful imagery, supported by vivid sound associations, can elevate slangy wordplay into an art form, a distinction that has earned slang the label of "the people's poetry" as mentioned earlier. Consequently, in the next section, we take an even deeper dive into the aesthetics of slang.

5 The aesthetics of slang expressions

As this section highlights, central to the expressive dimension of slang creation is analogy (attraction to pattern), one of the most powerful cognitive capabilities available. Douglas R. Hofstadter, author of the award-winning *Gödel, Escher, Bach* (1979), described it as the core of cognition[16] – historical morphologist Raimo Anttila went even further, characterizing it as "the warp and woof of cognition" (Anttila 2003). Analogy-making drives many of phonological and grammatical changes, and it is a major force in the creation of new words (Burridge/Bergs 2017).

To explore these expressive qualities of slang, we draw on the results of a 2021 survey, in which participants supplied slang terms for specific meanings such as 'stupid', 'very good', 'intoxicated' and so on. Aligned with areas typically linked to lexical creativity, these findings reveal that slang expressions thrive around taboo and face-threatening topics, such as stupidity, drunkenness, unattractiveness and (bawdy) body parts. The abundance of such expressions is unsurprising – humour and playfulness serve as powerful tools for mitigating anxiety and discomfort surrounding sensitive issues (see Burke/Manns 2024).

Our focus here is on a small subset of expressions for stupidity, a rich source of linguistic inventiveness. For this meaning alone, the participants' responses totalled

---

Words of high frequency are easier to access (the priming effect), and listeners don't require the same amount of phonetic detail (Fowler/Housum 1987).

16 https://www.youtube.com/watch?v=n8m7lFQ3njk (last access: 29 April 2025).

2,220 words and phrases; excluding idiomatic expressions (such as *a brick short of a load*), this figure yielded an impressive 219 unique single words (see Burridge 2024 for a full set of these expressions). The expressions vary considerably in the magnitude of the insult and in the nature of the foolishness, hopelessness, loopiness, incapacity, eccentricity and ineptitude that comes under verbal scrutiny (terms generally don't distinguish the nuances but rely on context). The list ranges from gentle jabs such as *drongo* (the favourite in the survey at 42% of the total number of expressions) and (potentially) much more potent taunts such as *dickhead* (third in popularity, but a long way behind *drongo* at only 6%). More than half of the 219 expressions appeared only once, and many had meanings not obviously connected with an intelligence deficiency (except perhaps in the mind of the survey respondent); examples include *scomo* (nickname for the former Australian Prime Minister Scott Morrison); *demented blowfly*; *grass parrot*; *tail light* (with the explanation "too dim to be a headlight"). Many of these are probable occasionalisms, or one-off expressions, that include expressions unique to the individual's speech.

5.1 Creative etymology – patterns of sound and meaning

Tellingly, favoured words for 'stupid person' cluster around a limited number of initial consonants, and there are two large groups that particularly stand out for their alliterative aspects and sound-sense associations – expressions beginning with "d" and "n" total 85 of the 219 expressions; four of these are in the top five most frequently cited insults: *drongo* (931 mentions); *dickhead* (139 mentions); *dill* (67 mentions); *nong* (54 mentions). The fact that insults beginning with "n" and "d" account for nearly 40% of all expressions is significant; first letter frequencies of words in dictionaries show "n" to one of the least common starting letters at 2.2% (so almost as rare as J, K, Q, V, X, Y, Z); "d" has a relative frequency of 6.1%[17].

As these "d" and "n" expressions show, the world of slang is awash with what Bolinger (1940: 65) described as "kinships of sound-to-sense" – constellations of words united in similarity of sound and "partly or wholly *induced* similarity of meaning". Speakers make associations between the sounds of words and their meanings, and they may extend the connections (especially if there are no spelling reminders in the way), a phenomenon Joseph (1997: 12) dubbed "phonesthematic attraction". It is a snowballing process, which, as Bolinger (1940), Joseph (1997), Allan (2001), Benczes (2019; 2020) and others have shown, can result in complex patterns of mutual influences. Once integrated into the system, these can be powerful triggers for creating new forms and altering the shape and meaning of existing forms – as Joseph (1997: 12) describes:

17 https://en.wikipedia.org/wiki/Letter_frequency#Relative_frequencies_of_the_first_letters_of_a_word_in_English_language (last access: 29 April 2025).

> the phenomenon of "phonesthematic attraction" . . . refers to situations in which sound symbolic clusters of words, marginal though they may be, nonetheless can draw other words into their 'orbit', so that these other words change their form in the direction of the sound symbol.

For the remainder of this section, we will focus on expressive forms beginning with "n", which account for around 10.5% of the 219 distinct words. The survey terms listed in Table 2 gives just a taste of this densely entwined kinship system of insults relating to stupidity; the bracketed figures indicate the number of mentions in the survey (*nong* at 51 mentions is a clear favourite).

Table 2: Survey "n"-words for 'unintelligent person'.

1.	nanger (1)
2.	nidiot, (1)
3.	nigel (1)
4.	nimbat (1)
5.	nincompoop (6)
6.	ning nong (6)
7.	ninny (1)
8.	nit (1)
9.	nitwit (5)
10.	no hoper (1)
11.	nob (3)
12.	nonce (1)
13.	nong (51)
14.	noong (3)
15.	noofta (1)
16.	nuf-nuf (9)
17.	nuffie (6)
18.	nufty (2)
19.	numb nut (2)
20.	numbat (2)
21.	numbnuts (7)
22.	numbskull (6)
23.	numptie (13)

This "kinship of sound-to-sense" is a historically impressive phonesthetic *noodledom* ('set of unintelligent people'; 19th-century slang) dating back to at least the 1300s. It didn't really take off until the 1500s, however – at least this is what is suggested by the sudden flourishing at the time of terms with noticeable family resemblances. The list in Table 3 provides a historic overview, though it is by no means complete:

These entangled word clusters would have started with some standout expressions that just happened to share similar meanings and sounds – perhaps *nidget* (a condensed version of *an idiot*) and *nod/noddy/noddle/noodle* (slang words for 'head'). Serendipitous occurrences like these encourage people to start forging stronger sound-to-

Table 3: Some historical "n"-words for 'unintelligent person'.

1300s:	*nice* (noun)*; nysot*
1500s:	*nidiot; nigion; nidget; nod; noddy; noddypoll; niddipoll; nodcock; nodgecock, nodgecomb; niddicock; noddypoop; noddypeak; ninny; ninnyhammer; nit; ninny lobcock; numps*
1600s:	*nup; nupson; nincompoop; nizey; numbskull; nigmenog; nikin*
1700s:	*noddle; noodle, niddle, numbhead*
1800s:	*ning-nong; ning-nang; neddy; nig-nog, niddle-noddle*
1900s:	*nitwit; nob; nong; nong-nong; numpty; nimwit; numptie; numbnut(s); numby, nuff-nuff*
2000s:	*numbat; nimbat; numbwit; nuff; nuffie, noofta/noofter, ninky nonks*

sense links, which can then become powerful triggers for creating brand new words and altering the shape and meaning of existing ones (see Benczes 2020 on "coincidence-based" motivation and the emergence of phonesthemes). In the past when spoken language prevailed, these sound-meaning links could develop and proliferate more freely – writing was then a luxury for the elite few, and there were no reference works and no spelling reminders to constrain words (or rather their speakers).

The intricate, interconnected nature of the slang lexicon was poetically captured by Bolinger who described how "certain words naturally go together, and being encountered drag each other along a train of thought like the barbed atoms of Democritus" (1940: 62). Much like these hooked atoms, phonesthetic parts of words connect and interlock with one another, and words from this list of "n"-words have done this in number ways:

- Words have altered their phonological shape; for example, *dimwit* (early 1900s) changed to *nimwit* (late 1900s) – in fact, given English is awash with "n"-words that relate to slow-wittedness, any one of these (or perhaps all of them) could have inspired *nimwit.*
- Words have changed their meanings; for example, Australian English *numbat* has very recently shifted from 'the termite-eating marsupial' to 'unintelligent person' (although this latter sense doesn't yet appear in any dictionaries, even those of slang) – with strong echoes also of *numbskull, numbnut, dingbat* (to name a few), it is small wonder *numbat* has now joined the "noodledom" family.

For centuries, speakers have been having fun with these words, shifting them, reshaping them and shuffling them up. Many appear to involve blends although what make up the mix is often not clear-cut. Early *nincompoop* is a highly successful expression, and remains still very much alive (as our survey indicates). The word is a lexical salad of potentially many colloquial bits and pieces (e.g. *ninny, noddypoop*), even perhaps, as Samuel Johnson suggested, a hint of more lofty *non compos (mentis)* 'of unsound mind' (from early 1600s legal Latin). We have just suggested that *dimwit* morphed into *nimwit* on the inspiration of *nitwit* (or any of the other "n" words) – but equally it could be *dimwit* blending with *nitwit.* It is not clear whether *numptie* (1980s) is a blend of *humpty-dumpty* and *numps* or *numbskull* (as the OED also points out,

Numpy or *Numpey* occurs in early literature as a nickname for a person characterized as silly or stupid). *Nong* could be a straightforward shortening of older *ning-nong,* but it also has strong echoes of *dong, dongo* and so on – and its popularity in Australia (it was one of the top five in the survey) could also have been amplified by additional echoes of *drongo* (as one of the survey respondents even suggested). It is often impossible to pin down the sources that gave rise to these words and, not surprisingly, most dictionaries are cautious and opt for "of obscure origin".

This family of words includes a number of playful reduplications, including the older ablaut-motivated formations such as *ning nong* (cp. *ding dong*); *nig-nog*; *niddle-noddle,* as well as word pairs showing the same low-high vowel alternation such as *nimbat – numbat.* In Modern English ablaut reduplication is limited, and yet Australian children have recently created *ninky nonks* (not yet in any slang dictionary); while its inspiration was presumably Ninky Nonk, a toy train which features in the children's TV series *In the Night Garden* (first produced in 2007), this would not be an apt insult for a dim-witted person without the additional aesthetic factors.[18]

Australian English *noong* (< earlier *nong*) underscores the wildcard dimension (from a linguistic point of view) to the life-cycle of words. As a number of participants in the survey made clear, many Australians might love the word *nong,* but they now worry it is offensive ("I suspect that it has racist roots", wrote one survey respondent). When taboos are involved, the association of meaning and sound is always strong – such is the eye- and ear-catching nature of offensive words that innocent bystanders easily get caught up in their orbit to then be abandoned (see Hock 1991; Burridge/Benczes 2019). For example, the benign origins of *niggardly* were not sufficient to overcome its clang association with racist words; the early English word for 'rabbit' *coney/cunny* (originally rhyming with *honey*) eventually disappeared because of its phonetic similarity with *cunt* (a connection that has of course been played on throughout its history). *Nong* has no etymological connections with any ethnic slur, but if people's perceptions are that it is seriously offensive, then this is the kiss of death. Modern sensitivities will determine whether this phonesthetic family continues to draw in new members. There are signs that time is running out for some members of in the "noodledom" kinship.

18 We are extremely grateful to Koen Wright for bringing to our attention this recent addition to the "noodledom" family.

5.2 Creative etymology – adaptation

A second related aspect of slang aesthetics is adaption. For expressions to retain their appeal and to remain novel, they often have to adapt – in Darwin's terminology, "fit" items must also be responsive to their environment. The survey respondents provided over 400 longer idiomatic phrases for stupidity (Burke/Manns, 2024), and these revealed another way slanguage can adapt to improve the chances of survival. Many conformed to a number of different templates – sequences of words or linguistic routines that provide a kind of life support framework to maintain the vitality of an idiom, sometimes over centuries. For speakers, it is a matter of inserting a more vivid or up-to-date image into the template, perhaps even playing with it too – to adapt the old proverb, like pouring new wine into old bottles, the spirit of the idiom is kept alive (see Adams 2009: 119–120).

Consider the "X short of Y" idiom, and also its sibling "not the full X". It is a common formula that appears in a number of languages (e.g. German *nicht alle Tassen im Schrank* 'not all the cups in the cupboard' and Dutch *hij heeft ze niet allemaal op een rijtje zitten* 'he doesn't have them sitting all in a row'; *hij is er niet helemaal* 'he's not altogether there'). Generally, these expressions denote some specified deficiency in a desirable or standard quantity of something, as in *a shingle short* (of a roof), one of the earliest recorded expressions, *a brick short of a load, a few slices short of a loaf, sixpence short of a shilling, a few chips short of a happy meal, a stubby short of a six pack, a lamington short of a CWA meeting* (= Country Women's Association), *a snag short of a barbie, a shrub short of an herbaceous border,* to name a few (cp. English *not all there*). Since at least the early 1800s, speakers have been playing around with the "X short of a Y" pattern, turning missing (or loose) tiles on rooves into sandwiches (or ants) at a picnic, Tim-Tams (chocolate biscuits) in a packet, bars on a mobile phone, Holdens in a carpark, and so on. Someone who's *not the full quid* or *not the full shilling* is changed to become *not the full tin of Milo, not the full jar of vegemite, not the full tube of Dencorub* and so on. The survey revealed a number of these frames and even blended frames such as *a few kangaroos short in the top paddock* (a fusion of *a few roos loose in the top paddock* and *a few sheep short in the top paddock*) and *not the sharpest knife in the biscuit tin* (a play on *not the sharpest knife on the rack, not the brightest star in the sky, not the brightest crayon in the box* etc.).

This type of creative verbal play has been part of English for centuries, as it has for many languages. Often it involves unexpected mixes of terms to create humorous compounds and blends – and sometimes provocative combinations inspired by the cultural taboos of the time. Consider a pattern of compounding based on *arse/ass* that has been producing insults for stupidity since at least the 1500s; for example, *arsehole, arsewipe, dumbarse, dumbass, donkeys arse* to name a few (see Schweinberg/Burridge 2025): *arse/ass* is a tabooed body part and one at the opposite end from the head, both features rendering it an appropriate seat of stupidity. Creative *-head* compounds for stupidity have also been in the language and for a similarly long time. Hundreds of examples exist, and many are still used today (e.g. *blockhead* from the 1400s). Once again, the new wine is poured into old bottles – the turn-over of words combining with *head* that maintains the contemporary appeal of these expressions. Earlier examples include animals (*asshead* 1400s), fish and insects (*cod's head* and *dorhead* 1500s), vegetables (*cabbage head* 1600s), soft materials (*woollen head* 1700s), porridge-like substances (*pudding head* 1800s), and so on. More recent times, the words that combine with *head* involve bodily effluvia, tabooed body-parts and sexual past-times; for example, *poop-head, butthead, dickhead, fuckhead.* These most recent *-head* examples mirror the evolving taboos of modern times and are also reflected in current shifts in swearing patterns; e.g. *(God) damn X* provides the model for more potent modern imprecatives such as *Shit on X, Fuck X, Bugger X,* and so on.

Suffix-like *-head* appears prominently among the lively affixes in Morris's (2022) recipes for forming effective derogatory noun-noun compounds in English: he describes it as an incredibly versatile suffix that can be preceded by just about any taboo word. Morris's list of 140 affix-like forms (e.g. *butt-*, *fart-*, *poop-*, *-head, -face, -brains*) combine to form 4,800 possible pejorative compounds (e.g. *butthead, fuckwaffle, dicknose, assbag*), more than half of which appeared in Reddit comments from 2006 to the end of 2020. "The truly creative", as Morris describes, "can go outside the box with oddball constructions like *fucktrumpet*, or *wankpuffin*". However, with the waning potency of physically and sexually based taboos, the recent appearance of expressions such as *vaxhead* may well be forecasting another change in idiom. *Vaxhead* appeared on the survey as an option for 'unintelligent person' and is occasionally used online as a derogatory term for a person against vaccines and regulations mandating vaccination (or usually both) (cp. AusE *cooker* – a pejorative term for someone whose brain has been "cooked" by overexposure to conspiracy theories).

6 Concluding remarks

People appear naturally drawn to the curious details and quirky facets of the lexicon. When English language dictionaries release their respective "Words of the Year" there is always a flurry of media attention fuelling discussions about their meanings, origins – and of course whether or not they are truly deserving of this honour. The internet is home to many heavily trafficked websites devoted to the "most irritating words", "favourite words", "dead words", "new words", "peculiar words", "clichés" – and many other topics that cater to logophiles and word nerds. No other aspect of language garners this sort of excitement. Dictionary editors are among the new celebrities answering questions such as: What is the longest word in the language? Is there a word that describes pieces of soap too small to use but too large to throw away? How many words do speakers know? Is *skibidi* a real word? And who decides when it enters the dictionary? Words are the most visible aspect of any language, and this leaves them susceptible to the changing tastes and interests of those who use them.

The slang component of vocabulary comprises some of the most culturally significant words and is language at its messiest – born from many different forces and shaped by a web of overlapping influences that includes celebrity endorsement, usefulness, multiple origins (including popular genesis narratives) and aesthetics. These can launch the career of a slang term, although they do not guarantee long-term success. Expressions can take off, flourish but be short-lived – and they can take off, flourish and be long-lasting. There will also be always a tangle of internal and external factors involved. In the earlier discussion of convict slang, we argued that Vaux's *pins* triumphed over *stamps* as a colloquial term for 'legs'. *Pins* was always more frequently used than *stamps*, and appeared in a number of phrases such as *nice pins*, *king pair of pins* and so on; it also extended figuratively, appearing in idioms such as *on one's pins* 'up and about in good health' and *shaky on one's pins* 'unwell'. *Stamp*, on the other hand, fell out of favour and, like other *-amp* words (e.g. *champ, tramp*) was overcome by the more competitive *-omp* phonestheme – *stamping ground* became *stomping ground* (*champing at the bit* became *chomping at the bit*). Vaux's *pigs* has lived on as a derogatory term for 'police', but not *grunters* – however, shorter and catchier *grunts* is alive and well in military slang for common soldiers and more recently for general dogsbodies. Like Moore's "basic slang" described earlier, *pigs* and *grunts* remain in tune with the generational ethos of speakers, and importantly it maintains a rebellious vibe – as Moore (2004: 59) puts it, such slang terms do not wear out but continue to be "pervasively used [. . .] because those who use them in their heyday never tire of identifying themselves with the values they represented". Clearly, an important key to the longevity of slang expressions is their link to identity; however, even this special significance doesn't guarantee them eternal life. As we have seen, there is no shortage of evidence illustrating the powerful human appetite for novelty and creative expression, especially in those areas that connect with the cultural concerns of speakers. Our brains respond to innovation, and our social lives are rich with avenues for self-expression.

Accounts of linguistic change so often seek neat single factor solutions; yet the reality of any linguistic innovation and change is complex and multi-factored (Joseph 2013), involving networks of different intersecting pressures that work to coerce a language in a particular direction (Burridge/Bergs 2017). Clearly, the lexical components are the most volatile, with vocabulary addition and loss being particularly rapid. More than other aspects of language, words resonate (or not) with the social and cultural preoccupations of speakers, and this introduces an X-factor into the evolution of words, that can shape their development in unexpected ways. Not constrained by the literary standard and its prescriptive ethos, slang offers compelling examples of how meanings can transform phonemic shapes and how phonemic shapes can transform meanings. Etymythology (to use Horn's 2004 label) and the compulsive creativity of speakers offer persistent challenges to the lexicographer – and ensure there will always be perplexing elements around the aspects of endurance. The different lifespans of the two words *gab* and *gob* underscore these perplexing elements. Both started life alternative pronunciations for 'mouth' and while neither appeared in Vaux's glossary, they do have entries in Grose's *Dictionary of the Vulgar Tongue* (1785). *Gab* 'mouth' has not survived as the word, but slightly older *gob* is alive and well, managing to retain a fashionable shabbiness after nearly 500 years (especially in expressions such as *shut your gob, gobsmacked* and *gobstopper*). It was probably the fact that originally Gaelic *gob* 'mouth' collided with French-inspired *gob* 'a dollop of thick spit' (originally 'lump, mass'), while *gab* became entangled with another *gab* meaning 'talk'; it survives in the now high fallutin' expression *gift of the gab* 'an ability to speak eloquently' (first attested 1761).

It is evident that change schemas do not follow prescribed courses determined by exceptionless laws or principles. However, even for the lexicon it is possible to talk about preferred pathways of change – those "gutters" that channel language change, to use an image famously invoked by Kuryłowicz (1945: 9). Referring specifically to analogical change (appropriately for our discussion), Kuryłowicz likened these developments to episodes of rain: while we may not be able to predict when it will rain, or even if it will, once the rain has fallen, we know the direction the water will flow because of gutters, drainpipes and spouting. What we hope to have done here is to provide a clearer picture of the dynamics that shape the contours of lexical change – and, in particular, the life-cycle of slang.

Bibliography

Adams, Michael (2009): Slang: The people's poetry. Oxford: Oxford University Press.

Algeo, John (1991): Fifty years among the new words: A dictionary of neologisms 1941–1991. Cambridge: Cambridge University Press.

Allan, Keith (2001): Natural language semantics. Oxford: Blackwell.

Allan, Keith/Burridge, Kate (1991): Euphemism and dysphemism: Language used as shield and weapon. Oxford: Oxford University Press.

Allan, Keith/Burridge, Kate (2006): Forbidden words: Taboo and the censoring of language. Cambridge: Cambridge University Press.

Anttila, Raimo (2003): Analogy: The warp and woof of cognition. In: Joseph, Brian D./Janda, Richard D. (eds.): Handbook of historical linguistics. Oxford: Blackwell, 425–440.

Australian National Dictionary. Ed. by Moore, Bruce. Australian National Dictionary Centre: Oxford University Press, ^{2}2016.

Bailey, R.W. (1996): Nineteenth-century English. Ann Arbor: University of Michigan Press.

Bauer, Laurie (1994): Watching English change: An introduction to the study of linguistic change in standard Englishes in the 20th century. London: Routledge.

Bee, J. (pseudonym for John Badcock): (1823) Slang: A dictionary of the turf, the ring, the chase, the pit, of bon-ton, and the varieties of life, forming the completest and most authentic lexicon balatronicum hitherto offered to the notice of the sporting world, etc. T. Hughes.

Benczes, Réka (2019): Rhyme over reason: Phonological motivation in English. Cambridge: Cambridge University Press.
Benczes, Réka (2020): Sound symbolism and semantic change. In: Allan, Keith (ed.): Dynamics of language changes: Looking within and across languages. Berlin/Heidelberg: Springer, 253–264.
Blake, Barry (2010): Secret languages: Codes, tricks, spies, thieves, and symbols. Oxford: Oxford University Press.
Biber, Douglas/Finegan, Edward (1988): Drift in three English genres from the 18th to the 20th centuries: A multidimensional approach. In: Kytö, Merja/Ihalainen, Ossi/Rissanen, Matti (eds.): Corpus linguistics, hard and soft. Amsterdam: Rodopi, 83–101.
Bolinger, Dwight (1940): Word affinities. In: American Speech 15, 1, 62–73.
Bolinger, Dwight. (1980): Language: The loaded weapon. London: Longman.
Burke, Isabelle/Manns, Howard (2024): Australia's idiomatic expressions: "speaking the culture" to maintain social relations. In: The Australian Journal of Linguistics, 365–389.
Burchfield, Robert. (1989): Unlocking the English language. London: Faber & Faber.
Burridge, Kate (2019): The obelisk and the asterisk: views on language and change from the late modern period. In: Jansen, Sandra/Siebers, Lucia (eds.): Processes of change. Studies in late modern and present-day English. Amsterdam: Benjamins, 25–48.
Burridge, Kate (2023): Prescription and taboo: Australia's sensitivity towards American influence. In: Beal, Joan C./Lukač, Morana/Straaijer, Robin (eds.): The Routledge handbook of linguistic prescriptivism. London: Routledge, 246–263.
Burridge, Kate (2024): "Survival of the fittest" – the evolution of slanguage. In: The Australian Journal of Linguistics, 340–364.
Burridge, Kate/Bergs, Alex (2017): Understanding language change. London: Routledge.
Burridge, Kate/Manns, Howard (2018): "Get yer hand off it, mate", Australian slang is not dying. The Conversation. https://theconversation.com/get-yer-hand-off-it-mate-australian-slang-is-not-dying-90022 (last access: 10 October 2024).
Burridge, Kate/Manns, Howard (2020): "Iso", "boomer remover" and "quarantine": how coronavirus is changing our language. The Conversation. https://theconversation.com/iso-boomer-remover-and-quarantini-how-coronavirus-is-changing-our-language-136729 (last access: 20 December 2024).
Burridge, Kate/Benczes, Réka (2019): Taboo as a driver of language change. In: Allan, Keith (ed.): The Oxford handbook of taboo words and language. Oxford: Oxford University Press, 180–199.
Bybee, Joan (2001): Phonology and language use. Cambridge: Cambridge University Press.
Coleman, Julie (2004): A history of cant and slang dictionaries. Vol. 2: 1785–1858. Oxford: Oxford University Press.
Coleman, Julie (2014) (ed.): Global English slang: Methodologies and perspectives. London: Routledge.
Darwin, Charles (1872): The descent of man, and selection in relation to sex. New York: D. Appleton and company.
Djenar, Dwi Noverini/Ewing, Michael C./Manns, Howard. (2018): Style and Intersubjectivity in youth Interaction. Berlin/Boston: Mouton de Gruyter.
Douglas, Mary (1966): Purity and Danger: An Analysis of Concepts of Pollution and Taboo. London: Routledge & Kegan Paul.
Durkin, Phillip (2016): Etymology, word history, and the group and division of material in historical dictionaries. In: Durkin, Phillip (ed.): The Oxford handbook of lexicography. Oxford: Oxford University Press, 236–254.
Eble, Connie (1994): Slang and usage. In: Publications of the American Dialect Society 78, 1, 15–18.
Enfield, Nick (2015): The utility of meaning: What words mean and why. Oxford: Oxford University Press.
Fowler, Carol A./Housum, Jonathan (l987): Talkers signalling "new" and "old" words in speech and listeners' perception and use of the distinction. In: Journal of memory and language 26, 489–504.

Grieve, Jack (2018a): Natural selection in the modern English lexicon. Proceedings of the 12th International Conference on the Evolution of Language (Evolang12); DOI:10.12775/3991-1.037.
Grieve, Jack (2018b): R Analysis for Natural Selection in the Modern English Lexicon. International conference on the evolution of language (Evolang12).
Grieve, Jack/Nini, Andrea/Guo, Diansheng (2016): Analyzing lexical emergence in American English online. In: English language and linguistics 21, 1, 99–127.
Hock, Hans H (^{2}1991): Principles of historical linguistics. Berlin/New York: Mouton de Gruyter.
Horn, Laurence (2004): Spitten image: Etymythology and fluid dynamics. In: American Speech 79: 33–58.
Joseph, Brian D. (1997): On the linguistics of marginality: The centrality of the periphery. https://www.researchgate.net/publication/247042735 (last access: 9 October 2024).
Joseph, Brian D. (2013): Multiple sources and multiple causes multiply explored. In: Studies in language 37, 3, 675–691.
Kidd, Evan/Kemp, Nenagh/Kashima, Emiko S/Quinn, S. (2016): Language, culture, and group membership: An investigation into the social effects of colloquial Australian English. In: Journal of cross-cultural psychology 47, 713–733. doi:10.1177/0022022116638175.
Kiesling, Scott F. (2004): Dude. In: American Speech 79, 3, 281–305.
Kortmann, Bernd (2020): English Linguistics: Essentials. 2nd revised, updated and enlarged edition. Stuttgart: Metzler.
Kuryłowicz, Jerzy (1945): La nature des procès dits "analologiques". In: Acta Linguistica 5: 15–37.
Laugesen, Amanda (2024): Australian historical lexicography and the treatment of slang and colloquial language. In: The Australian Journal of Linguistics, 304–320.
Leunig, Michael (2024): Newspaper poems. Boho South, Victoria: Curly Press.
Lignos, Constantine/Prichard, Hilary (2015): Quantifying cronuts: Predicting the quality of blends. Paper presented at the LSA Annual Meeting, Portland, January 2015. http://lignos.org/blends (last access: 20 December 2024).
Lindblom, Björn (1990): Explaining phonetic variation: A sketch of the H&H theory. In: Hardcastle, W. J./ Marchal, Alain (eds.): Speech Production and Speech Modelling. Berlin: Springer, 403–439.
Macquarie Dictionary. https://www.macquariedictionary.com.au (last access: 14 January 2025).
Mair, Christian (2024): Colloquialisation: Twenty-five years on. In: Journal of Historical Pragmatics 25, 2, 193–214.
Manns, Howard (2020) The lexicon of Australian English. In: Willoughby, Louisa/Manns, Howard (eds.): Australian English reimagined: Structure, features and developments. London: Routledge, 84–100.
Manns, Howard/Burridge, Kate (2016): Slanguage and "dinky di" Aussie talk in elections. In: The Conversation. https://theconversation.com/slanguage-and-dinky-di-aussie-talk-in-elections-59967 (last access: 12 March 2024).
Manns, Howard/Musgrave, Simon/Burridge, Kate/Burke, Isabelle/Hughes, Dylan/Allan, Keith (2024): What is Australian slang? Is it really slang? In: The Australian Journal of Linguistics, 283–303.
Martin, Katherine C. (2013): What is the original of Twerk? https://web.archive.org/web/20141215002042/ http://blog.oxforddictionaries.com/2013/08/what-is-the-origin-of-twerk/ (last access: 28 December 2024).
Moore, Bruce (2008): Speaking our language. The story of Australian English. Oxford: Oxford University Press.
Moore, Bruce (2014): Australian slang. In: Coleman, Julie (ed.): Global English Slang: Methodologies and perspectives. London: Routledge, 175–192.
Moore, Robert (2004): We're cool, mom and dad are swell: Basic slang and generational shifts in value. In: American Speech 79, 1, 59–86.
Moore, Robert (2012): On swearwords and slang. In: American speech 87, 2, 170–189.
Morris, Collin (2022): Compound pejoratives on Reddit – from buttface to wankpuffin. https://colinmorris.github.io/blog/compound-curse-words (last access: 20 October 2024).

Oxford English Dictionary. www.oed.com (last access: 15 January 2025).
Pagel, Mark/Beaumont, Mark/Meade/Andrew/Verkerk, Annemarie/Calude, Andreea (2019): Dominant words rise to the top by positive frequency-dependent selection. Proceedings of the National Academy of Sciences of the United States 116, 15, 7397–7402. https://doi.org/10.1073/pnas.1816994116.
Partridge, Eric (1933): Slang To-Day And Yesterday. London: Routledge.
Read, Allen W. (1963): The first stage in the history of "O.K". In: American Speech 38, 1, 5–27.
Reyes, Angela (2005): Appropriation of African American slang by Asian American youth. In: Journal of Sociolinguistics 9, 4, 509–532.
Ripollés, Pablo/Marco-Pallarés, Josep/Hielscher, Ulrike/Mestres-Missé, Anna/Tempelmann, Claus/Heinze, Hans-Jochen/Rodríguez-Fornells, Antoni/Noesselt, Toemme (2014): The role of reward in word learning and its implications for language acquisition. Current biology DOI: 10.1016/j.cub.2014.09.044 (last access: 10 March 2024).
Sabbah-Taylor, Angela/Jenks, Christopher J. (2024): Okay in intercultural lingua franca interactions between Chinese and British postgraduate students. World Englishes, 1–12. https://doi.org/10.1111/weng.12715.
Schweinberger, Martin/Burridge, Kate (2025): Vulgarity in Online Discourse around the English–Speaking World. In: Lingua. https://www.sciencedirect.com/science/article/pii/S0024384125000713.
Stockwell, Robert P./Minkova, Donka (2001): English Words: History and Structure. Cambridge: Cambridge University Press.
Tagliamonte, Sali/Hudson, Rachel (1999): Be like et al. beyond America: the quotative system in British and Canadian youth. In: Journal of Sociolinguistics 3, 147–172.
Thorne, Tony (2020): #CORONASPEAK – the language of Covid-19 goes viral. https://language-and-innovation.com/2020/04/15/coronaspeak-part-2-the-language-of-covid-19-goes-viral/ (last access: 20 December 2024).
Vaux, James H. (1819): A New and Comprehensive Vocabulary of the Flash Language (in Volume 2 of Memoirs of James Hardy Vaux, Written by himself). W. Clowes. https://babel.hathitrust.org/cgi/pt?id=nyp.33433082394838&seq=14 (last access 24 March 2024).
Weinreich, Uriel/Labov, William/Herzog, Marvin I. (1968): Empirical foundations for a theory of language change. In: Lehmann, Winfred P./Malkiel, Yakov (eds.): Directions for historical linguistics. Austin: University of Texas Press, 95–188.
Wierzbicka, A. (1992): Semantics, culture and cognition: Universal human cognition in culture-specific configurations. Oxford: Oxford University Press.
Zimmer, Ben (2013): Getting worked up over "twerk". Language log (August 28): https://languagelog.ldc.upenn.edu/nll/?p=6481 (last access: 3 March 2024).
Zipf, George K. (1936): The psycho-biology of language. London: Routledge.

Iván Arias-Arias, María José Domínguez Vázquez,
Carlos Valcárcel Riveiro

People, machines and dictionaries: Is artificial intelligence killing dictionaries?

Abstract: This paper explores the relationship between humans, dictionaries, and computer systems in the context of lexicographic processes. It encompasses actions performed by both dictionary creators and users. Drawing on the latest research regarding the influence of artificial intelligence on lexicographic activities, we present results from new experiments assessing the reliability of AI-generated outputs based on the type of user consulting them. Finally, we examine the current social and cultural value of dictionaries and their impact on society.

Keywords: lexicography, dictionary, artificial intelligence, society

Schlagwörter: Lexikographie, Wörterbuch, künstliche Intelligenz, Gesellschaft

1 Introduction

The question of whether lexicography (Garriga 2023; Maldonado 2018) and dictionaries, as we traditionally know them, have a future (Klosa-Kückelhaus 2014; Klein 2015; Schierholz 2021) has been raised for some decades. The advent of artificial intelligence (AI) once again brings into focus the potential demise of lexicography (de Schryver/Joffe 2023; Jakubíček/Rundell 2023). Whether AI will completely replace lexicography, or whether lexicographic activity as we know it today will disappear, relates to the

---

Acknowledgements: The results of this work are part of the research project ESMAS-ES$_+$ (Grant PID2022-137170OB-I00), funded by MICIU/AEI/10.13039/501100011033 and ERDF/EU. Iván Arias-Arias is a beneficiary of a grant from the Spanish Ministry of Science, Innovation and Universities within the program "Formación de Profesorado Universitario" (grant no. FPU21/00188).

Iván Arias-Arias, Universidade de Santiago de Compostela, Department of English and German Philology and Instituto da Lingua Galega (ILG), Faculty of Philology, Avenida Castelao, s/n, 15705, Santiago de Compostela, e-mail: ivanarias.arias@usc.gal
María José Domínguez Vázquez, Universidade de Santiago de Compostela, Department of English and German Philology and Instituto da Lingua Galega (ILG), Faculty of Philology, Avenida Castelao, s/n, 15705, Santiago de Compostela, e-mail: majo.dominguez@usc.es
Carlos Valcárcel Riveiro, Universidade de Vigo, Department of English, French and German Philology, Faculty of Education and Sport Sciences, A Xunqueira, s/n, 36005, Pontevedra, e-mail: carlos.valcarcel@uvigo.gal

https://doi.org/10.1515/9783112216644-012

notion that only what is no longer important or useful is replaced or disappears. Therefore, as a starting point, it is worth asking the following questions:
- Do we need lexicographic knowledge today?
- Can AI perform a lexicographic task?
- Can AI replace the work of a lexicographic team?
- Is AI considered an authority in society?
- Does AI have cultural, social, and emotional value?

To answer such broad questions, it is necessary, among other things, to narrow down the specific field of reference or research fields of lexicography and AI. For example, is lexicography important for agriculture? Perhaps not as important as irrigation technology for strawberry cultivation, but it is important if one wants to create a terminological work on irrigated plants. Therefore, the first question to be asked should not be whether lexicography is important, but for which purposes and tasks it is important and where it cannot be replaced by machines. Similar questions should be asked in the case of AI.

Therefore, we will present reflections on the participation of humans and machines in the lexicographic process, considering dictionaries as products of human-machine interaction (section 2). Section 3 explores key concepts related to humans and AI, such as intelligence, mental processes, reasoning, and behaviour. Section 4 provides data from some exploratory case studies on large language models (LLMs) like ChatGPT, leading to conclusions about the efficiency of LLMs in performing lexicographic tasks. Finally, section 5 addresses the cultural, emotional, and social value of dictionaries.

2 About people and lexicography

Concerning the relationship between humans and lexicography, it is important to distinguish the processes and actors involved in different actions, such as the elaboration and the consultation of resources (see section 4) as well as the social relevance of lexicographic data (see section 5). These processes typically require at least three participants: an agent, an instrument, and an addressee. Agents and addressees are thinking participants (see section 3), emulating the sender-receiver relationship in communication. The instrument is the computer, understood here also as the programming systems and rules that support the elaboration, editing, and consultation of resources. In computer-assisted lexicography, computers aid lexicographic work (Storrer 1996: 240) and serve as indispensable consultation devices, as do tablets and mobile phones in today's digital age. Therefore, computer-assisted lexicography (Storrer 1996: 240) has among its end products dictionaries for human users. Computational lexicography, on the other hand, focuses on developing resources and programs for machine processing, meaning that the interaction between agent and addressee differs. Here, the primary addressee of the products is a machine or system, which, as an instrument, subsequently offers data in various formats or products to a secondary human addressee or another system. Thus, the primary recipient of AI is usually a non-thinking entity -a machine- while the secondary recipients are both machines and human beings. Figure 1 summarises this approach.

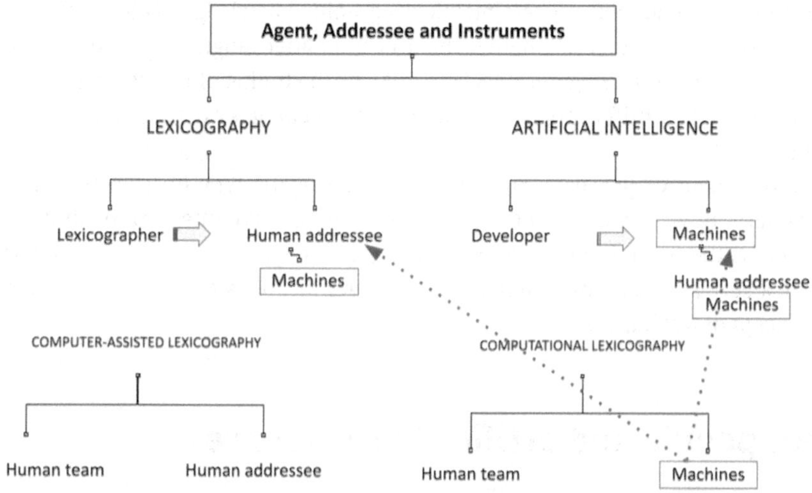

Figure 1: Actors and instruments in lexicographic processes.

If lexicography is defined as "Menge aller Aktivitäten, die auf die Erstellung lexikographischer Nachschlagewerke gerichtet ist" (WLWF-3 2020: 224), it can be concluded that the central task of a specialised lexicographic team is the design of a resource for a target group. To achieve this ultimate goal, various tasks are performed, all of them linked to hypothesis setting and decision-making processes, such as the selection and sorting of data, establishment of criteria, setting the structure of the resource, evaluation of the quality, etc. Cognitive processes are not only essential for the development of a lexical system or dictionary, but also for its consultation. Looking up information in a dictionary is not an innate ability. Even if we had the ideal dictionary user, they would still need to perform various steps to conduct a successful search: What do I specifically want to look up? Which work should I consult for my question? How do I navigate the selected dictionary? How can I be sure that I am proceeding correctly? What should I do if my search is unsuccessful? (cf. Domínguez/Valcárcel 2015). This process is also influenced by one's own culture and how one has learned to use the dictionary.

Concerning the role of humans in lexicography, several distinctions are to be made. Among dictionary makers, we can distinguish between a lexicographic team (with its internal roles and hierarchies) and laypeople in lexicography (within the hierarchies of collaborative resources). Based on the competence in dictionary use, a distinction can be made between learners (people who are learning and practising to use of a dictionary) and users with different experience levels (people who can use a dictionary effectively). The latter can be further divided into competent users (those who know how to use a dictionary well), skilled users (those who have the potential to use a dictionary well), and experienced users (those who not only know how to use a resource in practice but also possess metalexicographic knowledge). Other differences can also be observed, such as whether the user is a native language speaker or not (for more information, see Wiegand 1998: 505–508), or the timing of the user's interaction with the resource, differentiating between users *in-actu, ex-actu,* and *post-actu* (Wiegand 1998: 501).

Therefore, cognitive processes are linked to the specific type of user and their particular query. However, prior to the query itself, there is the intention behind the query as well as the formulation of a hypothesis (Müller-Spitzer et al. 2018b). This is followed by a series of decision-making processes. All of this is therefore connected with the concept of intelligence.

3 About people and artificial intelligence

One of the purposes of artificial intelligence is the development of machines and systems of different types that emulate human actions and capabilities by means of algorithms (cf. section 2 in Arias-Arias/Domínguez/Valcárcel 2024a). According to Russell/Norvig (2004: 2), definitions of artificial intelligence may be organised into four categories, which we reproduce as follows:

As shown in Figure 2, the Russell/Norvig proposal sets mental processes and reasoning (top row) in relation to behaviour (bottom row). In the image (top left, from top to bottom), success is measured in terms of how well a system can reproduce the way a human being acts (see section 2), as opposed to the information on the right, which refers to an ideal concept of intelligence that the authors call "rationality". According to this classification, we can include neural networks in the group of systems that think like humans, although they do not "think" but automate activities. Systems that act like humans are robots. Systems that "think" rationally are those that attempt to emulate the rational logical thinking of humans. And finally, systems that act rationally are those that try to rationally imitate human behaviour, such as intelligent agents.

In this context, the question arises whether machines -i.e., bots such as ChatGPT and robots- are intelligent. If we understand intelligence as the ability to achieve certain goals or solve specific problems, we could say that both humans (Sternberg 2012) and machines are intelligent (McCarthy 2007: 2) or, in the case of machines, "some-

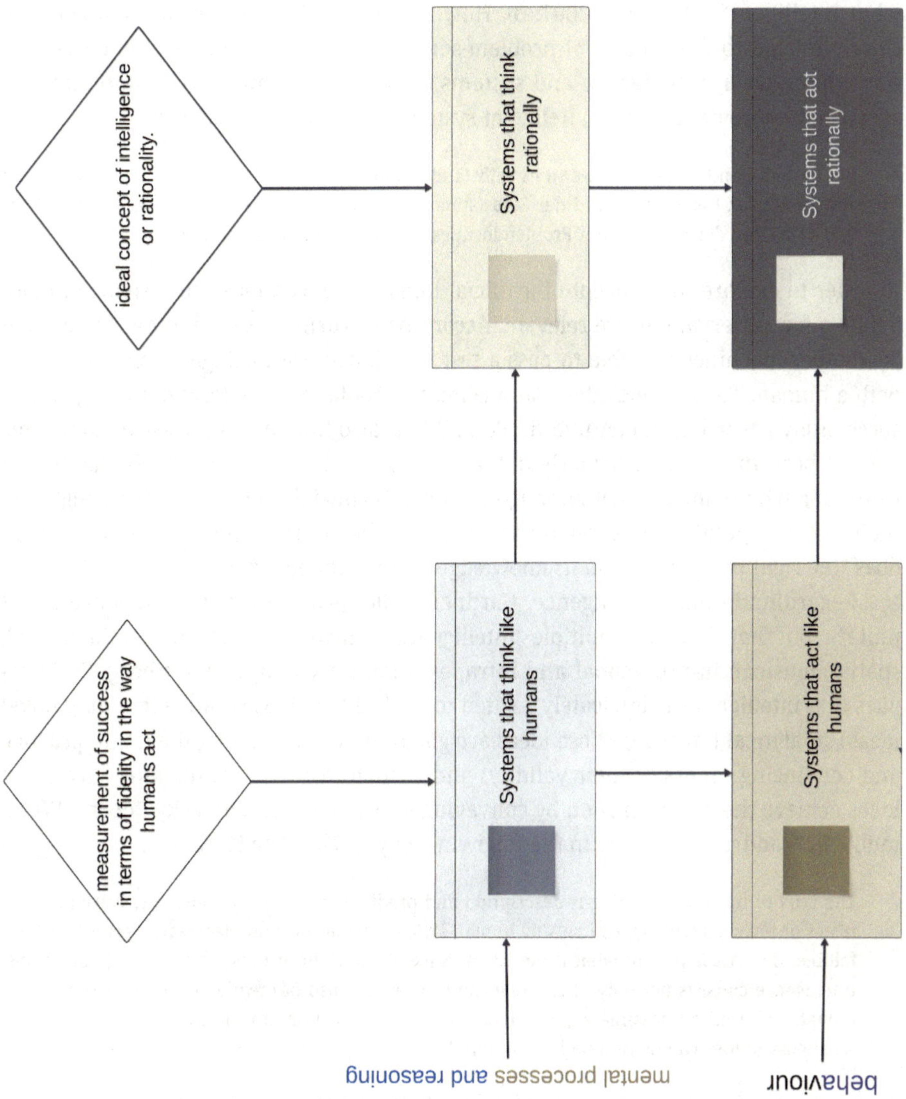

Figure 2: Definitions of artificial intelligence.

what intelligent" (McCarthy 2007: 3). However, since the concept of intelligence is closely related to the process of problem-solving, it is necessary to examine the relationship between intelligence and systems or machines from a computational perspective in more detail. Thus, intelligent systems are defined as follows:

> Ein System heißt intelligent, wenn es selbständig und effizient Probleme lösen kann. Der Grad der Intelligenz hängt vom Grad der Selbstständigkeit, dem Grad der Komplexität des Problems und dem Grad der Effizienz des Problemlösungsverfahrens ab. (Mainzer 2019: 3)

In order to explore the concept of artificial intelligence as applied to systems in more depth, a few observations are relevant. According to Turing (1950), the central question is whether machines are able to pass a test of behavioural intelligence by interacting with a human. Turing concludes that a computer could only be deemed intelligent if it successfully tricked a human into thinking it was also human. As far as we know, this has not been the case. Particularly noteworthy is also the statement by Russell/Norvig (2004: 48), who point out that although the term "artificial intelligence" has caught on, the term "computational rationality" would have been more appropriate: if a system does "the right thing" based on its knowledge, this would be "rationality".

Regarding human intelligence, Gardner (2006) proposes that intelligence is not unitary, but that there are multiple "intelligences", including linguistic, mathematical, spatial, musical, interpersonal and intrapersonal, for example. Sternberg (2012) argues that intelligence is intricately related to skill sets such as creative (creating novel ideas), analytical (ensuring those ideas are good), practical (putting them into practice and convincing others of their validity) and wisdom-based skills (making sure those ideas achieve the common good by conveying ethical values). Chomsky/Roberts/Watumull (2023) address this issue in the following way in *The New York Times*:

> The crux of machine learning is description and prediction; it does not posit any causal mechanisms or physical laws. Of course, any human-style explanation is not necessarily correct; we are fallible. But this is part of what it means to think: To be right, it must be possible to be wrong. Intelligence consists not only of creative conjectures but also of creative criticism. Human-style thought is based on possible explanations and error correction, a process that gradually limits what possibilities can be rationally considered.

Therefore, it seems that a human being is able to create a theory *ex-novo*, perform hypotheses and argue a critique, while a machine could analyse or solve hypotheses according to the data at its disposal and find answers to questions formulated by humans, thus emulating human behaviours or processes. But humans also possess knowledge of the world:

> Weltwissen – auch Hintergrundwissen, konzeptionelles oder enzyklopädisches Wissen – beschreibt das einem Menschen verfügbare allgemeine Wissen, Kenntnisse und Erfahrungen über Umwelt und Gesellschaft [*sic*], enthält also die im Gedächtnis gespeicherten Informationen über die Welt, in der er lebt und ohne die er nicht überleben könnte. Das Weltwissen ermöglicht es auch, neue Tatsachen einzuordnen und entsprechend zu handeln, auch wenn detaillierte Informationen noch

> fehlen und man sich etwa in deiner neuen Umgebung zurecht finden muss. Zum Weltwissen gehören zum Beispiel Hintergrundwissen und enzyklopädisches Wissen. (Stangl 2024)

Therefore, it is evident that the capabilities and skills of humans and AI are different (cf. Korteling et al. 2021). What happens then with the relationship between humans and AI regarding lexicographic purposes? Do they exclude each other, do they complement each other, will one lead to the disappearance of the other?

4 About people and ChatGPT for lexicographic purposes

Since its release in November 2022, the revolution caused by ChatGPT has given rise to several scientific publications which deal with the extent to which AI (in this case, represented by a chatbot) can replace lexicography or, at least, a part of the practical lexicographic work (cf. de Schryver/Joffe 2023; Jakubíček/Rundell 2023; Huete-García/Tarp 2024, to mention but a few). In this section, we intend to shed light on the relationship between AI systems (specifically, ChatGPT-3.5)[1] and humans taking different lexicographic tasks (either to create or to consult a lexical resource) as a starting point. Some of the conducted experiments (cf. Arias-Arias/Domínguez/Valcárcel 2024a) have already demonstrated that the lack of metalexicographic knowledge is one of the main weaknesses of ChatGPT, since the system is not capable of recognising a lexicographic text typology and it cannot consequently generate a lexicographic article.

When asked to create a "lexicographic article" in German, Galician and Spanish without further specifications,[2] the chatbot automatically interprets "article" as in 'prose composition published in a newspaper/magazine' and generates the output accordingly. The outcome of ChatGPT is thus formatted with appealing headings and an extensive paragraph division, which is not a common practice in lexicography. Furthermore, ChatGPT varies its response in each session, even when the same prompt is used, which is indicative of its lack of coherence. In each session a different sample of the underlying database may be activated and the answer is generated according to the selected set. The experiments conducted for the language pair German-Galician (Arias-Arias/Domínguez/Valcárcel 2024a) seem to suggest that ChatGPT can be considered to be "biased" in the understanding of the prompt, since the system starts generating lan-

1 It should be observed that the umbrella term AI does not only refer to chatbots or to ChatGPT and that more systems are included therein (e.g., virtual assistants, robots, healthcare management systems, etc.).

2 Arias-Arias/Domínguez/Valcárcel (2024a) have asked the system to create a lexicographic article without prior instructions, as any general user could do when using ChatGPT as a source of lexical knowledge.

guage taking the given prompt as unique starting point. Moreover, as aforementioned, this study has accounted for the low degree of efficiency of the system concerning its metalexicographic abilities, and this conclusion is based on the following descriptors:

a) ChatGPT is pseudoscientific (cf. Chomsky/Roberts/Watumull 2023) and pretentious in the sense that it convincingly answers lexicographic questions and solves lexicographic tasks without reasoning the automatically generated output (which, after all, is not its aim). The system does not have lexicographic knowledge, it just generates linguistic information based on the prompt provided as input to the system and on the training data. Users might mistakenly rely on the information given by ChatGPT, as it seems highly convincing. One piece of evidence to support this claim is that the answer to the same prompt is never constant in two parallel sessions of ChatGPT.
b) The output and response of ChatGPT constantly depend on two core aspects: (a) the strategy of prompt-shooting which is used and (b) the language in which the prompt is written (cf. Yu et al. 2024). Regarding the former, it has been shown in the field of prompt engineering that different prompting strategies can lead to very different results. Thus, the outcome will be different if we use a zero-prompt shooting strategy, in which we ask the system to perform a task without further examples (the one used in the discussed case study, Arias-Arias/Domínguez/Valcárcel 2024a) or other strategies in which we use examples so that the system can learn from them (cf. Arias-Arias/Domínguez/Valcárcel 2024b). As for the latter, most of the datasets (approximately 90%, according to Jakubiček/Rundell 2023) upon which ChatGPT has been trained are only available in English. This means that the system applies cross-lingual strategies and translates from English to other languages but the quantity of data available in, for example, German, Galician or Spanish is likely to be reduced.
c) As ChatGPT is not fine-tuned to conduct lexicographic tasks, the output it generates based on lexicographic questions is never systematised or coherent. With respect to the elements within the microstructure, for instance, ChatGPT might offer paraphrases of meaning and examples of use in one session, and idiomatic expressions or conjugation paradigms in a parallel session with the same prompt.[3]
d) Users remain essential in the evaluation of the system's efficiency. The interactive relation between the system and the user is one of most important aspects. In this sense, Fuertes-Olivera (2024) advocates the use of ChatGPT to enhance productivity[4] and states that ChatGPT, as well as other AI-based systems, can be very useful

3 The study of Arias-Arias/Domínguez/Valcárcel (2024a) illustrates how ChatGPT offers, for example, information on the pronunciation of lexical units just in the second session with German, whereas information on lexical derivation ("Verwandte Begriffe") is only provided in the first session for German.

4 Productivity, according to Fuertes-Olivera (2024: 131), refers to "the rate at which lexicographic data are produced per unit of time, labor, or resources".

for lexicographers. Huete-García/Tarp (2024) thematise the utility of ChatGPT for developing writing assistants for Spanish learners and they emphasise the relation between human and machine, where lexicographers as users of the system might induce the chatbot to regenerate or readapt the given responses. Thus, we shall consider that the users in both cited studies are expert lexicographers who have the required skills to convert the "raw" data provided by ChatGPT into lexicographic data.

It is particularly pertinent to elaborate on the last descriptor, since the efficiency of ChatGPT's outputs can only be evaluated when taking into consideration how expert the human user interacting with the system is. Even though we lack studies that analyse the behaviour or mental processes of users *in-actu* in the case of ChatGPT (cf. Müller-Spitzer et al. 2018a), we can try to outline the users' performance in different situations. For this purpose, we will present two hypothetical scenarios based on sessions with ChatGPT. When coping with how humans consult chatbots for lexicographic purposes, it is crucial to take into account the competence level of the user that is described. Three major distinctions should be drawn in this regard: a) learners, as people who are learning to use a dictionary, b) users with lexicographic background, as people who already know how to adequately use a dictionary, and c) expert users or lexicographers, as people with both experience and theoretical background knowledge (see section 2). The third group would include people not only with practical lexicographic skills, but also with metalexicographic knowledge.

4.1 Less experienced users and ChatGPT

The first hypothetical scenario would consider a less experienced dictionary user (e.g., a language learner) whose purpose is to find information, for instance, on the German lexical unit *abholen* ('to collect, to pick up'). Previous studies into dictionary use (cf. Müller-Spitzer et al. 2018a) have shown that users tend to choose and consult different tools or resources, among them general search engines, translation tools and lexicological information systems, based on their needs. ChatGTP serves in this regard as a general search engine which might offer a response to any potential lexicographic question. Assuming that a less experienced user would work with an initial hypothesis and may consult ChatGPT in order to confirm it (cf. Müller-Spitzer et al. 2018b; Wolfer et al. 2018), it is relevant to evaluate the quality of the data ChatGPT offers in this case and to what extent this user could finally confirm the hypothesis. The initial hypothesis could be broadly formulated, as the user might just intend to gain information about the meaning of the verb in a receptive situation or about its combinatorial potential. With a general prompt such as "Create a dictionary article for *abholen*", the user could expect to get a formatted dictionary entry containing the information they are looking for, but might get other results, since ChatGPT just generates text based on the formulation of the prompt (section 4). When analysing the output of ChatGPT for a prompt like the aforementioned,[5] following conclusions can be drawn for a less experienced user and considering the hypothesis formulation:

a) Less experienced users would trust the output of ChatGPT if it allows them to confirm their initial hypothesis or, if not, they might keep searching until they confirm their hypothesis (cf. Müller-Spitzer et al. 2018b; Wolfer et al. 2018). In the case of ChatGPT, they could be incorporating less accurate information in their foreign language repertoire if the response of the system allows them to confirm their working hypothesis. For instance, the third meaning paraphrase that ChatGPT offers in one of the analysed sessions (cf. session 2) for *abholen* is 'etwas oder jemanden als Gewinn, Erfolg oder Vorteil erlangen' (Eng. 'to gain something or someone as a profit, success or advantage'), not contemplated in some reference dictionaries such as *Duden online* or *DWDS*. If dealing with a receptive context with a sentence like *Nach dem Marathon könnt ihr sofort eure Medaille abholen* (Eng. 'After the marathon you can pick up your medal right away'), the user could accept the aforementioned meaning paraphrase as being the most adequate and construct knowledge based on this false assumption.
b) Different users in similar consultation situations and using the same prompt could come to different conclusions. Considering the example mentioned in a), another user would not incorporate this information in their repertoire, because in session 1, for instance, this meaning paraphrase is not mentioned. This accounts for the low reliability of the information ChatGPT offers and we shall bear in mind that, according to studies into dictionary use (cf. Müller-Spitzer et al. 2018b; Wolfer et al. 2018), at a certain point users consult different resources just to confirm their initial hypothesis. In the case of session 1, the delimitation in three presumably different meanings[6] could be confusing for language learners, since ChatGPT spins around the same core meaning of the verb, 'to collect'. Moreover, it should be stated that ChatGPT offers different types of information, which would make it impossible -or, at least, very difficult- to choose the chatbot as a reference resource for language activities, since each student would be getting different information.
c) It is true that ChatGPT can perform slightly better if the prompt is more precise and if users merely ask for the information they need (for instance, combinatorial potential, inflected forms, pronunciation, etc.) and based on which they construct

5 Two sessions in ChatGPT have been used as starting point for these reflections (Arias-Arias/Domínguez/Valcárcel 2024a):
a) https://chatgpt.com/share/9c89990d-7e65-4173-9578-d8e613b3a880?oai-dm=1
b) https://chatgpt.com/share/c087e4f4-2069-4605-aead-268c9ea1cd47?oai-dm=1.

6 The three different meanings are delimited as follows: "1. Etwas von einem Ort oder einer Person nehmen; 2. Etwas in Empfang nehmen; 3. Jemanden von einem Ort abholen." (Eng. '1. to take something from a place or a person; 2. to receive something; 3. to collect someone from a place.').

their consultation hypothesis. Nevertheless, users have no guarantee that the provided information is correct (cf. Ding et al. 2023; Reiss 2023; Jakubíček/Rundell 2023) and if they trust the chatbot, they might be constructing knowledge on a false premise.

d) Based on previous studies into dictionary use (cf. Domínguez/Valcárcel 2015; Müller-Spitzer et al. 2018a; 2018b; Wolfer et al. 2018), it can be confirmed that, due to their lack of lexicographic-linguistic knowledge, users might trust the data they receive from the chatbot without double-checking it. In this regard, less experienced lay users should be trained to learn to adequately use such systems. It should not be forgotten that lexicography is still struggling to develop a comprehensive dictionary culture (Gouws 2022).

4.2 Expert users and ChatGPT

The second hypothetical scenario would include an experienced dictionary user (e.g., a lexicographer) whose purpose is to resort to ChatGPT as a working tool to gather linguistic data and compile dictionary articles. Some studies on ChatGPT and its lexicographic applications have demonstrated that this system can assist lexicographers in different phases of their work (cf. Jakubíček/Rundell 2023; Fuertes-Olivera 2024; Arias-Arias/Domínguez/Valcárcel 2024b). ChatGPT serves in this regard as an AI tool that can inspire lexicographers in the phase of data acquisition, computerisation, data processing and data analysis (cf. Klosa-Kückelhaus 2013). Nevertheless, both lexicographers and chatbots need training to carry out lexicographic tasks effectively. This is shown in some articles that advocate the integration of ChatGPT in the lexicographic practice (cf. de Schryver 2023; Fuertes-Olivera 2024). The prompting strategy experts use differs considerably from the strategies lay people would formulate. The generative system underlying ChatGPT is, in such cases, "fine-tuned" to perform according to the lexicographer's instructions, but this is only possible because experts work with different hypotheses compared with less experienced users. The following aspects should be of particular interest in this case:

a) Lexicographers, or expert users, have both linguistic knowledge to prove that the data provided by ChatGPT is correct and the ability to consult other resources, such as lexicological information systems, so as to double-check for reliability. If an expert is not sure, for instance, whether the structure *den Sieg abholen* (Eng. 'to collect the victory', cf. session 2) can function as a collocation in German or not, they have the skill and expertise to consult other resources. A look into the combinatorial behaviour of *Sieg* in the *DWDS-Wortprofil* allows us to conclude that the combination of these two words is not as strong as it may appear from the data offered by ChatGPT. It can thus be concluded that domain expertise is required for making decisions (see section 2) when dealing with lexicographic-linguistic data so that the data can be adapted for lexicographic representation and therefore transformed into information by future potential users.

b) In some cases, ChatGPT can be useful during the phase of data acquisition, since lexicographers can obtain data *ad libitum* by adapting the prompt to their needs. In the case of example generation, lexicographers can ask the system to directly produce usage examples and this might increase its efficiency. Nonetheless, as Jakubíček/Rundell (2023) point out, there are linguistic technologies (such as the GDEX[7] algorithm) that have been conceived and trained for that purpose and this generally accounts for a higher level of accuracy. Some of the examples that are put forward by ChatGPT are not illustrative of a lemma's occurrence in natural language contexts.

c) When presenting ChatGPT as a sustainable resource for lexicographers (cf. Fuertes-Olivera 2024), we should be aware of the fact that AI systems are only sustainable from an internal point of view, since they constantly reutilise the data on which they were originally trained. From an external point of view, some articles (Bender et al. 2020; Spada 2023; Fan/Stinckwich 2023) have called attention to the fact that LLMs can enormously contribute to greenhouse gas emissions. Sustainability should also be contemplated from a social point of view, as different authors have demonstrated (cf. Spada 2023; Möller 2024), LLMs are trained on already biased data and therefore contribute to the perpetuation of stereotypes within modern societies. Taking this into consideration, we could state that it is more sustainable to develop lexicological information systems *ad hoc* when the lexicographic team is aware of social diversity which is further reflected on the dictionary. In this sense, Gouws (2022: 47) emphasises the importance of dictionaries as authorities in multilingual communities for contributing to the normalisation and consequent sustainability of minoritized languages (see section 5).

d) It cannot be denied that ChatGPT could imply an increase in lexicographic productivity if it is adequately integrated in the lexicographic process, because some phases within the lexicographic process are, to a certain extent, easily automatable. However, the phase of data analysis requires a greater human intervention, since the data needs to be compiled and the dictionary entries need to be written in a way that potential future users can obtain information from the lexicographic data presented. Considering this, lexicographers must double-check the working data in all phases of the lexicographic process and it is expected that the way in which ChatGPT presents its outputs leads to situations of overreliance on the data provided. In the same way, Huete-García/Tarp (2024) have made explicit the "indispensability of human-assisted intelligence" (see section 3), in the sense that lexicographers need to have the expertise to both interact with AI systems

7 GDEX stands for "Good Dictionary EXamples" and refers to a computational system that evaluates sentences based on their suitability to serve as representative dictionary examples.

and to evaluate the data provided. Regarding linguistic knowledge, ChatGPT often fails at generating linguistically accurate data, but it is the duty of the expert to validate and double-check the responses of the chatbot.

To sum up, we could answer the question regarding the efficiency of LLMs at performing lexicographic tasks by stating that this enormously depends on the type of user who interacts with the AI system. Figure 3 illustrates how the establishment of roles (agents, instruments, addressees; see section 2) differs in the two hypothetical situations presented, that is, one with the described user having less experience and another one with the described user being an expert. It can be clearly observed that expert users, and especially lexicographers, are actively involved in the lexicographic process, whereas less experienced users would give up their search once the initial hypothesis is confirmed. Figure 3 applies in particular in the case of computer-assisted lexicography, since computational lexicography, whose aim is to develop machine-readable dictionaries, has computers as final addressees as well (see section 2).

Furthermore, this representation confirms that humans, when they have the knowledge and required abilities, can create theories *ex-novo* and rationally process the data provided by the machine (see section 3). Needless to say, expert human review is still required when asking chatbots to carry out a lexicographic task and machines can partially assist lexicographers with more time-consuming tasks, such as programming, formatting or editing (cf. Jakubíček/Rundell 2023). We cannot forget either that dictionaries, rather than ChatGPT, are associated with social and cultural values, which are still crucial in today's world.

5 About people and dictionaries

The rise of new technologies often leads to fears that old things will become obsolete, like streaming services replacing vinyl records or e-readers making paper books disappear. However, these predictions haven't always come true – vinyl records are popular again and people still love paper books. This is because these things offer unique experiences beyond just the needs they satisfy. The same is likely to be true of dictionaries. While AI may revolutionise the way we access information, dictionaries serve important social, political and cultural purposes that AI cannot, for now. In short, dictionaries have a lot to offer beyond definitions, and that is why they may be here to stay.

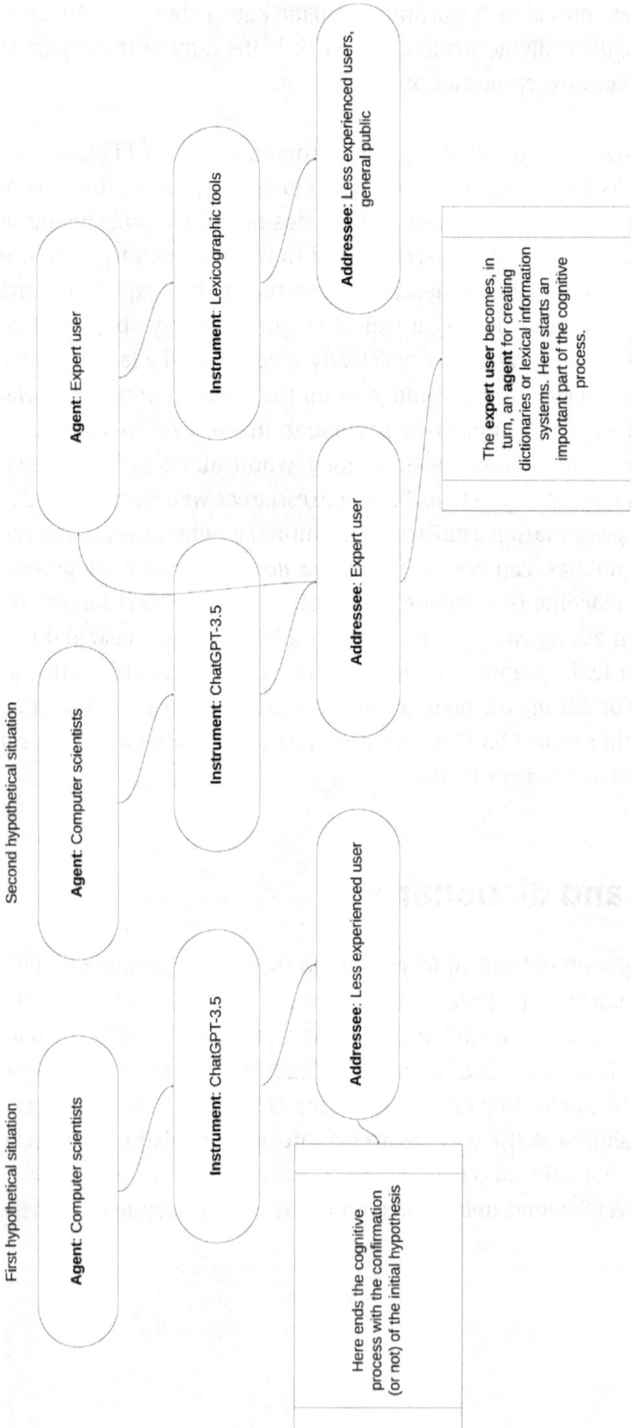

Figure 3: Representation of two hypothetical representations in terms of agents, instruments and addressees.

5.1 People trust dictionaries

Dictionaries carry with them a sense of authority and trust. People respect them as arbiters of meaning and reliable sources of information. This lies in the rigorous editing process that dictionaries often undergo, which establishes them as reliable sources of information on correct usage, spelling and definitions. This respect is manifested in many ways. First of all, it is remarkable how often people invoke the authority of a dictionary in arguments and debates, relying on it to settle disputes and ensure clarity. Thus, in the recent *European Survey of Dictionary Use and Culture*, resolving a dispute is the second most common use of dictionaries mentioned by informants (65.1%) (Kosem et al. 2019: 102). It is no wonder, then, that paper dictionaries can still be found on the shelves of living rooms in many homes.

But beyond these private uses of dictionaries, their arbitrating role in the public sphere seems visible and prevalent. Human-made dictionaries play a vital role in institutions such as schools, courts and administrations, legitimising texts and ensuring the accuracy of language usage. Teachers rely on them to assess students' work, judges and lawyers use them to interpret legal documents, and legislators consult them when drafting laws. This public importance of dictionaries is even reflected in movies, such as the French film *Le procès Goldman*, which shows how the famous *Littré* dictionary is used in the sessions of a trial (Danflous 2024).

Among the public uses that dictionaries still retain, those related to linguistic policy are perhaps the most obvious and relevant. The development of normative and prescriptive dictionaries is crucial to the development and maintenance of the standard variety of a language (McLelland 2021). For languages such as Spanish and French, prescriptive dictionaries are produced by language academies, institutions responsible for language regulation, which are often public bodies. Conversely, for English, this role is played by prestigious publishers (Mugglestone 2006; Spolsky 2011). Whatever the compiling body, it is essential that these dictionaries are produced and, crucially, validated by human experts. This necessity arises from the significant social and political implications associated with the inclusion or exclusion of words in these dictionaries. While there may be debate regarding the authority or infallibility granted to human-made dictionaries by users, it is clear that they retain a significant practical authority (Kosem et al. 2019).

The authority of dictionaries, in particular prescriptive ones, makes them a key aspect of other aspects of language policy, such as the revitalisation and standardisation of minority languages. Without a fixed and updated standard variety, a language could hardly be used for social functions in the public sphere, such as education, justice or administration. In the field of language policy studies, this phase of standard language development is known as codification. Dictionaries seem to play a key role in this process, as experts have highlighted (Cooper 1989; Muljačić 1986). It could therefore be said that the constitution and legitimation of a language implies the production of reference dictionaries by human experts. A well-known example of this is the Romance languages (Muljačić 1993), for many of which, such as Galician or Catalan (Colón 2014; Sánchez 2003; Fernández Rei 2018), the production of normative dictionaries by language academicians was essential to assume the social functions they have today. The same could be said of other languages that aspire to a similar status and legitimacy, such as Occitan or Asturian (D'Andrés 2018; Naro 2015).

5.2 Monuments of linguistic heritage

In addition to their importance in the elaboration and political legitimation of languages, dictionaries of all kinds remain a useful tool for storing, structuring and presenting linguistic information. Extensive research in historical lexicography has shown how dictionaries serve as meticulous archives of a language's evolution. Over the centuries they have recorded vocabulary, grammar and usage – snapshots of a language at one point in time (Durkin 2016). This documented history is invaluable not only to linguists studying language change and development, but also to a wide range of humanists interested in exploring social and cultural processes.

In such a task, dictionaries cover not only standardised languages, but also dialects and the linguistic expressions of specific social groups and local communities. Unsurprisingly, research in dialect lexicography is still extensive, as glossaries and dialect dictionaries for these communities find a place in bookshops and remain relevant to people. They celebrate the richness and diversity within a language and preserve the unique voices of local communities (Upton 2016; Van Keymeulen 2016). Alongside the great dictionaries of the language schools, these lexicographic works are a real repository of linguistic heritage and a source of identity for many communities. This has proved to be particularly important in helping to preserve endangered languages (Garrett 2018; Prinsloo 2012). By raising awareness of these languages within their communities and beyond, they promote recognition and appreciation.

In addition, dictionaries of endangered languages bridge geographical divides, enabling the sharing of linguistic resources and knowledge, which promotes cross-cultural understanding and cooperation. In fact, the process of compiling dictionaries for minority languages is often a collaborative effort involving linguists, local community members and non-governmental organisations (Ogilvie 2011). The efforts of these actors tend to focus on the production of bilingual dictionaries, as they can be instrumental in the development of educational materials that facilitate the transmission of these languages to future generations. Moreover, as mentioned above, the production of dictionaries itself contributes significantly to standardisation, raising the status of the language and empowering its speakers.

And last but not least, this prominence that dictionaries compiled by experts can give to minority languages improves the attitudes and perceptions of their speakers towards their heritage and culture, which can also promote a sense of well-being within their communities (Boerger 2017). Because of this social and political significance, dictionaries have often become an integral part of the cultural identity of many communities (Dollinger 2016; Margalitadze 2020). The *European Survey of Dictionary Use and Culture* (Kosem et al. 2019) has shown that in countries with minority languages, dictionaries are often perceived as national monuments or symbols, reflecting the deep connection between dictionaries, culture and community.

5.3 Dictionary lovers

The enduring relevance of dictionaries as cultural artefacts extends beyond their utility as reference tools. Indeed, a dedicated community of enthusiasts, distinct from professional lexicographers, find genuine passion in dictionaries and their contents. These people engage with dictionaries as much for consultation as for pleasure, not only in the process of looking up words but also in the process of compiling them. The lively forums that users have developed around popular online dictionaries such as *WordReference* are evidence of this (Crespi 2017). Another important example of the existence of such online learning communities related to dictionaries can be found in lexicographic portals, which offer different activities and content for their users to interact with (Murano 2014). These portals are often developed as a complement to reference dictionaries, such as the *Portal das Palabras*, which is generated from content in the *Dicionario da Real Academia Galega* (Fernández Casal 2022).

But user participation goes beyond the interaction of commenting or learning lexicographic content and reaches into the process of dictionary creation itself. Emerging research in the field of collaborative lexicography has already analysed different experiences such as the *Urban Dictionary* or the *DDF*, where users edit the dictionary entries themselves (Abel/Meyer 2013; Mabrak 2023; Sajous/Josselin-Leray 2022). Perhaps the best example is *Wiktionary* and the volunteer communities that develop its different editions (Meyer/Gurevych 2012). The European Master in Lexicography[8] itself, funded by the Erasmus Mundus programme, organises an annual hackfest around *Wiktionary*.[9] This event, held at the Pontevedra campus of the University of Vigo, brings together the students of this Master's degree with the community of editors and users of *Wiktionary*, all of them enthusiasts of dictionaries and languages. Together, they go on a journey to edit the entries in the different editions of this collaborative lexicographic project.

Regardless of the accuracy of these amateur lexicographers, there is no doubt that dictionary entries are a familiar type of text, encountered by most people during their education. Indeed, personal experiences with dictionaries are often vivid, encompassing memories of childhood (Neufeldt 2022). These experiences solidify the

8 https://www.emlex.eu.usc.gal/ (last access: 2 May 2025).

9 https://bit.ly/emlex-hackfest (last access: 2 May 2025).

presence of dictionaries in daily life, even inspiring the creation of social games centred on paper dictionaries. It is not surprising, then, that dictionaries can transcend their primary function as reference tools and become sources of artistic inspiration. Lexicographic texts are not only used directly in works of art; their influence also extends to the realm of decorative objects. Reproductions of dictionary entries adorn a wide range of objects, including posters, shower curtains, mugs, and even clothing such as T-shirts and hoodies (Klosa-Kückelhaus/Stähr 2019; 2020). This integration of dictionaries into popular culture highlights their continuing importance beyond the confines of academia.

6 Concluding remarks

In this paper, we have thoroughly examined the relationship between humans, dictionaries and artificial intelligence (AI), focusing in particular on the impact of AI on lexicographic processes. In order to answer the question of whether or not AI will replace dictionaries, our work has highlighted a number of key issues and brought to light some important findings.

First, the need for lexicographic knowledge in today's society remains undisputed. Despite advances in AI, the role of human expertise in creating, maintaining and using dictionaries is still indispensable. AI can assist with various lexicographic tasks, such as data acquisition and initial text generation, but it lacks the nuanced understanding and critical judgement that human lexicographers are skilled at. This difference is particularly evident in the accurate interpretation and contextualisation of lexicographic data, which AI systems currently cannot reliably replicate.

Second, while AI systems such as ChatGPT demonstrate impressive capabilities in text generation and rapid access to information, they are not yet able to perform large-scale lexicographic tasks independently. Our experiments have shown that AI-generated output often lacks consistency, coherence and the necessary metalexicographic knowledge. These shortcomings underline the importance of human supervision and intervention in ensuring the quality and reliability of lexicographic resources.

Furthermore, the role of AI as an authority in society is fundamentally different from that of traditional dictionaries. Dictionaries are perceived as cultural and social artefacts with a long-standing reputation for accuracy and trustworthiness. They play a critical role in education, legal contexts and cultural preservation. AI, on the other hand, while increasingly influential, does not yet carry the same weight of authority and trust. Its results are seen as utilitarian rather than trusted sources of knowledge.

In terms of cultural, social and emotional value, dictionaries offer much more than mere definitions. They are repositories of cultural heritage and linguistic diversity, reflecting the evolution of language and society. They serve as educational artefacts, historical records and symbols of linguistic identity. While AI is capable of processing and generating language, it does not yet capture these deeper values inherent in human-made dictionaries.

Overall, our research suggests that AI is not killing dictionaries, but rather transforming the landscape of lexicography. AI and human expertise can coexist, with AI increasing the efficiency and scope of lexicographic work, while human lexicographers ensure the depth, accuracy and cultural significance of dictionaries. The integration of AI into lexicography offers opportunities for innovation and collaboration, but it also reinforces the enduring importance of human expertise and cultural context in the creation and use of dictionaries. The future of lexicography is therefore more likely to lie in a balanced blend of technological enhancement and human knowledge, ensuring that dictionaries continue to evolve while maintaining their essential role in society.

Long live the dictionaries!

Bibliography

Monographs and articles

Abel, Andrea/Meyer, Christian M. (2013): The dynamics outside the paper: user contributions to online dictionaries. In: Kosem, Iztok, et al. (eds.): Electronic lexicography in the 21st century: Thinking outside the paper. Proceedings of the eLex 2013 Conference, 17–19 October 2013, Tallinn, Estonia. Ljubljana/Tallinn: Institute for Applied Slovene Studies/Eesti Keele Instituut, 179–194.

Arias-Arias, Iván/Domínguez Vázquez, María José/Valcárcel Riveiro, Carlos (2024a): Der Effizienz- und Intelligenzbegriff in der Lexikographie und künstlichen Intelligenz: kann ChatGPT die lexikographische Textsorte nachbilden? In: Lexikos 34, 1, 51–76.

Arias-Arias, Iván/Domínguez Vázquez, María José/Valcárcel Riveiro, Carlos (2024b): Sustainability and lexicography: Evaluating the methodological approach for the development of an automatic multilingual semantic tagger. Poster presented at the 21st EURALEX International Congress: Lexicography and Semantics, 8–12 October 2024, Cavtat, Croatia.

Bender, Emily M./Gebru, Timnit/McMillan-Major, Angelina/Shmitchell, Shmargaret (2020): On the dangers of stochastic parrots: Can language models be too big? In: FAccT '21, Proceedings of the 2021 ACM Conference on Fairness, Accountability, and Transparency, 610–623.

Boerger, Brenda (2017): Rapid word collection, dictionary production, and community well-being. In: 5th International Conference on Language Documentation & Conservation. Mānoa: 2–5 March 2017. http://hdl.handle.net/10125/41988 (last access: 2 May 2025).

Chomsky, Noam/Roberts, Ian/Watumull, Jeffrey (2023): The false promise of ChatGPT. In: The New York Times. https://www.nytimes.com/2023/03/08/opinion/noam-chomsky-chatgpt-ai.html (last access: 10 June 2024).

Colón, Germà (2014): La lexicografía histórica catalana a partir de fines del siglo XIX. In: Córdoba, Félix/González, Ernesto/Sánchez, María Dolores (eds.): Lexicografía de las lenguas románicas: Perspectiva histórica. Volumen I. Berlin/Boston: De Gruyter, 115–124. https://doi.org/10.1515/9783110310313.115.

Cooper, Robert L. (1989): Language planning and social change. Cambridge: Cambridge University Press.

Crespi, Patrizia (2017): Wordreference: une Wikipédia lexicographique. In: Revue française de linguistique appliquée 22, 1, 103–115. https://doi.org/10.3917/RFLA.221.0103.

Danflous, S. (2024): Le procès Goldman. César des lycéens. Dossier pédagogique. Paris: Ministère de l'Éducation nationale, de la Jeunesse, des Sports et des Jeux olympiques et paralympiques. https://eduscol.education.fr/document/56223/download (last access: 2 May 2025).

de Schryver, Gilles-Maurice & David Joffe (2023): The end of lexicography, welcome to the machine: On how ChatGPT can already take over all of the dictionary maker's tasks. Paper presented at the 20th CODH Seminar, ROIS–DS Center for Open Data in the Humanities, Tokyo, Japan, 27 February 2023. http://codh.rois.ac.jp/seminar/lexicography-chatgpt-20230227/

de Schryver, Gilles-Maurice (2023): Generative AI and lexicography: The current state of the art using ChatGPT. In: International Journal of Lexicography 36, 4, 1–33.

Ding, Bosheng/Qin, Chengwei/Liu, Linlin/Chia, Yew K./Joty, Shafiq/Li, Boyang/Bing, Lidong (2023): Is GPT-3 a good data annotator? In: arXiv:2212.10450, 1–21. https://arxiv.org/abs/2212.10450 (last access: 10 June 2024).

Dollinger, Stefan (2016): National dictionaries and cultural identity: Insights from Austrian, German, and Canadian English. In: Durkin, Philip (ed.): The Oxford handbook of lexicography. Oxford: Oxford University Press, 590–604. https://doi.org/10.1093/oxfordhb/9780199691630.013.42.

Domínguez Vázquez, María José/Valcárcel Riveiro, Carlos (2015): Hábitos de uso de los diccionarios entre los estudiantes universitarios europeos: ¿nuevas tendencias?. In: Domínguez Vázquez, Mª José/ Gómez Guinovart, Xavier/Valcárcel Riveiro, Carlos (eds.): Lexicografía de las lenguas románicas II. Aproximaciones a la lexicografía contemporánea y contrastiva. Berlin/Boston: De Gruyter, 165–189.

Durkin, Philip (2016): Etymology, word history, and the grouping and division of material in historical dictionaries. In: Durkin, Philip (ed.): The Oxford handbook of lexicography. Oxford: Oxford University Press, 236–252. https://doi.org/10.1093/oxfordhb/9780199691630.013.15.

D'Andrés, Ramón (2018): El procesu d'estandardización del asturianu. In: Giralt, Javier/Nagore, Francho (eds.): Lenguas minoritarias en Europa y estandarización. Zaragoza: Prensas de la Universidad de Zaragoza, 113–142.

Fan, Xia/Stinckwich, Serge (2023): On the unsustainability of ChatGPT: Impact of large language models on the sustainable development goals. In: UNU Macau. https://unu.edu/macau/blog-post/unsustainability-chatgpt-impact-large-language-models-sustainable-development-goals (last access: 10 June 2024).

Fernández Casal, Iolanda (2022): Los recursos digitales y la proyección del gallego en la red: la experiencia de la Real Academia Galega. In: Sargana, Andoni/Urkia, Miriam (eds.): Ingurune digitala, hizkuntzen estandarizazioa eta euskara. Madrid/Frankfurt am Main/Bilbao: Iberoamericana/Vervuert/ Euskaltzaindia, 177–190.

Fernández Rei, Francisco (2018): A codificación do galego moderno. O papel do Instituto da Lingua Galega e da Real Academia Galega neste proceso. In: Giralt, Javier/Nagore, Francho (eds.): Lenguas minoritarias en Europa y estandarización. Zaragoza: Prensas de la Universidad de Zaragoza, 77–112.

Fuertes-Olivera, Pedro A. (2024): Making lexicography sustainable: Using ChatGPT and reusing data for lexicographic purposes. In: Lexikos 34, 1, 123–140.

Gardner, Howard (2006): Multiple intelligences: New horizons in theory and practice. New York: Basic Books.

Garrett, Andrew (2018): Online dictionaries for language revitalization. In: Hinton, Leanne/Huss, Leena/ Roche Gerald (eds.): The Routledge handbook of language revitalization. New York, London: Routledge, 197–206.

Garriga Escribano, Cecilio (2023): La lexicografía ha muerto: viva la lexicografía. In: IX Congreso Internacional de Lingüística Hispánica (27 de septiembre–1 de octubre). Leipzig: Universität Leipzig, Philologische Fakultät

Gouws, Rufus H. (2022): Dictionaries: Bridges, dykes, sluice gates. In: Dictionaries and society. Proceedings of the XX EURALEX International Congress, 36–52.

Huete-García, Ángel/Tarp, Sven (2024): Training an AI-based writing assistant for Spanish learners: The usefulness of chatbots and the indispensability of human-assisted intelligence. In: Lexikos 34, 21–40.
Jakubíček, Miloš/Rundell, Michael (2023): The end of lexicography? Can ChatGPT outperform current tools for post-editing lexicography?. In: Medveď, Marek/Měchura, Michal/Tiberius, Carole/Kosem, Iztok/Kallas, Jelena/Jakubíček, Miloš (eds.): Electronic lexicography in the 21st century (eLex 2023): Invisible Lexicography. Proceedings of the eLex 2023 conference. Brno: Lexical Computing, 518–533.
Klein, Wolfgang (2015): Das Wörterbuch der Zukunft ist kein Wörterbuch. In: Eichinger, Ludwig (ed.): Sprachwissenschaft im Fokus: Positionsbestimmungen und Perspektiven. Berlin/München/Boston: De Gruyter, 277–296.
Klosa-Kückelhaus, Annette/Stähr, Lotta (2019): Lexikographie an der Wand: Wörterbuchartikel als Wandtattoos und Poster. In: IDS Sprachreport 35, 4, 26–35.
Klosa-Kückelhaus, Annette/Stähr, Lotta (2020): T-Shirt lexicography. In: Dictionaries: Journal of the Dictionary Society of North America 41, 2, 93–113. https://doi.org/10.1353/dic.2020.0024.
Klosa-Kückelhaus, Annette (2013): The lexicographical process (with special focus on online dictionaries). In: Gouws, Rufus H./Heid, Ulrich/Schweickard, Wolfgang/Wiegand, Herbert Ernst (eds.): Supplementary volume dictionaries. An international encyclopedia of lexicography. Berlin/Boston: De Gruyter Mouton, 517–524.
Klosa-Kückelhaus, Annette (2014): Gibt es eine Zukunft für Wörterbücher? In: IDS Sprachreport 4, 2014, 28–37.
Korteling, Johan Egbert/van de Boer-Visschedijk, Gillian/Blankendaal, Romy A.M./Boonekamp, Rudy/Eikelboom, Aletta (2021): Human versus Artificial Intelligence. In: Frontiers in Artificial Intelligence 4, 1–13.
Kosem, Iztok et al. (2019): The image of the monolingual dictionary across Europe. Results of the European survey of dictionary use and culture. In: International Journal of Lexicography 32, 1, 92–114.
Mabrak, Sami (2023): La lexicographie francophone collaborative à l'épreuve: le cas du *Dictionnaire des francophones*. In: Lynx 86. https://doi.org/10.4000/linx.10054.
Mainzer, Klaus (2019): Künstliche Intelligenz – wann übernehmen die Maschinen? Berlin/Heidelberg: Springer.
Maldonado González, Mª Concepción (2018): ¿Hay futuro para la lexicografía comercial? In: Revista de filología de la Universidad De La Laguna 36, 249–267.
Margalitadze, Tinatin (2020). Language and ecology of culture. In: Lexicographica 36, 225–240. https://doi.org/10.1515/lex-2020-0012.
McCarthy, John (2007): What is AI? Basic questions. Interview with Prof. John McCarthy. http://jmc.stanford.edu/artificial-intelligence/what-is-ai/index.html (last access: 20 December 2023).
McLelland, Nicola (2021): Grammars, dictionaries and other Metalinguistic texts in the context of language standardization. In: Ayres-Bennett, Wendy/Bellamy, John (eds.): The Cambridge handbook of language standardization. Cambridge: Cambridge University Press, 263–293. doi:10.1017/9781108559249.010.
Meyer, Christian M./Gurevych, Iryna (2012): Wiktionary: a new rival for expert-built lexicons? Exploring the possibilities of collaborative lexicography. In: Granger, Sylviane/Paquot, Magali (eds.): Electronic lexicography. Oxford: Oxford University Press, 259–291.
Möller, Hanna (2024): KI, geht das auch fair? In: Rudolphina. Wissen aus erster Hand. https://rudolphina.univie.ac.at/kuenstliche-intelligenz-fairer-gestalten (last access: 10 June 2024).
Mugglestone, L.C. (2006): Academies: dictionaries and standards. In: Brown, Keith (ed.): Encyclopedia of language and linguistics. Amsterdam: Elsevier, 12–14.
Muljačić, Žarko (1986): L'enseignement de Heinz Kloss (modifications, implications, perspectives). In: Langages 84, 53–63.

Muljačić, Žarko (1993): Standardization in Romance. In: Posner, Rebecca/Green, John N. (eds.): Trends in Romance linguistics and philology. Vol. 5: Bilingualism and linguistic conflict in Romance. Berlin/New York: De Gruyter Mouton, 77–114. https://doi.org/10.1515/9783110848649.77.
Müller-Spitzer, Carolin/Domínguez Vázquez, María José/Nied Curcio, Martina/Dias, Idalete/Wolfer, Sascha (2018a): Recherchepraxis bei der Verbesserung von Interferenzfehlern aus dem Italienischen, Portugiesischen und Spanischen: Eine explorative Beobachtungsstudie mit DaF-Lernenden. In: Lexicographica 34, 157–182.
Müller-Spitzer, Carolin/Domínguez Vázquez, María José/Nied Curcio, Martina/Dias, Idalete/Wolfer, Sascha (2018b): Correct hypotheses and careful reading are essential: Results of an observational study on learners using online language resources. In: Lexikos 28, 287–315.
Murano, Michela (2014): La lexicographie 2.0: nous sommes tous lexicographes?. In: Cahiers de recherche de l'école doctorale en linguistique française 8, 147–162.
Naro, Guilhem (2015): La lexicografía occitana entre recuperación del idioma y tresor sentimental. In: Domínguez, María José/Gómez, Xavier/Valcárcel, Carlos (eds.): Lexicografía de las lenguas románicas: Aproximaciones a la lexicografía moderna y contrastiva. Vol. II. Berlin/München/Boston: De Gruyter, 337–358. https://doi.org/10.1515/9783110310337.337.
Neufeldt, Victoria (2022): Writing children's dictionaries: A personal adventure. In: Dictionaries: Journal of the Dictionary Society of North America 43, 33–53. https://doi.org/10.1353/dic.2022.0008.
Ogilvie, Sarah (2011): Linguistics, lexicography, and the revitalization of endangered languages. In: International journal of lexicography 24, 4, 389–404. https://doi.org/10.1093/ijl/ecr019.
Prinsloo, Daniel J. (2012): Electronic lexicography for lesser-resourced languages: The South African context. In: Granger, Sylviane/Paquot, Magali (eds.): Electronic lexicography. Oxford: Oxford University Press, 119–144.
Reiss, Michael V. (2023): Testing the reliability of ChatGPT for text annotation and classification: A cautionary remark. In: arXiv:2304.11085, 1–12. https://arxiv.org/pdf/2304.11085 (last access: 10 June 2024).
Russell, Stuart/Norvig, Peter (^{2}2004): Inteligencia artificial. Un enfoque moderno. Madrid: Pearson Educación.
Sajous, Franck/Josselin-Leray, Amélie (2022): Issues in collaborative and crowdsourced lexicography. In: Jackson, Howard (ed.): The Bloomsbury handbook of lexicography. London: Bloomsbury Academic, 343–358.
Sánchez, María Dolores (2003): O papel dos diccionarios na conformación e difusión da variedade estándar da lingua. In: Álvarez, María/González, Ernesto X. (eds.): A estandarización do léxico. Santiago de Compostela: Consello da Cultura Galega/Instituto da Lingua Galega, 387–418.
Schierholz, Stefan J. (2021): Die Villa Vigoni Thesen. In: Lexicographica 37, 303–305 (see also https://www.emlex.phil.fau.eu/about-us/publications/other/, last access: 10 June 2024).
Spada, Alice (2023): ChatGPT is cool, but not that sustainable. In: ZeroCO2 magazine. https://zeroco2.eco/en/magazine/curiosities/chatgpt-sutainability/ (last access: 10 June 2024).
Spolsky, Bernard (2011): Language academies and other language management agencies. In: Language policy 10, 285–287.
Stangl, Werner (2024): Weltwissen. In: Online Lexikon für Psychologie & Pädagogik. https://lexikon.stangl.eu/31196/weltwissen (last access: 10 June 2024).
Sternberg, Robert J. (2012): Intelligence. In: Dialogues in clinical neuroscience 14, 1, 19–27.
Storrer, Angelika (1996): Metalexikographische Methoden in der Computerlexikographie. In: Wiegand, Herbert Ernst (ed.): Wörterbücher in der Diskussion II. Vorträge aus dem Heidelberger Lexikographischen Kolloquium. Tübingen: Niemeyer, 239–255.
Turing, Alan M. (1950): Computing machinery and intelligence. In: Mind 59, 236, 433–460.
Upton, Clive. 2016. Regional and dialect dictionaries. In: Durkin, Philip (ed.): The Oxford handbook of lexicography. Oxford: Oxford University Press, 381–392.

Van Keymeulen, Jacques (2016): Dialect lexicography. In: Hanks, Patrick/de Schryver, Gilles-Maurice (eds.): International handbook of modern lexis and lexicography. Berlin/Heidelberg: Springer, 1–15. https://doi.org/10.1007/978-3-642-45369-4_29-1.
Wiegand, Herbert Ernst (1998): Wörterbuchforschung: Untersuchungen zur Wörterbuchbenutzung, zur Theorie, Geschichte, Kritik und Automatisierung der Lexikographie. Berlin/New York: De Gruyter.
Wolfer, Sascha/Nied Curcio, Martina/Dias, Idalete/Müller-Spitzer, Carolin/Domínguez Vázquez, María José (2018): Combining quantitative and qualitative methods in a study on dictionary use. In: Lexicography in global contexts. Proceedings of the XVIII EURALEX International Congress, 101–112.
Yu, Danni/Li, Luyang/Su, Hang/Fuoli, Matteo (2024): Assessing the potential of LLM-assisted annotation for corpus-based pragmatics and discourse analysis: The case of apologies. In: International journal of corpus linguistics 29, 4, 534–561.

Dictionaries

DDF = Dictionnaire des francophones. Ed. by Institut international pour la Francophonie and Université Jean Moulin Lyon 3. https://www.dictionnairedesfrancophones.org/ (last access: 10 June 2024).
Duden online = Duden Wörterbuch der deutschen Sprache. Ed. by Cornelsen Verlag GmbH. https://www.duden.de/woerterbuch (last access: 10 June 2024).
DWDS = Digitales Wörterbuch der deutschen Sprache. Ed. by Berlin-Brandenburgische Akademie der Wissenschaften. https://www.dwds.de/d/wb-dwdswb (last access: 10 June 2024).
DWDS-Wortprofil = DWDS-Wortprofil für “Sieg”, Digitales Wörterbuch der deutschen Sprache. Ed. by Berlin-Brandenburgische Akademie der Wissenschaften. https://www.dwds.de/wp/?q=Sieg (last access: 10 June 2024).
Urban Dictionary = Urban Dictionary. https://www.urbandictionary.com/ (last access: 10 June 2024).
Wiktionary = Wiktionary. The free dictionary. Ed. by Wikimedia. https://www.wiktionary.org/ (last access: 10 June 2024).
WLWF-[3] = Wörterbuch zur Lexikographie und Wörterbuchforschung. Vol. 3. Ed. by Wiegand, Herbert Ernst/Gouws,Rufus H./Kammerer, Matthias/Mann, Michael/Wolski, Wolski. Berlin/Boston: De Gruyter, 2020.

Konan J-M Kouassi

Profilex: Kognitive Leistungen des Lexikographen und die Qualität im Wörterbuchartikel

Abstract: This article deals with the lexicographer's tasks in modern lexicographic practice. These tasks are divided into concrete and abstract elements and determine the role and importance of the lexicographer as well as his knowledge and competences for successful lexicographic practice. The lexicographer's cognitive performance is linked to the *quality* of the dictionary article, with quality being the goal and cognitive processes the prerequisite.

Keywords: Profilex, practical lexicography, cognitive processes, article quality, lexicographer

Schlagwörter: Profilex, praktische Lexikographie, kognitive Leistung, Artikelqualität, Lexikograph

1 Einleitung

Der folgende Beitrag beinhaltet zwei wesentliche Fragestellungen: 1) Was ist Qualität im Rahmen der lexikographischen Praxis? 2) Wie entsteht die Qualität von Wörterbuchartikeln? Dies erfolgt unter der Annahme, dass der Lexikograph[1] und dessen Background, Kompetenzen und Persönlichkeit eine wichtige und unumgängliche Rolle spielen. Moderne Technologien (Computer, Bildschirm, Software u. a.) haben zwar einen erheblichen Einfluss auf die traditionelle Arbeit des Lexikographen, schaffen aber auch Raum für neue Einstellungen und eine andere Arbeitsdynamik des Lexikographen. In seiner lexikographischen Praxis hat der Lexikograph mit einer Vielzahl von Entscheidungsknoten und Ermessensfragen zu tun, welche er mit kognitiv begründbaren Arbeitsschritten und mithilfe hermeneutischer Schlüsselkompetenzen löst. Welche das sind, ist empirisch untersucht worden, sodass Hinweise zu den kogni-

1 Im Text wird das generische Maskulinum verwendet und bezeichnet so Personen aller Geschlechter.

Acknowledgements: Profilex-Projekt „Gefördert durch die Deutsche Forschungsgemeinschaft (DFG) – 494892119".

Konan J-M Kouassi, Friedrich-Alexander-Universität Erlangen-Nürnberg, Bismarckstraße 1, 91054 Erlangen, e-mail: konan.kouassi@fau.de

https://doi.org/10.1515/9783112216644-013

tiven Grundlagen der Lexikographentätigkeiten vorliegen. Diese werden hier präsentiert und mit dem Merkmal *Wörterbuchartikelqualität* verknüpft. Die empirische Analyse hat darin bestanden, bei der Erstellung von Wörterbuchartikeln den Bildschirm des Arbeitscomputers des Lexikographen im Sinne eines Think-Aloud-Protokolls aufzuzeichnen. D. h. der Lexikograph sagt laut, was er tut, woran er denkt, was er empfindet und wie er seine Entscheidungen trifft. Denn es wird davon ausgegangen, dass die ausgesprochenen Worte des Lexikographen (in dem Bezug im Weiteren *Proband*) in Kombination mit den Bildschirmeffekten die kognitiven Geschehnisse und Entscheidungsprozesse des Lexikographen einsehbar machen. Dies wird als Hintergrund zur Qualität von Wörterbuchartikeln betrachtet.

Der Beitrag gliedert sich wie folgt: Zunächst erfolgt in Kapitel 2 eine kurze Beschreibung des Forschungsprojekts *Profilex*. Kapitel 3 enthält eine Darstellung der konkreten und abstrakten Leistungen des Lexikographen als Voraussetzung zu dessen kognitiven Leistungen. In Kapitel 4 werden die Ergebnisse der empirischen Untersuchung der kognitiven Leistungen auf der Basis der Bildschirmaufnahmen vorgestellt, und abschließend wird die kognitive Leistung des Lexikographen für die Bedeutung der Qualität im Wörterbuchartikel reflektiert.

2 Profilex: Kurzbeschreibung

Das Projekt *Profilex* steht als Akronym für *Der professionelle Lexikograph* und beschäftigt sich allgemein mit den Tätigkeiten des Lexikographen im lexikographischen Prozess zu modernen lexikalischen Informationssystemen. Es ist ein metalexikographisches Projekt, das am *Interdisziplinären Zentrum für Lexikographie, Valenz- und Kollokationsforschung*[2] der Friedrich-Alexander-Universität Erlangen-Nürnberg angesiedelt ist. Die zentrale Frage ist die Rolle bzw. die Notwendigkeit des Lexikographen vor dem Hintergrund der modernen Entwicklungen auf dem Gebiet der Informationstechnologien. Damit verknüpft sind weitere Fragen wie die Kompetenzen des Lexikographen, der Weg zum professionellen Lexikographen, die Interaktion zwischen technischen und intellektuellen Möglichkeiten sowie die Zukunft der lexikographischen Praxis. Wiegand (1997: 178) beschreibt die gesellschaftliche Verantwortung der wissenschaftlichen Lexikographie und bemängelt, dass über die Verantwortlichkeiten des Lexikographen zu wenig geforscht wird:

> Es muß daher überraschen, daß der Themenbereich, der mit Syntagmen wie lexikographische Verantwortung oder Verantwortlichkeit der Lexikographen aufgerufen wird, bisher in der Wörterbuchforschung – soweit ich sie übersehe – nicht in grundlegender Weise bearbeitet wurde, sondern stets nur aus der Sicht gewisser Aspekte der Verantwortungslosigkeit, nämlich im Zusammenhang mit Problemen des Plagiarismus und der Wörterbuchkriminalität.

---

2 URL: http://www.lexi.uni-erlangen.de/de.

Die Forschungsfragen des Profilex-Projekts und die Arbeit des Lexikographen als Themenbereich sind bis heute in der lexikographischen Fachliteratur nur teilweise, oberflächlich und wenig präzis angegangen worden. Die (meta)lexikographischen Arbeiten befassen sich vornehmlich mit der Lexikographie als Theorie und Praxis, mit den Wörterbuchstrukturen, der Wörterbuchforschung, der Bedeutung der Lexikographie, den Wörterbüchern für menschliche Benutzer sowie mit der Verbindung der Lexikographie zu benachbarten Disziplinen. Neuere Beiträge legen den Fokus auf die Verhältnisse zwischen Technologien wie ChatGPT und die lexikographische Praxis (z. B. bei Phoodai/Rikk 2023; de Schryver/Joffe 2023; Arias-Arias et al. 2024). Nur wenige wissenschaftliche Abhandlungen haben den Lexikographen zum Kernpunkt (z. B. Bergenholtz/Gouws 2012; Gouws 2012). Dabei gehen alle an der Persönlichkeit, den Fertigkeiten und Kompetenzen des professionellen Lexikographen, der Bedeutung und Konstitution seines Vorwissens vorbei, sodass festzustellen ist: Es fehlt eine metalexikographisch begründete und empirisch fundierte Übersicht zu der Rolle, d. h. den Verantwortungen, Aufgaben und Entscheidungsprozessen über den lexikographischen Prozess hinweg, die nur der ausgebildete Lexikograph leisten kann. Auch eine bestimmende und geprüfte Abgrenzung von Technologie und intellektueller Leistung fehlt.

Die Arbeit bzw. die Leistungen des Lexikographen als Themenbereich werden im Rahmen des Profilex-Projekts durch unterschiedliche Methoden untersucht: Experteninterviews, kritische Wörterbuchforschung, Fragebögen und Bildschirm-Tracking-Experimente. Letztere haben geholfen, die kognitiven Entscheidungsprozesse beim Lexikographen in Hinblick auf die Erzeugung von Qualität im Wörterbuchartikel aufzuspüren.

3 Konkrete und abstrakte Leistungen des Lexikographen

Dass die technische Unterstützung in der lexikographischen Praxis immer weiter zunimmt, ist in der Metalexikographie wie auch in den lexikographischen Werkstätten kein neues Thema. Christian Lehmann (2006: 26) schreibt: „Wenn irgendetwas technisch machbar ist, wird es gemacht“. Da die modernen lexikographischen Prozesse, insbesondere für Online-Wörterbücher, vorwiegend auf Computertechnik und informatische Technologien angewiesen sind und unabhängig davon, wie die Qualität der erzeugten Daten ist, kann davon ausgegangen werden, dass bei den Lexikographen die Aufgaben verbleiben, die nicht ohne Weiteres durchführbar sind. Die Beschäftigung mit der Arbeit des modernen Lexikographen lässt feststellen, dass diese sich wesentlich in zwei Kategorien aufteilt: *konkrete* und *abstrakte Leistungen.*

3.1 Konkrete Leistungen des Lexikographen

Die *konkrete Leistung* ist das, was der Lexikograph beim Projektleiter als erledigte Aufgaben einreicht. Sie werden dem Lexikographen vom Projektleiter oder dem Projektteam explizit als Aufgaben gegeben. Sie werden oft auch genutzt, um das Aufgabenspektrum in einem Stellenangebot zu beschreiben, sodass bei einer Einstellung für den Lexikographen klar ist, wozu er eingestellt ist und was konkret zu tun ist. Dazu gehören u. a. a) die Erstellung von Wörterbuchartikeln zu neuen Lemmata, b) das Korrekturlesen von neuerstellten Wörterbuchartikeln, c) das Ausbauen vorhandener Wörterbuchartikel, d) die Korpus-Annotation, e) die Nachexzerptionsarbeit (für neu editierte bzw. neu aufgefundene Quellentexte), f) die Mitwirkung beim Konzipieren neuer Wörterbuchprojekte, g) die Mitwirkung bei Auswahl und Bestimmung von neuen Lemmakandidaten, h) die Ermittlung neuer Lesarten zu bestimmten Lemmata, i) die Ermittlung veraltender/veralteter Lesarten, j) die Qualitätsprüfung von vorhandenen Artikeln, k) das Verfassen bzw. die Überarbeitung von Umtexten (z. B. Einleitung, Benutzungshinweise, Artikel des Tages). Als Ergebnis eines abgeschlossenen lexikographischen (Teil-)Prozesses trägt der Lexikograph die volle Verantwortung für die zuverlässige Erledigung dieser Aufgaben. Sie erfordern originelle Fähigkeiten, die Computerprogramme bzw. Algorithmen nicht leisten können, was aber für eine lexikographische Praxis für menschliche Benutzer prägend und unumgänglich ist. Dazu gehören das *Denkvermögen und Dinge reflektieren*, das *Beurteilungsvermögen*, die *Kenntnis der Benutzergruppe, deren Kultur und Einbeziehung ihrer Wünsche*, aber auch die *Angst, Fehler zu machen*, die *Begründbarkeit der Zuverlässigkeit des Datenangebots*. Diese Elemente weisen auf die *Hermeneutik* als Kunst des Verkündens, Dolmetschens, Erklärens und Auslegens von Texten verschiedener Autoren von einem Informationssender – hier vom Lexikographen – zu einer Empfängergruppe – hier die Wörterbuchbenutzer hin (vgl. Gadamer 1974: 1061). Um den Ansprüchen der Wörterbuchprojekte gerecht zu werden, können sich Lexikographen zwar auf technische Recherche- und Analysetools sowie weitere Technologien stützen, müssen jedoch hermeneutisch arbeiten, um qualitative und sichere Datenergebnisse zu erzielen.

3.2 Abstrakte Leistungen des Lexikographen

Die *abstrakten Leistungen* des Lexikographen bilden das Gesamt derjenigen Aufgaben und Arbeitsprozesse, die der Lexikograph vollzieht, damit die konkreten Aufgaben zustande kommen können. Dabei geht es u. a. um Arbeitsschritte wie a) die lexikalische Wortforschung in der Sekundärliteratur bzw. Wörterbüchern, Korpora und Internet, b) der Durchgang von Beleglisten, c) die Interpretation von Belegen, d) die Zuordnung von Belegen zu Lesarten, e) das Ermessen und die Bestimmung der Reihenfolge von Belegen, f) die Zuordnung von Daten bei homographen Lemmata, g) die Aussortierung von unzutreffenden Daten, h) die Erarbeitung der Konstitution der Bedeutungsangaben, i) die Entscheidung für jedwede Information im Wörterbuchartikel, j) die Betrachtung der Voraussetzungen und Wünsche der potenziellen Benutzer, k) die textuelle Formulierung des Artikels im Hinblick auf den Adressatenkreis, l) Absprachen mit Kollegen und externen Fachleuten. Die Erledigung dieser Aufgaben und Prozesse basiert auf den Erfahrungen, Erkenntnissen und dem Leistungsvermögen des einzelnen Lexikographen. Dem Projektleiter, der den Auftragt gibt, sind die abstrakten Leistungen bewusst. Ob und in welcher Weise und Intensität der Lexikograph davon Gebrauch macht, unterscheidet sich von Lexikograph zu Lexikograph, denn in der beruflichen Entwicklung eines jeden Lexikographen gibt es Abweichungen.

Somit ist die Rolle des modernen Lexikographen aus der Perspektive von konkreten und abstrakten Leistungen zu betrachten. Die vorliegenden fachlexikographischen Definitionen des Wortes *Lexikograph* sind zwar nicht falsch, bleiben aber doch zu allgemein und liefern wenig über die konkrete und praktische Leistung des Lexikographen. Einige der Bedeutungsangaben lauten wie folgt:

a) *‚One who engages in LEXICOGRAPHY, either as a COMPILER or as a METALEXICOGRAPHER.‘* (Hartmann/James *[Dictionary of Lexicography]* 2002:84)
b) *‚Person, die für die Erstellung eines lexikographischen Nachschlagewerks verantwortlich ist‘* (Wiegand et al. *[WLWF]* 2020: 223)

Wiegand et al. (2020: 223) geben in ihrem Wörterbuchartikel zu LEXIKOGRAPH einen Erläuterungsteil und beziehen den Status *Lexikograph* auf Personen,

> die durch herausragende Leistungen dadurch hervorgetreten sind, dass sie ein bedeutendes Wörterbuch publiziert haben [...]. Auch bezogen auf die Gegenwart lassen sich an vielen wichtigen und längerfristigen Projekten Beteiligte zweifellos als *Lexikograph(inn)en* bezeichnen, wenn bei ihnen entsprechende fachliche Voraussetzungen als gegeben anzusehen sind.

Autoren und Autorinnen der vielfältigen kleinen Wörterbücher zu ganz unterschiedlichen Bereichen sowie Personen, die in dem einen oder anderen Verlag dazu eingestellt oder abgestellt sind, als Projektleiter(innen) für Wörterbücher zu dienen, lassen Wiegand et al. (vgl. ebd.) kaum als Lexikographen bezeichnen, obwohl sie über lexikographisches Erfahrungswissen (meist konventioneller Art) verfügen, aber ihre Qualifikation für die Ausübung des Berufs aus ganz anderen oder bestenfalls benachbarten Disziplinen (z. B. der Sprachwissenschaft) beziehen. Auf die Natur der Voraussetzungen, die sprachlichen, fachlichen, methodischen und sozialen Kompetenzen zur lexikographischen Praxis, die für die Bestimmung des Lexikographenstatus auch relevant sind, gehen Wiegand et al. nicht ein. Im Profilex-Projekt sind sie jedoch die wesentlichen Fragestellungen.

Gouws/Bergenholtz (2012) versuchen ebenfalls, das Spektrum der Bedeutung des Wortes *Lexikograph* sowie Kategorien von Lexikographen zu erfassen. Sie vergleichen hierzu mehrere Bedeutungsangaben aus verschiedenen Wörterbüchern miteinander und grenzen sie voneinander ab. Sie kommen dann zu folgendem Schluss:

> Within the broad field of lexicography, a diverse range of participants can be identified. These include people writing dictionaries—dictionaries dealing with both language for general purposes and languages for special purposes, someone writing about dictionaries, someone reviewing dictionaries, someone teaching lexicography as a subject, someone being trained in theoretical lexicography and someone with a degree or diploma in lexicography. All these people can be referred to as lexicographers. (Gouws/Bergenholtz 2012: 73–74)

Dies beantworten die Forschungsfragen des Profilex-Projekts (die konkreten und abstrakten Leistungen, die kognitiven Leistungen, die Verantwortungen, Hintergründe und Kompetenzen des Lexikographen etc.) nicht. Im Folgenden werden die kognitiven Leistungen des Lexikographen präsentiert.

4 Empirische Erforschung von kognitiven Leistungen durch Bildschirm-Tracking

Die Probanden der Untersuchung sind insgesamt vier und stammen von den Wörterbucheinrichtungen DWDS und Duden; jeder der Probanden hat ein Lemma lexikographisch bearbeitet, sodass am Ende vier Aufnahmedateien (zu WUNDERFITZIG, FREIHÄNDIG, FLASCHENDEPOT, JDM. AUF DEN PELZ RÜCKEN erstellt worden sind. Jeder Proband hat ein Lemma ausgewählt und für das Experiment vorbereitet.[3] Die vier Aufnahmen dauern im Durchschnitt 65 Minuten und die Probanden haben keine Pausen eingelegt. Bei der Aufnahme sitzt der Lexikograph am Rechner und arbeitet. Sein Arbeitsmaterial hat er überwiegend im Computer (Redaktionssystem, Korpora, digitale Wörterbücher, Suchmaschinen); die Software ist für die Aufnahme bereits geöffnet. Gedruckte Wörterbücher sind teilweise im Arbeitsraum oder im Gebäude zu finden. Der Lexikograph sagt laut, was er tut, woran er denkt und was er empfindet. Begegnet ihm etwas Neues, wird das als Anlass für eine bestimmte Reaktion (z. B. nach etw. suchen, etw. lesen, verstehen, interpretieren, Ergebnis weiter berücksichtigen oder ignorieren, weil uninteressant) genommen. Es wird bei der Bildschirmaufnahme davon ausgegangen, dass die ausgesprochenen Worte des Probanden in Kombination mit den Bildschirmeffekten die kognitiven Geschehnisse und Entscheidungsprozesse beim Lexikographen widerspiegeln.

---

3 Um Zeit zu sparen und den Fokus auf die inhaltliche Seite des Experiments zu legen, wurden die Stichwörter vorab ausgewählt und als neue Einträge im Redaktionssystem eingetragen.

4.1 Kognitive Leistungen: Definition

Die kognitiven Leistungen sind hier Geschehnisse und Prozesse im Kopf des Lexikographen, die im Kontext der Artikelerstellung entstehen. Sie tauchen im lexikographischen Prozess auf, wenn der Lexikograph bestimmte Sachverhalte bedenkt, beurteilt und reflektiert. Sie werden im Profilex-Projekt durch Bildschirm-Tracking-Experimente ermittelt und im Hinblick auf die Entstehung von Qualität im Wörterbuchartikel untersucht.

4.2 Kognitive Leistungen: Verortung

Zur Verortung der kognitiven Leistungen wird Abb. 1 herangezogen.

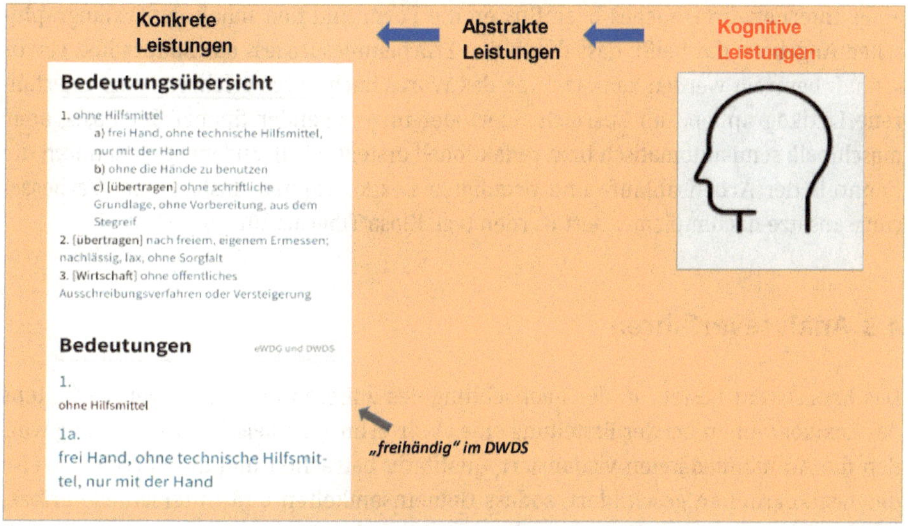

Abb. 1: Kognitive Leistungen: Verortung.

Auf der linken Seite steht ein Auszug des Wörterbuchartikeltextes zum Lemma FREIHÄNDIG[4] aus dem DWDS-Wörterbuch; dieser Artikeltext steht als Beispiel für die Kategorie der möglichen konkreten Leistungen, also der konkreten Aufgaben (vgl. 3.1), die der Lexikograph im Rahmen des Projekts leistet und einreicht. Der Wörterbuchartikeltext kennzeichnet im engeren Sinn das Ziel der lexikographischen Praxis; er liegt in einer bestimmten Qualität vor, die je nach Betrachter *gut*, *schlecht*, *sehr gut*, *passend* sein kann. Im Hinblick auf qualitative Wörterbuchartikel zieht der Lexikograph abstrakte

4 „freihändig", bereitgestellt durch das Digitale Wörterbuch der deutschen Sprache, https://www.dwds.de/wb/freih%C3%A4ndig, abgerufen am 20.6.2024.

Leistungen (vgl. 3.2 bzw. in der Mitte von Abb. 1) heran; sie gehen den konkreten Leistungen voraus. Der Lexikograph schreibt also seinen Artikel durch abstrakte Leistungen vor dem Hintergrund von Prozessen in seiner Kognition (rechte Seite von Abb. 1). Die Kognition beschreibt das *Oxford Dictionary of Psychology* als „The mental activities involved in acquiring and processing Information“ (Colman 2001: 140). Diese Definition ist hier besonders geeignet, weil sie sich auf den arbeitenden Lexikographen genauer übertragen lässt. Der Lexikograph nimmt die Korpusdaten wahr, erkennt die Zusammenhänge und verarbeitet die Daten durch kognitive Prozesse und Handlungen (diese sind in 4.4 detailliert aufgeführt) zu Wörterbuchartikeln. Dabei verfolgt er qualitative Wörterbuchartikel. In dieser Hinsicht ist die Qualität des Wörterbuchartikels nicht nur am Wörterbuchartikel zu beurteilen, sondern auch am Entstehungsprozess. Klosa/Tiberius (2018) stellten zu Recht Gründe dar, warum es notwendig ist, dass der lexikographische Prozess ständig untersucht und beschrieben wird. Die Entstehungsbedingungen eines Internetwörterbuches beeinflussen die Form und den Inhalt des lexikographischen Angebots; das heißt, dass durch den Erarbeitungsprozess das Endprodukt gewissenhaft beurteilt werden kann (z. B. ob das Wörterbuch durch erfahrene oder unerfahrene Lexikographen, mit ausreichender oder ungenügender finanzieller Basis, oder maschinell, semi-automatisch bzw. redaktionell erstellt wird). Zudem können durch die Kenntnis der Arbeitsabläufe und beteiligten Lexikographen Ausbau- und Verbesserungsansätze nachimplementiert werden (vgl. Klosa/Tiberius 2018: 67–68).

4.3 Analyseverfahren

Das Experiment besteht in der Beobachtung des äußeren und kognitiven Verhaltens des Lexikographen bei der Erstellung eines Wörterbuchartikels. Zur Auswertung werden die Aufnahmedateien visualisiert, qualitativ betrachtet und die Vorgehensweise des Lexikographen geschildert, sodass Gemeinsamkeiten und Unterschiede erfasst werden können. Die qualitative Analyse wird von drei Fragestellungen unterstützt: 1) Um welche konkrete Aufgabe/Leistung geht es bei der Aufnahme? 2) Wie geht der Lexikograph vor bzw. was macht er gerade?[5] und 3) Wie lassen sich die ausgesprochenen Worte mit den gedanklichen Prozessen im Lexikographen verbinden? Die Fragen werden für die Interpretation der gedanklichen Geschehnisse beim Lexikographen verwendet und spiegeln die nachfolgende Auswertung wider.

5 Hier erfolgt eine Protokollierung der abstrakten Leistungen, die der Lexikograph im Hinblick auf den fertigen Artikel leistet.

4.4 Ergebnisse der Analyse

In den Aufnahmen ist zu beobachten, wie der Lexikograph nicht nur Daten anbieten will, sondern nach den besten Daten sucht; er bringt sich ein und das fordert bei ihm eine gewisse kognitive Leistung. Es geht um *Denkprozesse* bzw. *kognitive Handlungen*, die den Lexikographen in seiner Arbeit prägen. Weil sie sowohl in den ausgesprochenen Worten als auch am Bildschirm des arbeitenden Lexikographen wiederholt zu beobachten sind, werden sie hier als besondere Kollokationen zum Wort *Lexikograph* gefasst und betrachtet. Das Muster hierfür lautet: *Der Lexikograph* + *Verb* (Handlung mit kognitivem Bezug). Die erfassten Denkhandlungen und Denkprozesse sind *vermuten, lesen, interpretieren, denken, überlegen, sich (etw.) merken, (etw.) ignorieren, finden/einschätzen, zweifeln, prüfen, überzeugt sein, entscheiden.* Diese Verben haben eine allgemeine Bedeutung in der Standardsprache, haben aber mit der fachlichen Bereicherung der lexikographischen Arbeit eine spezifische terminologische Ausprägung.

- Der Lexikograph **vermutet**: Der Lexikograph geht an die Daten mit persönlichen Vorstellungen heran bzw. er hat Vorannahmen, die er an den Daten prüfen kann. So vermutet er z. B. im Voraus, was ein bestimmtes Wort (das Lemma), eine bestimmte Wortkombination oder Wortgruppe (mit dem Lemma) bedeuten könnte. Für seine Vermutungen holt er sich zunächst eine Bestätigung in anderen Wörterbüchern, bevor er seine eigenen Recherchen startet. Beim Durchgang von Belegen macht sich der Lexikograph genauso Vermutungen darüber, was die einzelnen Belege in Kombination mit dem Stichwort bedeuten. So kann er am Ende bestimmte Belege als interessant oder uninteressant einstufen.
- Der Lexikograph **liest**: Er liest implizit ohne auszusprechen. Dabei ist er ruhig; er nimmt die Daten wahr und liest die schriftlichen Zeichen, auf die seine Aufmerksamkeit stößt oder die für den Artikel, der verfasst wird, eine Rolle spielen. Gelesen werden zum Beispiel Informationen in Suchergebnissen, Belegen, statistischen Resultaten, Metadaten, anderen Wörterbuchartikeln, enzyklopädischen Texten, Google-Einträgen. Beim Lesen solcher Texte denkt er gleichzeitig darüber nach, inwieweit die Daten ihm helfen können, sein Ziel (den Artikel in guter Qualität schreiben) zu erreichen.
- Der Lexikograph **interpretiert**: Die Interpretation geschieht systematisch bei oder nach der visuellen oder kognitiven Wahrnehmung von Daten, die ihm begegnen. Die Daten können Belege, Wörterbuchartikel, Bilder oder statistische Daten sein. In der großen Datenmenge findet intuitiv eine qualitative Kalkulation statt, um die Daten zu erkennen, die für den Artikel relevant sind. Die wichtigste Frage für den Lexikographen ist: *Was bedeuten diese Daten für mich, für das Lemma und für meinen Artikel?* bzw. *inwieweit sind die Daten für meinen Artikel relevant?* Die gedankliche Konfrontation mit diesen Fragen mündet auf Schlussfolgerungen wie die *Erschließung von Bedeutungen und Synonymen, Aufnahme von Belegen, Daten anmerken oder ignorieren, weil sie uninteressant sind, Weiterrecherchieren.*

- Der Lexikograph **denkt:** Das Denken als kognitive Leistung hier in Hinblick auf den fertigen Wörterbuchartikel verbindet den Lexikographen ständig mit seiner Arbeit. Er denkt ständig an die geeignete Möglichkeit, in seiner Arbeit voranzukommen und Lösungen für die verschiedenen Fälle zu finden (z. B. ob bestimmte Wörterbücher oder Webseiten zur Aufklärung bestimmter Fälle herangezogen werden sollen, das Korpus für weitere Recherchen gewechselt werden soll, oder eine Absprache mit Kollegen/Fachexperten heranzuziehen ist). Genauso denkt er an die Rezeption der Informationen beim potenziellen Benutzer, indem er sich in die Benutzerperspektive versetzt.
- Der Lexikograph **überlegt:** Diese kognitive Handlung gehört zum allgemeinen Denkprozess, dauert sekundenlang, oder kann länger dauern, weil der Lexikograph über etwas nachdenkt, bei dem er unsicher ist; er überlegt, was ihn bei bestimmten Daten stört. Das Ziel bei seinem Überlegen ist immer, dass er sich Klarheit über einen Sachverhalt verschaffen will, bevor er eine Entscheidung treffen kann (er überlegt bspw. was gut, besser bzw. schlecht ist).
- Der Lexikograph **zweifelt:** Bei Unsicherheiten oder Unklarheit in seiner Arbeit reagiert der Lexikograph mit Zweifel. Solange er Zweifel hat, hält er sich zurück, und das schützt ihn davor, falsche Entscheidungen zu treffen. Das ist der Fall, wenn er etwas nicht weiß, oder wenn er unsicher bzgl. der eigenen Vorannahmen und Vorstellungen, bestimmter Daten oder Sachverhalte ist. Der meist verwendete Ausdruck hierfür ist das Wort *vielleicht,* oder auch die Verwendung von Konjunktivformen. Die Unsicherheiten beschäftigen ihn, erschaffen in ihm das Verlangen nach Klarheit, Sicherheit und Überzeugung. Als Folgen davon sucht der Lexikograph im Korpus nach einer Bestätigung; er geht in den Austausch mit Kollegen oder er fragt Sachkundige bzw. Experten.
- Der Lexikograph **findet/schätzt ein:** Dies ist mehr ein Empfinden; nach Einsicht in die Daten und Abschluss der Denkprozesse erhält der Lexikograph eine persönliche Meinung oder Einschätzung über eine bestimmte Sache bzw. über die Daten vor ihm. Das drückt er in Form von Aussagen oder Beurteilungen aus. Dabei verwendet er Attribute wie *schön, interessant, richtig, seltsam, merkwürdig, passend, gut, besser, schlecht.* Das Einschätzen kommt im Anschluss an eine intellektuelle Analyse bzw. bevor er eine Entscheidung trifft. Außerdem nutzt der Lexikograph das Einschätzen, um Daten für korrekt zu erklären.
- Der Lexikograph **merkt sich** etwas für später: Dies ist eine aktive kognitive Handlung. Es geht um Daten oder bestimmte Dinge, die ihm bei seinen Recherchen begegnet sind. Er merkt sie sich, um sie später heranzuziehen oder noch einmal darauf zu kommen für eine nähere Untersuchung (z. B. bestimmte Kollokationsangaben, Satzbeispiele, Bedeutungsnuancen, Angabevarianten), wenn sie später für relevant befunden werden; ansonsten werden sie ignoriert. Er schreibt sie auf Papier oder digital auf bzw. behält sie im Hinterkopf.
- Der Lexikograph **ignoriert**: Das Ignorieren ist beim Lexikographen ein kognitiver Prozess, der darin besteht, bestimmte Daten als irrelevant, unnötig, unrichtig oder

nicht wahr einzustufen, um sich leichter auf andere Elemente zu konzentrieren, die in Hinblick auf den Artikel, der verfasst wird, interessanter sind oder zu sein scheinen. Je nach Art der ignorierten Daten bleiben sie trotzdem einige Zeit im Gedächtnis, weil sie bereits wahrgenommen sind.

- Der Lexikograph **prüft:** Das Prüfen ist hier ein kognitiver Vorgang bzw. ein Versuch, die Richtigkeit oder Tauglichkeit von bestimmten Daten, oder (Vor)annahmen, Vorstellungen, Erkenntnissen und Sachverhalten zu ermessen und zu bestätigen. Dabei werden die Gegebenheiten mit den erwünschten Zielen (benutzerorientiert) konfrontiert. Das heißt, der Lexikograph fragt sich z. B.: *Ist das Ergebnis meiner Mühen (fertig verfasster Artikel) das, was ich dem Benutzer zeigen will?* Wenn die Antwort „nein" ist, überlegt er sich, wie das gelöst werden kann; ansonsten geht der Lexikograph zum nächsten Arbeitsschritt.
- Der Lexikograph **ist überzeugt; ihm sagt etwas zu**: Die Überzeugung ist ein innerlicher Zustand, der in Verbindung mit der Kognition des Lexikographen steht. Er nimmt Daten erst an, wenn er überzeugt ist. Denn die Überzeugung erschafft in ihm die Sicherheit, dass alles gut ist. Die Überzeugung gilt als einer der letzten Denkprozesse, die im Lexikographen passieren, bevor er eine bestimmte Entscheidung trifft, z. B., ob er bestimmte Daten auswählt, ignoriert oder anmerkt, oder ob er eine neue Lesart aufnimmt oder eine weiterführende Recherche anstellt.
- Der Lexikograph **entscheidet:** Dies ist der finale Schritt bei der Erstellung einer lexikographischen Angabe, einer Aufgabe oder eines Wörterbuchartikels. Der Lexikograph nimmt innerlich an, dass die gewonnenen Daten für seinen Wörterbuchartikel gelten sollen; das sollen die Daten sein, die veröffentlicht werden. Somit sind z. B. die lexikographischen Angaben Aussagen und Urteile, die der Lexikograph im Anschluss an seine Recherchen intuitiv fällt. Er hält sie für gut, ja bestens. Die Entscheidungen, die der Lexikograph trifft, können in zwei Gruppen geteilt werden: 1) die Entscheidungen für den nächsten Schritt, d. h., was in einer bestimmten Situation zu tun ist. Das ist der Fall, wenn der Lexikograph in einer bestimmten Sache sicher oder unsicher ist, etwas nicht weiß, oder wenn er eine bestimmte Vermutung hat oder von einer Sache überzeugt ist etc. 2) Entscheidungen, die zwischen mehreren Variablen gewählt werden.

Diese charakteristischen Denkprozesse, kognitiven Geschehnisse und innerlichen Zustände (z. B. die Überzeugung) sind allen Probanden gemeinsam und tragen erheblich zur Schaffung einer guten *Qualität* für den Artikel bzw. das gesamte Wörterbuch bei. Hierzu müssen diese Denkprozesse stattfinden, um gute Ergebnisse zu liefern. Bei der lexikographischen Praxis sind die Lexikographen von Vorstellungen, Vorkenntnissen, Vorannahmen, also *Vorwissen* sowie von Vermutungen, Zweifelfällen und einem gewissen Grad an Beurteilungsvermögen geprägt. Letzteres wird in der Wirtschaftsbranche – das gilt dem Lexikographen nicht weniger –beschrieben als das Vermögen, „Wissen gut mit der aktuellen Situation in Verbindung zu bringen und diese dadurch sicher und selbstständig richtig einzuschätzen.“[6] Mit den eigenen Zielen (konkreten Aufgaben/Leistungen) fest im Blick scheinen die Lexikographen zu wissen, worauf es ankommt. Sie wägen also schnell und dennoch organisiert und kontrolliert zwischen verschiedenen Möglichkeiten ab. Ein solches Vermögen bedarf eines gewissen Erfahrungsschatzes; und wie jede Kompetenz wächst auch das Beurteilungsvermögen des Lexikographen mit der Zeit.

Die Verantwortung für den Lexikographen ist hoch, denn Belege können von Lexikograph zu Lexikograph unverständlich, falsch verstanden oder unterschiedlich interpretiert werden. Zudem ist zu erwähnen, dass der Lexikograph seine Entscheidungen so trifft, dass er sie begründen bzw. nachvollziehbar machen kann. Er kann z. B. begründen, warum er einen bestimmten Beleg aussortieren oder für den Artikel aufnehmen würde. Zuletzt ist in den Aufnahmen zu beobachten, wie der Lexikograph bei seinen Recherchen auf viele sprachliche Phänomene und sprachliche Möglichkeiten stößt, die für ihn neu sind, sodass er das Spektrum seiner Sprach- und Sachkenntnisse ständig erweitert.

5 Schlussfolgerungen

Die präsentierten kognitiven Leistungen lassen sich aus der Beobachtung und Analyse des Verhaltens der Probanden erschließen. Die kognitiven Leistungen zeigen, wie der Lexikograph auf der Basis von Korpusdaten, Wörterbuchdaten sowie dem Internet die Erzeugung von Qualität für seinen Artikel bedenkt, plant, umsetzt und evaluiert. Das Vorwissen und die Kompetenzen, insbesondere die Beurteilungskompetenzen des einzelnen Lexikographen, spielen neben den Bestimmungen im Instruktionsbuch eine wichtige Rolle in Hinblick auf die Qualität eines Wörterbuchartikels. In Anlehnung an Wiegand et al. (2010: 23) besteht der genuine Zweck eines Wörterbuchartikels darin, dass er solche Daten enthält, anhand derer Benutzer ihre sprachbezogenen oder sachbezogenen Wissenslücken erfolgreich schließen können. Gelingt dies, hat ein Wörterbuchartikel eine gute Qualität. Die Herausforderung für den Lexikographen besteht darin, die richtigen Daten zu finden und mit Kenntnis der Benutzervoraussetzungen in angemessener Weise darzustellen, so dass die Wörterbuchbenutzer das Qualitätsmerkmal erfahren. Qualität wird also erzeugt, und zwar durch die Anstrengung des Lexikographen (konkrete, abstrakte und kognitive Leistungen), richtige und effektive Daten darzustellen, mit denen Benutzer ihre Wissenslücken erfolgreich schließen können. Die Qualitätserzeugung ist daher von der Rolle des Lexikographen

6 Wirtschaftswerkstatt, Glossar zur Aufklärung von Begriffen aus der Finanzwelt; URL: https://www.wirtschaftswerkstatt.de/Glossar/B/230/Beurteilungsvermoegen#:~:text=Beurteilungsverm%C3%B6gen%20hei%C3%9Ft%2C%20sein%20Wissen%20gut,sicher%20und%20selbstst%C3%A4ndig%20richtig%20einzusch%C3%A4tzen (Abruf vom 22.7.2024).

nicht zu trennen. Bevor der Lexikograph Entscheidungen trifft, denkt und überlegt er, vergleicht und prüft er Daten, um eine gewisse Überzeugung von der Datenqualität bzw. vom erstellten Artikel zu erhalten. Wenn der Artikel seinen Wünschen für den Benutzer entspricht, bestätigt er sein Datenergebnis, indem er ihn für die weiteren Prozesse zur Artikelveröffentlichung speichert. Beim Lexikographen wird Qualität erzeugt; ob bei automatisch erstellten Artikeln von *Qualitätserzeugung* gesprochen werden kann, das muss hier offenbleiben. Außerdem beruht die Analyse in diesem Beitrag hauptsächlich auf der Phase der praktischen Artikelerstellung, sodass die übrigen Phasen des lexikographischen Gesamtprozesses nicht berücksichtigt worden sind.

Literatur

Monographien, Sammelbände und Beiträge in Sammelbänden oder Zeitschriften

Arias-Arias, Iván/Domínguez Vázquez, Maria José/Valcárcel Riveiro, Carlos (2024): Der Effizienz- und Intelligenzbegriff in der Lexikographie und künstlichen Intelligenz: kann ChatGPT die lexikographische Textsorte nachbilden? In: Lexikos 34, 1, 51–76. https://doi.org/10.5788/34-1-1879.

Bergenholtz, Henning/Gouws, Rufus (2012): Who is a lexicographer?. In: Lexicon *42*, (Iwasaki Linguistic Circle), 68–78.

Colman, Andrew M. (2001). A dictionary of psychology. Oxford University Press.

de Schryver, Gilles-Maurice/Joffe, David (2023): The end of lexicography, Welcome to the machine: On how ChatGPT can already take over all of the dictionary maker's tasks. 20th CODH Seminar, Center for Open Data in the Humanities, Research Organization of Information and Systems, Tokyo, Japan, 27 February 2023. Tokyo: National Institute of Informatics. https://youtu.be/watch?v=mEorw0yefAs (letzter Zugriff: 17.6.2024).

Gadamer, Hans-Georg (1974): Hermeneutik. In: Ritter, Joachim/Gründer, Karlfried/Gabriel, Gottfried (Hrsg.): Historisches Wörterbuch der Philosophie. Bd. 3, Darmstadt: Wissenschaftliche Buchgesellschaft, 1061–1073.

Gouws, Rufus (2012): Who can really be called a lexicographer? In: Lexikos *22* (AFRILEX-reeks/series 22), 217–225.

Hartmann, Reinhard R.K./James, Gregory (2002): Dictionary of Lexicography. [2. überarb. Aufl.]. London/New York: Routledge.

Klosa, Annette/Tiberius, Carole (2018): Der lexikografische Prozess. In: Klosa, Annette/Müller-Spitzer, Carolin (Hrsg.): Internetlexikografie. Ein Kompendium. Berlin/Boston: De Gruyter, 65–110.

Lehmann, Christian (2006): Linguisten brauchen Korpora und Korpora Linguisten. Wege zu wohl dokumentierten und verlässlichen Aussagen über Sprache. In: Kallmeyer, Werner/Zifonun, Gisela (Hrsg.): Sprachkorpora – Datenmengen und Erkenntnisfortschritt. Berlin (= Institut für Deutsche Sprache, Jahrbuch 2006) 1–8.

Phoodai, Chayanon/Rikk, Richárd (2023): Exploring the capabilities of ChatGPT for lexicographical purposes: A comparison with *Oxford Advanced Learner's Dictionary* within the microstructural framework. In: Medved', Marek, et al. (Hrsg.): Electronic Lexicography in the 21st Century (eLex 2023): Invisible Lexicography. Proceedings of the eLex 2023 Conference. Brno, 27–29 June 2023. Brno: Lexical Computing CZ s.r.o., 345–375.

Wiegand, Herbert Ernst (1997): Über die gesellschaftliche Verantwortung der wissenschaftlichen Lexikographie. In: Hermes 18 (Journal of Linguistics), 177–202.
Wiegand, Herbert Ernst, et al. (2010): Systematische Einführung. In: Wiegand, Herbert Ernst, et al. (Hrsg.): Wörterbuch zur Lexikographie und Wörterbuchforschung. Mit englischen Übersetzungen der Umtexte und Definitionen sowie Äquivalenten in neun Sprachen. Berlin/New York: De Gruyter, 1–105.

Wörterbücher

Cambridge = Cambridge Dictionary. Cambridge: Cambridge University Press. https://dictionary.cambridge.org/ (letzter Aufruf: 2.5.2025).
Duden = Duden online: https://www.duden.de/. Hrsg. von dr Dudenredaktion. Berlin.
DWDS = Digitales Wörterbuch der deutschen Sprache: https://www.dwds.de/. Hrsg. v. d. Berlin-Brandenburgischen Akademie der Wissenschaften.
Merriam-Webster = Merriam-Webster Dictionary: https://www.merriam-webster.com/. Hrsg. v. d. Encyclopædia Britannica, Inc.
Oxford = Dictionary of Psychology 1. Auflage, v. Andrew M. Colman, 2001). New York: Oxford University Press Inc.
Wiegand, Herbert Ernst, et al. (2020) (Hrsg.) = Wörterbuch zur Lexikographie und Wörterbuchforschung. Mit englischen Übersetzungen der Umtexte und Definitionen sowie Äquivalenten in neun Sprachen. Band 3: I–U. Berlin/Boston: De Gruyter.
Wirtschaftswerkstatt = Glossar (Alle Begriffe aus der Finanzwelt): https://www.wirtschaftswerkstatt.de/Content/115/Themen/Glossar/Begriffe_A_Z.html (letzter Aufruf: 2.5.2025).

Christine Ganslmayer

Dialektwörterbücher als Wörterbücher der Zukunft

Abstract: This article explores the significance of dialect dictionaries from the perspective of the early 21st century. Following a brief overview of the current state of academic German-language dialect lexicography, the fifteen "Villa Vigoni Theses on Lexicography" (2018) are applied to dialect dictionaries covering the Bavarian region. This analysis considers dialect dictionaries as "dictionaries of the future" and highlights their potential for future-oriented lexicography.

Keywords: dialect dictionary, Bavarian Dictionary, Franconian Dictionary, Bavaria's Dialects Online

Schlagwörter: Dialektwörterbuch, Bayerisches Wörterbuch, Fränkisches Wörterbuch, Bayerns Dialekte Online

1 Einführung: Warum Dialektwörterbücher wichtig sind

Die Frage nach der Relevanz oder Wichtigkeit eines Gegenstandes kann als Rechtfertigungsdiskurs missverstanden werden, oder aber sie kann dazu beitragen, den betreffenden Gegenstand in seiner Spezifik näher zu fassen. Dies soll in diesem Beitrag bezogen auf „Dialektwörterbücher" aus der Perspektive des frühen 21. Jahrhunderts versucht werden. Einen solchen Versuch haben natürlich schon andere vorher unternommen, beispielsweise vor ca. 50 Jahren Margot Dietrich (1975) und Hans Friebertshäuser (1976b) unter den Titeln „Dialektwörterbücher – wozu?" und „Relevante Aspekte der Dialektlexikographie". Auch auf den Webseiten aktueller Wörterbuchprojekte kann man mehr oder weniger ausführlich entsprechende Informationen finden: „Wozu die wissenschaftliche Beschäftigung mit Dialektwörtern?" (= DIBS, Wozu Dialektwörterbücher),[1] „Kulturgut Dialekt erforschen, sichern, weitergeben" (= WBF, Zielsetzung),[2] „Erforschung und Dokumentation der Mundarten Altbayerns"

1 Unter https://dibs.badw.de/das-projekt/wozu-dialektwoerterbuecher.html (letzter Zugriff: 30.1.2025).
2 Unter https://wbf.badw.de/zielsetzung.html (letzter Zugriff: 30.1.2025).

Christine Ganslmayer, Department Germanistik/Komparatistik, Friedrich-Alexander-Universität Erlangen-Nürnberg, Bismarkstraße 1, D-91054 Erlangen, e-mail: christine.ganslmayer@fau.de

https://doi.org/10.1515/9783112216644-014

(= BWB, Projekt),[3] „Mittelelbisches Wörterbuch: Aufgaben und Ziele" (= MeWb),[4] „Sudetendeutsches Wörterbuch: Ziele" (= SdWb).[5]

Welche Aspekte führen die Kolleginnen und Kollegen im Detail an?

Dialektwörterbücher

1. „bewahren eine eigenständige Sprachform" (Dietrich 1975: 73; aufgegriffen von Friebertshäuser 1976b: 8; vgl. auch WBF, Zielsetzung; MeWb).
2. „erschließen eine Landschaft und ihre Kultur" (Dietrich 1975: 74; aufgegriffen von Friebertshäuser 1976b: 8; vgl. auch WBF, Zielsetzung; MeWb; SdWb).
3. sind Geschichtsdokumente, und zwar bezogen auf Sprach- und Sachwelt (Dietrich 1975: 74; aufgegriffen von Friebertshäuser 1976b: 8; vgl. auch DIBS, Wozu Dialektwörterbücher?; WBF, Zielsetzung; BWB, Projekt; MeWb; SdWb).
4. tragen zur Mundartpflege bei und unterstützen die Sprachdidaktik (Dietrich 1975: 75–76; aufgegriffen von Friebertshäuser 1976b: 8; vgl. auch WBF, Zielsetzung).
5. sind identitätsstiftend (vgl. DIBS, Wozu Dialektwörterbücher?).
6. sind spracherhellend (vgl. DIBS, Wozu Dialektwörterbücher?).
7. sind Teil der sprachlichen Grundlagenforschung (vgl. DIBS, Wozu Dialektwörterbücher?; WBF, Zielsetzung; BWB, Projekt).
8. stellen „wissenschaftlich basierte Informationen [...] einem möglichst breiten Publikum frei zur Verfügung" (WBÖ, Lexikalisches Informationssystem).[6]
9. sind Nachschlage- und Forschungsmittel für Sprachwissenschaft (v.a. Sprachgeschichte), aber auch für die Geschichts-, Kultur- und Rechtswissenschaften und sogar für das Bundeskriminalamt bei der Erstellung von Verbrecherprofilen (vgl. DIBS, Wozu Dialektwörterbücher?; SdWb).

Seit 50 Jahren begegnen also in unterschiedlicher Schwerpunktsetzung und mehr oder weniger ausführlich ähnliche Argumente. Die Dokumentationsfunktion bezogen auf regionale Wortschätze steht heute wie damals im Vordergrund. Teils finden sich aber je aktuelle Paradigmen widergespiegelt: Das Argument der „Sprachdidaktik" hat sich vor dem Hintergrund der Entwicklung zu Regiolekten bzw. dem zunehmenden Abbau der Basisdialekte seit den 1970er Jahren abgeschwächt und bedarf aus heutiger Perspektive einer Revision. Andere Ideen, z.B. zu sprachlicher Identitätsbildung beizutragen oder transdisziplinär nutzbare Informationen zur Verfügung zu stellen, sind eher ein Reflex jüngerer Argumentationsmuster. Es ist interessant, dass im „Vorbericht" eines der ältesten Idiotika, dem *Versuch eines schwäbischen Idiotikon*, schon Johann Christoph Schmid (1795: 1–2) den Nutzen seines Vorhabens reflektiert. Er findet teils weitere Argumente, mit der die obige Liste weiter ergänzt werden kann:

---

3 Unter https://bwb.badw.de/das-projekt.html (letzter Zugriff: 30.1.2025).

4 Unter https://mew.uzi.uni-halle.de (letzter Zugriff: 30.1.2025).

5 Unter https://www.collegium-carolinum.de/forschung/grundlagenforschung/sudetendeutsches-woerterbuch (letzter Zugriff: 30.1.2025).

6 Unter https://lioe.dioe.at (letzter Zugriff: 30.1.2025).

1. Dialektkenntnis schließt Benennungslücken: „Die Kenntniß der provinziellen Dialekte verschafft uns einen großen Vorrath von brauchbaren Wörtern, um Begriffe zu bezeichnen, für die wir in der allgemeinen Sprache keine Benennungen haben." (Schmid 1795: 1)
2. Dialektkenntnis verschafft Einblick in den Sprachbau.
3. Dialektkenntnis vermittelt einen Eindruck von der Mentalität der Dialektsprecher/-innen: „[...] geben sie ein sicheres Kennzeichen von dem Geiste und Charakter des Volkes ab, welches sich ihrer in seinem Umgange bedient." (Schmid 1795: 2)
4. Dialektbasierte Sprachvergleiche bereiten Vergnügen.

Aus einer metalexikographischen Perspektive heraus kann man Wörterbücher unter anderem ausgehend von ihren Benutzungsmöglichkeiten klassifizieren, was wiederum Rückschlüsse auf Relevanz und Funktionen von Wörterbüchern zulässt. In Kühns systematisierender Typologie erscheinen Dialektwörterbücher in zweifacher Hinsicht: erstens als „Nachschlagewerk" zur „Textrezeption" und hier zur „Verständigungssicherung" und zweitens als „Lesebuch" zu „Erbauung und Belehrung" gerichtet an „Sprachinteressierte" bzw. „Bildungsbürger" (Kühn 1989: 121). Auch diese stark schematisierte Betrachtungsweise vermag die funktionale Vielfalt von Dialektwörterbüchern nicht vollständig abzudecken, zu unterschiedlich sind denkbare Nutzergruppen. Beispielsweise fehlt die Perspektive der Forschenden, denn Dialektwörterbücher können selbst Forschungsgegenstand sein, oder man kann Dialektwörterbücher auch als Speicher lexikalischer Daten begreifen, aus denen bei entsprechenden Auswertungen Ergebnisse zu unterschiedlichen wissenschaftlichen Fragestellungen abgeleitet werden können. Nicht zu vergessen ist außerdem, dass mit Sprachlexikographie auch stets bestimmte gesellschaftliche Interessen verbunden sind (vgl. Wiegand 1998: 59). Auch aus diesem Blickwinkel ließen sich weitere Aspekte ergänzen, denen in der Geschichte der Dialektlexikographie zu unterschiedlichen Zeiten je unterschiedliches Gewicht beigemessen wurde. Beispielsweise spielte in den Anfängen die „Stärkung des Nationalbewußtseins" mit Sicherheit eine größere Rolle. Auch die „Stabilisierung einer Standardsprache als Leitvarietät relativ zu anderen Varietäten" bzw. die „Durchsetzung von Sprachnormen" ist heute mit dem fortgeschrittenen Abbau der Basisdialekte von geringerer Relevanz. Heute dienen Dialektwörterbücher eher zur „Stabilisierung von Gruppenbewußtsein", der „Durchsetzung sonstiger sprachkultureller oder kulturpädagogischer Anliegen" oder verhindern den „drohenden oder angeblich drohenden Untergang" von Sprachvarietäten. Die „Förderung wissenschaftlicher Bestrebungen" freilich spielte (aus Perspektive der schreibenden Wissenschaftler/-innen) stets eine zentrale Rolle, und man kann bezogen auf Dialektwörterbücher auch einen Beitrag zu „gesellschaftliche[r] Integration durch Abbau von sprachbedingten Kommunikationsstörungen" erkennen (vgl. Wiegand 1998: 59).

Im vorliegenden Beitrag soll nun ein aktueller Versuch unternommen werden, vielfältige Funktionen und dadurch auch die Relevanz von Dialektwörterbüchern im 21. Jahrhundert darzulegen (vgl. Abschnitt 3). Unter „Dialektwörterbüchern" verstehe ich im Wesentlichen die sogenannten „großlandschaftlichen Dialektwörterbücher“ der deutschen Sprache, die den wissenschaftlich bearbeiteten Wortschatz eines größeren sprachlichen Areals beinhalten. Unter den verschiedenen Ausprägungen der Dialektwörterbücher handelt es sich hierbei vor allem um „Territorialwörterbücher“ (vgl. Wiegand 2017: 38). Diese zählen zu den diatopischen Dialektwörterbüchern, für die grundlegend das Raumkriterium leitend ist. Ein Territorialwörterbuch umfasst dabei ein großes sprachlandschaftliches Areal, in das kleinräumige Dialekte integriert sind (vgl. Mann 2020: 912). Solche diatopischen Gebietswörterbücher sind in der Regel groß angelegte wissenschaftliche Projekte, deren Genese teils Jahrzehnte in Anspruch nimmt und die oft als Akademiewörterbücher drittmittelfinanziert erarbeitet werden. Die deutschen Territorialwörterbücher sind traditionsreiche Unternehmungen, deren Geschichte teils bis ins 19. Jahrhundert zurückreicht. Entsprechend disparat ist ihre makro- und mikrostrukturelle Konzeption, wenngleich sie gegenstandsbedingt auch durch grundlegende Gemeinsamkeiten verbunden sind. Ein kurzer Überblick zum gegenwärtigen Stand der deutschsprachigen Dialektwörterbücher findet sich in Abschnitt 2. Auf dieser Grundlage erfolgt in Abschnitt 3 die Beantwortung der Frage, warum Dialektwörterbücher aus Perspektive des frühen 21. Jahrhunderts wichtig sind. Leitend sollen hierfür die „15 Villa Vigoni-Thesen zur Lexikografie“ sein, die im Dezember 2018 auf dem Workshop „Wörterbücher für die Zukunft – Die Zukunft der Wörterbücher. Herausforderungen an die Lexikografie in einer digitalen Gesellschaft“ verabschiedet worden sind.[7] Diese Thesen repräsentieren in ihrem Querschnitt die multiplen Anforderungen an eine moderne, reflektierte Lexikographie und skizzieren zentrale Ideen für Wörterbücher der Zukunft. Im vorliegenden Beitrag werden diese Thesen auf die Dialektwörterbücher des Deutschen bezogen. Bei dieser Betrachtung wird keineswegs systematische Vollständigkeit angestrebt. Vielmehr ist intendiert, beispielorientiert anhand der großlandschaftlichen Dialektwörterbücher in Bayern das Potenzial dieses Wörterbuchtyps für eine zukunftsorientierte Lexikographie aufzuzeigen.

2 Überblick zu den wissenschaftlichen Dialektwörterbüchern des Deutschen

Einen ersten komprimierten Überblick zum Bearbeitungsstand der „landschaftlichen deutschen Mundartwörterbücher der Gegenwart“ im reichsdeutschen Gebiet hat Mitzka (1937) erarbeitet. Niebaum (1979) bietet in einem „Sammelbericht“ eine Aktualisierung sowie eine vergleichende Betrachtung. Hier ist auch erstmals eine Karte mit

7 Online verfügbar unter https://www.emlex.phil.fau.de/files/2019/01/Villa-Vigoni-Thesen-2018.pdf (letzter Zugriff: 30.1.2025). Vgl. Schierholz (2021).

den Arealen der großlandschaftlichen Mundartwörterbücher des Deutschen integriert (1979: 373). Entsprechende Karten finden sich auch in Friebertshäusers zentralem Handbuchartikel (1983: 1287) sowie bei Niebaum/Macha (2002: 37) und im *dtv-Atlas Deutsche Sprache* (zuletzt König 2007: 138). Landolt (2007) beschreibt neuere Entwicklungen in der historischen Dialektlexikographie. Eine letzte zusammenfassende Beschreibung des Bearbeitungsstands der Dialektwörterbücher kann Moulin (2010) entnommen werden. Hieran anschließend erfolgt eine erneute Aktualisierung.

Die Bearbeitungsgebiete der mehr als 30 Dialektwörterbücher des Deutschen bilden insgesamt ein Netz, das den gesamten historischen deutschsprachigen Raum (vor 1914) mit nur wenigen Überlappungen abdeckt (vgl. schraffierte Flächen im Kartenbild in Abb. 1). Diesbezügliche systematische Bemühungen wurden durch die Gründung eines Wörterbuchkartells im Jahr 1921 befördert. Von Anfang an wurde – dem zentralen Raumparadigma des 19. Jahrhunderts entsprechend – die Finanzierung durch die damaligen Feudalstaaten (oft in Form von wissenschaftlichen Akademie-Projekten) geleistet. Jüngere Wörterbuchprojekte mussten allerdings bereits zu Beginn des 20. Jahrhunderts „oft unglücklich geformte Raumlücken schließen" (Mitzka 1937: 96). Wie man Abb. 1 entnehmen kann, werden zu den großlandschaftlichen Dialektwörterbüchern auch die Wörterbücher des Luxemburgischen bzw. des Friesischen gerechnet, obgleich es sich hier genau genommen um eigenständige Sprachen handelt. Einige Wörterbücher (z.B. *Deutschbaltisches Wörterbuch, Siebenbürgisch-Sächsisches Wörterbuch, Wörterbuch der Ungarndeutschen Mundarten*) beziehen sich auf deutsche Sprachinselmundarten in Estland, Rumänien bzw. Ungarn, deren Bearbeitungsgebiet bereits vor 1914 außerhalb der geschlossenen Grenzen des deutschsprachigen Raums lag. Weiterhin ist es üblich, auch wissenschaftlich erarbeitete Dialektwörterbücher zu Stadtmundarten (*Hamburgisches Wörterbuch, Frankfurter Wörterbuch*) zu integrieren, auch wenn es sich dabei streng genommen um syntopische Dialektwörterbücher handelt (vgl. Wiegand 2020: 822). Die Farbgebung in Abb. 1 zeigt den aktuell erreichten, jeweiligen Publikationsstand an: Grün markierte Wörterbücher liegen bereits vollständig bearbeitet vor, rot und lila markierte werden aktuell noch bearbeitet, wobei die lila markierten Wörterbücher nicht mehr als gedruckte Wörterbücher erscheinen, sondern ausschließlich digital.[8]

In Tab. 1 sind die wissenschaftlichen Dialektwörterbücher gesamthaft zusammengestellt, und zwar in chronologischer Reihenfolge nach dem jeweiligen Publikationsbeginn (ab Lieferung 1 bzw. ab öffentlichem Online-Zugang). Es sei darauf hingewiesen, dass die modernen Projektgründungen, die Planungsphase und der Beginn der Sammeltätigkeiten in der Regel noch viel weiter zurückreichen (vgl. Mitzka 1937: 92–94). Nur ein Beispiel: Den Auftakt machte das *Schwäbische Wörterbuch*, das von

8 Die Karte in Abb. 1 basiert auf Niebaum/Macha (2006: 37, Abb. 9) und bietet zugleich eine inhaltliche Aktualisierung der Karte von König (2007: 138), auf welcher der Publikationsstand farblich differenziert dargestellt ist.

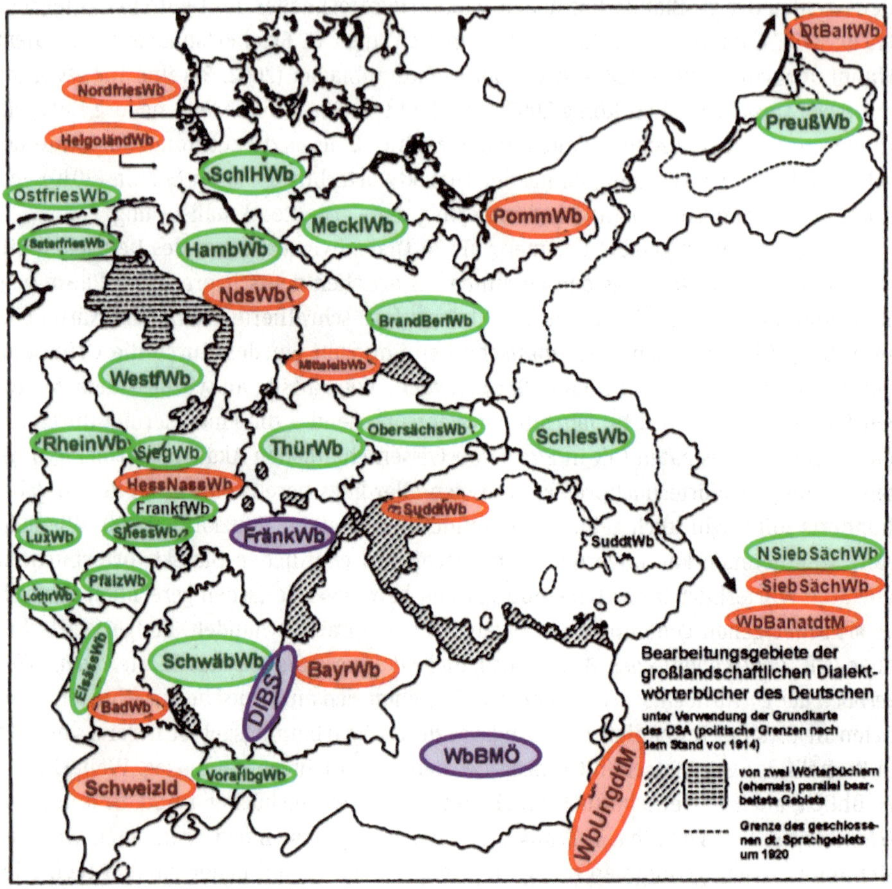

Abb. 1: Bearbeitungsgebiete und -stand deutscher Dialektwörterbücher (unter Verwendung von Niebaum/Macha 2006: 37, Abb. 9).

Keller um 1854 begründet hat; die sukzessive Publikation begann 1901 (Lfg. 1) und wurde 1936 mit insgesamt sechs Bänden abgeschlossen (vgl. Mitzka 1937: 92). Weiterhin kann man Tab. 1 Informationen zur Veröffentlichungsform (Print, Retrodigitalisat, Digital-Version) entnehmen sowie gegebenenfalls zu Projektwebseiten, teils mit Zugang zu weiteren Materialien. Dass zwischenzeitlich auch die Vernetzung zwischen einzelnen Wörterbüchern über das „Wörterbuchnetz" des Kompetenzzentrums für elektronische Erschließungs- und Publikationsverfahren in den Geisteswissenschaften der Universität Trier (vgl. Moulin 2010: 601–607) weiter fortgeschritten ist, wird anhand der integrierten Hyperlinks ebenfalls deutlich.

Die in Tab. 1 zusammengestellten Informationen basieren auf eigenen Internetrecherchen sowie auf Sekundärliteratur (Mitzka 1937; Friebertshäuser 1983: 1286–1288; Niebaum/Macha 2006: 36–38; König 2007: 138–139; Moulin 2010: 594–596; Lenz/Stöckle

2021). Nicht integriert sind entsprechende Wikipedia-Artikel, wie sie zu den meisten der Wörterbuchprojekte existieren. Sie zeichnet im Wesentlichen aber ein hohes inhaltliches Niveau aus, und gerade für ältere, bereits abgeschlossene Projekte ohne eigene Webseite werden dort wichtige Informationen gebündelt bereitgestellt.

Die Bezeichnungen der Wörterbücher machen deutlich, dass der Konzeption je unterschiedliche geographische, historische oder sprachlich basierte Raumvorstellungen zugrunde liegen (vgl. bereits Mitzka 1937: 95; Moulin 2010: 595). Teils wurden die Wörterbücher im Laufe ihrer langen Geschichte infolge einer Neuausrichtung oder Neubewertung des zugrundeliegenden Raumkonzepts auch umbenannt: Dies betrifft beispielsweise das *Mittelelbische Wörterbuch* (ehemals *Ostfälisches Wörterbuch*), das 1935 den Wortschatz der niederdeutschen Provinz Sachsen erfassen sollte, um eine entsprechende Lücke in den Bearbeitungsgebieten der deutschen Mundarten zu schließen. Bereits 1940 erfolgte aber eine Erweiterung um Teile des anhaltischen Gebiets, was eine Umbenennung nötig machte: Statt der sprachlich basierten Bezeichnung „Ostfälisch" wurde eine geographische Bezeichnung „Mittelelbisch" leitend. Das zu bearbeitende Gebiet rund um Magdeburg (nördlicher und mittlerer Teil Sachsen-Anhalts) umfasst seitdem unterschiedliche niederdeutsche und mitteldeutsche Mundarten auf niederdeutscher Grundlage (vgl. „Wörterbuchbereich und Quellen" auf der Projekthomepage).[9] Erst im Jahr 2012 erfolgte die Umbenennung des ehemals *Ostfränkischen Wörterbuchs* in *Fränkisches Wörterbuch* (WBF). Diese Benennung bot der interessierten Öffentlichkeit ein höheres Identifizierungspotenzial, da die laiensprachliche Dialektbezeichnung „Fränkisch" in der Region usuell ist. Da im WBF außerdem der Wortschatz der bayerischen Regierungsbezirke Mittel-, Ober- und Unterfranken (vor der Gebietsreform 1972, daher inklusive Landkreis Eichstätt) erfasst wird, ist eine politisch-administrativ basierte Bezeichnung mit Bezug auf die Region „Franken" korrekter als die sprachlich basierte Benennung „Ostfränkisch". Zwar nehmen die ostfränkischen Dialekte den größten Teil des Untersuchungsgebiets ein, an den Rändern ragen aber andere Mundarten (Hessisch, Thüringisch, Nordbairisch, Schwäbisch) herein, und Ostfränkisch in Thüringen oder Baden-Württemberg wird im WBF beispielsweise nicht miterfasst (vgl. „Untersuchungsgebiet" auf der Projekthomepage).[10]

Die Datenbasis sämtlicher Dialektwörterbücher wurde in langwieriger Sammeltätigkeit empirisch aufgebaut. Im Detail unterscheiden sich diese Materialien in ihrer Form, ihrem Alter, ihrem Umfang und hinsichtlich der Methodik bei den Erhebungen. Auch die Wörterbücher selbst weisen einen stark abweichenden Umfang auf (ein bis mehr als zehn Bände) und wurden bzw. werden teils von einzelnen Bearbeitern, teils von Teams in größeren Arbeitsstellen erarbeitet. Während einige Wörterbücher längst fertiggestellt sind, hat bei anderen die Publikation erst jüngst begonnen. Manche Wörterbücher werden seit mehr als 100 Jahren erarbeitet, andere konnten in ver-

9 Unter https://mew.uzi.uni-halle.de/info (letzter Zugriff: 10.3.2025).
10 Unter https://wbf.badw.de/gebiet.html (letzter Zugriff: 10.3.2025).

Tab. 1: Wissenschaftliche Dialektwörterbücher des Deutschen.

Wörterbuch	Publikation (Zeitraum)	Form der Veröffentlichung	ggf. weitere Informationen online
OstfriesWb = *Wörterbuch der ostfriesischen Sprache*	1879–1884	*Print* (3 Bde.)	
Schweizid = *Schweizerisches Idiotikon*	1881–	*Print; digital*: https://www.idiotikon.ch/woerterbuch/idiotikon-digital	https://www.idiotikon.ch/
ElsässWb = *Wörterbuch der elsässischen Mundarten* (ElsWb)	1899– 1907	*Print* (2 Bde.); *digital*: https://woerterbuchnetz.de/?sigle=ElsWB&lemid=A00001	
SchwäbWb = *Schwäbisches Wörterbuch*	1901–1936	*Print* (6 Bde., 1 Nachtragsbd.)	
LothrWb = *Wörterbuch der deutsch-lothringischen Mundarten* (LothWb)	1909	*Print* (1 Bd.); *digital*: https://woerterbuchnetz.de/?sigle=LothWB&lemid=A00001	
RheinWb = *Rheinisches Wörterbuch* (RhWb)	1923–1971	*Print* (9 Bde.); *digital*: https://woerterbuchnetz.de/?sigle=RhWB&lemid=A00001; https://woerterbuchnetz.de/?sigle=RhWBN&lemid=A00001 (Nachträge)	
Siebenbürgisch-Sächsisches Wörterbuch	1924–	*Print* (aktuell 10 Bde.)	https://icsusib.ro/de/forschungsprojekte/siebenbuergisch-saechsisches-woerterbuch
BadWb = *Badisches Wörterbuch*	1925–	*Print* (aktuell 4 Bde., Teile von Bd. 5)	https://uni-freiburg.de/badwb/; http://rudolf-post.de/bwb_index.html; https://www.leo-bw.de/themenmodul/alltagskultur-im-suedwesten/sammlungen-und-quellen/fragebogen-zur-volksuberlieferung
SchlHWb = *Schleswig-Holsteinisches Wörterbuch*	1925–1935	*Print* (5 Bde.); *Retrodigitalisate* über UB Kiel: https://dibiki.ub.uni-kiel.de/viewer/toc/PPN1750113996/1/LOG_0000/	

Tab. 1 (fortgesetzt)

Wörterbuch	**Publikation (Zeitraum)**	**Form der Veröffentlichung**	**ggf. weitere Informationen online**
HessNassWb = *Hessen-Nassauisches Wörterbuch* (HNWb)	1927–	*Print* (aktuell 3 Bde., Bd. 1 in Bearb.); *Retrodigitalisate* über Landesgeschichtliche Informationssystem Hessen (LAGIS): https://www.lagis-hessen.de/de/subjects/browsepages/sn/hnwb; *digital*: https://www.lagis-hessen.de/de/subjects/gsform/sn/hnwb	https://www.uni-marburg.de/de/fb09/dsa/projekte/aktuelle-projekte/hessen-nassauisches-woerterbuch; https://www.lagis-hessen.de/de/subjects/intro/sn/hnwb
MecklWb = *Mecklenburgisches Wörterbuch* (MeckWB)	1937–1992	*Print* (7 Bde.); *Digitalisat* i.V.	https://www.wossidlo.uni-rostock.de/wossidlo-forschungsstelle/forschung/aktuelles-forschungsprojekt-wossidlo-teuchert-online/wossidlo-teuchert-online/
SiegWb = *Siegerländer Wörterbuch*	1938 (^{2}1968)	*Print* (1 Bd.)	
LuxWb = *Luxemburger Wörterbuch* (LWB)	1950–1977	*Print* (5 Bde.); *digital*: https://dico.uni.lu/?sigle=LWB#0; *Zugang auch über* https://www.woerterbuchnetz.de/	
NdsWb = *Niedersächsisches Wörterbuch*	1953–	*Print* (aktuell 10 Bde., Teile von Bd. 11, 12)	https://www.uni-goettingen.de/de/219054.html
HambWb = *Hamburger Wörterbuch*	1956–2006	*Print* (5 Bde.)	https://www.slm.uni-hamburg.de/niederdeutsch/ueber-die-abteilung/hamburgisches-wb.html
HelgoländWb = *Helgoländer Wörterbuch*	1957–	*Print* (A–L, Helgoländisch–Deutsch); *digital* (Deutsch-Helgoländisch): http://www.helgolaendisch-halunder.de/103.html	http://www.helgolaendisch-halunder.de/projekt.html
VorarlbgWb = *Vorarlbergisches Wörterbuch*	1955–1965	*Print* (2 Bde.)	

Tab. 1 (fortgesetzt)

Wörterbuch	**Publikation (Zeitraum)**	**Form der Veröffentlichung**	**ggf. weitere Informationen online**
SchlesWb = *Schlesisches Wörterbuch*	1963–1965	*Print* (3 Bde.)	
WbBMÖ = *Wörterbuch der bairischen Mundarten in Österreich* (WBÖ)	1963–	*Print* (A–E, 5 Bde.); *digital* (ab F/V) über Lexikalisches Informationssystem Österreich (LIÖ): https://lioe.dioe.at/; *Zugang auch über* https://www.woerterbuchnetz.de/	https://www.oeaw.ac.at/de/acdh/wboe-projektcluster
PfälzWb = *Pfälzisches Wörterbuch* (PfWb)	1965–1998	*Print* (6 Bde., 1 Beiheft); *digital*: https://woerterbuchnetz.de/?sigle=PfWB&lemid=A00001	
ShessWb = *Südhessisches Wörterbuch*	1965–2010	*Print* (6 Bde.); *Retrodigitalisate* über Landesgeschichtliche Informationssystem Hessen (LAGIS): https://www.lagis-hessen.de/de/subjects/discover/sn/shwb; *digital*: https://www.lagis-hessen.de/de/subjects/gsform/sn/shwb/; *Zugang auch über* https://www.woerterbuchnetz.de/	https://www.lagis-hessen.de/de/subjects/intro/sn/shwb
ThürWb = *Thüringisches Wörterbuch* (ThWb)	1966–2006	*Print* (6 Bde.)	https://www.gw.uni-jena.de/440/arbeitsstelle-thueringische-dialektforschung
BrandBerlWb = *Brandenburg-Berlinisches Wörterbuch* (BBW)	1968–2001	*Print* (4 Bde.)	Brandenburg-Berlinisches Spracharchiv (BBSA): https://www.bbsa-potsdam.de/
WestfWb = *Westfälisches Wörterbuch* (WWb)	1969–2021	*Print* (5 Bde.); *digital*: https://woerterbuchnetz.de/?sigle=WWB&lemid=A00001	https://www.mundart-kommission.lwl.org/de/forschung/westfaelisches-woerterbuch/
FrankfWb = *Frankfurter Wörterbuch*	1971–1988	*Print* (5 Bde., 1 Registerbd.)	
PreußWb = *Preußisches Wörterbuch*	1974–2005	*Print* (6 Bde.)	

Tab. 1 (fortgesetzt)

Wörterbuch	Publikation (Zeitraum)	Form der Veröffentlichung	ggf. weitere Informationen online
ObersächsWb = *Obersächsisches Wörterbuch*	1994–2003	*Print* (4 Bde.)	
SaterfriesWb = *Saterfriesisches Wörterbuch*	1980 (^{2}2015); 1992–;2017	*Print* (1 Bd.); *Print* (A–E, 1 Bd.) mit *Retrodigitalisat*: https://www.seeltersk.de/wp-content/uploads/Kramer_Nai_Seelter_Woudebouk.pdf; *digital* und *App*: https://www.xn-saterfriesisches-wrterbuch-tvc.de/	https://www.seeltersk.de/archiv/woerterlisten/
NSiebSächsWb = *Nordsiebenbürgisch-Sächsisches Wörterbuch*	1986–2006	*Print* (5 Bde.)	https://www.siebenbuerger.de/zeitung/artikel/saksesch/6304-radio_tipp-nordsiebenbuergisch.html#google_vignette
NordfriesWb = *Nordfriesisches Wörterbuch*	1986–	*Print* (verschiedenen Teilwörterbücher)	https://www.uni-kiel.de/de/universitaet/detailansicht/news/friesisch; https://www.isfas.uni-kiel.de/de/frisistik/dokumentation
SuddtWb = *Sudetendeutsches Wörterbuch* (SdWb)	1988–	*Print* (aktuell 5 Bde., Teile von Bd. 6); *Retrodigitalisate* über MDZ, z.B. Bd. 1: https://daten.digitale-sammlungen.de/0015/bsb00152744/images/index.html?fip=193.174.98.30&id=00152744&seite=1	https://www.collegium-carolinum.de/forschung/grundlagenforschung/sudetendeutsches-woerterbuch
BayrWb = *Bayerisches Wörterbuch* (BWB)	1995–	*Print* (aktuell 3 Bde., Teile von Bd. 4); *Retrodigitalisat* Bd. 2: https://publikationen.badw.de/de/bwb; *digital*: https://lexhelfer.bwb.badw.de/index.php; https://bdo.badw.de/; *Zugang auch über* https://www.woerterbuchnetz.de/	https://bwb.badw.de/das-projekt.html

Tab. 1 (fortgesetzt)

Wörterbuch	Publikation (Zeitraum)	Form der Veröffentlichung	ggf. weitere Informationen online
PommWb = *Pommersches Wörterbuch* (PWB)	1997–	*Print* (aktuell 1 Bd., Teile von Bd. 2)	https://germanistik.uni-greifswald.de/pommersches-woerterbuch/
MittelelbWb = *Mittelelbisches Wörterbuch* (MeWb)	2002–	*Print* (aktuell 2 Bde., Teile von Bd. 3); *digital*: https://mew.uzi.uni-halle.de/	https://mew.uzi.uni-halle.de/; https://leucorea.de/forschung/mittelelbisches-woerterbuch/
WbBanatdtM = *Wörterbuch der Banater deutschen Mundarten*	2013–	*Print* (aktuell 2 Bde.); *Digitalisat* Bd. 2: https://www.ikgs.de/wp-content/uploads/2020/04/OpenBook-Woerterbuch-der-Banater-Deutschen-Mundarten-II-D-F.pdf	
FränkWb = *Fränkisches Wörterbuch* (WBF)	12/2016–	*digital*: https://lexhelfer.wbf.badw.de/index.php; https://bdo.badw.de/; *Zugang auch über* https://www.woerterbuchnetz.de/	https://wbf.badw.de/das-projekt.html
DtBaltWb = *Deutschbaltisches Wörterbuch* (DBWb)	2019–	*digital*: https://arhiiv.eki.ee/dict/bss/index.cgi	https://arhiiv.eki.ee/dict/bss/bss.html
DIBS = *Dialektologisches Informationssystem von Bayerisch-Schwaben*	12/2020–	*digital*: https://lexhelfer.dibs.badw.de/; https://bdo.badw.de/; *Zugang auch über* https://www.woerterbuchnetz.de/	https://dibs.badw.de/das-projekt.html
WbUngdtM = *Wörterbuch der Ungarndeutschen Mundarten* (WUM)			Wörterbuchkorpus in Datenbank (passwortgeschützter Zugang): https://wum.elte.hu/

hältnismäßig kurzem Zeitraum abgeschlossen werden. Die kriegsbedingt schwierigen Umstände im 20. Jahrhundert und die daraus erwachsenen Folgen haben die praktische Erarbeitung und die institutionellen sowie finanziellen Rahmenbedingungen mehr oder weniger stark beeinflusst. Für mehrere Wörterbücher (u.a. WBF, WBÖ) wurde zwischenzeitlich die Entscheidung getroffen, diese nur noch digital erscheinen zu lassen. So blickt jedes der Wörterbücher auf eine individuelle Geschichte und Genese zurück. Was jedoch die lexikographische Arbeitsweise betrifft, so sind die Projekte durch ähnliche Prinzipien und teils analoge Praktiken miteinander verbunden:

Bereits die Planungsphasen erfolgten methodisch reflektiert, in Konzeption und Methodik orientierte man sich am damaligen aktuellen Standard. Bei aller dialektologischer Methodenvielfalt gilt besonders das wortgeographische Prinzip als leitend (vgl. Friebertshäuser 1983: 1283–1286).

Die großlandschaftlichen Dialektwörterbücher sind als Wörterbuchprojekte also äußerst traditionsreiche Unternehmen und verfügen über teils enorme Archiv- und Materialsammlungen, auf deren Basis Wortartikel erarbeitet werden. Dabei sind sie aber keineswegs beim Zettelkasten stehen geblieben, sondern haben frühzeitig bereits seit den 1980er Jahren die modernen EDV-gestützten Möglichkeiten für die Wörterbucharbeit ebenso genutzt wie für die Archivierung und Sicherung der Materialien. Moulin (2010: 601) weist darauf hin, dass rechnergestütztes Arbeiten in sämtlichen noch aktiven Wörterbuchprojekten zum Standard geworden ist, dass sich hinsichtlich des Grades beim Einsatz moderner digitaler Verfahren im Detail jedoch deutliche Unterschiede zeigen. Das Spektrum reicht hier vom Rechnereinsatz bei der Erstellung der Wörterbuchartikel bis hin zum Aufbau komplexer Datenbanken, der Entwicklung eigener Programme für die Artikelerstellung oder der Integration digitaler Tools (z.B. für Kartenerstellung). Auch was das Format der Veröffentlichung betrifft, unterscheiden sich die einzelnen Wörterbücher deutlich: Während einige ältere Wörterbücher „nur" im Druck und noch nicht einmal in retrodigitalisierter Form vorliegen, erscheinen andere inzwischen im Druck und zugleich digital oder sogar nur noch digital (vgl. oben). Dies hängt im Einzelfall natürlich von der jeweiligen finanziellen Ausstattung und den Fördermöglichkeiten ab.

Für einen Überblick zu aktuellem Stand und Genese der noch laufenden Wörterbuchprojekte sind abgesehen von Einzelberichten die Sammelbände von Friebertshäuser (1976a) sowie Lenz/Stöckle (2021) äußerst hilfreich: Hier präsentieren sich die einzelnen Unternehmungen in Selbstdarstellungen, berichten über den aktuell erreichten Stand und informieren über die jeweilige Projektgeschichte, das Bearbeitungsgebiet, die Materialgrundlage, die makro- und mikrostrukturelle Konzeption sowie die Methodik bei Materialerfassung und Artikelerstellung, zuletzt inklusive der Adaption moderner digitaler Verfahren. Im Folgenden wird ein Fokus auf die wissenschaftlichen, noch im Arbeitsprozess befindlichen Wörterbuchprojekte in Bayern gelegt.

Die Grundlagenforschung zu den Dialekten Bayerns an der Bayerischen Akademie der Wissenschaften (BAdW) blickt bereits auf eine über hundertjährige Geschichte zurück: Den Auftakt zur Erarbeitung der modernen Dialektwörterbücher bildet die Gründung der „Kommission für Mundartforschung" im Jahr 1911, die mit der Erarbeitung von Wörterbüchern zu den bairischen, ostfränkischen und rheinpfälzischen Mundarten im damaligen Königreich Bayern beauftragt wurde. Da das Schwäbische in Bayern zu diesem Zeitpunkt bereits im *Schwäbischen Wörterbuch* (SwWb) von Hermann Fischer bearbeitet wurde, war es aus diesem Arbeitsauftrag ausgenommen. Für die Mundarten Bayerns existierte ein berühmtes Vorgängerwerk, das *Bayerische Wörterbuch* (1827–1837) von Johann Andreas Schmeller, der mit diesem Pionierwerk als Begründer der modernen wissenschaftlichen Dialektlexikographie gilt. Die Materialbasis (Schwerpunkt auf Altbayern, keine systematischen Erhebungen, großer

Anteil historischer schriftlicher Quellen) genügte aber schon zu Beginn des 20. Jahrhunderts den wissenschaftlichen Ansprüchen nicht mehr, auch war das Wörterbuch in überarbeiteter zweiter Auflage vergriffen. Während das SwWb bereits 1936 mit sechs Bänden und einem Nachtragsband abgeschlossen werden konnte, werden die Wörterbücher zum Bairischen und Ostfränkischen in Bayern nach wie vor erarbeitet. Sie zählen zu den ältesten Langzeitvorhaben der BAdW.

Das aktuelle Projekt *Bayerisches Wörterbuch* (BWB)[11] leistet mit inzwischen vier wissenschaftlichen Mitarbeiterstellen Grundlagenforschung zum bairischen Wortschatz in Oberbayern, Niederbayern, der Oberpfalz und den bairischen Gebieten in Bayerisch-Schwaben sowie Mittel- und Oberfranken. Mit der Materialsammlung wurde bereits 1913 begonnen, und sie hält noch immer an. Inzwischen beinhaltet das Wörterbucharchiv ca. 9 Mio. Belege aus unterschiedlichen Erhebungen und Exzerpten aus der Literatur (vgl. zur Materialgrundlage Tab. 2). Nach dem Zweiten Weltkrieg wurde das ursprüngliche Konzept eines gemeinsamen Wörterbuchs für die bairischen Mundarten in Bayern und Österreich aufgegeben, so dass das Bearbeitungsgebiet für die Münchner Arbeitsstelle seit den 1960er Jahren auf die bairischen Mundarten in Deutschland begrenzt ist. Mit der Publikation wurde 1995 (Lfg. 1: *A–Acker*) begonnen. Mittlerweile liegen die Bände I (*A–Bazi*), II (*Be–Boxhamer*) und III (*Prä–törmisch*) in Printfassung und als Digitalisate komplett vor, von Band IV mehrere Einzellieferungen (mit Stand 10/2024: *Dorn–türeln*), außerdem ein digitales Stichwortverzeichnis. Insgesamt soll das gedruckte Gesamtwerk zehn bis zwölf Bände umfassen; der Projektabschluss ist für 2064 geplant.

Die Anfänge des *Ostfränkischen Wörterbuchs* (seit 2012: *Fränkisches Wörterbuch*, WBF)[12] waren eng verbunden mit dem BWB (Wörterbuchkanzlei in München ab 1913). Mit der Materialsammlung wurde daher ebenfalls 1913 begonnen, sie ist für das *Fränkische Wörterbuch* aber seit 2001 eingestellt (vgl. zur Materialgrundlage Tab. 2). Der Initiative des Erlanger Sprachhistorikers Friedrich Maurer ist es zu verdanken, dass schließlich ab 1934 eine eigene Wörterbuchkanzlei mit einer Mitarbeiterstelle in Erlangen eingerichtet wurde. Im Zweiten Weltkrieg kam die Arbeit vollständig zum Erliegen, ein Neubeginn mit neufinanzierter Redaktorstelle (zunächst wieder in Erlangen) erfolgte ab 1963. Seitdem war die Arbeitsstelle zwischenzeitlich in Bayreuth verortet. In den Jahren 2003 bis 2007 entstand mit dem *Handwörterbuch von Bayerisch-Franken* (Wagner/Klepsch 2007) ein einbändiges Auswahlwörterbuch mit ca. 4000 Lemmata und damit überhaupt erstmals ein wissenschaftlich erarbeitetes Wörterbuch zum (ost-)fränkischen Wortschatz. Dieses wird das einzige Druckwerk bleiben, denn im Jahr 2003 fasste die „Kommission für Mundartforschung“ der BAdW den Beschluss, auf eine Buchpublikation des WBF zugunsten eines digitalen Wörterbuchs zu verzichten. Das aktuelle Projekt *Fränkisches Wörterbuch*, seit 2012 wieder in Erlangen,

---

11 Vgl. zum BWB Schnabel/Raaf/Schwarz (2021) sowie die Projektwebseite unter https://bwb.badw.de und den von der Arbeitsstelle gepflegte Wikipedia-Artikel „Bayerisches Wörterbuch“ (Stand: 9.7.2024).

12 Vgl. zum WBF König/Raaf/Klepsch (2021) sowie die Projektwebseite unter https://wbf.badw.de. Für viele Detailinformationen danke ich Almut König sehr herzlich.

Tab. 2: Materialgrundlage von BWB und WBF.

<table>
<tr><th></th><th>Bayerisches Wörterbuch (BWB)</th><th>Fränkisches Wörterbuch (WBF)</th></tr>
<tr><td>1913–1933</td><td colspan="2">„Systematischer Fragebogen"
(gesamtbayerische, indirekte Fragebogenerhebungen mit dem Ziel systematischer Wortschatzerhebungen; 109 Serien mit thematischen Bögen; Schwerpunkt bis 1915; ca. 2/3 Sammler in Altbayern, 1/3 in Pfalz und Franken)
→ ges. 780.000 Belegzettel, davon ca. 64.000 im Zweiten Weltkrieg verloren</td></tr>
<tr><td>1927–1933 (BWB)</td><td>„Kundfahrtenkatalog"
(direkte Befragungen)
→ ges. 108.000 Belegzettel</td><td></td></tr>
<tr><td>1927 (BWB)/ 1928 (WBF) -1940</td><td colspan="2">„Mundartgeographischer Fragebogen"
(indirekte Fragebogenerhebungen für die Erstellung sprachgeographischer Karten;
294 Serien mit thematischen Bögen, je ca. 20–30 Fragen)
Rücklauf BWB ca. 80.000 Bögen Rücklauf WBF ca. 57.000 Bögen
→ ges. ca. 1,3 Mio. Belege (BWB)</td></tr>
<tr><td>1932–1934 (WBF), 1934 (BWB)</td><td colspan="2">„Maurer-Fragebogen"
(indirekte Fragebogenerhebung; 1 Serie, 90 Fragen zu Lautung und Wortschatz)
Rücklauf WBF 2812 Bögen
→ ges. ca. 250.000 Belege (BWB)</td></tr>
<tr><td>seit 1958 (BWB)</td><td>„Wörterlisten"
(indirekte Fragebogenerhebung zum Schließen kriegsbedingter Lücken; bisher über 300 Serien)
→ ges. weit über 4 Mio Belege</td><td></td></tr>
<tr><td>1960–2001 (WBF)</td><td></td><td>„Nachkriegsbögen"(indirekte Fragebogenerhebungen; 123 Serien)
Rücklauf ca. 48.000 Bögen</td></tr>
<tr><td>1967 (WBF)</td><td></td><td>„Mündliche Befragungen" (825 Ortserhebungen)</td></tr>
<tr><td>Literarische Quellen</td><td>Exzerpte aus historischer und zeitgenössischer bair. geschriebene Texte seit dem 8. Jh. bis ca. 1800
→ ges. ca. 800.000 Belege
Zettelarchiv:ges. ca. 8 Mio. Belege</td><td>1933–1940: Kartei mundartlicher Wortbelege (literarische Quellen, lokale Wörterbücher, Wörtersammlungen)
→ ges. ca. 648.000 Belege
Zentralkartei ohne literarische Quellen: ges. ca. 1,2 Mio. Belege</td></tr>
</table>

erarbeitet mit einer wissenschaftlichen Mitarbeiterstelle die Online-Datenbank, die die Grundlage für die digitale Version des WBF darstellt. Dabei handelt es sich um eine Belegdatenbank, d.h. sämtliche erhobene Belege werden wissenschaftlich erfasst und lemmatisiert. Seit Dezember 2016 ist diese Volltextdatenbank online öffentlich zugänglich. Sie wird sukzessive ergänzt. Aktuell sind in der Datenbank 1.566.671 Datensätze (Material der sog. „Nachkriegsbögen", vgl. Tab. 2) recherchierbar. Der Projektabschluss ist für 2064 geplant.

Durch gemeinsamen IT-Support durch die BAdW sind BWB und WBF inzwischen wieder eng verbunden: In beiden Projekten erfolgt die Belegbearbeitung digital mit dem webbasierten Redaktionstool LexHelfer, der verschiedene Grundfunktionen bietet, um digitalisierte Fragebögen (Beleggrundlage) oder maschinell erfasste Belege zu durchsuchen und zu edieren (vgl. Raaf 2017). LexHelfer wird in beiden Projekten je spezifisch eingesetzt (vgl. Raaf 2017): Im BWB-Projekt werden in der Datenbank halbautomatisiert erstellte „Schnipsel", d.h. Ausschnitte aus den digitalisierten, handschriftlich ausgefüllten Fragebögen als Bilddigitalisate erfasst (ges. 6 Mio.). Das Redaktionstool unterstützt hier eine schnelle Lemmatisierung und die Artikelvorbereitung sowie via XML-Export und Weiterverarbeitung in Oxygen eine direkte Veröffentlichung der bearbeiteten Belege. Derzeit beinhaltet die Datenbank des BWB 27.564 Stichwörter, die mit 370.098 Bilddigitalisaten verknüpft sind. Im WBF-Projekt basiert LexHelfer auf Excel-Listen, in denen die Belege manuell erfasst sind. Über LexHelfer erfolgt hier der Zugriff auf das komplette Belegmaterial, die relationale Datenbank bildet die Grundlage für eine automatisierte Artikelerstellung. Beide Datenbanken sind für Recherchen in öffentlichen Versionen zugänglich.[13]

BWB und WBF sind alphabetisch konzipierte Bedeutungswörterbücher, in denen anders als bei einem Idiotikon nicht nur dialektale Wörter erfasst werden, sondern auch allgemeinsprachliche Lexeme, sofern sie im Belegmaterial vorkommen. Die Lemmata werden, sofern sie nicht nur mundartlich belegt sind, in standardsprachlicher Schreibweise geboten; andernfalls orientiert man sich an der Lemmatisierung in anderen mundartlichen Wörterbüchern bzw. gestaltet einen eigenen Lemmaansatz, der sich an der mundartlichen Lautung orientiert.

Im gedruckten BWB erfolgt die makrostrukturelle Anordnung der Haupt- sowie Verweislemmata initial- und nischenalphabetisch, wobei einzelne Buchstabenpaare (B/P, D/T, F/V) in Entsprechung zur mundartlichen Lautung zusammengefasst sind. Hauptlemmata, bei denen es sich um Wortbildungen handelt, werden im Anschluss an das Grundwort integriert. Betroffen sind hiervon nicht nur Komposita und Suffigierungen, sondern auch Präfix- und Partikelbildungen; Mehrfachkomposita werden im Anschluss an das entsprechende einfache Kompositum eingeordnet, auch wenn dieses nicht selbst lemmatisiert ist, vgl. z.B. folgende Lemmaabfolge in Bd. II (Sp.

13 Online unter <https://lexhelfer.bwb.badw.de> bzw. <https://lexhelfer.wbf.badw.de> (letzter Zugriff: 10.3.2025).

49–89): *Pedell, Beefsteak, Beere, [Amel]b., [Amsel]b., [Ananas]b.,* [...] *[Au]b., [Rausch-au] b., [Äuglein]b., [Seidel-bast]b., [Brom-beer(en)]b., [Rot-brom]b., [Schwarz-brom-beer]b., [Ernte-beers]b., [Heid-beer]b., [Kran-beer(en)]b., [Lor-beer]b., [Schlingen-beerlein]b., [Schwarz-beer]b., [Beiß]b.,* [...] *[Hecken]b., [Heid]b., [Heidel]b.,* [...] *[Zwaltsch]b., beereln, [ab]b., [abher]b.,* [...] *[wein]b., [ein-wein]b., beeren,* [...] *Beff, -beff, Beffel, beffen, Beffzger.* Durch diese Anordnung werden Wortbildungsnester ersichtlich. Die Wörterbuchmikrostruktur berücksichtigt maximal folgende Positionen (Abb. 2):

Birling M., †F., (v.a. kleiner) Heuschober, °westl.OB, °OP, °MF, °SCH vereinz.: °*der macht Bierling, er rechnet s Hai auf und macht Hauferl* Weilhm; *Die Birling* „Heuschober“ SCHMELLER I,278; *pürlịŋ* nach SCHWEIZER Dießner Wb. 157.– Auch: °*Birling* „Haufen Gras, der früher mit der Sichel gesammelt wurde“ Berching BEI.	**Artikelkopf** mit Lemmazeichengestaltangabe in Fettdruck (Hauptlemma, ggf. Nebenlemmata als wichtige Varianten des Hauptlemmas) (kurzer) **Formkommentar** (morphologische Position: Wortart, bei Subst. nur Genus) **semantischer Kommentar** (bei Polysemie ggf. mit Positionsangabe in Fettdruck und einzelnen semantischen Subkommentaren) mit Bedeutungsposition, Pragmatikposition (Frequenzangaben, diatopische, diachrone, diastratische Angaben), Belegposition inklusive Phraseologieposition, enzyklopädische Angaben (sach- und volkskundliche Angaben), Synonymangabe(n)
Etym.: Mhd. *birlinc* stm., zur gleichen Wz. wie →*bären*[3]; Schw.Id. IV,1503 f. Ltg: *bialịŋ* u.ä., daneben *-ir-* westl.OB, SCH, *-ur-* u.ä. (LL, WM). SCHMELLER I,278.– Tir.Wb. 81; Schwäb.Wb. I,1132 f.; Schw.Id. IV,1502–1504.– DWB II,40; Frühnhd.Wb. IV,457 f.; LEXER HWb. I,397.– W-26/35. Abl.: *birlingen.* E.F.	**teilartikelexterner Postkommentar**: etymologische Angabe; Angaben zur Lautung, zu Formen und Syntax; Literaturangaben und Angaben zu Erhebungsphasen; wortbildungsmorphologische Angaben (Ableitungen, Komposita, Präfix-/Partikelbildungen); Siglenangabe des Autorennamens

Abb. 2: Beispielartikel BWB (Bd. II, Sp. 900, s.v. *Birling*).

Die relationale SQL-Datenbank des WBF erlaubt vielfältige Abfragemöglichkeiten, Sortier- und Filterfunktionen. Folgende Informationen können systematisch abgefragt werden: *Lemma* (lemmatisiertes Kernlexem, u.a. um Wortbildungsnester abzubilden), *Grundform* (eigentliches Lemma in standardnaher Verschriftung), *Bedeutung*, *Grammatik* (bei Belegen im Satzzusammenhang vollständige grammatische Angaben), *Originaltext* (originalgetreue Belegwiedergabe, ggf. mit Kontext), *Umschrift* (gesamter Originaltext in standardnaher Verschriftung), *Ort* (Erhebungsort), *Planquadrat* (bezogen auf die zugrunde gelegte Ortsnetzkarte), *Kommentar Gewährsperson* (ggf. erläuternde Anmerkungen der Gewährsperson), *Kommentar Bearbeiter* (ggf. Hinweise zur Belegerfassung, zu anderen Wörterbüchern, zur Etymologie), *Gewährsperson* (Nummer pro Planquadrat), *Bogen* (Seriennummer des Fragebogens), *Frage* (Nummer der Frage), *Bild* (aufrufbare Bilddatei des gescannten Originalbelegs) (vgl. Abb. 3).

Lemma ▾▴	Grundform ▾▴	Bedeutung ▾▴	Grammatik ▾▴	Originaltext ▾▴	Umschrift ▾▴	Ort ▾▴	Planquadrat ▾▴	Kommentar Gewährsperson ▾▴	Kommentar Bearbeiter ▾▴	GP ▾▴	Bogen ▾▴	Frage ▾▴	Bild
Katharina	Patschkäthel	Schulkind, das dem Lehrer immer alles verrät	Sn NomSg	a 'Badschkädl	eine Patschkäthel	Zirndorf	c32,6			2	31	20	
patschen	Patschkäthel	Schulkind, das dem Lehrer immer alles verrät	Sn NomSg	a 'Badschkädl	eine Patschkäthel	Zirndorf	c32,6			2	31	20	

Abb. 3: Beispiel WBF-digital (*Patschkäthel*).

Seit Juli 2021 sind die Daten aus BWB, WBF sowie DIBS (vgl. unten) in einem von der IT-Abteilung der BAdW erarbeiteten Online-Portal „Bayerns Dialekte Online" (BDO) abrufbar. Dadurch kann man sich dialektregionenübergreifend zur dialektalen Lexik in Bayern informieren und Erkenntnisse u.a. zu Gemeinsamkeiten bzw. Unterschieden im Lexembestand gewinnen. In diesem Sprachinformationssystem sind die Primärdaten der drei bayerischen Dialektwörterbücher über eine gemeinsame Oberfläche und mittels eines einheitlichen Layouts vereint (vgl. Raaf 2022b: 16). Möglich wurde dies durch die aufwändige Homogenisierung der unterschiedlichen Datenbestände und anschließende Integration (vgl. Raaf 2025). In BDO erscheinen die Printwörterbuchartikel des BWB im digitalen Format, im Falle des WBF werden auf Basis der Belege in der WBF-Datenbank Wörterbuchartikel automatisiert erstellt. Bei polysemen Lexemen erfolgt hierfür lemmabezogen eine automatische Gruppierung identischer Belege und Bedeutungen. Die Anordnung der Bedeutungen orientiert sich an der aktuell in der Datenbank erfassten Belegzahl. Die einfachen und kombinierten Suchmöglichkeiten in BDO sind äußerst vielfältig: Die erweiterte Suche ermöglicht nicht nur Abfragen zu Stichwort (Lemma), Bedeutung, Dialektbeleg, Grammatik oder zur geographischen Verbreitung, sondern auch zu onomasiologischen Themengebieten, zu Wortfamilien, zu Etymologie (Herkunftssprache) und zum Sprachgebrauch (Pragmatik). Hier kann nach Kategorien gesucht werden wie „abwertend", „Ausruf", „ältere Sprache", „Bauernregel", „Fachsprachen" (z.B. Jägersprache, Soldatensprache), „Fluch", „Kosename", „Lied", „Phraseologie" und vielen anderen. Ein nächster Meilenstein wurde im Januar 2022 erreicht: Seitdem ist BDO in das Trierer „Wörterbuchnetz" integriert, sodass der recherchierte Datenbestand auch mit dem von anderen Wörterbüchern verglichen werden kann. Ein Daten-Update erfolgt monatlich (vgl. Abb. 4).

Ein weiteres, kleineres Projekt wird an der BAdW seit 2017 realisiert (geplanter Abschluss: 2044): Das „Dialektologische Informationssystem von Bayerisch-Schwaben" (DIBS)[14] begann zunächst als *Digitales Wörterbuch von Bayerisch-Schwaben*. Hierzu erschien ein einbändiges Auswahlwörterbuch *Dialektwörterbuch von Bayerisch-Schwaben* (König/Schwarz 2013) mit ca. 3000 Lemmata. Schon seit 1998 werden in einer Datenbank mundartliche Belege erfasst, um den schwäbisch-alemannischen Wortschatz Bayerns zu dokumentieren. Hintergrund dieses Projekts ist es, Fischers *Schwäbisches Wörterbuch*, das für den schwäbischen Teil Bayerns sehr große Lücken aufweist, zu ergänzen. Auch in DIBS wird LexHelfer als Redaktionstool verwendet. Die Datenbank ist seit 2020 öffentlich zugänglich und ebenfalls in BDO integriert.[15]

Im Anschluss an diesen Zustandsbericht sollen im Folgenden anhand der „15 Villa Vigoni-Thesen zur Lexikografie" Nutzbarkeit, Nützlichkeit und Zukunftsfähigkeit der

---

14 Vgl. zum DIBS Schwarz/Funk/Raaf/Welsch (2021) sowie die Projektwebseite unter https://dibs.badw.de (letzter Zugriff: 5.5.2025).

15 Online unter <https://lexhelfer.dibs.badw.de> bzw. <https://lexhelfer.wbf.badw.de> (letzter Zugriff: 10.3.2025).

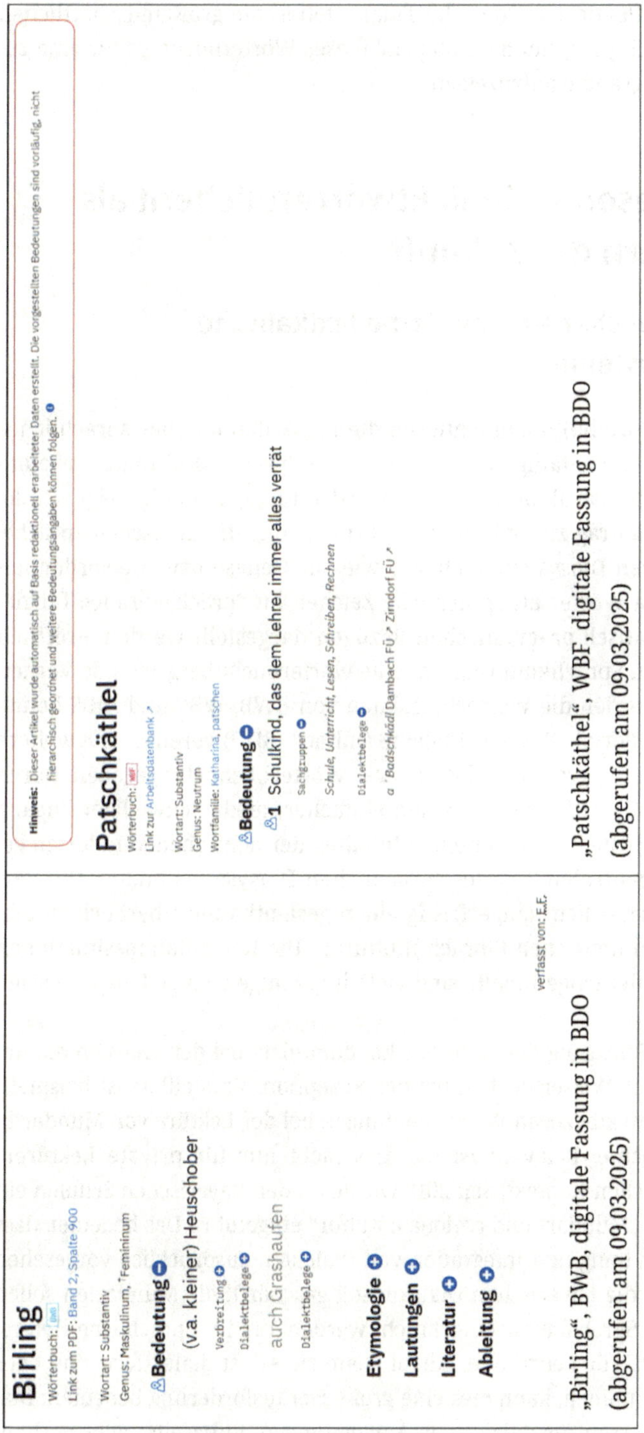

Abb. 4: Beispiele aus „Bayerns Dialekte online" (BDO).

Dialektwörterbücher reflektiert werden. Im Fokus stehen die großlandschaftlichen Dialektwörterbücher in Bayern, um das Potenzial dieses Wörterbuchtyps für eine zukunftsorientierte Lexikographie aufzuzeigen.

3 Fünfzehn Thesen zu Dialektwörterbüchern als Wörterbüchern der Zukunft

3.1 Dialektwörterbücher sind moderne lexikalische Informationssysteme

Dialektwörterbücher (DiaWbb) dokumentieren die Lexik diatopischer sprachlicher Varietäten und beinhalten vielfältige Informationen zu Sprache und Kultur, wie anhand der Wörterbuchmikrostrukturen von BWB und WBF (vgl. 2) aufgezeigt wurde. Sie leisten damit einen Beitrag zur vollständigen Erforschung der deutschen Sprache, zu einzelnen diatopischen Diasystemen ebenso wie zur Genese bzw. Gewordenheit der Standardsprache. Da Wörter als sprachliche Zeichen im Sprachgebrauch fungieren und in ihren semantisch-pragmatischen Bezügen dargestellt werden, eröffnen DiaWbb einen Zugang zu Sprachkulturen. Um eine wörterbuchübergreifende Vernetzung zu ermöglichen, wurden die Wörterbuchdaten von BWB, WBF und DIBS homogenisiert und im Online-Portal „Bayerns Dialekte Online“ (BDO) vereint. Eine weitere Vernetzung ist durch die Integration in das „Trierer Wörterbuchnetz“ gegeben. Durch diese moderne, digitale Zugriffsstruktur ist ein einfacher, niederschwelliger Zugang zu wissenschaftlich erarbeiteten, lexikalischen Inhalten der deutschen Mundarten gewährleistet, die einen zentralen Teil des sprachlichen Diasystems bilden. Die Verknüpfung der Inhalte ermöglicht längerfristig einen gesamthaften Überblick zu dialektalen bzw. regionalen deutschen (Sprach-)Kulturen. Die Konsultationssituationen und Nutzergruppen für derartige Inhalte sind vielfältig. Einige wenige Beispiele seien skizziert:

Mit zunehmendem Rückgang der Basisdialekte dominiert bei den DiaWbb die unterstützende Funktion für Wissenslücken bei der Rezeption. Vorstellbar ist beispielsweise, dass man sich kontextbezogen Wortbedeutungen bei der Lektüre von Mundartliteratur erschließen möchte. Relevant ist die dies nicht nur für private Lektüren, sondern auch im schulischen Kontext: Seit 2018 wurde an den bayerischen Schulen ein Unterrichtsschwerpunkt „Mundart und regionale Kultur“ eingeführt. Das bedeutet, dass im Schulalltag die Behandlung und Integration von Dialekten ausdrücklich vorgesehen ist. Das Bewusstsein für die bayerischen Dialekte soll geschärft, die Mundarten sollen positiv erlebt und in die Sprachkultur eingebracht werden, um für sprachliche Heterogenität zu sensibilisieren. Für Lehrkräfte, zumal wenn sie selbst dialektfern sind oder aus anderen Regionen stammen, kann dies eine große Herausforderung bedeuten: Dialektale Sprachformen müssen für didaktische Anwendungen aufbereitet oder vorhandene Materialien müssen selbst reflektiert und verstanden werden, um sie sachgerecht in den Unterricht einbinden zu können (vgl. StMUK 2015 und 2019). In den DiaWbb ist veraltende oder veraltete Lexik bewahrt, die nicht selten mit Veränderungen in der Sachwelt einhergeht (vgl. *Birling* in BWB). Dies macht DiaWbb zu einer zentralen Nachschlagequelle sowohl für Sprachhistoriker/-innen als auch für Volkskundler/-innen und Historiker/-innen. Aus einer kontrastiven Perspektive können DiaWbb außerdem konsultiert werden, um Aufschluss über von der Standardsprache abweichenden lexikalischen Gebrauch zu erhalten. Ein Beispiel hierfür aus den bayerischen DiaWbb ist *Bengel*, das in sämtlichen Mundarten Bayerns zwar auch die standardsprachliche Bedeutung 'ungezogenes Kind' aufweist, das aber häufiger als 'Holzprügel' und 'Gerät zum Dreschen bzw. Teil davon' belegt ist. Diese eigentliche Bedeutung wird metaphorisch auf Personen übertragen, sodass auch 'grobe, unkultivierte Burschen', 'große, kräftige Männer' und eben 'ungezogene Kinder' damit bezeichnet werden (vgl. BDO, s.v. *Bengel*).

Es ist davon auszugehen, dass für DiaWbb die unterstützende Funktion bei Schreib- und Formulierungsprozessen weniger relevant ist, handelt es sich bei Dialekten bzw. Regiolekten ja um in der Regel gesprochene, nähesprachliche Varietäten. Auch hier ist aber im Kontext von Mundartliteratur ein mögliches Nutzungsszenarium durch Autorinnen oder Autoren vorstellbar, und im Kontext der Wiederbelebung gesprochener Mundarten bzw. der Förderung regional begrenzter Minderheitensprachen können durch die DiaWbb durchaus auch sprachproduktive Prozesse unterstützt und angeregt werden, wie z.B. anhand einer App zum Saterfriesischen deutlich wird, die von der Gemeinde Saterland, gefördert durch die Beauftragte der Bundesregierung für Kultur und Medien und das Niedersächsische Ministerium für Wissenschaft und Kultur, seit 2017 bereitgestellt wird.[16]

3.2 Dialektwörterbücher sind im öffentlichen Diskurs präsent

Mit wachsendem Interesse an Dialekten und regionalen Umgangssprachen geht einher, dass auch DiaWbb öffentliche Aufmerksamkeit zuteilwird. Dieser Effekt wird durch den Ausbau der lexikographischen Online-Angebote verstärkt, die niederschwellig erreichbar sind. Für das öffentlich zugängliche Redaktionssystem LexHelfer des WBF beispielsweise wurden seit Beginn der Statistikführung für öffentliche Seitenaufrufe 8.459.258 einzelne Zugriffe registriert, für LexHelfer des BWB 1.048.025.[17] Für das „Informationssystem Bayerns Dialekte online“ (BDO) wurden für das Jahr 2022 bereits 105.000 Suchanfragen verzeichnet. Damit hat sich BDO innerhalb der Online-Angebote der BAdW schon im ersten Jahr nach seiner Einführung im Vorderfeld

16 Vgl. unter <https://apps.apple.com/de/app/saterfriesisch/id6469493604> (letzter Zugriff: 10.3.2025).
17 Vgl. unter <https://lexhelfer.wbf.badw.de/index.php?section=stats> und <https://lexhelfer.bwb.badw.de/index.php?section=statistik> (letzter Zugriff: 10.3.2025).

platziert. Für das Jahr 2023 wurden bereits 2,2 Mio. Suchanfragen von mehr als 70.000 Besucherinnen und Besuchern registriert.[18]

Außerdem engagieren sich die Mitarbeiter/-innen in den laufenden Projekten in der Wissenschaftskommunikation und geben den Wörterbüchern in der Öffentlichkeit ein Gesicht: In der seit vielen Jahren beliebten Rubrik „Host mi?“ im Nachmittagsmagazin „Wir-in-Bayern“ (BR Fernsehen) wird während der Woche täglich die Bedeutung bairischer Dialektwörter erraten. Diese werden anschließend von Anthony Rowley, Projektleiter und Ausschussvorsitzender des BWB, erklärt. Ein ähnliches Format, auch als Podcast abrufbar, funktioniert mit Almut König, Redaktorin des WBF, im Frankenfernsehen. An Aktionstagen wie dem „Tag der offenen Tür an der BAdW“ (Dialekt-Quiz im Mai 2024) oder der „Langen Nacht der Wissenschaften der Friedrich-Alexander-Universität Erlangen-Nürnberg“ präsentieren sich die Wörterbuchprojekte oder veröffentlichen über Social-Media-Kanäle Beiträge, z.B. Erklärungen zu interessanten Wörtern am „Tag der Muttersprache“ (21.2.2024).

3.3 Dialektwörterbücher zeigen gesellschaftliche Verantwortung

Im Datenmaterial der DiaWbb sind (besonders im Zusammenhang mit Personenbezeichnungen) auch brisante Wörter enthalten (z.B. bei der Bezeichnung für People of color), oder aber Wörter werden im Belegmaterial diskriminierend gebraucht (z.B. antisemitische Ausführungen). Wie geht man bei der praktischen Wörterbucharbeit in solchen Fällen vor? Das Thema wurde im Rahmen eines Online-Netzwerktreffens der großlandschaftlichen DiaWbb im Juli 2021 breit diskutiert. Wissenschaftlich anzustrebende Objektivität und akademische Integrität machen es erforderlich, auch unangenehme Inhalte zu dokumentieren. Es ist aber auch zu bedenken, dass ein heute als diskriminierend empfundenes Wort mit historischem Abstand andere Konnotationen im Sprachgebrauch aufweisen kann. Um diese einschätzen zu können, sind Anschlussrecherchen notwendig, um eine entsprechende Kontextualisierung zu leisten (vgl. Ganslmayer 2022: 284–286). Grundsätzlich ist es aber möglich, entsprechende Lexeme metasprachlich zu kommentieren. Im WBF (vgl. Ilter 2023 und für die folgende Passage Klepsch/König 2022: 56) erfolgt in eindeutigen Fällen in der Bedeutungsspalte der Zusatz „pejor“, in nicht eindeutigen Fällen „evtl. pejor“. Ethnophaulismen und personenbezogene Schimpfwörter werden im Bearbeiterkommentar mit „#diskriminierende Bezeichnung“ und einem Link zu folgendem Kommentartext versehen: „Die Bezeichnung diskriminiert eine bestimmte Bevölkerungsgruppe, die Verwendung des Wortes sollte vermieden werden. Der Ausdruck spiegelt nicht den Sprachgebrauch der Redaktion wider, sondern wurde im Zuge der Befragungen von einer Gewährsperson angeführt.“ Werden Ethnika abwertend metaphorisch gebraucht, erfolgt der Zusatz „#pejorative Metapher“.

18 Vgl. unter <https://bdo.badw.de/info/neuigkeiten> (letzter Zugriff: 10.3.2025).

3.4 Dialektwörterbücher werden kritisch diskutiert und evaluiert

Üblicherweise werden wissenschaftliche Publikationen in der jeweiligen wissenschaftlichen Gemeinschaft rezensiert. Kritische Rezensionen haben sowohl eine informative Funktion als auch die Aufgabe, den wissenschaftlichen Ertrag im Kontext der fachinternen Diskussion zu beurteilen. Für laufende Projekte bieten sie die Chance, die geleistete Arbeit zu reflektieren und gegebenenfalls auf Kritik zu reagieren. Selbstverständlich wurden und werden auch die großlandschaftlichen DiaWbb meist bei Erscheinen eines Bandes in Fachrezensionen entsprechend gewürdigt (vgl. z.B. zu BWB I, Bergmann 2003).

Darüber hinaus sind die großlandschaftlichen DiaWbb häufig drittmittelfinanzierte Akademieprojekte, was auch für BWB, WBF und DIBS gilt. Das Akademienprogramm ist das wichtigste Förderprogramm für Langzeitprojekte geistes- und sozialwissenschaftlicher Grundlagenforschung in Deutschland. Um die wissenschaftliche Qualität zu gewährleisten, sind regelmäßige Projektevaluationen und Durchführungskontrollen ein integraler Bestandteil des Programms (vgl. Stock/Zwies 2014: 45–46): Bei den „Projektevaluationen" werden die erzielten Ergebnisse, der erreichte Arbeitsstand und die weitere Arbeitsplanung überprüft. Die Höhe der Personal- und Sachausstattung wird in Beziehung zur zu leistenden Arbeit gesetzt, die Tragfähigkeit der Projektkonzeption beurteilt (vgl. Stock/Zwies 2014: 48). Zwischen den größeren Projektevaluationen finden sogenannte „Durchführungskontrollen" statt, bei denen vorrangig der Bearbeitungsstand geprüft wird: In Zielerreichungskontrollen wird berichtet, wie in den letzten drei Jahren gearbeitet wurde und welche Ergebnisse erzielt wurden. In „Zielvereinbarungen" wird die Projektplanung (Arbeits- und Veröffentlichungsplan) der kommenden drei Jahre skizziert. Ergeben sich Rückfragen der Wissenschaftlichen Kommission, müssen Stellungnahmen der Projekte erfolgen, die zur Kommissionssitzung vorzulegen sind (vgl. Stock/Zwies 2014: 49). Durch dieses engmaschige Evaluationsverfahren ist gewährleistet, dass die Akademieprojekte über ihre gesamte Laufzeit hinweg von ausgewiesenen Expertinnen und Experten wissenschaftlich begleitet werden, sodass eine hohe wissenschaftliche Qualität garantiert ist.

3.5 Dialektwörterbücher dokumentieren Änderungen in Online-Informationssystemen

Veränderungen im Datenbestand (sukzessive Erweiterung der Primärdaten) werden offengelegt und Fortschritte im Erfassungsstand statistisch dokumentiert: In der WBF-Datenbank erfolgten Datenuploads bis 2023 in halbjährlichem Rhythmus (jeweils Ende März und Ende September). Seit Herbst 2023 konnte der Workflow gestrafft werden, so dass eine Aktualisierung der Daten wöchentlich oder sogar täglich erfolgt. Die aktuell enthaltenen Einzelbelege werden genau beziffert.[19]

Auch für das BDO sind die Datenbankupdates in Zeit und Umfang dokumentiert:[20] Zu Beginn der Pretest-Phase im März 2021 enthielt BDO bereits über 100.000 Stichwörter, im März 2023 schon 125.930. Seitdem wurden monatlich weitere Artikel integriert: + 4.400 Artikel (04/2023), + 350 (05/2023), + 245 (06/2023), + 416 (07/2023), + 3.827 (08/2023), + 213 (09/2023), + 861 (10/2023), + 791 (11/2023), + 105 (01/2024), + 803 (02/2024), + 666 (03/2024), 7.287 (04/2024), + 5.625 (05/2024), + 1.853 (06/2024), + 785 (07/2024), + 442 (08/2024), + 5.000 (09/2024), + 1.386 (10/2024), + 59 (11/2024), + 243 (12/2024), + 828 (01/2025), + 447 (02/2025), + 548 (03/2025). Besonders hohe Zuwachszahlen stehen in Zusammenhang mit der Integration retrodigitalisierter Inhalte des BWB: Mit September 2024 war diese abgeschlossen, so dass sämtliche frei verfügbaren Hefte des BWB in BDO integriert waren. Auch die Einführung neuer Suchfunktionen in BDO wird dokumentiert, und Nutzer/-innen des BDO finden auf der Eingangsseite den Hinweis, dass die Wörterbücherprojekte noch nicht abgeschlossen sind und es daher sein kann, dass ein gesuchtes Wort noch nicht verfügbar ist.

3.6 Dialektwörterbücher bilden ein Netzwerk

Schon 1913, als in Marburg die Idee zu einem „Wörterbuchkartell“ (ab 1921) entstand, existiert eine Interessensvertretung der deutschsprachigen Mundartlexikographie. Man koordinierte nicht nur die Abgrenzung der Bearbeitungsgebiete, sondern trat auch in einen inhaltlich-methodischen Austausch, um gemeinsame methodische Ansätze bei der Datenerhebung umzusetzen (Entwicklung eines Fragebogens), die DiaWb inhaltlich ähnlich zu konzipieren und Fachliteratur auszutauschen (vgl. Bremer/Hoffmann 1982: 207). Durch die deutsche Akademienlandschaft, in die viele der aktiven DiaWbb integriert sind, besteht ein wissenschaftlich koordinierter Austausch.

In jüngerer Zeit haben sich die noch aktiven DiaWbb in „Lexikonet“ zusammengeschlossen, dem „Netzwerk großlandschaftlicher Dialektwörterbücher“.[21] In bislang vier Netzwerktreffen (Wien 2017, Gießen 2018, online 2021 und organisiert durch Erlangen, Budapest 2024) wurden konkrete Probleme der lexikographischen Arbeit und im Zusammenhang mit der technologischen Weiterentwicklung der Datenbanken diskutiert.

19 Vgl. unter <https://lexhelfer.wbf.badw.de/index.php?section=stats> (letzter Zugriff: 10.3.2025).

20 Vgl. unter <https://bdo.badw.de/info/neuigkeiten> (letzter Zugriff: 10.3.2025).

21 Vgl. unter <https://www.oeaw.ac.at/de/acdh/institut/netzwerke-kooperationen/netzwerke/lexikonet> (letzter Zugriff: 10.3.2025).

Für die übergreifende digitale Vernetzung der DiaWbb ist das „Wörterbuchnetz" des Kompetenzzentrums für elektronische Erschließungs- und Publikationsverfahren in den Geisteswissenschaften der Universität Trier zentral (vgl. Moulin 2010: 601–607).[22]

3.7 Dialektwörterbücher agieren digital zukunftsorientiert

Die meisten der aktiven DiaWbb haben bereits vor mehreren Jahrzehnten mit Planung, Materialerhebung und Erstellung von Wörterbuchartikeln begonnen (vgl. 2); kontinuierliches Arbeiten und sukzessives Publizieren lassen bei derartigen Langzeitprojekten relativ wenig bis nahezu keinen Spielraum für Änderungen der ursprünglichen Konzepte zu, weder in Inhalt noch Design des Endprodukts. Dennoch wurden für die DiaWbb frühzeitig und umfänglich die Möglichkeiten der Digitalisierung genutzt, wie am Beispiel von WBF und BWB und der Entwicklung von BDO gezeigt wurde (vgl. 2).

Betroffen sind hier unterschiedliche Dimensionen der Digitalisierung: Digitale Softwareanwendungen wurden adaptiert oder entwickelt und in die bestehenden Arbeitsabläufe integriert. Für die Belegverwaltung und -bearbeitung ergab sich hieraus ein enormer Zeitgewinn; digitale Vernetzung ermöglicht in den Arbeitsstellen ein synchrones Arbeiten an den jeweiligen Datenbanken; beim WBF konnten bestimmte Arbeitsschritte der Wörterbucherstellung als digitaler Prozess modelliert werden: Die Wörterbuchartikel werden hier automatisiert auf Basis der Datenbank erstellt. Die umfangreichen Archivmaterialien (handschriftlich ausgefüllte Fragebögen, Belegzettel, Wortschatzsammlungen, lautschriftliche Protokolle, handgezeichnete Karten und vieles mehr) wurden bzw. werden gescannt und damit nachhaltig gesichert.[23] Bilddigitalisate werden in die Datenbanken integriert und ermöglichen bei der Nutzung im Projekt, aber auch darüber hinaus einen unmittelbaren Zugang zum Quellenmaterial und damit auch eine Überprüfbarkeit der wissenschaftlichen Analysen, die der Wörterbucharbeit zugrunde liegen.

BDO wurde von Anfang an als ergänzende Publikationsplattform verstanden, bei deren Entwicklung die redaktionellen Arbeitsabläufe nicht behindert, sondern indirekt

22 In das „Trierer Wörterbuchnetz" sind derzeit folgende regionalsprachliche Wörterbücher integriert: ElsässWb, Lothr Wb, PfälzWb, RheinWb, WestfWb, LuxWb, *Wörterbuch der Luxemburgischen Mundart* (WLM), *Lexikon der Luxemburger Umgangssprache* (LLU), *Letzebuerger Online Dictionnaire* (LOD), ShessWb, Regionalsprache.de (REDE), BDO und WBÖ. Vgl. unter <https://www.woerterbuchnetz.de/> (letzter Zugriff: 10.3.2025). Aktuell wird an der Integration des MecklWb gearbeitet, vgl. unter <https://tcdh.uni-trier.de/de/projekt/wossidlo-teuchert-online> (letzter Zugriff: 10.3.2025).

23 Teilweise stehen diese Materialien online zur Verfügung, wie z.B. handgezeichnete Sprachkarten, vgl. unter <https://wbf.badw.de/sprachkarten.html> und <https://bwb.badw.de/sprachkarten.html> (letzter Zugriff: 10.3.2025).

unterstützt werden sollten (Raaf 2025: 64–65). Da für BDO die Primärdaten standardisiert und homogenisiert werden mussten, trug die Entwicklung der Plattform zugleich zur Datenverbesserung in allen Teilprojekten bei: Die heterogenen Datenbestände der drei Wörterbuchprojekte wurden teils korrigiert, in ein einheitliches XML-Format konvertiert und implementiert. Beim WBF und DIBS erfolgte hierfür ein automatisierter Zugriff auf die Daten in den relationalen SQL-Datenbanken; beim BWB wurden die Bände I bis III (ursprünglich Wörterbuchartikel im Word-Format) retrodigitalisiert und automatisiert in XML transformiert (vgl. Raaf 2025). Die standardisierten Daten wurden und werden gegebenenfalls um weitere Analysedimensionen angereichert. Beispielsweise sind alle Belege mit Georeferenzdaten versehen, so dass sie in Sprachkarten automatisiert visualisiert werden können. Um die definierten Anforderungen bestmöglich realisieren zu können, wurden bei der Implementierung von BDO verschiedene etablierte Technologien bzw. Programmiersprachen kombiniert (XML, XQuery, Python, XSL, Bash-Script, JavaScript/HTML/CSS, TeX, PHP, vgl. Raaf 2019; 2025: 99–109).

Die Standardisierung der Daten ist die grundlegende Voraussetzung für mögliche Erweiterungen und Verknüpfungen (wie z.B. Einbindung ins „Wörterbuchnetz"). Längerfristig ist so auch eine Verdichtung des Datenbestandes möglich: So hat man beispielsweise am WBF, gefördert aus Mitteln der Mittelfrankenstiftung, der Oberfrankenstiftung und der Unterfränkischen Kulturstiftung, zwischen Mai 2018 und Juni 2021 Daten aufbereitet, die im Rahmen des Bayerischen Sprachatlas (BSA) in den Fränkischen Regierungsbezirken erhoben wurden (Sprachatlas von Nordostbayern, Sprachatlas von Unterfranken, Sprachatlas von Mittelfranken). Diese können später in die Datenbank und in BDO integriert werden.[24] Denkbar ist auch, BDO zu einer Multimediadatenbank auszubauen (vgl. Raaf 2025: 167).

Was den korpuslinguistischen Anspruch an die Datenbasis von Wörterbüchern betrifft, so basieren die DiaWbb durchgängig auf empirisch erhobenen Sprachdaten und/oder Exzerpten aus schriftlichen Quellen. Diese Materialbasis stellt selbstverständlich kein repräsentatives, ausgewogenes Textkorpus im strengen Sinne dar: Die Erhebungen erfolgten auf Basis von thematisch ausgerichteten Fragebögen oder Fragebüchern, so dass eine onomasiologische Ausrichtung der Datenbasis erkennbar ist. Mitunter werden Antworten durch die Fragestellungen auch bewusst evoziert, so dass frequenzbasierte Auswertungen der Tokenzahlen nicht repräsentativ sein können. Dennoch handelt es sich um wertvolle, authentische Sprachdaten mit unterschiedlicher historischer Tiefe, die für weitere Anschlussforschungen zur Verfügung stehen. Die Datenbank des WBF ist eine Belegdatenbank, d.h., es sind nicht nur exemplarische Belege erfasst, sondern sämtliche Vorkommnisse im Material, was eine forschungsbezogene Nachnutzung der Daten in vielerlei Hinsicht ermöglicht (vgl. 3.8).

Eine Nachnutzbarkeit der Primärdaten ist in mehrfacher Hinsicht gewährleistet: Die Forschungsprimärdaten der Wörterbücher sind über LexHelfer online zugäng-

24 Vgl. unter <https://lexhelfer.wbf.badw.de/> (letzter Zugriff: 10.3.2025).

lich, bei DIBS und WBF können die Suchergebnisse mittels CSV-Export für die individuelle Weiterarbeit genutzt werden. In BDO können die Suchergebnisse als XML-Datei heruntergeladen bzw. über einen Permalink abgespeichert und somit auch in wissenschaftlichen Publikationen zitiert werden. (vgl. Raaf 2019; 2022b: 19; 2025). Seit November 2024 ist BDO auch ein Teil von „open.bydata – Offene Daten aus Bayern". Neben dem gesamten Datenbestand können auch einzelne Wörterbücher im XML-Format zur freien Nachnutzung heruntergeladen werden.[25]

3.8 Dialektwörterbücher ermöglichen Wörterbuchforschung

Wörterbuchforschung beinhaltet zum einen Forschung über Wörterbücher, aber auch mit Wörterbüchern: Die Inhalte der DiaWbb, die zugrundeliegenden Primärdaten und die DiaWbb selbst regen vielfältige weitere Forschungsfragen an, wie anhand einiger Beispiele gezeigt werden soll: Aus einer linguistischen Perspektive können die Daten beispielsweise für die Erforschung von Wortbildungsphänomenen und -systemen genutzt werden, sowohl innerdialektal als auch dialektübergreifend und im Kontrast zur Standardsprache. So wurde von der Fritz Thyssen Stiftung in den Jahren 2018 bis 2020 an der Friedrich-Alexander-Universität Erlangen-Nürnberg das Projekt „Produktivität und Kreativität in der Lexik des Ostfränkischen" gefördert, das als Pilotprojekt u.a. auf Basis der WBF-Daten durchgeführt wurde (vgl. Ganslmayer/Müller 2022).

Darüber hinaus bieten sich die Daten der DiaWbb natürlich für viele weitere lexikalisch-semantische Studien (semasiologisch und/oder onomasiologisch ausgerichtet), aber auch für lautliche oder morphosyntaktische Untersuchungen als mögliche Grundlage an. Durch die historische Tiefe des Materials werden außerdem diachrone Fragestellungen unterstützt. Die vielfältigen Such- und Filtermöglichkeiten in den Datenbanken des WBF bzw. in BDO initiieren die Entwicklung unterschiedlichster Fragestellungen und ermöglichen zudem eine Verbindung mit pragmatischen Aspekten wie z.B. Sprach- und Kulturkontaktphänomenen, volkskundlichen Fragestellungen oder Sprechereinstellungen. Beispielsweise wird in Ganslmayer (2025) ausgehend von Movierungsbildungen und Sexusmarkierungen im WBF gezeigt, wie sich geschlechtsspezifische Stereotypisierungen im dialektalen Sprachgebrauch rekonstruieren lassen. In Ganslmayer (2022) werden anhand von WBF-Material verschiedene Formen sprachlicher Ausgrenzung in der Dialektlexikographie im Kontext diskriminierender Personenbezeichnungen untersucht, und zwar im Belegmaterial, durch Gewährspersonen und bei der Materialerhebung. Wie alle Wörterbücher sind auch DiaWbb selbst kulturelle Dokumente, in denen sich historische Entwicklungen, gesellschaftliche Veränderungen und Einstellungen der beteiligten Akteure widerspiegeln. Daher kann es auch

25 Vgl. unter <https://bdo.badw.de/info/neuigkeiten> (letzter Zugriff: 10.3.2025).

darum gehen, die historischen Diskurse zu untersuchen, in denen DiaWbb geplant, erstellt und genutzt wurden und werden.

3.9 Dialektwörterbücher sind theoriegeleitet und standardisiert

Dass DiaWb dialektale und lexikographische Theorien und Methoden seit mehr als hundert Jahren adaptieren und ihrerseits anregen, wurde bereits hinlänglich aufgezeigt. Im Kontext der digitalen Transformation wurden bei BWB und WBF die Wörterbuchdaten korrigiert und weiter standardisiert. Projektübergreifendes Arbeiten und die Zusammenarbeit mit IT-Spezialisten ist ohne die Verwendung einer metalexikographisch basierten, einheitlichen Kernterminologie nicht denkbar.

3.10 Dialektwörterbücher sind visuell kreativ

Bereits im Printformat (vgl. 2) nutzt das BWB typographische Strukturanzeiger, um die Wörterbuchmikrostruktur funktional zu unterstützen (z.B. Fettdruck zur Herausstellung der Lemmaposition, Kursivierung für Belegtextangaben, Kapitälchen für Belegstellenangaben, kleiner Schriftgrad für Postkommentar etc.). Außerdem sind einzelne Illustrationen integriert, um enzyklopädisch-kulturelle Informationen zu vermitteln (vgl. z.B. BWB II, Sp. 257, *Benne* (Leiteraufbau) auf dem Schlitten), sowie mitunter wortgeographische Karten, um die diatopische Verteilung sinn- bzw. sachverwandter Wörter zu visualisieren (vgl. z.B. BWB II, Sp. 65–66: Verbreitung der Synonyme von „Heidelbeere").

Ein gelungenes Design zieht nicht nur Aufmerksamkeit auf sich, sondern unterstützt inhaltliche Funktionen und verbessert die Nutzererfahrung. Das Webdesign von BDO orientiert sich grundsätzlich an Erkenntnissen der Usability-Forschung und wurde von einer extern beauftragten Dienstleisterin optimiert (vgl. Raaf 2025: 33–48, 273). Die Gestaltungsmöglichkeiten eines Online-Wörterbuchs werden in sämtlichen Belangen (Farbcodierung, statische/dynamische Elemente, Zugriffsstrukturen, interaktive Elemente, Suchoptionen etc.) reflektiert ausgenutzt. Die visuelle Kreativität zeigt sich z.B. darin, dass die Startseite nur ein Suchfeld im Zentrum beinhaltet und ansonsten von einer Wortwolke aus zufällig ausgewählten Stichwörtern der Datenbank dominiert wird. Klickt man ein Stichwort an, wird der zugehörige Artikel aufgerufen. Dies ermöglicht interessierten Laien einen niederschwelligen Zugriff (vgl. Raaf 2019; 2025: 65). Durch die Georeferenzierung der integrierten Belege können zu jedem Lemma Karten aufgerufen werden, auf denen die räumliche Verteilung visualisiert wird. Ist ein Wort in allen drei Wörterbüchern belegt, können die jeweiligen Belege separat oder gemeinsam auf einer Karte angezeigt werden.

3.11 Dialektwörterbücher sind nutzerorientiert konzipiert

Die Konzeptionsphase der meisten DiaWbb liegt bereits lange zurück, und die Publikationsphase hat vor längerer Zeit begonnen oder ist bereits abgeschlossen. Daher sind DiaWbb üblicherweise als klassische Printwörterbücher konzipiert. Auch wenn diese DiaWbb inzwischen teilweise retrodigitalisiert vorliegen, ändert dies nur wenig an der ursprünglichen Konzeption. D.h., dass die mit Online-Wörterbüchern verbundenen Möglichkeiten der Nutzerorientierung in der Regel nicht ausgenutzt werden können.

Innovative Formate können lediglich dort realisiert werden, wo Publikationskonzepte erst jüngst entwickelt und die Wörterbücher bereits für die digitale Nutzung konzipiert worden sind. Ein Beispiel hierfür ist die digitale Version des WBF im Kontext der Online-Plattform BDO, in die auch BWB und DIBS integriert sind (vgl. 2). Die Entwicklung von BDO erfolgte nutzerorientiert unter Berücksichtigung von Erkenntnissen der Wörterbuchbenutzungsforschung und einer eigenen Nutzerstudie zur Internetlexikographie (vgl. Raaf 2022a; 2025: 129–162): Mittels Online-Fragebogen und persönlicher Online-Interviews wurden Bedürfnisse der primären Nutzergruppe (interessierte Laien) eruiert und evaluiert. Hierfür war die Frage zentral, welche Eigenschaften ein Online-Wörterbuch aufweisen muss, um eine hohe Nutzerfreundlichkeit für unterschiedliche Nutzergruppen gewährleisten zu können. Als entsprechende Eigenschaften wurden ermittelt: laienfreundliche Sprache in Beschriftungen und Informationstexten (möglichst Verzicht auf Fachterminologie, da die interessierte Öffentlichkeit als Zielgruppe eingebunden ist), schlichtes Design, klare Informationsstruktur mit Beschränkung auf das Wesentliche, niederschwelliger Zugang über mehrere Zugriffsmöglichkeiten (einfache und erweiterte Suche, Stichwortliste, Wortwolke), schnelle, intuitive Suche und ein responsives Design, um eine Adaption an unterschiedliche Bildschirmformate und mobile Endgeräte zu ermöglichen (Raaf: 2025: 163–164). Die Nutzerorientierung zeigt sich auch in der Integration von direkten Suchmöglichkeiten in Auswahlmenüs, der Einbindung von Informationstexten und der Bereitstellung eines Einführungsvideos, in dem Grundfunktionen der Suche demonstriert werden.[26]

Eine Herausforderung für Ressourcen im Aufbau sind „Leere Suchergebnisse“, die bei Suchabfragen von den Nutzerinnern und Nutzern in der Regel als unbefriedigend wahrgenommen werden. Um das Frustrationserlebnis abzumildern, wird vorgeschlagen, einen erläuternden Hinweis („Dieser Artikel ist ein Platzhalter für dieses Stichwort, da es sich noch in Bearbeitung befindet und künftig in die BDO eingespeist wird.“) oder Dummy-Artikel zu integrieren (Raaf 2025: 185). Auch die unscharfe Suche nach Dialektausdrücken soll weiter verbessert werden (vgl. Raaf 2025: 183).

26 Vgl. unter <https://bdo.badw.de/info/videos> (letzter Zugriff: 10.3.2025).

3.12 Dialektwörterbücher berücksichtigen metalexikographische Erkenntnisse

Für sämtliche Phasen des lexikographischen Prozesses (Vorbereitungs-, Datenbeschaffungs-, Datenaufbereitungs-, Datenauswertungs-, Satz- und Druckvorbereitungsphase, vgl. Wiegand et al. 2010: 10) der DiaWbb waren und sind metalexikographische Erwägungen leitend (vgl. 2). Durch die digitale Wende wurden teils nachträglich, teils von Beginn an Teilphasen des lexikographischen Prozesses computergestützt umgestaltet. Wie bei der digitalen Konzeption von BDO metalexikographische Erkenntnisse berücksichtigt wurden, wurde ebenfalls in Abschnitt 2 gezeigt; ein Fokus lag dabei auf den Forschungsergebnissen zur Wörterbuchbenutzung (vgl. 3.11). Die inhaltliche Konzeption der DiaWbb liegt teils Jahrzehnte zurück. Daher konnten Erkenntnisse der modernen Unterrichts- und Übersetzungspraxis nicht gezielt integriert werden, werden aber dennoch teils umgesetzt. Indem beispielsweise Dialektbegriffe mit sach- und volkskundlichen Hintergrundinformationen enzyklopädisch erläutert werden, werden in den DiaWbb Strategien umgesetzt, wie sie für die moderne Kulturvermittlung in zweisprachigen Wörterbüchern genutzt werden.

3.13 Dialektwörterbücher setzen eine produktive Nutzerbeteiligung um

Die DiaWbb bemühen sich darum, die Nutzer/-innen aktiv und produktiv in die laufenden Projekte einzubinden. Interesse besteht an deren sprachlicher Kompetenz, aber auch an möglichen weiteren materiellen Quellen zu den Dialekten in Bayern. Beispielsweise ist im horizontalen Navigationsmenü in BDO „Mitmachen" anklickbar. Hier finden sich Aufrufe zur Mitwirkung bei einem wissenschaftlichen Experiment zum dialektalen Wortschatz im Ostfränkischen, zum Ausfüllen von Fragebögen des BWB (vgl. unten) und um die Zusendung von Wortlisten an DIBS, vor allem aber auch von anderen Materialien zum schwäbisch-alemannischen Wortschatz Bayerns (Zeichnungen, Fotografien, Ton- oder Videoaufnahmen), da DIBS künftig um multimediale Inhalte erweitert werden soll. Eine partizipative Einbindung der interessierten Öffentlichkeit in Form von „Sprachspenden" wird also bereits realisiert und für eine Ergänzung und Erweiterung der Daten und Quellen genutzt. Für das BWB sammeln aktuell ca. 230 Mundartsprecher/-innen in Altbayern Belege, indem sie Fragebögen (Wörterlisten) ausfüllen und zurücksenden. Neue Sammler sind jederzeit willkommen.[27]

Weitere kreative Mitmachaktionen wären denkbar, um den Einbindungsgrad noch zu erhöhen und digital verfügbare Ressourcen zu dynamisieren. Dies erfordert aber einen erhöhten personalen Mehraufwand für Konzeption, Kommunika-

27 Vgl. unter <https://bwb.badw.de/materialsammlung.html> (letzter Zugriff: 10.3.2025).

tion und Qualitätskontrolle, der bei den engen Zeitplänen des lexikographischen Prozesses nicht ohne Weiteres aufgebracht werden kann. Einige Anregungen für denkbare Community-Beiträge, Citizenship-Projekte oder Gamification-Elemente seien hier skizziert: BDO könnte um eine offene Plattform für nutzergenerierte Inhalte ergänzt werden, auf der Dialektwörter eingereicht oder persönliche Anekdoten im Zusammenhang mit Dialektwörtern geteilt werden können; Nutzer/-innen könnten Einträge liken, kommentieren oder ergänzen und dadurch zu einer besseren Einschätzung der Datenrelevanz beitragen; in interaktive Dialektkarten könnten Wortvarianten eingetragen werden, um in Ergänzung zum erfassten Datenbestand die aktuelle wortgeographische Verbreitung dialektaler Lexik zu eruieren; regelmäßige Dialekträtsel (gegebenenfalls mit Bereitstellung von Preisen) könnten integriert werden; Nutzer/-innen könnten um die Teilnahme an Rankings oder Akzeptabilitätstests gebeten werden, um den Bekanntheits- oder Beliebtheitsgrad dialektaler Wörter zu ermitteln; in den Social-Medial-Kanälen könnte wöchentlich ein Dialektwort der Woche diskutiert werden; Dialektwörter könnten in lustigen Kontexten dargestellt und Internet-Memes erstellt werden. Eine Vielzahl entsprechender Ideen ist am Beispiel von DIBS und seiner Transformation zu einem „dialektologischen Informationssystem“ in Schwarz/Funk/Raaf/Welsch (2021: 125–127) skizziert.

3.14 Dialektwörterbücher unterstützen die Digitalisierung der Gesellschaft

Das digitale Datenangebot der DiaWbb ist niederschwellig erreichbar und kann von der interessierten Öffentlichkeit kostenfrei genutzt werden. DiaWbb erfüllen damit nicht nur ihren kulturpädagogischen Auftrag, sondern leisten zugleich einen zentralen Beitrag zur Digitalisierung der Gesellschaft und sind Hilfsmittel im Prozess des „Lebenslangen Lernens“. Die Motivation, in den digitalen Dialektressourcen zu lesen, zu recherchieren oder sie bei Wissenslücken gezielt zu konsultieren, steigt, wenn die DiaWbb nutzerorientiert und modern gestaltet sind (vgl. 3.10, 3.11). Das pädagogische Konzept des „Lebenslangen Lernens“ fußt auf individuellen Selbst- und Informationskompetenzen. Gelingt es, die Nutzung von DiaWbb durch die breite Öffentlichkeit anzuregen, können DiaWbb dergestalt dazu beitragen, sprachliches und kulturelles Wissen zu mehren, für sprachliche Variation und Diversität zu sensibilisieren und zugleich Medienkompetenzen zu verbessern. Durch nutzerorientiert gestaltete digitale Angebote wie WBF, DIBS oder BDO steigt die Akzeptanz digitaler Informationssysteme in der Öffentlichkeit.

Um die kritische Nutzung digitaler Informationssysteme nachhaltig als Schlüsselkompetenz in der Gesellschaft zu verankern, ist es unabdingbar, digitale Ressourcen in die schulischen Curricula zu integrieren und Lehrkräfte entsprechend aus- bzw. weiterzubilden. Bezogen auf DiaWbb bedeutet dies, dass diese bekannt gemacht werden, dass deren Nutzung erklärt und angeregt wird und dass didaktische Anwendungsszenarien für den Schulunterricht entworfen werden. In Ganslmayer/Nied (i. V.) zu „Digitalen Wörterbüchern“ im Deutschunterricht werden auch DiaWbb berücksichtigt.

3.15 Dialektwörterbücher sind in pädagogisch-didaktische Konzepte eingebunden

Im Kontext schulischer Initiativen zur Stärkung der Dialekte bzw. Regiolekte wurden die DiaWbb bereits in schulische Projekte eingebunden und in pädagogischen Handreichungen (vgl. StMUK 2015; 2019) berücksichtigt, um eine weitere Nutzung im schulischen Kontext anzuregen. In der Handreichung „Dialekte in Bayern“, die das Münchner Staatsinstitut für Schulqualität und Bildungsforschung“ in Zusammenarbeit mit dem Bayerischen Rundfunk erarbeitet hat, sind die bayerischen DiaWbb vielfältig eingebunden. Sie erscheinen mehrfach in einzelnen Filmsequenzen der Sendereihe „Dialekte in Bayern“: In „Dialektforschung heute“ erläutert beispielsweise Prof. Dr. A. Rowley, Projektleiter des BWB, die Arbeit am BWB. Die zugehörige Aufgabenstellung lautet: „Beschreibe die Ziele, Methoden und Schwierigkeiten bei der Erstellung des Bayerischen Wörterbuchs“ (StMUK 2015: 22). Oder in „Reichtum der schwäbischen Mundart, Arbeitsweisen der Dialektforschung, „Merkdatei“ Kempten“ beschreibt Dr. Brigitte Schwarz ihre Arbeit. Danach lässt sich die Frage beantworten, wie es links und rechts des Lechs heißt, wenn der Hahn seine Hennen begattet (StMUK 2015: 47). In der Handreichung für Lehrer (StMUK 2015) erscheint der Begriff „Wörterbuch“ auf ca. 390 Seiten insgesamt 102-mal, und über die DiaWbb sind zahlreiche Basisinformationen eingebunden bzw. sie erscheinen in Unterrichtsmodellen: Für verschiedene Altersstufen und Lernbereiche des Faches Deutsch werden Unterrichtseinheiten vorgestellt (vgl. Übersicht in StMUK 2015: 107), in die die DiaWbb integriert sind. Beispielsweise ist in einem Unterrichtsmodell zum Bairischen ein Eintrag aus dem BWB aufgenommen (Lernziel: Die Schüler „eruieren den Aussagewert eines Lemmas des „Bayerischen Wörterbuchs“, StMUK 2015: 131). Oder aber, die DiaWbb entfalten eine Vorbildwirkung, indem Schülerinnen und Schüler eigene themenspezifische „Dialekt-Wörterbücher“ erstellen (vgl. StMUK 2015: 165).

Derartige Aktivitäten spielen verstärkt eine Rolle im Rahmen des Projekts „MundART WERTvoll“ (StMUK 2019). Hier sind konkrete Schulprojekte beschrieben, in denen u.a. kleine Dialektwörterbücher entstanden sind, wie beispielsweise an der Gregor-von-Scherr-Schule (Staatliche Realschule Neunburg vorm Wald in der Oberpfalz) ein illustriertes Sachgruppenwörterbuch, das sich als „Lexikographisches Lesebuch“ versteht (StMUK 2019: 51) und „Lebendige Mundart“ in der Oberpfalz darstellt. Im Fazit wird herausgestellt: „Die intensive und aktive Auseinandersetzung mit der bairischen Mundart konnte bereits in den ersten Monaten erreicht werden. Dies gelang vor allem durch die Verschriftlichung der Dialektwörter in Form eines Wörterbuchs. Handlungsorientiert und kreativ konnte der eigene Dialekt erfahren und sowohl im Klassenzimmer als auch auf dem Schulhof bewusst angewendet werden.“

(StMUK 2019: 34). An der Hallertauer Mittelschule in Mainburg wurde ein neuartiges Wörterbuch „Migraboarisch©" erarbeitet, „das etwas andere Wörterbuch für alle heimischen und zuagroastn Buama und Madln in Bayern" (StMUK 2019: 34). Hier wurden Mundartausdrücke recherchiert und in einem eigenen Wörterbuch „mit verschiedenen Übersetzungen" aufgelistet (StMUK 2019: 48). Als besondere Erkenntnis wird u.a. Dialekt als großer integrativer Faktor herausgestellt: Anders als zunächst vermutet, war keine Mischsprache aus den unterschiedlichen Sprachen der Jugendlichen unterschiedlicher Nationen feststellbar: ein neuer „Jugend-Dialekt" war nicht nachweisbar (StMUK 2019: 44, 46).

Auch in der Hochschullehre spielen die DiaWbb eine Rolle. Beispielsweise werden in einem variationslinguistischen Schwerpunkt an der Friedrich-Alexander-Universität in Erlangen regelmäßig Lehrveranstaltungen zum *Fränkischen Wörterbuch* von der Redaktorin des WBF, PD Dr. Almut König, angeboten, wie z.B. „Dialektologie und Lexikographie am Beispiel des *Fränkischen Wörterbuchs*" (Wintersemester 2024/25) oder „Dialekt ins Museum?" (Wintersemester 2023/24). Letztere wurde in Zusammenarbeit mit der museumspädagogischen Leitung des „Museums für Franken" (Staatliches Museum für Kunst- und Kulturgeschichte) in Würzburg veranstaltet. Ziel war, das Museum mit „Dialekt-Exponaten" auszustatten und auf Grundlage des WBF „Ausstellungsstücke" in Form von Wortartikeln zu erarbeiten, die längerfristig in die Museumsausstellung integriert werden.

Was die Zukunft der DiaWbb im schulischen Kontext anbelangt, so müsste in den Didaktisierungskonzepten die fortgeschrittene digitale Transformation der DiaWbb noch einbezogen werden. Eine Aktualisierung der Unterrichtsmodelle ist also notwendig. Durch das digitale Angebot der DiaWbb könnte inzwischen die Medienkompetenz der Schüler/-innen in unterschiedlichen Dimensionen in erweiterter Form berücksichtigt werden: Dies betrifft das Wissen über Medien (digitale DiaWbb) und ihre Handhabung ebenso wie die Mediennutzung, also das rezeptive und interaktive Handeln mit Medien. Durch digitale Mitmachformate kann außerdem die Mediengestaltungskompetenz aufgebaut werden. Der reflexive Umgang mit den dialektalen Medieninhalten kann weiterhin dazu beitragen, für sprachliche Vielfalt zu sensibilisieren.

4 Fazit

In diesem Beitrag wurden vielfältige Funktionen von Dialektwörterbüchern im 21. Jahrhundert aufgezeigt. Dialektwörterbücher sind mehr als erinnernde historische Kulturdokumente. Sie sind Teil lebendiger regionaler Sprach- und Lebenswelten, spiegeln soziales Handeln wider, wirken sprachsensibilisierend und identitätsvermittelnd und können einen toleranten Umgang mit Diversität befördern: Dialektwörterbücher machen die Vielfalt sprachlichen Handelns sichtbar und können ihrerseits als rezeptive, produktive und interaktive Handlungsmittel zur Erkenntnis kultureller Differenz und somit zu einer offenen Gesellschaft beitragen, die wertungsfrei das Andere in ihrem eigenen Wert anerkennt und Diversität ermöglicht.

Die „15 Villa-Vigoni-Thesen zur Lexikografie“ wurden auf Dialektwörterbücher bezogen. Damit konnte gezeigt werden, dass Dialektwörterbücher nicht traditionsverhaftet sind, sondern eine Transformation zu „Wörterbüchern der Zukunft“ vollziehen und die Möglichkeiten der Digitalisierung weitestgehend ausschöpfen. Dies gilt insbesondere für diejenigen Dialektwörterbücher, die sich noch im Entstehungsprozess befinden. Als Beispiel wurden die wissenschaftlichen Dialektwörterbücher Bayerns herangezogen.

Literatur

Wörterbücher und lexikalische Informationssysteme

BDO = Bayerns Dialekte Online. Hg. von der Bayerischen Akademie der Wissenschaften. 2019–. https://bdo.badw.de/ (letzter Zugriff: 30.1.2025).

BWB = Bayerisches Wörterbuch (BWB). https://lexhelfer.bwb.badw.de/ (letzter Zugriff: 30.1.2025).

DIBS = Dialektologisches Informationssystem von Bayerisch-Schwaben (DIBS). https://lexhelfer.dibs.badw.de/ (letzter Zugriff: 30.1.2025).

König/Schwarz (2013) = Dialektwörterbuch von Bayerisch-Schwaben. Vom Allgäu bis zum Ries. Hg. von Werner König. Bearbeitet von Brigitte Schwarz. Augsburg: Wißner.

Schmid, Johann Christoph (1795): Versuch eines schwäbischen Idiotikon oder Sammlung der in verschiedenen schwäbischen Ländern und Städten gebräuchlichen Idiotismen mit etymologischen Anmerkungen. Berlin/Stettin: Nicolai.

Wagner/Klepsch (2007) = Handwörterbuch von Bayerisch-Franken. Hrsg. von der Kommission für Mundartforschung der Bayerischen Akademie der Wissenschaften. Bearbeitet von Eberhard Wagner und Alfred Klepsch. Bayreuth: Verlag Fränkischer Tag.

WBF = Fränkisches Wörterbuch (WBF). https://lexhelfer.wbf.badw.de/ (letzter Zugriff: 30.1.2025).

Internetquellen

Art. Bayerisches Wörterbuch. In: Wikipedia – Die freie Enzyklopädie. Bearbeitungsstand: 9.7.2024. https://de.wikipedia.org/wiki/Bayerisches_W%C3%B6rterbuch (letzter Zugriff: 21.2.2025).

Bayerisches Wörterbuch (BWB), Projektwebseite. https://bwb.badw.de (letzter Zugriff: 10.3.2025).

Dialektologisches Informationssystem von Bayerisch-Schwaben (DIBS), Projektwebseite. https://dibs.badw.de (letzter Zugriff: 10.3.2025).

Fränkisches Wörterbuch (WBF), Projektwebseite. https://wbf.badw.de (letzter Zugriff: 10.3.2025).

Lexikonet. [https://www.oeaw.ac.at/de/acdh/institut/netzwerke-kooperationen/netzwerke/lexikonet (letzter Zugriff: 10.3.2025).

Lexikalisches Informationssystem Österreich (LIÖ), Projektwebseite. https://lioe.dioe.at (letzter Zugriff: 10.3.2025).

Mittelelbisches Wörterbuch (MeWb), Projektwebseite. https://mew.uzi.uni-halle.de (letzter Zugriff: 10.3.2025).

Saterfriesisches Wörterbuch, Infoseite. https://www.xn–saterfriesisches-wrterbuch-tvc.de/index.php?suche=Infoseite (letzter Zugriff: 10.3.2025).
Sudetendeutsches Wörterbuch (SdWb), Projektwebseite. https://www.collegium-carolinum.de/forschung/grundlagenforschung/sudetendeutsches-woerterbuch (letzter Zugriff: 10.3.2025).
Wörterbuchnetz. Trierer Initiative zum digitalen Verbund von Wörterbüchern, Projektwebseite. https://tcdh.uni-trier.de/de/projekt/woerterbuchnetz (letzter Zugriff: 10.3.2025).
Wörterbuchnetz. Kompetenzzentrum – Trier Center for Digital Humanities. https://woerterbuchnetz.de/ (letzter Zugriff: 10.3.2025).

Monographien und Aufsätze

Bergmann, Gunter (2003): Rezension zu BWB, Bd. I. In: Beiträge zur Namenforschung NF 38, 3, 346–348.
Bremer, Ernst/Hoffmann, Walter (1982): Wissenschaftsorganisation und Forschungseinrichtungen der Dialektologie im deutschen Sprachgebiet. In: Besch, Werner/Knoop, Ulrich/Putschke, Wolfgang/Wiegand, Herbert Ernst (Hrsg.): Dialektologie. Ein Handbuch zur deutschen und allgemeinen Dialektforschung. Erster Halbband. Berlin/New York: De Gruyter, 202–231.
Dietrich, Margot (1975): Dialektwörterbücher – wozu? In: Sprachdienst 19, 73–76.
Friebertshäuser, Hans (1976a) (Hrsg.): Dialektlexikographie. Berichte über Stand und Methoden deutscher Dialektwörterbücher. Festgabe für Luise Berthold zum 85. Geburtstag am 27.1.1976. Wiesbaden: Steiner.
Friebertshäuser, Hans (1976b): Relevante Aspekte der Dialektlexikographie. In: Friebertshäuser, Hans (Hrsg.): Dialektlexikographie. Berichte über Stand und Methoden deutscher Dialektwörterbücher. Festgabe für Luise Berthold zum 85. Geburtstag am 27.1.1976. Wiesbaden: Steiner, 5–10.
Friebertshäuser, Hans (1983): Die großlandschaftlichen Wörterbücher der deutschen Dialekte. Areale und lexikologische Beschreibung. In: Besch, Werner/Knoop, Ulrich/Putschke, Wolfgang/Wiegand, Herbert Ernst (Hrsg.): Dialektologie. Ein Handbuch zur deutschen und allgemeinen Dialektforschung. Zweiter Halbband. Berlin/New York: De Gruyter, 1283–1295.
Ganslmayer, Christine (2022): Sprachliche Ausgrenzung in der Dialektlexikographie. In: Lexicographica 38, 281–306.
Ganslmayer, Christine (i. Dr.): „Di Kipfenbergeri hout a böisa Nachbari". Movierung und Sexusmarkierung im Ostfränkischen. In: Werth, Alexander (Hrsg.): Die Movierung. Formen, Funktionen, Bewertungen. Berlin/Boston: De Gruyter.
Ganslmayer, Christine/Müller, Peter O. (2022): Wortschatzausbau im Ostfränkischen. Wortbildung – Bedeutungsbildung – Entlehnung. In: Vergeiner, Philip C./Elspaß, Stephan/Wallner, Dominik (Hrsg.): Struktur von Variation zwischen Individuum und Gesellschaft. Akten der 14. Bayerisch-Österreichischen Dialektologietagung 2019. Stuttgart: Steiner, 13–38.
Ganslmayer, Christine/Nied Curcio, Martina, (Hrsg.) (i. V.): Digitale Wörterbücher [erscheint als Der Deutschunterricht Heft 1/2026].
Ilter, Hülya (2023): Umgang mit diskriminierender Sprache im Fränkischen Wörterbuch (WBF). In: Ferstl, Christian (Hrsg.): Namenphilologie trifft Dialektlexikographie. Beiträge aus dem Arbeitskreis für bayerischösterreichische Namenforschung und dem Netzwerk der großlandschaftlichen Dialektwörterbücher – LexikoNet. Teil 2: Großlandschaftliche Dialektwörterbücher zwischen Tradition und Innovation. Hrsg. von Almut König und Mechthild Habermann. Regensburg: edition vulpes: 299–309.
Klepsch, Alfred/König, Almut (2022): Datenerfassung und Datenbeschreibung im WBF. Ein Redaktionshandbuch. Mit einem Kapitel zum Umgang mit diskriminierenden ethischen Beschreibungen von Elisabeth Demleitner. 3., erweiterte und überarbeitete Fassung. Erlangen.

https://wbf.badw.de/fileadmin/user_upload/Files/WBF/Redaktionshandbuch_Stand_11_22.pdf (letzter Zugriff: 28.2.2025).
König, Werner ([16]2007): dtv-Atlas Deutsche Sprache. München: dtv.
König, Almut/Raaf, Manuel/Klepsch, Alfred (2021): Das Fränkische Wörterbuch (WBF). In: Lenz, Alexandra N./Stöckle, Philipp (Hrsg.): Germanistische Dialektlexikographie zu Beginn des 21. Jahrhunderts. Stuttgart: Steiner, 77–103.
Kühn, Peter (1989): Typologie der Wörterbücher nach Benutzungsmöglichkeiten. In: Hausmann, Franz Josef/Reichmann, Oskar/Wiegand, Herbert Ernst/Zgusta, Ladislav (Hrsg.): Wörterbücher. Ein internationales Handbuch zur Lexikographie. Erster Teilband. Berlin/New York: De Gruyter: 111–127.
Landolt, Christoph (2007): Neuere Entwicklungen in der historischen Dialektlexikographie des Deutschen. In: Lexicographica 23, 151–172.
Lenz, Alexandra N./Stöckle, Philipp (2021) (Hrsg.): Germanistische Dialektlexikographie zu Beginn des 21. Jahrhunderts. Stuttgart: Steiner.
Mann, Michael (2020): Art. Territorialwörterbuch. In: Wörterbuch zur Lexikographie und Wörterbuchforschung. Bd. 3, hrsg. und bearb, von Herbert Ernst Wiegand et al. Berlin/Boston: De Gruyter, 912–913.
Mitzka, [Walther] (1937): Die landschaftlichen deutschen Mundartwörterbücher der Gegenwart. In: Zeitschrift für Mundartforschung 13, 2, 91–99.
Moulin, Claudine (2010): Dialect dictionaries – traditional and modern. In: Auer, Peter/Schmidt, Jürgen Erich (Hrsg.): Language and Space. An International Handbook of Linguistic Variation. Bd. 1: Theories and Methods. Berlin/New York: De Gruyter, 592–612.
Niebaum, Hermann (1979): Deutsche Dialektwörterbücher. In: Deutsche Sprache 4, 345–373.
Niebaum, Hermann/Macha, Jürgen (2006): Einführung in die Dialektologie des Deutschen. 2., neubearbeitete Auflage. Tübingen: Niemeyer.
Raaf, Manuel (2017): LexHelfer: die Digitalisierung der 6 Millionen Belege des Bayerischen Wörterbuchs. Forschungsposter: Data First!? 4. Digital Humanities Austria Konferenz. 4.–6.12.2017 Universität Innsbruck. https://www.uibk.ac.at/congress/dha2017/bilder-und-dateien/poster_lexhelfer.pdf (letzter Zugriff: 10.3.2025).
Raaf, Manuel (2019): Bayerns Dialekte Online: Ein Sprachinformationssystem zu den drei bayerischen Dialektwörterbüchern sowie zur Bayerischen Dialektdatenbank BayDat. Forschungsposter: 14. Bayerisch-Österreichische Dialektologentagung, 7.11.2019, Salzburg. https://dhmuc.hypotheses.org/files/2019/11/B%C3%96DT_Poster_Raaf.pdf (letzter Zugriff: 10.3.2025).
Raaf, Manuel (2022a): Evaluation des User-Centered Designs eines Sprachinformationssystems – Planung, Durchführung und Ergebnisse einer Benutzerumfrage zu Usability und User Experience. In: Klosa-Kückelhaus, Annette/Engelberg, Stefan/Möhrs, Christine/Storjohann, Petra (Hrsg.): Dictionaries and Society. Book of Abstracts of the XX EURALEX International Congress, 12–16 July 2022, Mannheim, Germany. Mannheim: IDS-Verlag, 149–151. https://ids-pub.bsz-bw.de/frontdoor/deliver/index/docId/11078/file/Book_of_Abstracts_Euralex_XX_2022.pdf.
Raaf, Manuel (2022b): Bayerns Dialekte Online. In: Bayerische Akademie der Wissenschaften (Hrsg.): Jahrbuch 2021. München: Pinsker, 16–19. https://badw.de/fileadmin/user_upload/Files/BADW/07-04_Jahrbuecher/Jahrbuch_2021/epaper_jb_2021/#16.
Raaf, Manuel (2025): Bayerns Dialekte Online. Ein dynamisches Sprachinformationssystem zu den Dialektwörterbüchern Bayerisches Wörterbuch, Dialektologisches Informationssystem von Bayerisch-Schwaben und Fränkisches Wörterbuch. Diss. Erlangen. https://open.fau.de/handle/openfau/34909.
Schierholz, Stefan J. (2021): The Villa Vigoni Theses on Lexicography. In: Lexicographica 37, 303–305.
Schnabel, Michael/Raaf, Manuel/Schwarz, Daniel (2021): Bayerisches Wörterbuch (BWB). In: Lenz, Alexandra N./Stöckle, Philipp (Hrsg.): Germanistische Dialektlexikographie zu Beginn des 21. Jahrhunderts. Stuttgart: Steiner, 47–76.

Schwarz, Brigitte/Funk, Edith/Raaf, Manuel/Welsch, Ursula (2021): Dialektologisches Informationssystem von Bayerisch-Schwaben (DIBS). In: Lenz, Alexandra N./Stöckle, Philipp (Hrsg.): Germanistische Dialektlexikographie zu Beginn des 21. Jahrhunderts. Stuttgart: Steiner, 105–141.

StMUK (2015) = Bayerisches Staatsministerium für Unterricht und Kultus (Hrsg.): Dialekte in Bayern. Handreichung für den Unterricht. 2., erweiterte und aktualisierte Auflage. Erarbeitet vom Staatsinstitut für Schulqualität und Bildungsforschung (ISB). Furth: MDV Maristen.

StMUK (2019) = Bayerisches Staatsministerium für Unterricht und Kultus (Hrsg.) (2019): MundART WERTvoll. Lebendige Dialekte an bayerischen Schulen. Handreichung. Erarbeitet vom Staatsinstitut für Schulqualität und Bildungsforschung (ISB). Schneckenlohe: Appel & Klinger.

Stock, Günter/Zwies, Sebastian (2014): Bedeutung und Funktion von Evaluationen im Akademienprogramm. In: Akademie Aktuell 2, 44–49.

Wiegand, Herbert Ernst (1998): Wörterbuchforschung. Untersuchungen zur Wörterbuchbenutzung, zur Theorie, Geschichte, Kritik und Automatisierung der Lexikographie zur Lexikographie. 1. Teilband. Berlin/New York: De Gruyter, 57.

Wiegand, Herbert Ernst (2017): Art. Dialektwörterbuch. In: Wörterbuch zur Lexikographie und Wörterbuchforschung. Bd. 2, hrsg. und bearb. von Herbert Ernst Wiegand et al. Berlin/Boston: De Gruyter, 38–39.

Wiegand, Herbert Ernst (2020): Art. Syntopisches Dialektwörterbuch. In: Wörterbuch zur Lexikographie und Wörterbuchforschung. Bd. 3, hrsg. und bearb. von Herbert Ernst Wiegand et al. Berlin/Boston: De Gruyter, 822–823.

Wiegand, Herbert Ernst, et al. (2010) (Hrsg.): Systematische Einführung. In: Wörterbuch zur Lexikographie und Wörterbuchforschung. Bd. 1. Berlin/New York: De Gruyter, 1–121.